# Religious Diversity in Europe

Also Available from Bloomsbury:

*French Populism and Discourses on Secularism*
Per-Erik Nilsson

*Religious Pluralism and the City*
Edited by Helmuth Berking, Silke Steets and Jochen Schwenk

*Secular Bodies, Affects and Emotions*
Edited by Monique Scheer, Nadia Fadil, and Birgitte Schepelern Johansen

# Religious Diversity in Europe

## Mediating the Past to the Young

Edited by

Riho Altnurme, Elena Arigita and Patrick Pasture

BLOOMSBURY ACADEMIC

LONDON • NEW YORK • OXFORD • NEW DELHI • SYDNEY

BLOOMSBURY ACADEMIC
Bloomsbury Publishing Plc
50 Bedford Square, London, WC1B 3DP, UK
1385 Broadway, New York, NY 10018, USA
29 Earlsfort Terrace, Dublin 2, Ireland

BLOOMSBURY, BLOOMSBURY ACADEMIC and the Diana logo are
trademarks of Bloomsbury Publishing Plc

First published in Great Britain 2022
This paperback edition published 2023

Copyright © Riho Altnurme, Elena Arigita, Patrick Pasture and contributors, 2022, 2024

Riho Altnurme, Elena Arigita and Patrick Pasture have asserted their rights under the
Copyright, Designs and Patents Act, 1988, to be identified as Editors of this work.

For legal purposes the Acknowledgements on p. xv constitute an
extension of this copyright page.

Cover design: Tjasa Krivec
Cover image © M. Jazwiecki / POLIN Museum

A catalogue record for this book is available from the British Library.

Library of Congress Control Number: 2021950375

ISBN: HB: 978-1-3501-9858-6
PB: 978-1-3501-9862-3
ePDF: 978-1-3501-9859-3
eBook: 978-1-3501-9860-9

Typeset by Newgen KnowledgeWorks Pvt. Ltd., Chennai, India

To find out more about our authors and books visit www.bloomsbury.com and
sign up for our newsletters

This volume has received funding from the European Union's Horizon 2020 research and innovation programme under grant agreement No 770309. The contents of this publication are the sole responsibility of the authors and do not necessarily reflect the opinion of the European Union.

# Contents

List of Illustrations                                                           ix

List of Contributors                                                            xi

Acknowledgements                                                                xv


Introduction    Religious diversity in Europe: Meditating the past to the young    1
*Patrick Pasture*

1    Religious diversity in Europe: The challenges of past and present          15
*Patrick Pasture and Christophe Schellekens*

2    Views of the young: Reflections on the basis of European pilot studies     33
*John Maiden, Stefanie Sinclair, Päivi Salmesvuori, Karel Van Nieuwenhuyse*
*and John Wolffe*

3    Representing European religious diversity in textbooks for history education    51
*Karel Van Nieuwenhuyse, Madis Maasing and Laura Galián*

4    Society exhibited: Museums, religions and representation                   67
*Merve Reyhan Kayikci, Tamara Sztyma-Knasiecka, Naum Trajanovski*
*and Marija Manasievska*

5    Religious diversity and generation Z: TV series and YouTube as
     instruments to promote religious toleration and peace                     91
*Mikko Ketola, Ivan Stefanovski, Kaarel Kuurmaa and Riho Altnurme*

6    Refugees and the politics of memory: Political discourses of religious
     toleration and peace                                                      113
*Laura Galián, John Maiden, Stefanie Sinclair and Árpád Welker*

7    Commemorating the Good Friday Agreement (1998) and the Ohrid
     Framework Agreement (2001)                                                137
*Lidija Georgieva, Naum Trajanovski and John Wolffe*

8    Religious pluralism in the Islamic tradition in late al-Andalus and in
     contemporary Islamic transnationalism: A conceptual approach             159
*Nadia Hindi Mediavilla, Antonio Peláez Rovira and*
*María Dolores Rodríguez Gómez*

9   From dialogue to peace: Organizations for interreligious and
    interconvictional dialogue in Europe                                175
    *Elina Kuokkanen and Patrick Pasture*

10  Religious toleration in the new spirituality subculture: The Estonian case   191
    *Lea Altnurme*

Notes                                                                       207
References                                                                  213
Index                                                                       261

# Illustrations

## Figures

4.1   Institut du Monde Arabe                                                       75

4.2   Reconstruction of the roof of the synagogue in Gwoździec at the core
      exhibition of the Museum of the History of Polish Jews POLIN                    79

4.3   The Museum of the Macedonian Struggle and the Archaeological
      Museum in Skopje                                                                86

7.1   A commemorative plaque in Lenište near Prilep                                  145

7.2   Monument 'Macedonian Defenders' in Skopje                                      147

7.3   'Skenderbeg Square' in Skopje                                                  148

7.4   Clonard Martyrs Memorial Garden                                               154

7.5   Mural on the Shankill Road                                                     155

8.1   Capitulations of Granada, Archivo de los Duques de Frías (Sección
      Nobleza, Archivo Histórico Nacional)                                           163

## Tables

1.1   Agnostics and atheists in Europe per UN region
      (percentages, 1900–2020)                                                        24

1.2   Muslims in Europe per UN region (percentages, 1900–2020)                         25

1.3   Religious diversity in Europe (index, 2010)                                      26

# Contributors

**Lea Altnurme** is Associate Professor of Sociology of Religion at the School of Theology and Religious Studies, University of Tartu (Estonia). She is the principal investigator of H2020 project Religious Toleration and Peace (RETOPEA) at the University of Tartu. Her research focuses on changes in spirituality on the individual level, new phenomena in the religious landscape and the role of religion in Estonian cultural history. She is the founder and editor-in-chief of the series *Mitut usku Eesti* (Multireligious Estonia).

**Riho Altnurme** is Professor of Church History at the School of Theology and Religious Studies, vice dean for research at the Faculty of Humanities and Arts, University of Tartu (Estonia) and also visiting professor at the University of Latvia (2019–21). His research is concentrated on nineteenth- and twentieth-century church history, in the context of church-state-society relations. He is the editor of *History of Estonian Ecumenism* (2009) and *Old Religion, New Spirituality: Implications of Secularisation and Individualisation in Estonia* (2021).

**Elena Arigita** is a permanent Lecturer of Arab and Islamic Studies at the Department of Semitic Studies, University of Granada (Spain). Earlier, she was a language lecturer at Cairo University and al-Azhar (Egypt), postdoctoral researcher at the International Institute for the Study of Islam in the Modern World-ISIM in Leiden (The Netherlands) and senior researcher at the International Institute for Arab and Muslim World Studies-IEAM Casa Arabe (Spain). She is the principal investigator of RETOPEA at the University of Granada. Her research interests and publications deal with religious authority and institutionalization of Islam and the politics of inclusion and exclusion of Islam in Europe.

**Laura Galián** is assistant professor at the Department of Arab and Islamic Studies and Oriental Studies, Autonomous University of Madrid (Spain). Earlier, she was a postdoctoral researcher at Universidad de Granada and a Juan de la Cierva research fellow. Her research interests and publications deal with history of concepts, history of ideas and the Middle East. She has recently published the book *Colonialism, Transnationalism and Anarchism in the South of the Mediterranean* (2020).

**Lidija Georgieva** is Professor in Peace and Conflict Studies at the Faculty of Philosophy, Ss. Cyril and Methodius University in Skopje. She is a UNESCO chair in Intercultural Studies and Research and principal investigator of RETOPEA for Ss. Cyril and Methodius University.

**María Dolores Rodríguez Gómez** is Associate Professor of Arab and Islamic Studies at the Department of Semitic Studies, University of Granada (Spain). Earlier, she was a postdoctoral researcher at the University of Abdelmalek Essaâdi (Tetouan, Morocco). She is assistant editor-in-chief of the journal *Miscelánea de Estudios Árabes y Hebraicos: Sección Árabe-Islam*, and director of the group of research 'Ciudades Andaluzas Bajo el Islam' (HUM-150 PAIDI). Her research focuses on economic and social history of al-Andalus (thirteenth and fifteenth centuries), and particularly its relations with the Maghreb.

**Merve Reyhan Kayikci** is a postdoctoral research fellow at the Department of Semitic Studies, University of Granada (Spain) and collaborator at the Interculturalism, Migration and Minorities Research Centre (IMMRC), KU Leuven (Belgium). She obtained her PhD from the IMMRC, KU Leuven. Her doctoral work investigated the intersections of volunteering and ethical self-becoming among Belgian Muslim female volunteers. She is the author of *Islamic Ethics and Female Volunteering Committing to Society, Committing to God* (2020) and co-editor of *Muslim Volunteering in the West: Between Islamic Ethos and Citizenship* and *European Muslims and New Media* (2020).

**Mikko Ketola** is Adjunct Professor and University Lecturer in Church History at the Faculty of Theology, University of Helsinki (Finland). He is the principal investigator of RETOPEA at the University of Helsinki. He is also secretary of CIHEC (International Commission for History and Studies of Christianity) and editor of the Finnish opinion journal *Vartija*. His research interests include Finnish and Baltic church history, religion and popular culture, post-communist Ukrainian church politics, and contemporary papacy. He has published several articles in Finnish and international scholarly journals and has edited eight volumes of the *Yearbook of the Finnish Society of Church History*.

**Elina Kuokkanen** holds a BA in Social Work from Jyväskylä University of Applied Sciences (Finland) and an MA in European Studies: Transnational and Global Perspectives from KU Leuven. She is project assistant at Beyond the Horizon ISSG, and is a founding member of Bonding Beyond Borders.

**Kaarel Kuurmaa** is a doctoral fellow at the School of Theology and Religious Studies, University of Tartu (Estonia), and film programmer, critic and consultant (artistic director of the Arvo Pärt Centre film nights, as well as programmer for Tallinn Black Nights Film Festival, DocPoint – Documentary Film Festival in Helsinki and Tallinn and film commissioner for the Estonian Film Institute).

**Madis Maasing** is research fellow at the Institute of History and Archaeology, University of Tartu (Estonia). His main research interests and publications deal with the history of sixteenth century in Estonia and Latvia (then known as Livonia), including the political consequences of the Reformation. This subject also featured prominently in his doctoral dissertation *The Role of the Bishops in the Livonian Political System (in the First Half of the 16th Century* (2016). He is also co-author of a two-volume Estonian textbook about Medieval times (*Keskaeg: ajaloo õpik 7. klassile* (Middle Ages: History Textbook for the 7th Grade), 2016–17).

**John Maiden** is head of department and senior lecturer in Religious Studies at the Open University, UK. He is a historian of twentieth-century religion with a particular interest in transnational evangelical and Pentecostal Christianities. He is co-editor of *Transatlantic Charismatic Renewal, 1950–2000* (2021) and *Evangelicalism and the Church of England in the Twentieth Century: Reform, Resistance and Renewal* (2014).

**Marija Manasievska** is a PhD candidate in Classical Studies and researcher at the Ss. Cyril and Methodius University in Skopje (North Macedonia).

**Nadia Hindi Mediavilla** is Assistant Professor of Arab and Islamic Studies at the Department of Semitic Studies, University of Granada (Spain) and research associate at the RETOPEA. Her research interests and publications deal with feminism and gender and its relation to nationalism and sectarianism in Iraq.

**Patrick Pasture** is Professor of European and Global History and director of the Centre for European Studies at KU Leuven (Belgium). He is the project leader of the European H2020 project RETOPEA and principal investigator of the Jean Monnet Network European Transoceanic Encounters and Exchanges (ETEE). He has published extensively on European and Global History and in particular the social, political and cultural history of religion in a global perspective, including *Histoire du syndicalisme chrétien international: la difficile recherche d'une troisième voie* (1999), *Imagining European Unity since 1000 AD* (2015) and *Ontmoetingen in het Oosten: een wereldgeschiedenis* (Encounters in the East: A Global History), 2019).

**Antonio Peláez Rovira** is Associate Professor of Arab and Islamic Studies at the Department of Semitic Studies, University of Granada (Spain). Earlier, he was a postdoctoral researcher at the University of Genoa (Italy) and had other research stays in Arab countries. He coordinates the master's programme in Arabic and Hebrew Cultures: Al-Andalus and the Contemporary Arab World, and he is the principal investigator of SONADE Project (Nasrid Society in the 15th Century: Application of the Law and State Administration) at the University of Granada. His research interests and publications deal with political structures and power in al-Andalus (thirteenth–fifteenth centuries), Nasrid intellectuals and relationships with other states.

**Päivi Salmesvuori** is university researcher and lecturer at the Faculty of Theology and board member of the Doctoral Programme in History and Cultural Heritage, University of Helsinki, Finland. She has researched issues of gender, power, authority and religion from the Middle Ages to present times. She has been awarded the membership of the Teachers' Academy of University of Helsinki for her achievements in university pedagogics.

**Christophe Schellekens** is a historian working at the intersection of teaching, research and research management. He was researcher for the RETOPEA project at the Leibniz Institute for European History in Mainz and coordinator of RETOPEA at KU Leuven until September 2021. Since August 2020, he is a lecturer at the University of Utrecht (The Netherlands).

**Stefanie Sinclair** is Senior Lecturer in Religious Studies and director of the Centre for Scholarship and Innovation at the Faculty of Arts and Social Sciences at the Open University (UK). She has a special research interest in religion, identity, politics and education in Germany and the UK, and is the Teaching and Learning representative on the executive committee of the British Association for the Study of Religions.

**Ivan Stefanovski** holds a PhD in law from the Scuola Normale Superiore in Florence and is currently researcher at the Ss. Cyril and Methodius University in Skopje (North Macedonia).

**Tamara Sztyma-Knasiecka** is a postdoctoral fellow at the Faculty of 'Artes Liberales', University of Warsaw and curator at the Museum of the History of Polish Jews (Polin) in Warsaw (Poland).

**Naum Trajanovski** is a PhD candidate in sociology at the Institute for Philosophy and Sociology, Polish Academy of Sciences in Warsaw, and a doctoral research fellow at the University of Ss. Cyril and Methodius in Skopje (North Macedonia). His major academic interests include memory politics in North Macedonia and sociological knowledge-transfer in 1960s Eastern Europe. He is the author of a book in Macedonian on the Museum of the Macedonian struggle and the Macedonian memory politics (2020).

**Karel Van Nieuwenhuyse** is Associate Professor in Historical Education and director of the Specific History Teacher Training Programme (MA), Faculty of Arts, KU Leuven (Belgium). He is president of the Flemish Association of History Teachers and vice president of the International Research Association for History and Social Sciences Education. He was involved as an expert in the development committee for new standards for (primary/secondary school) history education in Flanders. He has published extensively on the history of history education and historical representations in history education and popular historical culture, and on research about teaching and learning processes within history education.

**Árpád Welker** is currently a policy officer at the European Commission. He was previously affiliated with the University of Helsinki where he researched topics related to anti-Semitism, history of Jewry and interconfessional relations.

**John Wolffe** is Professor of Religious History at The Open University (UK), where he was also associate dean (Research Enterprise and Scholarship) in the Faculty of Arts and Social Sciences from 2016 to 2021. He is the principal investigator of RETOPEA at the Open University. He is the author of numerous publications on North Atlantic Evangelicalism, anti-Catholicism, responses to death and, most recently, *Sacred and Secular Martyrdom in Britain and Ireland since 1914* (2020).

# Acknowledgements

This book is a result of the European H2020 research project RETOPEA to promote religious toleration and peace, particularly among youth. This project involves scholars from eight academic institutions all over Europe – the KU Leuven (Belgium), the University of Tartu (Estonia), the University of Helsinki (Finland), the Leibniz Institute for European History in Mainz (Germany), Ss. Cyril and Methodius University in Skopje (UKIM, North Macedonia), the University of Warsaw (Poland), the University of Granada (Spain) and Open University, Milton Keynes (UK) – as well as three centres for civic education: the Euro-Arab Foundation (FUNDEA, Granada), Le Foyer in Brussels and the Macedonian Center for International Cooperation (MCIC).

The premise of the project is that insight into historical religious peacemaking offers a prism for interpreting contemporary issues related to religious diversity, including the use of the public space. From this perspective, we first explored the different ways in which religious coexistence was thought of and achieved in different historical environments. Second, we delved into how religious plurality in the past and in the present is represented in the context of different media today. This volume presents the conclusions of this part of the research. We have also developed a new tool – making 'docutubes' in the way of vlogs – to stimulate religious literacy and active learning among young people. For more information, please visit our website https://retopea. eu/s/start/page/home.

We would like to thank all the authors and the entire RETOPEA team for their enthusiastic collaboration. The production of this book – not to speak of the making of docutubes – was seriously hampered by the Covid-19 pandemic in 2020 and 2021, but we managed to go forward. We are blessed with a project officer at the European Commission, Jarkko Siren, who is particularly supportive of this project, for which we would like to express our particular appreciation. Thanks also to Nigel Walkington and Chun Gan for their assistance as well as to Lalle Pursglove, Lily McMahon and their collaborators at Bloomsbury, who have warmly welcomed this book.

Introduction

# Religious diversity in Europe: Mediating the past to the young

Patrick Pasture[1]

*God Is Back* is the title of a bestselling book about an alleged return to religion in the world (Micklethwait and Wooldridge 2009). But rather than the return of one single God, what we in fact seem to be witnessing is the appearance of many different gods and a plurality of competing world views, both religious and secular. It raises discussions, with deep historical roots, about the place of religion in society and in particular in what is labelled as 'the public space'. Also religious violence has returned, in Europe, mainly from Islamist terrorists. Furthermore, Islamophobia and anti-Semitism led to violence and oppression. At the same time an awareness that religion can connect people and may contribute to peace and toleration emerged as well. History in this context is often invoked as a motivation or legitimation for divergent actions and policies.

Young people in particular are exposed to such narratives and experience their effects in their daily lives. However, as the authors of Chapter 2 (John Maiden, Stefanie Sinclair, Päivi Salmesvuori, Karel Van Nieuwenhuyse and John Wolffe) emphasize, on the basis of a series of pilot studies in different places and contexts in Europe, young people are usually quite open-minded with regards to religious (or convictional) diversity, and are willing to discuss their experiences, reflect on them and learn from them. At the same time, it is also obvious how little historical and religious knowledge they have and how much their vision of the past is twisted by presentism, that is, the backward projection of present experiences into the past (Borries 1994; Angvik and Borries 1997). In fact, they get their information from a wide variety of sources, from their close, personal circle (family, friends, religious community) to schools and various mediating contexts, most of which are covered in this book.

This book sets out to offer a critical assessment of contemporary representations of the history of religion and religious – or broader, 'convictional' – pluralism, particularly with regards to young people. It is part of a wider project that aims to improve the understanding of religious pluralism and to facilitate peaceful coexistence and toleration among young people,[2] although in this book we will be focusing particularly on assessing these representations and how they are mediated to the young.

## Defining Europe

Unlike many studies that refer to Europe's history and identity, this book adopts a broad, inclusive view of Europe. We use the term first of all as a geographical concept, referring to a generally accepted definition which situates the continent between (including) the British Isles in the west, the Nordic countries in the north and the northern Mediterranean (Portugal, Spain, Italy, Greece) in the south. Europe's eastern borders are perhaps less easy to agree on: for practical purposes in this volume we have excluded both Russia and present-day Turkey (but not the 'European part' of the former Ottoman Empire). We are aware that such a meta-geographical concept is far from being 'objective' (see extensively Lewis and Wigen 1997), but it is workable. We also decided to work within a limited time frame: our historical references do not go back beyond the European Middle Ages, thereby avoiding possible discussion about the 'Europeanness' of Ancient Roman and Greek civilizations. At the same time, this time frame encompasses the history of al-Andalus and the Ottoman lands in Eastern Europe as well as that of European Christendom, to which most studies of European identity tend to be confined. This is important in many respects, not least because the experiences and memories of these Muslim lands resonate strongly in the present, albeit in quite diverse ways, as will become clear in the following chapters.

Such an inclusive view of Europe raises other issues though: to what extent is it meaningful to group together such diverse countries and (sub)regions? Is there 'enough' homogeneity or similarity to isolate them as a separate continent? For outsiders (and for Europeans living elsewhere) the answer is obvious enough, even if the question of the exact boundaries remains unsolved. From a religious perspective, we can nevertheless easily distinguish between an Orthodox Europe, born out of the Byzantine Empire, a Catholic and a Protestant Europe, divided into Lutheran, Calvinist and Anglican areas (a careful observer will also recognize patterns in early and late Christianization). For its part, Islam dominated much of the Iberian Peninsula for centuries, until its final conquest by Catholics at the end of the fifteenth century and the subsequent expulsion of Muslims (and Jews). Islam also held sway in Southeast Europe after the conquests of the Ottoman Turks spanning the fourteenth and sixteenth centuries. Since then (until the twentieth century, that is), the latter region has been a mixed Islamo-Christian zone, a multi-ethnic, multi-confessional concoction which did not just include Orthodox Christians and Muslims but also Catholics, Protestants and Jews, to name just the main religious categories. Secularization patterns, the Cold War, post-war migrations and the increasing attraction of Asian and Amerindian spiritual cultures and New Age have also had a profound impact on the religious fabric of Europe, and are perhaps even more prevalent today (Pasture 2013; see also Chapter 1). The main issue is whether the contemporary divisions within Europe are less significant than those distinguishing Europe from the rest of the world. An answer to that question, however, lies beyond the scope of this book and would require a global comparative study, including 'outside-in' perspectives.

It does seem remarkable, however, that many contemporary narratives about Europe, even secular(ist) ones, emphasize the Christian dimension, somehow marginalizing or blatantly ignoring the fact that large swathes of Europe were under Islamic rule for centuries. Antiquity, by contrast, is normally included within European history. Many claim that Europe is rooted in Christianity and treat Islam as the 'external other' against which Europe has defined itself (Wintle 2016; Delanty 2013). At first sight, these views appear to encompass Jewish history, as they often refer to a Judeo-Christian heritage, but appearances can be deceptive: the notion of Judeo-Christianity has ambiguous, if not deeply anti-Semitic, roots, and does not prevent anti-Judaic or even anti-Semitic stances, for example, with regards to ritual slaughter (see in particular Nathan and Topolski 2018; Kluveld 2018; Topolski 2018). The contemporary use of Judeo-Christianity has another obvious downside in that it effectively excludes Muslims from Europe's identity construction.

A different set of questions arises regarding the distinction with America, to which Europe is connected as part of what is called 'the West' – a concept with an even more complex history even though the Atlantic Ocean is clearly vast enough to act as a boundary (Corm 2005, 2009; Nemo 2010). There are no such links between Europe and the East, however. The exclusion of Russia from Europe may appear bizarre: as the heir to the Orthodox legacy and to that of communism (that quintessentially European ideology), it is in many ways undoubtedly European, and its exclusion is a political and cultural construction based on complex, largely geopolitical considerations and reasons (Neumann 1995, 1998a, 1998b; see also Pasture, forthcoming). In this book we would have liked to buck this trend and to have included Russia in our analysis, but the huge scale of this task rendered this impractical.

The European perspective is also a way to overcome the trap of methodological nationalism, although the national straitjacket is difficult to escape from, as media and mediating contexts are often structured along national lines and are highly dependent on language (itself an important barrier for effective transnational or pan-European research). As Laura Galián, Madis Maasing and Karel Van Nieuwenhuyse remark in Chapter 3, history textbooks, for example, often take a strongly national perspective, and focus almost exclusively on national history. Significantly, some smaller Northwest European countries, however (with Germany as an interesting exception as a larger country), adopt a broader European perspective, which in fact is part of their national identity. Likewise, in this book most chapters contain a national dimension, although we have tried to offset this as far as possible by making comparisons between different countries.

Before continuing our investigation, a few more observations are required – first about the meaning of religion as defined in this volume. In reality, we leave the definition rather open-ended. Most contributions deal with the main religious institutions or communities, although non-institutional forms such as New Spirituality are covered as well. We also touch on non-religious world views, albeit without discussing all their possible interpretations, definitions and boundaries. As Lois Lee (2015) demonstrated, the non-religious encompasses a wide variety of positions, from agnosticism to atheism, and many variations in between, which include personal searches for meaning and individualistic bricolage. A similar story could also be told about religious people: they too display a wide variety of positions and practices. This is the case for all beliefs, and applies just as well to Muslims, Christians, Jews and Buddhists. As it happens, even the boundaries between religious and non-religious have become porous, and appear increasingly irrelevant for many. This is what we observed in different settings, among the young people that took part in the pilot studies (Chapter 2) and in our study of interconvictional associations (Chapter 9). This, to be sure, is completely at odds with the polarization that appears to dominate the media, although, in this case too, appearances can be misleading. In the current populist discourses about a Christian civilization under threat, for example, religion is rarely the issue, but it is politicized as an identity-marker (Marzouki, McDonnell and Roy 2016); hence blurring the boundaries between politics and religion.

## Religious diversity in Europe: Different narratives and interpretations

It is widely accepted that Europe has become a multicultural, multireligious, even hyper-diverse region, mainly as a result of immigration, although huge differences exist within Europe: while the main Western European capitals such as London, Paris, Brussels or Berlin perfectly illustrate this assertion, the situation is much less diverse in more rural areas, and in Mediterranean countries – within which huge differences exist – as well as in Eastern Europe, even in capital cities such as Warsaw and Budapest. Although countries that belonged to the former communist bloc were interconnected to some extent and welcomed activists from all over the world (Mark, Kalinovsky and Marung 2020), they did not experience the same waves of immigration as in Northwestern Europe, which attracted large numbers of workers for their booming industries as well as refugees and fortune seekers after decolonization and other major upheavals.

The narrative that Europe has become a hyper-diverse region suggests that this is a largely recent phenomenon and therefore flies in the face of another discourse that has always identified Europe with pluralism and diversity, and in which Europe is represented as the cradle of toleration. The latter is certainly part of the self-identification of the EU, although this narrative has lost much of its appeal in the face of current debates about multiculturalism and immigration. To a large extent the discourse of 'unity in diversity' – from this perspective a highly ambiguous motto – actually refers to national and ethnic pluralism rather than cultural and religious, although these are obviously strongly connected. Elsewhere I have argued that although characterized by large internal migrations, for centuries and until recently, Europe was relatively homogenous compared to some other regions such as South and Southeast Asia or Africa, and actually developed an ideal of homogeneity that was rooted in the complex history of Christendom, through monopolistic claims over the truth as proclaimed by Christianity as well as the close association between church and state. Pluralism, and toleration as its alter ego, rarely was something that was valued positively, let alone something to strive for. This ideal has survived the gradual secularization of Europe (which also needs to be put into perspective) and particularly inspires modern and contemporary ideologies of nationalism and populism (see Pasture 2015 and Chapter 1 of this volume).

Secularization is certainly a dominant narrative when discussing the meaning of religion in society today – Paolo Costa considers it a 'modern foundational myth' (Costa 2019) – although it has become highly contested. There is, however, no consensus on the meaning of the term, referring most frequently to the declining social significance of institutional religion and in particular of Christian churches. When used with regards to Europe, the term 'secularization' could arguably therefore be replaced by 'de-Christianization' (e.g. Christie and Gauvreau 2013). The original theorists of secularization and their contemporary acolytes, however, clearly refer to religion in general when they imagine an inconsistency between religion and modernization, and claim that modernization, understood in widely divergent terms as social differentiation, rationalization and individualization, and as underlying an ideal of progress, would inevitably entail, and indeed bring about, a decline in the social significance of religion.

In this description it is hard not to discern an ideological component, and a conceptual history reveals the common origins of secularization and secularism in Christendom itself (Lübbe 2003; Quack 2017; see also Asad 2003 and Weir 2015). Notwithstanding extensive attention to trying to define the different concepts, the two are easily conflated. Rather than speaking about 'the ideological underpinning of secular society and politics' (Calhoun, Juergensmeyer and Van Antwerpen 2011: 9), I prefer to limit the use of the term secularism to the *ideology* advocating that 'religion ought to be separate from all or some aspects of politics or public life (or both)' and that the state has 'a *raison d'être* of its own and should not be subordinated to religious authority, religious purposes or religious reasons' (Fox 2015: 2; see also Modood and Sealy 2019: 6; Wohlrab-Sahr and Burchardt 2012). While secularism in the sense of emphasizing the neutrality of the state and a formal separation between religious institutions and the state is often presented as a tool promoting toleration – in India it is sometimes even identified with toleration (Keysar 2017: 40) – a more radical, political interpretation of secularism views it as a means of limiting the role of religion in the public sphere and subordinating religion to the interests and values of the state (Asad 2013). Speaking about the French *laïcité*, Étienne Balibar in this respect distinguishes between a position that respects 'the autonomy of civil society, to which belong the liberties of conscience and of expression', and a radical interpretation of *laïcité* as 'an essential piece of the "normative" primacy of public order over private activities and opinions' (Balibar 2018: 163). In this perspective, secularism risks becoming 'identitarian' and limiting the freedom of conscience and religion, excluding people who manifest their faith. It then has a lot in common with the positions of New Atheism, which basically considers religion incompatible with Western liberties and rationality (Lee 2015: 136; Modood and Sealey 2019). In that perspective, secularization is not only the inevitable result of social processes but also the desired outcome of secularism.

To be sure, few, if any, still endorse the normativity and inevitability of secularization as a process closely tied to modernity: secularization theory has been redefined and reinvented as a theory of religious change explaining why religions may actually resist decline and even expand in modern societies (the classic example being Inglehart and Norris 2004). Neo-secularization theorists also concede that secularization does not imply the eventual disappearance of religion (and thus is 'relative'), and may follow different paths: Karel Dobbelaere (2002), for example, distinguishes between macro-, meso-, and individual levels, while José Casanova (1994) recognizes that social differentiation led to the emancipation of 'the secular spheres' (the state, the economy and science are the prime examples) as well as to the parallel formation of a separate religious sphere. However, he argues that the latter is not confined to the private domain and that a process of de-privatization has taken place since the 1980s through which religions (re-)emerged as public actors.

Nevertheless, surveys and statistics do reveal the declining relevance of both institutionalized religious practices and 'churching' in Europe, with only minor variations and exceptions (see Chapter 1). Ronald Inglehart (2021) recently made a strong case that religion worldwide – not just Christianity – is receding, but his argument remains contested (see also Stolz 2020 and the reactions in this special issue of *Social Compass* for a state-of-the-art discussion).

What such surveys are largely unable to measure is the significance of non-institutionalized religion and individual spirituality, which are often said to have no significant societal impact (see e.g. Bruce 2002, esp. 95–9; for a poignant critique see Aupers and Houtman 2006; Houtman and Aupers 2007). The traditional literature on secularization interprets spirituality and non-institutionalized religion therefore as cyphers of secularization – illustrating in this way how much the concept of religion in secularization theories owes to Christianity (Asad 2003). These new trends could also be considered as signs of the vivacity of religions that are engaging with modernity in various ways. They may be viewed as expressions of individual liberty which lead to and legitimize a wide variety of spiritual alternatives to institutionalized religions. From this perspective, rather than as a sign of increasing secularization, New Spirituality should be considered as a form of 'democratization' of religion, as well as blurring the lines between the secular and the sacred (Cooper 2016). In this process, as Slavoj Žižek (2001) observed, *believing* and *believing in* became dissociated. Hence, adopting a long-term perspective, Ethan Shagan concluded that 'secularization has not segregated belief from the world, it has instead opened the world to belief liberating a central category of Western civilization from the demands that Christianity placed upon it' (Shagan 2019: 293).

The secularization of Europe is also put into perspective when migrants are added to the equation. In this case we are less concerned about whether the religiosity of migrants will decline in the same way as that of the autochthonous population or follow different paths, and are more interested in the fact that migrants bring in different religious traditions and hence increase the diversity of the religious landscape, thereby creating a need for societies to 'govern' this diversity. In a political perspective pluralism appears as the core of the liberal ideology according to which the state should 'not impose on all citizens one single view or way of doing things' (Bardon et al. 2015). For others, the difference between pluralism and diversity lies in pluralism's presumed 'engagement' and its evaluative or normative stance. In this respect religious pluralism refers to an imagined ideal state in which 'balance, harmony, mutual support and equality of opportunity between faith communities' prevails (Eck 2016; Beckford 2003: 101; see Giordan 2012; Bock and Fahy 2019).

In any case the ways in which European states have accepted religious diversity and pluralism vary quite considerably, giving way to different 'secularisms' or, to avoid the latter concept's ideological load, 'secularities', that is, secular state systems which in diverse ways govern religion and spirituality.[3] This refers to ways of guaranteeing religious freedom and the right to believe and worship as well as to proselytize, and affects the way religions may organize themselves, the relationships between religious institutions and secular authorities and with other organized world views, and the degree of reciprocity and equality shown to minority religions and world views. The latter is hardly an issue in Europe though, but not because European societies treat different world views in the same way. In fact quite the opposite is true (Roy 2019). In most states in Europe, (organized) religions, spiritualities and secular world views do *not* have equal status and do *not* enjoy the same rights and benefits (Fox 2015). Notwithstanding centuries of conflict and continued separation, historical Christian churches have privileged relationships with secular authorities, and concertation with other religious institutions is organized according to the same model applied with the Christian church(es). However, most religions, including New Spirituality and non-religious world views, do not have similar centralized church structures. Only recently, that is, roughly since the 1960s and, particularly, since the 1990s, has there been a growing tendency to treat different religions equally, although today this equality increasingly means that they all suffer from the same biases (Ferrari 2013; see Chapter 1). In this respect the late Alfred Stepan introduced a useful alternative approach, looking into the ways in which societies guarantee what he calls the 'twin tolerations', according to which democratic political institutions get 'sufficient space' from religious institutions to function, while the state allows its citizens to live their religion in peace. These twin tolerations effectively allow for several regimes of secularity (Stepan 2000, 2011).

Even if declining religious statistics may suggest otherwise, people, and young people in particular, are exposed to religious differences in their daily lives and are challenged in their beliefs – which can be religious but also non-religious and secularist – and in their search for identity. Sometimes they are faced with manifestations of intolerance and violence, in their own personal experiences or in their immediate surroundings, or through what happens elsewhere, both nearby and far away – as modern media has considerably reduced the significance of physical distance, while at the same time creating new opportunities for interaction. The gruesome murder of French secondary-school teacher, Samuel Paty, on 16 October 2020, which happened while we were working on this book, once again revealed to us all – including the young people we have in mind in this book – the power of religious fanaticism and the reality of apparently incompatible world views in Europe. Clearly the murder not only affected the local community of Conflans-Sainte-Honorine, but also resonated all over Europe and beyond.

Apart from the increased significance of diversity and pluralism, perhaps the most striking feature today is the enhanced public visibility of religions (Casanova 1994; Hjelm 2015; Furseth 2018a), even if the visibility question depends a lot on one's particular perspective and location: the position of religion in society looks quite different if you are analysing it from the perspective of a country like the Netherlands, where only a minority still considers themselves Christian, or Poland, where a militant Catholic Church is trying to help shape a nation after decades of communist oppression, or Ireland where the same Church dominated public life but has now entered a deep crisis after the exposure of major abuse scandals, or the United States, where the impact of evangelicalism and Christian nationalism has increased greatly since the Second World War,[4] let alone from the standpoint of China or Iran (Hjelm 2015; Beckford 2010, 2012).

The 'visibility' of religion in the public sphere is largely mediated through the media. An extensive literature has developed to assess the multiple ways in which various media function as intermediaries for processes of change within and between religious and other social institutions, and what the relationship is between the 'mediatization of religion' (Hjarvard 2008, 2012, 2013) and its changing public representation. A central issue here is whether religion itself is changed by this process: obviously religious institutions adapted in different ways, depending on issue and context (Furseth 2018b; Hellemans and Rouwhorst 2020). There is certainly also evidence that it becomes more diffuse and even 'banal' (as Michael Billig claims has happened with nationalism), in the sense of being present in everyday action, receiving its meaning not from grand manifestations but often from the simplest of daily events. Although in this book, we will not be dealing with these changes *an Sich*, they do coincide with our findings that religion is a reality and a practice that young people encounter in their daily lives, and not (only, not even particularly) in explicitly religious settings. An important finding of the research on the mediation of religion is that changes may not only be abrupt and immediate, provoked by specific incidents such as terrorist attacks, but that they also take place at a deeper, more gradual level. Another conclusion, more directly relevant for us, is that it is possible to 'use the media to engage with contentious issues in ways that may reduce ethnic and religious stereotypes' and polarization (Lövheim and Hjarvard 2019: 208; Hjarvard 2008, 2012, 2013). In the Nordic countries, in particular, the potential use of the media to improve relations between people, and particularly youngsters, with different world views and faiths has been extensively studied.

Nevertheless, the mainstream media, from newspaper and television headlines to the unrestrained clamour of social networks, continue to be dominated by often simplistic, black-and-white narratives. This is not surprising, as the media tend to focus on the spectacular and on issues that disrupt social order (Hjarvard and Lundby 2018). Nonetheless, a closer look at the representations of religion quickly reveals that there are more voices than may appear at first sight. A more nuanced picture soon emerges, showing different views of the meaning of religion, religious liberty and the separation of church and state as well as about the role of religion in society, the (il) legitimation of violence, and the past and present of religious diversity in Europe and elsewhere.

It could be argued that five, not entirely unrelated, issues dominate the public perception of religion in Europe today, which also suggests that religion has become a political factor again (Schwörer and Fernández-García 2020): (1) the occurrence of politically motivated religious violence, particularly by some Islamist movements; (2) the uses of religion in contemporary populism, often adopting a 'clash of civilizations' identity discourse between a 'Christian' *Abendland* and an Islamic East, fuelled by anti-Islamic images and cartoons that often seek to provoke and insult; (3) more generally the discussions on the place of religion and religious (mostly Islamic) symbols and practices in the public and the social sphere (the wearing of headscarves, the building of mosques and minarets, the ritual slaughter of animals); (4) to a lesser extent, the political clout of conservative Christian evangelicalism in US politics, especially since the presidencies of George W. Bush and Donald Trump and (5) the resurgence of religion in conservative ethics, in the pro-life movement, which is also gaining ground in Europe. The notion that religion might also be a force for good seems to have dissipated in European narratives – missionaries tend to be presented as colonialists or as 'aid workers', ignoring their religious motivation (Goddeeris 2021: 96–102). When religions, especially Islam, are referred to, it is often in a distorted, schematic way, either casting doubts about present-day political Islam or praising a decontextualized and idealized past of coexistence. In any case religion appears mostly within a context of tensions, if not conflict, which particularly emphasizes religious 'minorities' – including Jews, not only as an ethnic group (and associated with Israel), but also Judaism as a faith community (e.g. with regards to ritual slaughter).[5] The Covid pandemic has furthermore fuelled anti-Semitism, in various ways.

## Mediating contexts

This book assesses the representations of religion and religious interactions in Europe today. Rather than focusing exclusively on the media, we decided to look at different *mediating contexts* where religion is represented. In this case, 'mediating contexts' refer to places and instances in the public sphere where religion is (made) 'visible', and thus also mediated towards the public. Mediating contexts can not only be print, audiovisual and online media, in the widest sense – for example, also including books – but also places such as museums where religions are literally 'on display' (although this of course depends on the type of museum) as well as symbolic 'places' in civil society, including political parties, religious institutions, spiritual groups and (inter)faith associations.[6] The intended public of these representations are primarily, but not exclusively, young people. After all, young people also encounter images and representations that are not specifically targeted at them.

Our initial expectation was that this approach would provide a far more diverse picture of the presence of religion in contemporary society than the traditional sociological surveys, which inevitably argue that religion is in decline, even though this conclusion clearly runs contrary to the widely held perception that religion is increasingly visible in society. We do believe, however, that this increased visibility, if narrowed down to what is commonly referred to as the public sphere, is also incomplete. In fact, it pays to abandon the framing of secularization that underpins this notion, and to take the perception of religion seriously, appreciating that religion is a multifaceted phenomenon that is present in very different contexts. This corroborates Inger Furseth's approach towards religion, which is grounded in a social science complexity frame of reference and argues against reducing history to 'single dimensions' and basic evolutions in one or other direction: in reality there are (and actually always were) 'several seemingly contradictory religious trends at different levels' (Furseth 2018b: 16). This is also highlighted by this book, even if our aim is not to engage in this theoretical debate on the place of religion in society here. In this respect our ambition remains far more modest: assessing (albeit still to a limited extent) the multiple ways in which religion and religious coexistence are presented to the public and to the young in particular, and what we can learn from these experiences to improve our understanding of the issues inherent in living together with people of different faiths and world views.

Ever since we first imagined this book, we realized that the representation of religion would vary according to the particular mediating context. Indeed, you hardly have to be an expert to imagine that the way popular newspapers depict religion would differ from the representations in, for example, religious schoolbooks (see also Lundby et al. 2018; Christensen 2018). This may appear a self-evident truism, but it seriously questions some of the basic assumptions that dominate public debate and current scholarship. This book also brought together different approaches and perspectives. The results of our research certainly confirm our initial expectations, but also show that, once again, reality is more complex than anticipated. In fact, the phrasing of the example above already suggests as much: by specifically comparing the popular press and religious schoolbooks (rather than just the press and schoolbooks), we are already implying that differences exist within each of these quite different mediating contexts (RETOPEA 2020).

The fact that the press is diverse may not come as a surprise: indeed, the media landscape includes not only tabloids but also so-called quality press, as well as lifestyle magazines and explicitly religious journals, published either by secular publishing companies or by religious institutions and associations. National political and mediating contexts also play a role in how religions and religious and convictional plurality and interactions are covered: media coverage of the same subject in Scandinavia, the UK or Greece can vary considerably as a result of the different political and mediating contexts, in line with diverging institutional positions of religions and the way media position themselves within the media market (Christensen 2018). Moreover, religious actors are often active participants or mediators in the media representation of religion: they are publishers and intervene in the public debate (Hjarvard 2012, 2013). Contrasting representations of religion can also occur in situations in which religious actors are not involved and where one would perhaps expect there to be only minimal differences, as between religious and history schoolbooks, for example. Religious textbooks tend to be far more inclusive, discussing a variety of religious traditions from different places, than history textbooks – which focus on Christianity, conflict and largely lose their interest in religion after the French Revolution.[7]

That said, there are also quite a few parallels in the way history textbooks deal with religious diversity and interactions. Representations of religious diversity in history textbooks vary, but as Laura Galián, Madis Maasing and Karel Van Nieuwenhuyse argue in Chapter 3, there are also some important parallels between the almost fifty textbooks they analysed from four countries – they even suggest some sort of common 'canon', notwithstanding important national differences. Not surprisingly these representations focus on conflicts and take into account a relative variety of actors, even if they also tend to homogenize the different faiths. But this restricted focus on conflict and the implicitly positive depiction of secularism – which is not critically assessed – is, as the authors note, highly problematic, particularly because textbooks clearly constitute an important source of information for young people, as was also confirmed in the pilot studies; they are arguably the most 'pedagogical' tool through which young people can obtain information.

The same applies when we move on to museums, a large selection of which have been analysed by Merve Reyhan Kayikci, Tamara Sztyma-Knasiecka, Naum Trajanovski and Marija Manasievska in Chapter 4. Many national historical museums consider religion as constituent (if not identical) to civilization. Islam, for example, is presented in this way. But this also implies that Islam is homogenized and disconnected from both European history and the present-day world. The dialogue with the local community, particularly with a Muslim background, then becomes difficult. Some, more general, museums, while also 'exoticizing' religions, appear more successful. The Chester Beatty Museum in Dublin, one of the world's leading religious museums, offers a case in point. It organizes extensive activities aimed at promoting religious understanding among young people. However, it also illustrates the fact that museums, in contrast to history textbooks (but similar to religious textbooks), often neglect more contentious parts of religious history. Some museums are implicitly or even explicitly designed to encourage mutual understanding, as is the case with the Jewish museums studied in Chapter 4. Given the long history of persecution of the Jews, culminating in the Holocaust, Jewish museums in this respect constitute a particular case. Most of them engage very successfully with the pluralist past to convey a message of connection and unity. Some museums, however, prefer to remain silent about religion. For its part, the permanent exhibition at the House of European History in Brussels, an initiative of the European Parliament and open since 2017, recognizes the legacy of Christendom and – in passing – Islam and Judaism as parts of European heritage and as 'defining' features of Europe but gives them hardly any visible space (Cf. Rosenberg 2018; Settele 2015; Kaiser 2017). A guide explained to me that the museum considers religion as a divisive force in Europe, which clashes with its ideal of creating a common, unifying narrative.[8] These differences make the narrative of museums complex, and quite different from that presented in textbooks.

However, both textbooks and museums, although not all to the same extent and in different ways, share a certain secularist bias, associating religion rather with non-European cultures and, when talking about Europe, with pre-modern times, as if religion in Europe somehow ceased to be a significant political and societal factor after the French Revolution. Religious minorities – perhaps most obviously in the case of Jews – become 'ethnicized' or 'nationalized' and are presented (if at all) as national or ethnic minorities. This version of events has some historical basis: an evolution of this kind did happen, but to a much lesser degree than suggested, and in fact nation and religion were often intertwined (see Wood 2016 for a recent discussion). In the Yugoslav wars in the late twentieth century, religion again functioned as an identity-marker, and around the same time it re-emerged in the debate on multiculturalism, in which the word 'culture' was used to refer to migrant communities and was mainly associated with religion.

Remarkably, this secularist bias (which has largely been debunked by recent historical scholarship: see Chapter 1) paradoxically disappears if one moves away from mediating contexts that bear the mark of academic traditions (such as textbooks and museums) towards popular culture – an observation that points at the need for more self-reflexivity among the academia. Popular media (as expressions of popular culture) illustrate the new visibility of religion in different ways. They describe religion as quite widespread, even if it still depends a great deal on media and context (Lundby et al. 2018). Moreover, although very prominent in particular settings (particularly online and in extremist media, which hardly qualify as popular culture), the tensions that characterize political and academic discourses in general seem far less prominent in popular media. In fact, they could be considered 'post-secular' in that religious plurality, in all its different guises, is a reality that in itself is hardly viewed as problematic; attitudes appear far more relaxed. This may also relate to the prominent presence of non-institutional religious expressions, in particular (New) Spirituality (formerly called New Age), which appear in various popular media, including video games and lifestyle magazines (Lundby et al. 2018). Religious symbols moreover are often decontextualized and dissociated from their particular origins; they also show a wide variety of identities 'in between' religious and non-religious and atheism (Lee 2015). In fact, as Stef Aupers and Lars de Wildt (2019) recently argued, role playing in video games (in which religious references are very prominent) can actually contribute to mutual understanding and empathy towards the (non-)religious other and can bridge the gap between belief and non-belief.

In Chapter 5 Mikko Ketola, Ivan Stefanovski, Kaarel Kuurmaa and Riho Altnurme analyse two media that may be illustrative of popular culture: TV series and YouTube videos. TV series remain extremely popular among people of all ages, even if the ways of watching have changed since the first (mass) introduction of the medium in the 1950s. While religion is sometimes depicted in conflictual settings, this is not necessarily the case, as, for example, in the internationally successful series *Citizen Khan*, or even in the series from the Balkans. Although one tends to associate online media with radicalization and fundamentalism – particularly Islamist but also from other religious traditions – most online content is actually either neutral or promotes religious peace and toleration. YouTube offers a case in point, as indicated by the authors, who found a diverse range of video clips that promote religious literacy and toleration and in so doing also combat extremism and radicalism. In fact, this chapter nicely illustrates how TV series and YouTube videos can be used to educate young people.

Politics is the mediating context where one would expect the greatest emphasis on religious oppositions and an instrumentalization of religion in line with political agendas of conflict and identity-building, all the more so as political discourses are mediated to the public through the press, be they in print, audiovisual or online, which arguably tend to inflate tensions even more. In Chapter 6, taking political debates about the 'refugee crisis' between 2013 and 2017 as a case study, Laura Galián, John Maiden, Stefanie Sinclair and Árpád Welker compare how notions of national and transnational memory have been used to discursively frame contemporary understandings of toleration and peace. Their chapter focuses on political debates in Germany, Hungary, Spain and the UK as examples of quite different national contexts, with complex histories of religious coexistence, not necessarily peaceful, between Christians, Muslims and Jews. The results of this comparative study not only confirm our expectations, but also qualify them to some extent. References to religious history are indeed instrumentalized, but with different goals. Particularly interesting in this respect are the very divergent ways in which history is used to legitimize and provide support for very different political stances. Although not addressed in the chapter (nor in this book), one may also observe the difference in which the political press addresses religion through political debate and the way other popular media such as lifestyle magazines represent it (Cf. esp. Lundby 2018).

In Chapter 7, Lidija Georgieva, Naum Trajanovski and John Wolffe assess the representation and commemorative practices of two major examples of peace-making from recent times: the Good Friday Agreement (1998) and the Ohrid Framework Agreement (2001) that put an end to the civil wars in Northern Ireland and North Macedonia respectively. Although the cases differ in several respects, their analyses reveal the futile attempts made by academic or 'elitist' circles to propagate a supposedly inclusive narrative, but nevertheless show that cultivating collective memory, particularly through physical memorials and museums recalling the conflicts, can contribute at least to a sense of justice, as a first but not unimportant step towards more enduring peace. This is actually an important finding as it highlights the potential role heritage can play in promoting peaceful coexistence.

Contemporary debates about religion in society often treat Islam as the European other. As explicit religious violence in contemporary Europe appears to be largely carried out by Islamist terrorists, so Muslims in particular have been targeted by secularists and populists, who describe them as backward and criticize them for being dissociated from 'European values' of democracy, freedom (inter alia of expression) and (gender) equality and emancipation. There are also, however, counternarratives that emphasize Islamic traditions of toleration and *convivencia*. In Chapter 8, Nadia Hindi Mediavilla, María Dolores Rodríguez Gómez and Antonio Peláez Rovira discuss how in al-Andalus, especially during the Nasrid era of Granada (1230–1492), a relatively peaceful *convivencia* was enacted and legitimized on the basis of the Islamic legal and ethical tradition, and how concepts such as *dhimma* (the legal status of non-Muslims under Islam), *mudajjan* (the legal status of Muslims under Christianity), *dār al-islām* (the 'house' of Islam), *'adl* (justice), *istiḥsān* (the public good) and *tasāmuḥ* (mutual tolerance) are being used in contemporary initiatives to reimagine Islam in the current plural context.

By looking into the discourses in some prominent Islamic initiatives towards peaceful coexistence and toleration, Chapter 8 already introduces the theme of interfaith and interconvictional collaboration. Interfaith and interconvictional organizations offer a fascinating space for encounter and dialogue, often particularly addressing young people. While most research concentrates on interfaith movements, Elina Kuokkanen and Patrick Pasture argue in Chapter 9 that they should actually be viewed in a broader perspective and also include the non-religious. Their findings show a remarkable level of engagement in dialogue as a means of increasing mutual understanding and acceptance of difference, of setting up a conversation without – and that distinguishes them from ecumenical initiatives – arguing for a particular truth.

The purpose appears above all to be about reintroducing *civility* into the debate, which is reminiscent of a largely forgotten tradition associated with the Radical Reformation and in particular with arguably the earliest 'Western' experiment with religious pluralism, the 'holy experiment' of Roger Williams in Rhode Island and Providence Plantations (on Williams's significance for civility and the debate of toleration see esp. Bejan 2017). A more inclusive narrative can also be found among the New Spirituality subculture, as is studied by Lea Altnurme with regards to the Estonian case in Chapter 10. Altnurme, however, also points to continuing tensions between different understandings of religion, and to institutional and non-institutional spirituality.

In conclusion, and before we go on to discuss the mediating contexts in detail in the following chapters, we thought it would be useful to provide an additional perspective to this book. As we often refer to the representations of the past, we wanted to outline this past according to the latest historical scholarship. In Chapter 1, Patrick Pasture and Christophe Schellekens offer a wide-reaching essay of how Europeans dealt with the issue of religious diversity. They do not provide the usual narrative of Europe as a beacon of toleration though, and question the still-popular narrative about the alleged progress of secularization and the marginalization of religion, arguing that the role played by religion in society changes in far more complex ways. Instead, the authors emphasize a fundamental longing for homogeneity and a deep-rooted fear of diversity as a continuing legacy of Christendom, and the association between religion and politics. They present history as one of people who are struggling to find practical solutions to what they perceive as existential problems. They also include the history of al-Andalus and the Ottoman Empire in their assessment, noting the parallels, differences and interactions in dealing with religious differences.

# Religious diversity in Europe: The challenges of past and present

Patrick Pasture and Christophe Schellekens[1]

This book assesses historical and contemporary representations of religious diversity in Europe and how the past is mediated to the present and future generations. Indeed, present-day representations of this issue often invoke and refer to the past. Europe has a troubled history with religion, as manifested, for example, in the Wars of Religion. Nevertheless, Europeans have also learned to live together, and perhaps this was more often the case than we assume. In order to properly understand and grasp the full significance of contemporary representations of religion, we must also therefore have a reasonable understanding of the past. This chapter briefly outlines some of the salient features of Europe's long and complex history of religious coexistence and toleration, less as a yardstick to measure the accuracy of historical representations – though this objective, even if never fully attainable, is not entirely absent – and more as a means of comprehending and historically contextualizing these contemporary representations. It not only looks at Europe as the original centre of (or heir to) Christendom, but also explores the experiences of al-Andalus and the Ottoman Empire. Throughout this chapter, we will be focusing not only on practices and attitudes but also on the norms, beliefs and values held by a diverse set of actors and institutions.

## A history of (in)tolerance, war and peace-making

'We have learned that tolerance is the soul of Europe,' the German Chancellor Angela Merkel declared at a ceremony to mark the 500th anniversary of the Reformation on 31 October 2017, in Wittenberg (Merkel 2017). The place and timing of the statement suggest that she was mainly referring to religious toleration, without excluding tolerance in other walks of life.[2]

The underlying idea is that tolerance is Europe's answer to its remarkable diversity, an idea that is also expressed in the European Union's (EU's) motto, 'Unity in Diversity', which it adopted in 2005. It is perhaps worth pausing for a moment to look at these two assumptions. Is Europe really so diverse? Compared to South and Southeast Asia with their multitude of languages, ethnicities and religions, one may wonder. In fact, rather than being particularly diverse, one could argue that Europe, if anything, is obsessed with a drive towards unity and has an innate fear of diversity (Pasture 2015). From that perspective, perhaps the opposite is true: that *intolerance* lies at the heart of Europe's soul. The origins of this intolerance lie in the particular history of Christendom, in which an intense alliance was forged between church and state and their interests became closely aligned. It also explains why Europe never completely endorsed freedom of religion in the way the United States did – after all, tolerance is not the opposite of intolerance (although calling it its *counterfeit*, as Thomas Paine did, may be overstating it as well) (Paine 1791: 78).

The learning process invoked basically refers to the tolerance that allegedly emerged after the Wars of Religion. According to the standard narrative, these wars ended with the Peace of Westphalia (1648), which ushered in a new, stable European order based on sovereign states with fixed territorial boundaries, the 'Westphalian model' that is still referred to in most textbooks and analyses of the international system. It was also responsible, so the story goes, for the rise of religious toleration, for which the Enlightenment is mainly credited. Both narratives are highly problematic historically. The alleged Westphalian order, for example, is a nineteenth-century myth that describes an idealized political model that has no basis in the actual peace treaties or in political practice. Neither did it bring an end to religious violence, certainly not if one takes a pan-European perspective (e.g. Nexon 2009: 265–88). And as for its contribution to the rise of toleration, arguments in favour of religious freedom and tolerance had been formulated by various thinkers long before the Enlightenment, including Christian ones.[3]

The narrative furthermore ignores Europe's non-Christian and particularly Islamic pasts, and thus implicitly equates Europe with the history of Christendom, excluding other religions (Asad 2003). In this chapter, we will be focusing on how both Christendom and Europe's Islamic empires dealt with religious diversity, offering examples of their 'tolerance' and intolerance, and discussing their different ways of living together. While Classical Antiquity is usually associated with a tolerant attitude towards religious diversity (notwithstanding the persecution of Christians) (Marcos 2018), Christendom is notorious for its intolerance which goes back to the recognition of Christianity as a state religion in the late Roman Empire (Edict of Thessalonica in 380 AD). This also applies to the Christian kingdoms that were constituted in Western Europe in the Early Middle Ages, although at that stage religion appears to have been more of a social commitment than a belief system, and society seems to have been far more open to foreigners and religious diversity than in later times (Classen 2018; see also Brown 2013). It was not until the eleventh or twelfth centuries that Europe turned into a 'persecuting society' (Moore 2006). With few exceptions, European states demanded adherence to Catholicism as a sign of obedience (even though the different interpretations of religion allowed for considerable variation in practice).

The fear of diversity applied, among others, to 'heretics' as well as pagans and 'infidels', which explains why non-Christian advisors or experts (doctors, astronomers, mathematicians, etc.) were rarely to be found at European courts. Likewise, non-Christian merchants in Medieval and Early Modern Europe hardly travelled inland. This even extended to the Arabs, great travellers and merchants who in Asia and Africa ventured far beyond Islamic territories. Jews, however, could be found throughout

Christendom since Roman times. Though often harassed and persecuted, they were respected as people of the 'Old Covenant' and enjoyed the protection of canon law even if they were also condemned for their rejection of the New Covenant (*Sicut iudaei*, *c.* 1120) (Levy 2016). Sometimes they enjoyed royal protection in exchange for loyalty and for their services as moneylenders and scholars. Especially when Europe became more urbanized and moved towards more organized feudal states, however, Jews became systematically and massively persecuted. In 1290 they were expelled from England, and later also from France and Spain after the Reconquista (Moore 2000; [1987] 2006; see also Kaplan 2007: 294–330; Nirenberg 1996, 2014). Romani, although mostly Christians, faced similar difficulties. Itinerant descendants of military clans from northern India, they arrived in Europe in the fourteenth century, as wandering vagrants, tolerated sometimes with fascination, but more often despised, persecuted and expelled (Taylor 2014).

There were nevertheless times and places in Christendom, such as medieval Sicily, Hungary (between *c.* 1200 and *c.* 1300) and Christian Spain (until *c.* 1500), in which Muslims and Christians lived together in (relative) peace, and Catholic monarchs recognized Muslims as legitimate citizens, granting them a similar status to that afforded to Christians in Muslim countries (Catlos 2014). Resisting calls from the hierarchy to impose religious uniformity, the Catholic kings of the Polish-Lithuanian Union in 1368 granted religious freedom to all: Catholics, Orthodox, Jews, Shamanistic and Islamic Tatars (who settled in Lithuania in the fourteenth century), and increasingly Christian dissidents or heretics, such as Hussites, Lutherans, Calvinists and Anabaptists. It would be wrong though to consider the Polish kings as 'enlightened' advocates of religious freedom, as their power was tightly restrained by the powerful nobility (Forst 2018).

## Tolerance beyond Christendom

While in Christendom most of the time 'infidels' and heretics were persecuted, the situation in Europe's Muslim areas appears different. Although the history of the Islamic view on religious diversity is complex and varied from one place to the next and at different times in history, in Medieval and Early Modern times Muslim states adopted Islam as the state religion, while not only tolerating and protecting, but also discriminating against other religions to varying degrees.

The Umayyads conquered Visigoth Spain in the eighth century. In addition to instituting the *Sharia* as the political and judicial fundament of the state, they also laid the ground for a brilliant Arabic-Islamic culture. Non-Muslims received protection in return for paying a *jizya* (religious tax). They were nevertheless held in a subordinate position and were limited in what they could and could not do. They were also compelled to wear cultural markers that set them apart from the Muslims. They could not proselytize because for Muslims apostasy was punishable by death. The degree of protection and discrimination varied over time such that in the twelfth century non-Muslims were even banished (although in practice most stayed while enduring harsher discrimination). Pogroms of Christians and especially Jews did occur, although they remained rare compared to Christian Europe. In fact Christians and Jews were able to make significant contributions to the blossoming of arts and sciences. The conquest of al-Andalus by the Catholic monarchs eventually put an end to this relative toleration. Although initially a system of coexistence developed that was similar to that applied in al-Andalus, recognizing the right of Muslims to emigrate or to remain subject to restrictions (see Chapter 8 of this book), intolerance soon prevailed after the fall of the last independent Muslim state on the Iberian Peninsula, the Nasrid kingdom (Emirate) of Granada in January 1492. The Jews were expelled almost immediately in March 1492, and in the following decades Muslims were also forced to convert or emigrate; the Inquisition ruthlessly persecuted alleged false conversions. In 1609, converted Muslims (*Moriscos*) were also expelled. While some Jewish entrepreneurs set up businesses in major Western European ports such as Bordeaux, Livorno and Amsterdam, most Jews escaped to North Africa or the Ottoman Empire, where they were welcomed with open arms. Some found refuge in Poland-Lithuania (Kaplan 2007).

The Ottoman Empire, which from the fourteenth century onwards expanded across Eastern Europe and reached its maximum extent in 1683 at the gates of Vienna, was in effect a multireligious state in which diversity was 'managed' rather than suppressed; similar to al-Andalus or the Ancient Roman, the Russian and the Mongol Empires, the Ottomans believed that toleration contributed to internal peace and stability and was beneficial to the welfare of the empire. While guaranteeing the supremacy of Islam as the rock on which the state was built, they largely followed local customs of organization and granted certain freedoms, including freedom of worship, to the many religious and cultural minorities, albeit in exchange for the payment of religious taxes and the observance of certain codes of conduct under which Muslims were treated differently from those of other creeds. The specific degree of protection, liberty and discrimination varied widely across the empire, depending on the particular time, political context and the changes in the interpretation of Ottoman law. Although until the mid-seventeenth century the Ottomans sometimes captured Christian boys to raise them as Muslim soldiers in the elite corps of the Janissaries (where they could rise to the highest position in the empire), for most 'infidels' Ottoman rule was to be preferred over Catholic suzerainty, as in the Habsburg Empire. The Greek-Orthodox Church even enjoyed a privileged position at the centre of Ottoman power: it was allowed to levy its own taxes and the patriarch was appointed by the sultan. The Ottomans welcomed Jews as well as Christian refugees of all sorts, fleeing from the Wars of Religion. Although not always actively encouraged by the sultans, some non-Muslims did convert to Islam. Conversion in the opposite direction, however, was effectively prohibited, as it was everywhere else in the Muslim world. Overall an 'ecumenism of everyday life' existed, although from the late sixteenth century onwards a process of 'Ottoman confessionalization' (Tijana Krstić) took place, along similar lines to post-Reformation Christendom (see Gara 2017 for a brilliant discussion of the literature; also Barkey 2008: 110–11).

While in Christian Europe, Islam figured prominently in apocalyptic visions and the Ottoman invasions still haunt the imagination of the old Habsburg lands, the wars were more a clash of empires than faiths. Ottoman armies, for example, had a considerable number of Christian soldiers, even in positions of command (Almond 2009: 151–80). In spite of initial papal opposition, the French and the English concluded lasting alliances with the Ottoman Turks. Religion did not stand in the way of trade either. In fact, a rich imaginary of Islam as Europe's 'other' existed which was threatening to be sure, but at times also very much admired (Malcolm 2019).

## European Christendom between toleration and genocide

Although most wars in Europe's turbulent history had other origins, religion only slowly ceased to be a major issue during the seventeenth and eighteenth centuries (Kaplan 2007). Overall the authority of secular powers over the different religions was reinforced: Protestant Churches became state or 'national' churches in Protestant countries, while the monarch's authority over the church in Catholic states also increased. However, secular authorities also supported concerted efforts by the different confessions (churches) to impose orthodoxy (Ocker 2018; Nexon 2009; Gorski 2000). These campaigns achieved mixed results however: all authority was somewhat tainted and people had learned to think for themselves, particularly in Protestant areas (Marshall 2018).

In practice, therefore, limited multi-confessionalism, or 'tolerated diversity', became the norm in most of Europe. The American historian Wayne P. Te Brake (2017) distinguishes a plethora of different arrangements to secure peace after religious war. In reality, however, in most of these, religious homogeneity remained the ideal and the solution often tried to put this ideal into practice, albeit symbolically, for example, by imposing segregation, repression or, by contrast, partial integration of dissidents (involving restrictions on the public expression of religion). Sometimes other solutions were reached in which one church was favoured over others, or in which two, or more, different churches were granted equal status, or which included diverse forms of 'ad hoc tolerance' (Te Brake 2017; see also Kaplan 2007; Friedeburg 2011). But they never encompassed all churches, excluding new and radical religious communities.

Two of the states that became best known for their tolerant attitude towards religion were the Polish-Lithuanian Union and the Dutch Republic. The Dutch respected freedom of conscience and everyone was free to believe what they wanted in private, but the extent to which these beliefs could be practised in public depended on many factors. Commercial interests came before confessional concerns. Jews in Amsterdam were allowed to build a huge synagogue, but they could not join the guilds. Catholics were considered a liability, as were Anabaptists, and could at most practise their faith in 'hidden churches'. Elsewhere in Europe religious freedom was more restricted, although in many places mixed communities found ways of living together, mostly peacefully. In some, this meant living 'together apart', in separate communities. For Jews, and in very rare instances also Muslims, this implied living in a ghetto, a measure which also afforded them a degree of protection (Safley 2011; Kaplan 2007).

One should also emphasize that the general trend was not necessary towards extending toleration and when rulers felt strong enough, they rolled it back, as was the case of King Louis XIV of France, who in 1685 repealed the Edict of Nantes of 1598 that had granted religious freedom to Protestants. The dialectic between tolerance and persecution was played out in full in the British Isles, leading to the emergence of ideas about civil and religious liberty and later to the extension of the freedom of worship to Nonconformists in 1689 (Toleration Act), which paved the way for 'Protestant pluralism' (Coffey 2000; Stevens 2018; Walsham 2008; Worden 2013).

Toleration emerged mainly to guarantee a stable and peaceful political order and to maximize the contribution of all towards economic and political prosperity. But it was also advanced on philosophical grounds. The most radical proponents of religious freedom were members of the Radical Reformation such as Thomas Helweys and Roger Williams, who claimed that God was an advocate of separate religious and secular powers and of full religious freedom. Many of their arguments in favour of religious freedom were based on the ideas of ancient church fathers such as Tertullian and Lactantius as well as Medieval thinkers. More moderate theologians, such as the Swiss Reformed theologian Thomas Erastus, advocated that a strong monarch acting as God's representative should grant religious freedom in order to guarantee peace and stability. Increasingly, 'Enlightened' philosophers expressed doubts about the validity of religious claims altogether (Forst 2011; Laursen and Nederman 1998; Wilken 2019; Sorkin 2008; Zagorin 2003). Together with freedom of thought, they also called for control over the churches and over the Catholic Church in particular. Some Catholic thinkers actually welcomed the prospect of 'modernizing' the church (Lehner 2016). Enlightened monarchs followed suit. Emperor Joseph II of Austria, for example, issued a Toleration Edict in 1781–2 allowing Lutherans, Calvinists, Orthodox and Jews to hold private religious ceremonies.

The American Revolution, in response to the actual pluralism that had emerged in the New World and inspired by a mixture of Radical Reformation, Evangelical and Enlightened ideas, went even further and imposed the separation of church and state and religious freedom in the newly established United States of America (although a Christian nationalist current emerged which argued that the United States had been founded on Christian principles: Green 2010; Haselby 2015)).[4] In Europe the French Revolution adopted the Rights of Man and the Citizen (1789), which declared that all sovereignty originated with the people, and introduced freedom of opinion and religion. However, while pursuing a policy of active de-Christianization of state and society, the revolutionaries went so far as to create an alternative secular state religion (The Cult of Reason). The latter proved premature and soon afterwards Napoleon reinstated the Catholic Church as the 'majority church', although he maintained the freedom of religion. The Congress of Vienna (1815) restored the Ancien Régime while modernizing the international order; in the process the power balance between church and state was tipped a little further in favour of the latter.

## Secular Christendom in context

In the nineteenth century, religion apparently faded as political drive, class, ethnicity and nation came to the fore (see e.g. McLeod 2000; McLeod and Ustorf 2003; Hempton and McLeod 2017). Nevertheless, religion remained an important social and political factor in much of Europe and continued to impact upon the state, so giving rise to 'secular Christendom'. From the 1860s onwards nation and religion became increasingly intermingled. In continental Western Europe in the 1870s–90s conflicts arose between secularists and both the Reformed and (especially) the Catholic Church, which actively opposed liberal values and ideas of self-determination, democracy and sovereignty. In France this resulted in the separation between church and state and the obligation of the state to remain 'neutral' (*laïcité*), while more informal separations between church and state took hold in Germany, Belgium, the Netherlands, Austria (the Habsburg Empire) and, eventually, also Italy. Confessional political parties in these countries took on the defence of church interests, supporting their claims to remain active in education, social and health care. Secularists acted as a different 'confession' but pursuing an agenda of political secularization (Weir 2014). Different convictional movements constituted competing life-worlds, sometimes developing into extensive 'pillarized' communities in which 'believers' were nourished 'from the cradle to the grave' (Kaiser and Clark 2003; Hellemans 1990, 2020). After the First World War, the Vatican regained political clout as an international political actor, establishing concordats with various countries to secure the interests of the church (Chamedes 2019).

In the 1920s and 1930s, a period of strong political polarization between right and left, churches across Europe largely came down on the side of authoritarianism, Fascism and even Nazism. The Vatican actively and successfully promoted authoritarian Catholic confessional states, as happened in Hungary, Poland, Austria, Portugal and Spain, among others. This also encouraged anti-Semitism, particularly because Jews were branded as communists and secularists. At the same time, however, some Christian movements and individuals developed theologies and practices that upheld democracy and liberty (Chamedes 2019; Chappel 2018; Conway 2006; Hanebrink 2006, 2018; Weir 2015).

Meanwhile since the eighteenth century, conflicts emerged in the Ottoman Empire between Muslims and non-Muslims as a result of the latter's better economic and commercial connections with the burgeoning European economies. This led to more closed, 'bounded' ethno-religious identities, and each religious community was given a degree of autonomy to regulate its own affairs (often referred to as the 'millet-system', although it was never as systematic as imagined). Tensions were further fuelled by Western European economic success and religious-political interventions by Russia and other European empires in defence of Christian minorities. The Ottomans reacted by 'modernizing' and centralizing their state apparatus (Tanzimat Reforms, 1838–76), although in the end this only heightened the frictions between the ethno-religious communities. The introduction of religious equality introduced religious freedom, including for Christian missionaries, but stripped the minorities as well as the Muslim majority of their communal privileges, provoking frustration among all. For their part, the educational reforms fostered a spirit of competition and rivalry between ethnic and religious communities. Sultan Abdülhamid II (r. 1876–1909) in contrast promoted a modern Pan-Islamist ideology as the common source of identity for the empire, at the expense of non-Muslims. The Young Turks in the twentieth century reacted by formulating a secularist-nationalist alternative. This also failed to unite the various different populations and resulted in the 'genocide' of the Armenians. The new nation states that emerged in the wake of the disintegrating empire similarly tried to establish a common identity based on the fusion of religion and nation. Once again, the most common result was more suffering and death. The relatively peaceful coexistence that had existed between ethnic and religious communities in the Ottoman Empire was erased from memory and replaced by one of discrimination and conflict (Barkey 2008: 277–97; Gara 2017; Mazower 2000; Hajdarpašić 2008; Todorova 1997: 180).

It would be a mistake, however, to limit religious nationalism in Europe to the Balkans. Increasingly churches associated themselves with nations, while the new nation states and nation-empires themselves began to exorcise minorities (see e.g. Wood 2016; Weitz 2008). In spite of this, in most of Central and Western Europe nationalism in the nineteenth- and twentieth century appears more secular. Most Protestant countries retained their state churches, albeit merely symbolically, leaving room for religious dissent. This did not vaccinate them against racism however. The call for ethnic (and religious) homogenization in Germany and other parts of Central Europe ultimately culminated in the genocide of Jews and Romani. It is clear that the underlying anti-Judaism leading to the Holocaust was part of a centuries-old European tradition. However, anti-Judaism and anti-Semitism received a new impulse in the nineteenth century through scientific racism, which impregnated secular ideologies more than religious ones, most of all National Socialism in Germany, but also Marxism-Leninism in the USSR.

Meanwhile Christian churches, albeit with certain ambiguities, supported European imperialism and colonialism, and its underlying racist ideology. Nevertheless, respect for other religions in the colonies began to emerge in the late nineteenth century, first in Protestant, and later also in Catholic missionary circles. They also gave local people leadership roles in the local churches, and gradually and to varying degrees distanced themselves from colonialism. This allowed them to survive and even expand after decolonization.

The Second World War signalled the end of empire in Europe (although it took fifteen more years to acknowledge that colonial empires were also doomed), giving way to more homogenous nation states. The idea that ethnic and religious diversity constituted a risk for stability and peace remained strong initially, and the new nation states idealized ethnic and religious homogeneity (Ther 2015). The communists in Eastern Europe pursued their own purification politics by oppressing religion, which was considered divisive for both class and state interests. Forced secularization and ethnic and religious assimilation policies went hand in hand in communist countries, such as Bulgaria where the communist regime imposed dire measures on Muslims and Romani. Elsewhere in communist Europe religious freedom was also suppressed, even in Yugoslavia, which, in spite of this, largely retained its multireligious character (Mazower 2000: 116–42).

## A new start?

After the Second World War, Western Europe tried to distance itself from its tumultuous past in a different way. Most countries adopted the European Convention of Human Rights, which protected religious freedom as an *individual* human right and provided for the creation of a European Court of Human Rights to enforce its principles (albeit initially excluding the colonies). The freedom to believe, which included changing religion, and respect for the autonomy of religious institutions in matters of internal organization and doctrine became important features of state-church relations in Western Europe. Nevertheless, the impact of religion on politics and society remained high, as seen by the fact that the Cold War was presented as a conflict between secular materialism and Christian humanism (Betts 2020: 125–72). The Catholic Church continued its anti-communist crusade, backing authoritarian regimes in Spain and Portugal, while only belatedly accepting democracy elsewhere (Chamedes 2019: 265–9; Chappel 2018: 144ff.; Müller 2011: 132–43). Although Western European nation states emphasized their autonomy vis-à-vis the churches, multiple ties remained and Christian Democracy emerged as the most powerful political movement in continental Western Europe. The 'pillars' – which organized people into separate sociopolitical 'mental worlds' according to their world view (Hellemans 2020) – blossomed and, in the case of Christian pillars, were financed by official church taxes or even state subsidies. In Protestant countries with a state church, however, the monarchs – as formal heads of the state and the church – abstained from interfering in ecclesiastical affairs, limiting their role to confirming any decisions with regards to church organization and dogma. In the UK, a pluralistic model of church-state relations emerged in which diversity is valued as a source of national identity. One manifestation of this is that public servants are allowed to wear religious symbols (Ferrari 2013; see also Roy 2017).

Although religion was at the heart of a lasting conflict between Catholics and Protestants in Northern Ireland, in general Christian churches set out on a path of reconciliation and ecumenism, thereby reversing the mutual antagonism that had previously characterized their relations, as well as the anti-Semitism that had been part of Christian culture until 1945. Although late compared to Protestant churches, perhaps the most stunning *volte-face* was that of the Catholic Church which around the time of the Second Vatican Council (1962–5) cast off the anti-modernist approach that it had adopted a century earlier and accepted political and religious freedom, although in fact the church maintained its claims upon the truth and the obligation of the state to support it (see esp. Schindler and Healy 2015).

While the political reshaping of Europe after the Second World War and in particular the breakthrough of the nation state created smaller but culturally more homogenous political spaces, this homogeneity has since been shattered by at least three different processes, which are largely unrelated but do interact, and are significant with regards to religious coexistence: secularization, or rather the de-Christianization of politics and society; 'Easternization' or, more broadly, the impact of New Age and new spiritualities; and immigration of people with other faiths.

De-Christianization refers above all to the declining impact of Christian churches on society, especially since the late 1950s, affecting politics and moral and social life. It was also manifested in declining adherence to churches and participation in traditional Christian rituals and practices. In communist countries, the state, while in theory recognizing religious freedom, in practice actively promoted atheism and discriminated against religions, limiting their ways of expression and barring religious people from promotion at work. In Western Europe this decline happened more spontaneously, although particularly in France secularism was also actively promoted (Stanley 2018: 79–101). Although the debate on causes is still open, rising educational levels and prosperity increased the autonomy and liberty of individuals: it was no accident that especially young women took on a vanguard role (Brown 2001; McLeod 2010). From the 1980s onwards the 'pillarized' systems eroded; in Italy Christian Democracy collapsed. In Germany, Austria, Belgium and the Netherlands the 'pillars' largely remained intact, although their ideological sharpness became increasingly blurred (Hellemans 1990, 2020). French ideas about political secularism – the alleged 'neutrality' of the state – widely spread over Western Europe, leading to what Joseph Weiler (2005) termed 'Christianophobia' in the EU, where references to Europe's Christian past became viewed as problematic.

Surveys of Western Europe since the 1960s indicate a pronounced decline in Christianity, although the pace of decline has varied from one country to the next. Recent surveys that include Eastern Europe show that in most Central and Eastern countries the share of Christian affiliation has remained more or less stable in recent decades (Dargent 2017; Pew Research Center 2018a, 2018b; Inglehart 2020). In some Eastern European countries, and especially Orthodox countries where the association between nation and church has been re-established after the fall of communism (Belarus, Russia, Ukraine, Bulgaria), both participation and affiliation numbers in contrast have even been increasing, although the politicization of religion can also cause a backlash. The surveys moreover show changing patterns in belief in God that to a certain extent mirror those of religious affiliation and participation. Furthermore, while differences certainly remain, traditional distinctions between Protestants and Catholics – such as those regarding the paths to salvation (by faith alone or also by 'good deeds') – have lost much of their power to divide. Most Catholics and Protestants in Western Europe today believe that the similarities outweigh the differences (Pew Research Center 2017). These figures suggest that in Europe today there are various forms of 'believing without belonging' (Dargent 2017; Davie 2000).

Secularization and de-Christianization were, however, also expressed in an increase in atheism and agnosticism as well as adherence to alternative spiritual movements. The numbers of atheists and agnostics have augmented particularly in Northern and Western Europe since 1970, despite a decline after the demise of communism in Eastern Europe (see Table 1.1). New spiritualities – including local esoteric traditions,

**Table 1.1** Agnostics and Atheists in Europe per UN Region (Percentages, 1900–2020)

| UN Region | 1900 | 1970 | 2000 | 2015 | 2020* |
|---|---|---|---|---|---|
| Western Europe | 0.19 | 4.74 | 10.23 | 12.59 | 13.20 |
| Southern Europe | 0.13 | 4.70 | 5.06 | 5.63 | 5.78 |
| Northern Europe | 0.70 | 5.80 | 9.47 | 10.15 | 10.78 |
| Eastern Europe | 0.11 | 18.60 | 7.76 | 4.45 | 4.16 |

Amero-Indian shamanistic practices and highly secularized Indic religions – in Europe remain a minority interest. Nevertheless some 15–40 per cent in Western Europe declare that they believe in a 'higher power' or spiritual force, and in some surveys in Central and Eastern Europe over a third express a belief in reincarnation, an idea originating in Indic religions (Pew Research Center 2018a: 42–5, 119–38, 2018b: 19–20, 24; see also Campbell 2007; Pasture 2011). Interestingly, this development has led to a remarkable 'secularization' of religious symbols. This process started especially in popular (youth) culture and New Spirituality, which appropriated religious signs from different cultures, often enabling people to piece together some form of individual spirituality (Lee 2015).

The 1950s and 1960s saw an influx of migrants into (North)Western Europe. Intra-European migration from Eastern and Mediterranean countries to Western Europe remains hardly visible in the statistics, but did lead to perceptions of cultural difference even if newcomers shared the same faith as the population of the host country. Most non-European migrants were either postcolonial refugees or 'guest workers' for the expanding industries. Most of them were usually Christians or, to a lesser extent, Muslims as well as Hindus, Buddhists and Sikhs. Conversion does not appear to have been a major reason for the spread of non-European religions in Europe, including Islam. The Muslims belonged to different Islamic currents, and there were also ethnic divisions between them. The ways in which they integrated into European societies diverged, ranging from assimilation to radical opposition and many variants in between (creating many 'Euro-Islams', to use a concept that is usually interpreted in a normative and in our view inadequate way) (Dressing, Jeldtoft and Woodhead 2013; al-Azmeh and Fokas 2007; esp. Nielsen 2007 and Cesari 2007; al-Sayyad and Castells 2002; Bistolfi and Zabbal 1995) (see Table 1.2).

The unexpected collapse of the Soviet Empire and the subsequent 'liberation' of Eastern Europe reintroduced real religious and political liberty in these countries. Religious groups, which with the exception of Poland tended to be made up of quite small, non-institutionalized communities, became massively engaged in the civic protests. In some countries, most obviously in Poland, this was paralleled by a restoration of religious life and a revival which lasted for decades. A similar revival, however, did not take place in the Baltic States or indeed in most other Eastern

**Table 1.2**  Muslims in Europe per UN Region (Percentages, 1900–2020)

| UN Region | 1900 | 1970 | 2000 | 2015 | 2020* |
|---|---|---|---|---|---|
| Western Europe | 0.05 | 1.21 | 5.87 | 7.29 | 7.74 |
| Southern Europe | 2.75 | 3.14 | 6.59 | 7.61 | 8.26 |
| Northern Europe | 0.00 | 0.77 | 2.93 | 5.50 | 6.09 |
| Eastern Europe | 4.35 | 4.18 | 5.74 | 6.43 | 6.81 |

* Estimate

*Data source*: Johnson and Grim (2020) (accessed 20 July 2020). It should be noted that the classification of UN regions is rather counter-intuitive. The UK, for example, is classified as part of Northern Europe. See https://unstats.un.org/unsd/methodology/m49/#fn2.

**Table 1.3** Religious Diversity in Europe (Index, 2010)

| Country | Index | Country | Index | Country | Index |
|---|---|---|---|---|---|
| Netherlands | 6.4 | Slovenia | 4.0 | Greece | 2.5 |
| Bosnia-Herzegovina | 6.0 | Spain | 3.9 | Andorra | 2.2 |
| France | 5.9 | Austria | 3.8 | Lithuania | 2.1 |
| Belgium | 5.7 | Albania | 3.7 | San Marino | 1.8 |
| Latvia | 5.7 | Switzerland | 3.7 | Ireland | 1.7 |
| North Macedonia | 5.6 | Bulgaria | 3.5 | Liechtenstein | 1.7 |
| Estonia | 5.5 | Finland | 3.5 | Serbia | 1.6 |
| Sweden | 5.4 | Hungary | 3.5 | Croatia | 1.4 |
| Germany | 5.3 | Denmark | 3.3 | Portugal | 1.4 |
| UK | 5.1 | Italy | 3.3 | Poland | 1.2 |
| Luxembourg | 4.9 | Norway | 3.1 | Iceland | 1.1 |
| Russia | 4.9 | Ukraine | 3.1 | Malta | 0.7 |
| Belarus | 4.7 | Slovakia | 2.9 | Moldova | 0.6 |
| Czech Republic | 4.1 | Monaco | 2.8 | Romania | 0.1 |
| Montenegro | 4.0 | Kosovo | 2.6 | Vatican City | - |

*Data source*: Pew Research Center (2014). Johnson and Grim (2020) contains more recent statistics, but the figures are calculated very differently and the results are not as convincing (e.g. with Sweden as the religiously most diverse state in Europe).

European countries. With the break-up of Yugoslavia, a series of nationalist-religious conflicts erupted, leading to ethnic cleansing and even genocide. Of the countries since the end of this war, only Bosnia-Herzegovina and North Macedonia retain a somewhat precarious multi-ethnic and multireligious character. Another result of the fall of communism was that most former Eastern Bloc countries experienced an exodus of workers and young people in search of opportunities in Western Europe, increasing the sense of diversity there (see Table 1.3).

## Religion in a multicultural society

Although already in the making since the end of the 1960s and initially mainly in response to the enlargement of the European Community, the EU embraced multiculturalism as an ideal in the late 1990s (Prügl and Thiel 2009; Kastoryano 2009; Lähdesmäki 2012). Around the same time, however, multiculturalism became a target for extreme right-wing and emerging populist movements, even though until then it had hardly ever been actively encouraged as a political project (Schinkel 2017: 5–6; Chin 2017: 80–138). In fact, religious diversity, including the presence of Muslims, was not perceived as an issue until the end of the 1980s. The relative unimportance of this question is nicely illustrated by the European Values Study, which until 1989 did not even ask Europeans about their opinions about migrants and different religions. Culture, in a broad sense, began to be considered an issue in the 1980s, and only since the 2000s has this been narrowed down to religion, and especially Islam (Chin 2017: 3–4; Allievi 2005; Yilmaz 2016).

Religious communities had modified their stance towards others some time earlier. Some churches had been arguing for dialogue and unity for decades; ecumenism came to the fore with the establishment of the World Council of Churches in 1948 and the ecumenical shift of the Catholic Church with the Second Vatican Council. After the 9/11 attacks in 2001, interfaith and interconfessional movements emerged in an effort to combat religious extremism by establishing a dialogue based on mutual respect, appreciating difference as a positive value in itself (see Chapters 8 and 9).

The new EU member states, however, did not all share the same imaginary based upon the rejection of a past beset by nationalism and genocide, as symbolized by the Holocaust, which had emerged in the 1980s as the ultimate symbol of Europe's depravity against which the EU and its predecessors had been created. This was particularly true of the new member states from the East. Former communist European countries preferred to emphasize their own suffering under the Soviet yoke (Littoz-Monnet 2012; Leggewie 2011; Trimçev et al. 2020). Likewise, the ethically liberal and secular(ist) narrative of EU values incited increasing opposition. The debate in 2004 on the preamble to a proposed 'EU Constitution' (which was eventually dropped) laid bare tensions between those who thought it should contain a reference to Christian values and history and those who emphasized the humanistic-secular values of the Enlightenment and cherished the 'secular' nature of the political. An anti-Islamic dimension increasingly entered the debate, which crystallized around the possible accession of Turkey to the EU. Opponents of Turkey's membership highlighted either the legacy of Christendom or that of Enlightened secularism, and often both, disregarding the fact that Turkey was a secular state (in some ways even more so than most EU countries). Within this debate, the German-Syrian sociologist Bassam Tibi (1998: 154) proposed the idea – reminiscent of the traditional Islamic way of dealing with diversity – that Europe had a common *Leitkultur* (leading culture) which he associated with modernity: 'democracy, secularism, the Enlightenment, human rights and civil society'. In this context, religions (not without cause) were exposed as illiberal, undemocratic and intolerant, especially towards LGBTQ, and as regards liberal values of self-determination. Others, by contrast, associated European *Leitkultur* with (Judeo-)Christian values, or with a combination of Christian and secular, enlightened thinking. This leads to various and often paradoxical political stances, especially with regards to gender-related issues, for example, when wearing certain (allegedly religious) clothing is prohibited. Gender has indeed moved to the centre of the debate on the place of religion in society, and exposes the complex and divergent ways both are imagined (Furseth 2018).

Since the 2000s wearing religious clothing and symbols in the public space (a space that has gradually enlarged) has become contentious throughout Europe. The argument focuses on the need of the state in a multicultural society to remain 'neutral' – including teachers and pupils in public schools – but has increasingly spilled over to other domains such as the workplace and even 'public' free-time zones such as swimming pools. Especially female religious clothing, in particular the hijab, is viewed as inherently oppressing and opposite to Western values. In this perspective signs of worship have become contentious as well. Minarets were prohibited as were the calls to prayer by the muezzin. While Muslims were particularly targeted, other religions also shared the same fate in similar circumstances, although in general Christian symbols were spared: Christian church towers or church bells never faced the same criticism; the (disappearing) wearing of cassocks, habits or nuns' veils was not targeted either (it should be noted though that in public positions in France and Belgium all religious signs are prohibited). European courts have sanctioned discrimination mainly by interpreting Christian symbols (even the crucifix) as part of European 'culture' and denying their 'proselytizing' capacities, thus 'secularizing' them, as Elayne Oliphant (2012) observes (see also Roy 2020, 144–50; Bhuta 2014; Moyn 2014; Martínez-Torrón 2016; a different philosophical perspective in Forst 2011: 543–71). In the wake of the murder of a French schoolteacher by Islamist terrorists on 16 October 2020, the French government demanded clear adherence to its 'republican values', criticizing intellectuals and proponents of interfaith dialogue. Freedom of religion itself has come under fire – in 2013 several local councils in Moldova, for example, made it illegal to hold Islamic rites in public. Some forms of religious harassment have increased by about 70 per cent in Europe since 2007, often affecting not just religious people but society at large (Diamant 2019; Sägesser et al. 2018: 28–34). Religiously unaffiliated and non-religious people have also come under attack, as in Greece, while Islamist terrorists targeted particularly the freedom of expression (Villa 2019).

Populist Islamophobia has also resuscitated narratives of a decline of the Christian Occident. In fact, such narratives had already appeared during the final days of the communist regime in former Yugoslavia and Bulgaria in the late 1980s when Muslims were depicted as a threat to European civilization. Such rhetoric underpinned the expulsion in 1989 of approximately 350,000 Muslim 'Turks' (descendants of people that had migrated from Central-Asia to the Balkans in the fourteenth–fifteenth century) and motivated anti-Muslim violence during the Yugoslav Wars of the 1990s. In this respect the discourses of Serbian leaders such as Slobodan Milošević in 1989 are identical to those of contemporary populists such as Victor Orbán, the present prime minister of Hungary, in defence of 'European Christian civilization' (Mark et al. 2019: 154–72). These claims about a Christian European civilization under threat also appeared in Western Europe, as espoused by German Christian Democrats in Bavaria (Germany), British Brexiteers and the Italian populists of Matteo Salvini (see Chapter 6).

Even if they vary considerably between different populist parties, these discourses about a Christian European *Leitkultur* may suggest a growing politicization of religion (Caiani and Carvalho 2021). But they should not be confused with signs of re-Christianization or desecularization. In fact, the references to Europe's Christian past among populists are anything but consistent, and rarely mention faith. They illustrate what Olivier Roy termed, with regards to Muslim fundamentalists, as 'holy ignorance', the individualist, cultural-emotional reaction against secularization and elitism that underpins radicalization and fundamentalism of different persuasions (Roy 2010; Marzouki, McDonnell and Roy 2016; De Cesari 2020: 26–46). Moreover, Christian churches often resist such instrumentalization of Christian symbols, expressing their solidarity with embattled Muslims and Jews. That is not always the case though. Some local churches, most notably the Orthodox Church in Bulgaria and the Catholic Church in Poland and Hungary, strongly oppose Muslim immigration, which they describe as an 'invasion' (Sägesser et al. 2018: 28–34). In doing so, they actually support populist Islamophobia. One should, however, refrain from dismissing these resistances too easily: they are actually very much in line with a long tradition of confessional politics, and point to the continued prevalence of a persistent religious 'social imaginary' that is mobilized more effectively by populists than by the Christian Democratic parties, who often appear too much a part of the elite culture (Van den Hemel 2019). Other signs of a revival of political Christianity can be seen in the pro-life and anti-LGBTQ movements. Gender equality and sexual democracy have become core values of Western secular ethics (in Western Europe often presented as a litmus test for migrants, especially Muslims, and often also viewed as taking precedence over religious freedom: Furseth 2018), but they incite increasing opposition, particularly in Eastern Europe (Poland, Hungary) as well as in France and Italy (Bialasiewicz and Gentile 2020).

This raises the question about the degree of religious toleration in Europe. Surveys highlight huge differences in acceptance of the other, especially non-Christians, and reveal a deep East-West divide – with Greece clearly situated in the East. Notwithstanding the variations between the different surveys, the trends and relative positions largely correspond. It is interesting to note that people in Western Europe generally believe that religious discrimination is more widespread in their country than discrimination on the grounds of gender, age or disability, but less than for race/skin colour (Romani being perceived as the most discriminated against group), while Eastern Europeans think there is less religious discrimination. As regards acceptance of the other, the answers strongly suggest that religious discrimination may be far more widespread in Eastern than in Western Europe. But no doubt realities are more complex than these self-assessments suggest (GESIS 2019).

The surveys show that prejudices and negative stereotypes towards Muslims and, to a lesser extent, Jews, still hold strong support, even if they seem in general to be on the decline: in Western Europe 20–40 per cent, for example, agree that Muslims want to impose religious law in their country (Belgians in particular appear deeply alienated from the Muslim population), while about 11–36 per cent (median 21 per cent) hold negative stereotypes towards Jews. Those with negative attitudes towards religious others tend to reject all those of different persuasions, even if their specific attitudes towards Muslims (most difficult to accept as family members or neighbours), Jews, Indic religions, other Christians or even atheists do not entirely coincide. In general Europeans are more tolerant towards atheists and non-religious people than towards religious people, more tolerant towards Jews than towards Muslims, and more tolerant in terms of accepting the religious other as a neighbour than as a family member. Catholics are usually less tolerant than Protestants, but those who were raised Christian but left the church have more tolerant attitudes towards Muslims and Jews than those who were raised in a non-religious environment (Pew Research Center 2018a: 42). Acceptance of other Christians is quite common, also at a more intimate level. Ignorance about the others' religion, however, is widespread everywhere. There is extensive, though very divergent, support for restrictions on Muslim's 'religious' clothing and especially face coverings (though in Portugal and Sweden about half of the population say

'Muslim women should be allowed to wear whatever religious clothing they want')
(Pew Research Center 2017, 2018a).

# Conclusions

This overview of different ways of dealing with religious diversity in Europe cannot be summarized in terms of the usual narrative that increasing tolerance has emerged as a reaction to the intolerance of religions and their mutual exclusivism. Today secularism is viewed as the most effective way of dealing with religious and cultural diversity, but the term refers to quite different realities, and the more radical manifestations actually may hamper the inclusion of religious minorities (see also the introduction to this volume). Though not central to the analysis, our review of this issue moreover shows that arguments for toleration can be found within religious traditions themselves. It also makes clear that the concepts of tolerance or toleration can mean different things, and rarely imply that differing world views are considered of equal worth, in the past or in the present. Christendom, with its close but ambivalent association between the secular and the sacred, privileges homogeneity, but has always included countervailing forces.

The 'secularization' of politics in Europe has continued the search for homogeneity in different guises, to the point that, as Zygmunt Bauman (1991: 8, 53–74) argues, 'intolerance is, therefore, the natural inclination of modern practice', even if religion is not currently the driving force behind it. One may, however, also observe that it is easy to overestimate the significance of religion: it is just one of many sources of identity and alliance, perhaps not even the main one. And before arguing that religion surely mattered more in the past than in the present it is worth reminding that it did not always have the same meaning: for centuries religion referred more to relations and practices than to belief, and the meaning of belief itself also changed dramatically, transcending the traditional boundaries of faith (Shagan 2019).

We also looked at ways in which Muslim regimes dealt with religious difference. Muslims and Christians are often seen as opposites, particularly in contemporary representations. While evolution is mostly associated with Christendom – narrated in terms of progress – the worlds of Islam are usually (as will also appear in following chapters) portrayed as static. They are then viewed as either eternal enemies of Christendom and 'the West', or idealized for their capacity for *convivencia*, which in reality allowed for very divergent practices. Our analysis, by contrast, shows that both worlds changed profoundly over time and were characterized by unequal patterns of coexistence and inclusion, sometimes relatively peaceful, co-operative even, but also often violent, sometimes extremely so, while not exactly weaving a story of continuing progress in either case. Moreover, as one moves away from Medieval and Early Modern times, more similarities between faiths emerge: while Islamic empires disappeared from Europe, they were confronted with European, and later American, imperialism elsewhere. Muslim reactions throughout the globe varied from absolute rejection and opposition, to accommodation, and modernization – sometimes by not only reinventing fundamentalist traditions, but also by supporting secularism (as in

Turkey) and democracy: similar processes can be observed in 'Christian' and modern Europe as well. It is also worth noting that today there are more Muslims living in democracies than in autocratic regimes (the same perhaps cannot be said for atheists or Christians). Muslim democracies moreover appear more inclusive than European states, for example, by respecting the traditions and customs of different faiths and world views, such as recognizing their respective feast days (Stepan 2011, 2014).

Meanwhile, the longing for homogeneity remained a key component of European politics at least until the early post–Second World War period, although 'secularized' and dissociated from its origins. It is particularly visible in the population policies that became associated with the ideal of the nation state (even if they were first introduced in modern European *empires* of the late-nineteenth- and twentieth century). The current situation in the late twentieth-/early twenty-first century is sometimes labelled post-secular, but what that exactly means is open for debate (Beckford 2012; Hjelm 2015). One thing that is certain is that the social significance of Christianity in Europe (and in Canada and Australia, but not elsewhere) has declined considerably, to the point of it becoming a marginal social and political factor in some countries, although in recent times Christian references have been re-emerging as political and cultural signifiers. Secularism has also lost a lot of ground, but has made a forceful comeback in reaction to mainly Islamist terrorism and an increased public visibility of religions, in particular Islam. As will become clearer in the following chapters, currents in society that embrace more pluralist visions of society also certainly exist. Sometimes even the boundaries between religions and between the religious and the secular evaporate or are transcended, where religion becomes immanent or non-believers adopt religious symbols and spiritual practices. The contemporary religious landscape has become multiple and complex, even inconsistent, escaping any simplistic label.

So, tolerance unfortunately is not the soul of Europe. European history has too often been characterized by violence and intolerance to warrant such a claim, even if, in reaction, Europeans – using quite different arguments – have developed philosophies and practices that enable peaceful coexistence. But especially they have learned – although they also tend to forget – that dialogue is possible, which may lead to practical arrangements which may not be ideal, but guarantee peace and ways of living together nevertheless. Tolerance remains no less a challenge though in the twenty-first century than it did in the tenth, sixteenth or twentieth.

# Views of the young: Reflections on the basis of European pilot studies

John Maiden, Stefanie Sinclair, Päivi Salmesvuori,
Karel Van Nieuwenhuyse and John Wolffe

## Introduction

Although recent years have seen growing interest in views and understanding of religious diversity in European countries, one particular demographic has received markedly less attention: the young. This chapter examines data from the multinational RETOPEA project, collected between 2019 and 2020. It was intended as preparatory cross-European research for involving young people in making short films (docutubes) which explore religious diversity, tolerance and intolerance. A unique aspect of this data is that it concerns the perspectives of young people regarding both contemporary and historical religious diversity. We are therefore able to consider the ways in which European young people relate past and present in considering religious diversity. In particular, we examine the sources of information upon which they construct their understanding and the extent to which a 'presentist' epistemology shapes their attitudes. In what follows we will first survey the literature on young people's attitudes towards religious diversity; then, second, we describe the methodology used by RETOPEA for gathering data on young people's perspectives; third, we offer analysis of this data; and, fourth, we discuss its significance both in terms of our understanding of young people's thinking and, practically, in relation to pedagogical approaches.

## Existing literature of young people's views

Scholarly research on European young people and religious diversity is linked with a wider academic agenda to understand changing patterns of religiosity. One dimension of this is the significance of Christianity. This has been expressed by some, such as in Steve Bruce's *God Is Dead: Secularization in the West*, in terms of inexorable 'secularization' (2002). Others have tended to emphasize multiple and complex patterns and dynamics at play; for example, Grace Davie (2000, 2006) has adopted terms such as 'believing without belonging' and 'vicarious religion' while also pointing towards the significance of migration for both private and public expressions of religion. Concomitant to studies on pluralization are the expanding literatures on multiculturalism and national identity (Grever and Ribbens 2007). Here, however, our primary interest is the niche body of literature on the attitudes and experiences of young people regarding religious diversity. Larger European surveys of young people's attitudes, such as the European Commission's REDCo project (involving nine Universities, in England, Estonia, France, Germany, Netherlands, Norway, Russia and Spain), the University of Münster's 'Perception and Acceptance of Religious Diversity amongst the European Population' (PARD) survey and Ziebertz and Kay's earlier project 'Religion and Life Perspectives of Youth in Europe' (2005), offer, like RETOPEA, the potential for cross-European comparison. Other studies, such as the University of Warwick's 'Young People's Attitudes to Religious Diversity' project, have provided more detailed national and local analysis. Taken together, this literature offers three broad areas of insight.

First, young people, the qualitative and quantitative data gathered by REDCo underlines, have tended on one hand to be appreciative – at least in an abstract sense – of 'religious heterogeneity', but on the other could also express 'a range of prejudices' (Jackson and McKenna 2016: 7–8). Age could be a factor – the youngest age group (eighteen to twenty-four) in the PARD study of Denmark, France, Western and Eastern Germany, Netherlands and Portugal was found to be generally more positive about religious diversity, but some variation was also observable; for example, this age group in Germany was comparatively more sceptical towards religious plurality than the same cohort in the other nations, and, where Islam was concerned, less supportive of mosque building and more likely to support restrictions on the practice of the Muslim faith (Yendell 2016). A broader finding of REDCo was that, generally speaking, young people's appreciation of religious diversity was expressed in recognition of the importance of knowledge of different religious traditions, and a desire to see a range of religions taught in the classroom (Jackson and McKenna 2016: 7; see also Skeie 2009).

Second, existing literature offers insights into the multivariant factors shaping young people's attitudes towards religious diversity. Arweck and Penny described this in terms of 'concentric circles' (Arweck and Penny 2015), with family exerting the most important influence, followed by friends or school, and then faith community (Arweck 2016). It has also been suggested that where attitudes towards the 'Other' are concerned (and most clearly, it seems, attitudes towards Islam), contact, and *frequency* of contact, with those of other religions was significant in cultivating a more tolerant outlook (Arweck and Ipgrave 2016: 24–5; Yendell 2016). Regarding the role of the media, research on the young in the UK indicated that young people were 'shrewd and astute in identifying underlying agendas in media reporting', for example, in stereotypes and generalizations, but also noted 'that repetitiveness and the ubiquity of stereotypical portrayals had an effect on them, whether they were conscious of it or not'. It has also been suggested that television was a more influential medium than the internet in the shaping of young people's views about religion (Arweck and Penny 2015: 269).

Third, the research underlines the importance of local context. In the UK, the breadth of coverage of 'Young People's Attitudes Towards Religious Diversity' was able to highlight the ways in which local religious plurality, and the attitude of individual schools towards diversity and teaching of religion, produced variation in the views of the young (Arweck and Ipgrave 2016).

What remains underexplored in current research is how young people's opinions and attitudes towards religious diversity relate to levels of historical awareness and understanding. Rarely does the existing literature address young people's historical reference points. It is also unclear which sources of information shape young people's perceptions of religious diversity in the past, and how they regard the representation of historic religious diversity in popular media (in terms of trustworthiness, for instance). We do not know how understandings of religious diversity in the past and present are interconnected and how each informs the other. *Young Peoples' Attitudes Towards Religious Diversity* (Arweck 2016) includes very little discussion about social representations of religious diversity in the past. The same applies to one large multinational research project on European religious pluralism (Avest et al. 2009: 249–75), in which was found that young people themselves preferred to talk about present-day issues in relation to religious diversity rather than about its historical dimensions. More broadly, the major quantitative European-wide research *Youth and History: A Comparative European Survey on Historical Consciousness and Political Attitudes among Adolescents* (Angvik and Borries 1997) focused on young people's historical interests, their political attitudes, their attachment to human and civil rights, their attitudes towards migrants and ethno-cultural diversity, and their perception and appreciation of the school subject of history, but not their attitudes towards religious diversity.

However, if we step back from issues of religious diversity, the current literature does provide important insights more broadly into the ways in which young people's understanding of history is constructed and the interrelation between present and past, and it is very likely that some of these ways of thinking apply to religious diversity. A key finding is that young people often take a very presentist approach of the past, meaning they do not consider the past in its own right, but tend to look at it through a present-day lens (Borries 1994). They consider and understand past events through their own, again present-day, experiences. It is not for nothing that Sam Wineburg (2001) defines historical thinking as 'an unnatural act'.

This presentist approach often leads young people to moral judgements when dealing with the past. They often judge past events based on present-day societal, moral and personal opinions, thereby completely ignoring historical contexts. The result can be an unconsciously biased understanding of the past, being somehow inferior to the present (Borries 1994). In other words, they testify to a belief in progress.

The existing literature has some insights at an epistemological and procedural level, which are relevant to this research. Young people often demonstrate a naivety concerning ideas about historical knowledge and the role of sources in the construction of that knowledge. Wineburg (1991, 2001) and Nokes (2010), for instance, found that students do not spontaneously approach sources as evidence – accounts of authors that need to be interpreted – but rather treat them as authorless collections of historical facts. They consider and read sources as pure bearers of information, which they accept uncritically. Most students do not contextualize sources, hardly critique what they read or see, and rarely pay attention to the performative character of the (textual and visual) language used in the sources or to the rhetorical strategies. These findings are confirmed in many other studies (Britt and Aglinskas 2002; Hynd 1999; Nokes, Dole and Hacker 2007; Nokes 2010; Paxton 1999; Perfetti, Britt and Georgi 1995; Stahl et al. 1996).

Considering young people's historical reference knowledge, many studies have been conducted relating to different kinds of historical knowledge (on reference knowledge of the national past, see e.g. Van Havere et al. 2017). Often this kind of research is accompanied by lamentation concerning a decrease in historical knowledge. Wineburg (2004) firmly rejects the recurrent critiques against this (alleged) decrease in historical knowledge among young people – whose roots date even back to Classical Antiquity. These critiques seem to stem from a nostalgia for a very encyclopedic, factual dealing with the past. In his opinion, it is not a good idea to test factual knowledge of (young) people, 'only to discover – and rediscover – their "shameful" ignorance' (Wineburg 2004: 1406). He makes a plea for a different, reflective approach of the past (particularly in history education), more oriented towards fostering people's understanding of the past and fostering their historical thinking skills.

Finally, research indicates that – not surprisingly – students not only acquire historical knowledge at school, but also through popular historical culture (via films, television series, news, YouTube clips etc.) and through stories in their own family and community circles. Seixas (1993), in this respect, concluded that historical family stories and experiences play an important part in how students gather knowledge and attribute significance to the past, for those stories shed light on enduring or emerging issues in history or contemporary life. Between school history and family/community history as sources of historical knowledge, discrepancies and conflicts can occur. When students from minority groups do not recognize themselves and their history in school history, they will shove it aside – even reject school history – and they will only value the historical narratives within their own group (family/community). He hence issues a plea to seek for connections between both and to address family and social groups' stories within school history.

In summary, while there is valuable literature emerging on young people's attitudes towards religious diversity, there is minimal research specifically on their understanding of the religious (or non-religious) past. However, the wider literature on the ways in which young people understand the past – notably their presentist tendency – and both the pedagogical challenges and possibilities for engaging young people with the past offered important points of reference for our own research.

## Research context, questions and methodology

### Research context

The European teaching landscape for religious education and religious history is diverse and complex. In general, there are three broad patterns for teaching religion in European public schools and, to some extent, in private schools. The first pattern is a system where no teaching of religion is offered at schools operated by the state (e.g.

France, Hungary, Czech Republic), but religion can be taught if the parents or students ask for it – although not during school time or as part of the school curriculum. The second pattern comprises 'non-denominational' teaching about religion (e.g. the UK, although in cooperation with the religious organizations and institutions). Often these are compulsory courses; exceptions here are Estonia and Slovenia. Sometimes special attention is paid to Christianity (e.g. Denmark and the UK). The third pattern is 'denominational' teaching of religion – by which we mean teaching of a specific religion. This is often supported from the point of view of finance and logistics by the state (e.g. Belgium, Finland, Poland, the Netherlands, the Czech Republic, Spain, Italy, Romania). In some states the teaching of religion is granted only to recognized or registered religious communities and almost everywhere a minimum number of students is required (Ferrari 2013: 100–1). Germany represents a very special case with regards to religious education. After the fall of the Berlin Wall in 1989 and reunification in 1990, religious education in schools was intensely debated, due to the fact that religion previously had such different roles in the East and West German legal and educational system. Currently, each of the sixteen German states has their own legislation which provides the framework for imparting religious education; in addition to this religious education is the only subject mentioned by the German national constitution. In most states, denominational religious education exists (i.e. Roman Catholic, Protestant and, in some cases, Islamic), and ethics is offered as an alternative, though in some (e.g. in Berlin) ethics is a compulsory course for students and on request students may have classes in religious instruction (Eckhardt 2019: 20–1).

Despite the existence of the three aforementioned patterns, it can be discerned that the subject matter of denominational and non-denominational teaching on religion has recently become more alike than it has been historically (although the growing religious plurality in Europe raises the question of whether these models will adequately provide the breadth of teaching required to address the changing situation of religious diversity). Religious plurality is presented in religious education textbooks; very often the source is the World Religions Paradigm (WRP). While there is overall a moderate to high emphasis on interreligious dialogue, there is little to no attention on religious history (Štimac 2015).

What of teaching history in schools? History education has in general been considered very important. In a recent project, *Shared Histories for a Europe without Dividing Lines* (Council of Europe 2014), it has been said that History is 'key to the development of skills, attitudes and values such as critical thinking, open-mindedness, tolerance, an ability to appreciate the value of cultural diversity and to communicate peacefully with those who have different cultural and religious affiliations and who speak other languages' (18). However, recent studies show that very often such goals are dismissed and that the history curriculum has a narrower scope, often either nationally or Eurocentrically oriented. Furthermore, while different societal domains (politics, economy, culture, social) might be addressed, there is little reference to religious diversity in the past or to local history and family history (see e.g. Van Nieuwenhuyse 2017). Overall, in both the teaching of religious education and history, little attention is paid to religious diversity and interreligious contacts in the past.

**Research questions**

This study was conducted within the wider context of the RETOPEA project and in preparation for 'docutube' workshops that the project team is planning to run in schools, museums and youth groups across Europe. These workshops aim to engage young people (aged thirteen–eighteen) with themes of religious history, toleration and peace through the production of 'docutubes', that is, short documentary-style films produced by the teenagers themselves. In the preparatory phase, we attempt to gather some indicative snapshots of young people's perceptions and experiences of religious diversity (past and present) in Europe to help us pitch the development of the materials for the docutube workshops at an appropriate level.

This research aimed to achieve deeper insights into young people's perceptions, experiences and knowledge of religious diversity in the past and present. In particular, we aimed to gain a greater understanding of the following:

- young people's views on how religion and religious diversity (in the past and present) are represented in the media
- the sources and extent of young people's knowledge of and views on religious diversity in the past
- young people's perception of religious diversity in contemporary society
- how young people's knowledge and views of religious diversity in the past and present inform each other
- differences and similarities between young people's views on these issues in different national contexts.

**Participants**

The research was conducted with gender-balanced small groups of teenagers, with a maximum of sixteen participants (though most groups were smaller) per group. Some groups included a mix of young people of different ages; others consisted of students of the same age, though all participants were between thirteen and eighteen years old. Given that we were aiming to gain indicative, but relatively in-depth, snapshots, rather than a comprehensive, large-scale or representative overview of young people's views on these issues, we worked with a relatively small sample of young people who were invited via their schoolteachers to take part in this research project.

We approached and included a diverse mix of religious and non-religious schools, ranging from schools with very ethnically/religiously diverse to relatively homogeneous student populations, as well as schools from a range of urban and rural sociocultural settings. A total of 132 students participated from twelve schools in six countries. Participating schools included four schools in the UK (England), three schools in Belgium (Flanders), two schools in Germany and one school in Finland, Estonia and Spain each. We had also planned to include groups from Poland and North Macedonia in our research, but due to the sudden imposition of social-distancing restrictions and school closures linked to the Covid-19 pandemic, our planned research in these countries could unfortunately not be completed in time for the publication of this chapter.

Participation was voluntary, and all participants (and their parents, for students younger than sixteen years old) gave informed consent. In one instance, the parents of a group of young refugees did not consent for their children to participate in our research. While the teenagers of this group were happy to take part, their parents were suspicious and worried that anything their children would say as part of the focus group interviews might impact negatively on their outstanding applications for asylum or residency. Our assurances that all contributions would be anonymized did not unfortunately allay these parents' concerns; so we could therefore not include this group in our study.

## Methodology

Our research combined a range of methods, including a short questionnaire and semi-structured focus group interviews with small groups of students (Eliot & Associates 2005). We began by asking each individual participant to quietly spend five–ten minutes to complete a short, anonymized questionnaire. The questionnaire contained the following three multiple-choice questions:

1. How important (if at all) is religion to your life? Please circle a score between 1 (not important at all) and 5 (of great importance).
2. Have you ever observed prejudice or bias against religion in the area where you live? Please circle one of the following answers: Yes – No – Not sure.
3. Have you ever experienced bias against your religious or non-religious beliefs? Please circle one of the following answers: Yes frequently – Yes sometimes – No, but hardly ever – No – Not sure.

In addition to the provision of a selection of multiple-choice answers, participants were given the option of adding open comments or explanations, and many of them chose to do so. The questionnaires primarily served as a 'warm up' to the semi-structured focus group interviews. The idea was to introduce the topic of religious diversity, toleration and peace and give participants a moment of quiet time to activate their thoughts, reflect on the topic and start considering how it might relate to their personal views and experiences before engaging in small group discussions.

The quiet time for the completion of the questionnaire was followed by a semi-structured focus group interview that lasted for about one hour. If all participants (and their parents/guardians) consented, audio recordings were made of the focus group discussions. In cases where that was not possible, detailed notes were made by the researchers, though all reports were anonymized.

In advance of the focus group interviews, we established with teachers whether there were any sensitive issues concerning intercommunity relations the facilitators should be aware of in relation to each group that was interviewed. We also made sure that there were opportunities for participants who were in any way concerned or upset following the interview to speak to a teacher, youth worker or a member of our project team. Before the focus group interviews began, facilitators also asked participants to agree to the ground rules of (1) listening, (2) respecting different opinions and (3) not directing criticism at individuals.

For the focus group interviews, the research team worked with the same set of questions in all localities (translated into each local language). However, we were keen to allow local and national perspectives to come through in the discussions. The topics of the questions of the semi-structured interviews were aligned with our research questions, thoroughly discussed with the project team and pilot tested. These questions focused on four themes: that is, young people's perceptions of

1.  representations of religion and religious diversity in the media (including questions, such as 'How accurate or inaccurate, fair or unfair, do you think different types of media are when they discuss different religious groups?')
2.  religious diversity in the past (e.g. 'Historically, how religiously diverse do you think your city/town/ country/ Europe has been? Are there any particular 'turning points' when your city/town/ country/ Europe became more or less religiously diverse?')
3.  religious diversity in present-day society (e.g. 'In the present day, to what extent do you think religious diversity offers benefits or challenges to society?') and
4.  potential connections between approaches to religious diversity in the past and present (e.g. 'Are there ways in which we can learn from history?').

The interview questions were designed with the aim to trigger conversation, and facilitators were instructed to give as much agency as possible to participants to share and respond to views about their experiences and perceptions of religion and religious diversity. Facilitators were therefore asked (1) to give sufficient time for a discussion of each question, (2) if there is an awkward silence, to not immediately rush to the next question – but give participants time to think and (3) if tangential discussions develop, to not always 'shut these down', as they can 'break the ice', but to use their discretion as to when to return to more relevant conversation. While facilitators aimed to encourage participation, they were also advised to be careful not to put individual students 'on the spot' with any question. The aim was to facilitate a guided discussion, but not place any participant under pressure to speak, and allow individuals to withdraw from the discussion at any point.

As pointed out above, our aim was to gain insights into young people's perceptions and experiences of religious diversity. In particular, we hoped to establish to what extent and how participants made connections between religious diversity in the past and present. We started our analysis from a grounded theory approach. This meant that we did not apply an existing theoretical framework from the outset of our research, but developed theory through the analysis of data. After a thorough reading of all transcripts of the semi-structured interviews, we followed a dialectical approach to data analysis. This involved an iterative process of going back and forth between themes that we initially identified, and then refined or changed after rereading (Onwuegbuzie et al. 2009; Peck 2010; Weston et al. 2001). Emerging themes included the temporal dimension (Did participants talk about the past, present or connections between both?), sources of knowledge (Which sources of information did participants use and trust, and why?), a sense of value or judgement (What value did participants assign to religious diversity? Did they adopt a neutral, positive or negative view on religious diversity – and why?) and participants' awareness of the complexity and nuance of relevant issues and of their own positionality.

In light of the relatively small sample size, the research team was very aware of the limits of any general conclusions that could be drawn from the quantitative analysis of the responses to the multiple-choice questions that were part of the 'warm up' questionnaire, especially with regards to any specific national contexts. The analysis of the open comments submitted as part of the survey and the focus group discussions was much more conclusive as this qualitative data offered much more in-depth information about participants' perceptions. Regardless of the relatively limited value of the findings of the analysis of the questionnaire responses, the process of completing the questionnaires appears to have fulfilled a very useful function in itself by setting the scene or 'warming up' participants for the focus group discussions, where the issues could be explored in much more depth, detail and nuance. Participants reported that they found the quiet time spent completing the questionnaires useful to help them focus their minds at the start of the session. Many participants also commented positively on the format and set-up of the focus group discussions, and explicitly stated that they really appreciated the opportunity to discuss their views and experiences in this context with their peers and wished that such opportunities were facilitated more frequently in their schools.

Given that all of the questionnaire and focus group data had to be anonymized (as required by the funding agency), it was not possible for the research team to establish direct connections between questionnaire answers, specific student profiles and individual students' statements made during the focus group interviews.

## Research findings

### Young people and religious diversity in the past

Most young people showed awareness that religious diversity is not an exclusive phenomenon of the present. We noticed in all focus groups, however, that knowledge and understanding of the extent of religious diversity in the past was limited, usually based upon particular major events in their own national or regional context. During a discussion in one German school, for example, these events included the Roman occupation, the Protestant Reformation, the Nazi regime and the arrival of migrants (particularly Turkey) in the past seventy years. Participants in Flemish focus groups discussed Roman polytheism, the Crusades and the Reformation. In the English schools, references were made to the Tudors and the Reformation, the Second World War and Holocaust, and new commonwealth migration. Some students at a Roman Catholic school in England did describe a more distinctive narrative of growing Catholic emancipation over the past two centuries. Overall, a number of aspects of students' understanding of religious diversity in the past were striking. First, there was the tendency to underestimate religious diversity in the past; in the English schools, there were only two individual mentions of non-Christian religious diversity pre-1945, that of the nineteenth-century Jewish community. Second, there was a tendency to focus on larger events and with almost no discussion of lived history and everyday religious diversity. An exception here were the young people in Granada, who had a more sophisticated understanding, which reflected the heritage of Christian-Muslim interaction in that region. Third, historical understanding also tended to reflect students' positionality – whether it was nationally or regionally rooted – with very few students able to draw upon examples from wider global contexts, although because it involved a wider geographical sphere, the Second World War and Holocaust were mentioned in a number of different national contexts as an example of religious intolerance.

It was evident that while students often cited media representation when discussing contemporary religious diversity, they seldom mentioned examples of this for historic diversity, and where they did so it was with reference to costume dramas such as *The Tudors* and *The Medicis*. This may suggest, then, that it is school education which is the main factor in the formation of historical understanding. While more research is needed on different national curriculums, it seems possible that the narrowness and positionality of knowledge and understanding amongst English students may reflect the kinds of criticisms which some scholars made of the 2014 History national curriculum for the UK as 'largely exclusionary, monochrome' and as defending 'Britishness' (Alexander and Weekes-Bernard 2017). At the same time, where young people demonstrated knowledge of new commonwealth migration in relation to religious diversity, this may point towards the ways in which teachers have been able to intervene in the spaces for creativity in the curriculum, although it is acknowledged that 'such spaces are overly reliant on the commitment of individual schools and teachers' (Alexander and Weekes-Bernard 2017).

What was generally evident where students' understanding of the past was concerned was the lack of concrete examples of religious toleration. Our report on the focus group in Estonia, for example, observed, 'It did not seem that the students who were starting the course about religion had much knowledge about the history of coexistence of different confessions at the same time in Estonian history'. Rather, there was a strong tendency across nearly all the schools (with Granada being an exception) to associate religious diversity in the past with the absence of toleration and the presence of conflict. Where the former was concerned, one English student's view of the past was that 'it was very strict', and various students in England, Germany and Finland spoke of a lack of freedom to choose religion in the past. Our report of one English school observed that students spoke of religious diversity in the past 'in almost wholly negative terms', with mention of religion in relation to 'genocide', 'Holocaust', 'civil wars' and 'Christians against Muslims'. One key historical event mentioned across various national contexts was the Holocaust. Overall, the past was presented as one of intolerance, and history tended to be seen in terms of cautionary tales, such as the importance of not demonizing 'other' groups. We learn from the past so things 'won't happen again'.

## Young people's views on media representation of religious diversity in the present

When asked about various kinds of media coverage of religion and religious diversity, it was notable that the participants predominantly focused on the representation of religion rather than on that of religious diversity. The latter did emerge spontaneously in their answers. In general, young people acknowledged that religion is addressed in both television news and documentaries, and in several series, films, on Netflix, television, YouTube and other channels.

Some dramatic series were cited quite frequently, such as *Riverdale* or *Sabrina, the Teenage Witch*. However, the sheer – and surprising – range of references, including *Family Guy*, *Daredevil* and *Orange Is the New Black*, is a strong indication of the pervasiveness of representations of religion. Somewhat paradoxically, students tended to think that representations of religion within popular culture did not have a significant role in shaping their perceptions of religion; however, the ability of some young people to freely cite examples of representations of religion, and also articulate generalizations and biases suggests that popular culture may have a greater influence than previously thought. Some young people were able to articulate a feeling that drama series could represent religion in ways which might emphasize either caricatures or particular negative aspects of religion. One Black and Minority Ethnic (BAME) English student, for example, observed that Black people were 'always Pentecostal, singing, dancing, clapping their hands' in drama series. A white British student at an English Catholic school, in an overwhelmingly white British area, suggested that dramatic representations, such as *Citizen Khan*, could shape one's views of a BAME group before you even got to know someone from a particular community well. However, there was some mention of the ways in which drama could break down stereotypes: students in Finland, for example, mentioned the series *Skam*, which they believed helped viewers to understand Muslim viewpoints on different matters.

Our clearest observation is that there is a wide consensus among young people from the different countries with regards to their perception of how the news media represents religion. They all agreed that religion tends to be presented in a very simplified and superficial way. While some differentiated between the television news and social media – claiming that television news is more accurate as journalists apply at least some standards and provide evidence for the news they offer – many others questioned both without distinction. There was a strong feeling that media preferred to rather portray religion in a negative way. One English student argued with respect to the coverage of Islam: 'Bad news is good business.' In this respect, all focus groups, not only Muslim youth, referred to the portrayal of Islam. This specific religion, they argued, is often associated with terrorism and with violence. One student in Finland even described a 'media circus' where coverage of Islamicist terrorism was concerned. When a shooting is covered, for instance, the shooter is not particularly labelled, but as soon as the shooter is a Muslim, he is called a 'terrorist', the young people claimed. They were hence perfectly capable of deconstructing media discourses in this respect, and non-Muslim young people could display significant empathy with Muslim peers. Whereas media bias concerning Islam was mentioned in most focus groups, other groups also mentioned other biases. In the UK Catholic school, and also in the Finnish school, for example, various students believed that news media tended to highlight issues such as anti-abortion and child abuse, and that this could influence public perceptions of the church. 'A lot of people I know, when they think of Catholicism they think of paedophile priests, or when they think of Muslims they think of terrorists,' argued one student. In response to this representation of religion in the media, some young people held a firm plea that media should be more inclusive and nuanced. In their opinion, the common values and similarities between different religions should be stressed more, instead of solely focusing on differences (in particular between the Western world and Islam).

Not all young people, however, engaged in a debate about representation of religion in the news media; some felt that religion was hardly in the news at all. Furthermore, in all focus groups, young people stated that their beliefs and representations were not influenced primarily by television series and films, and media in general. According to them, (conversations with) family and friends, and in some cases, documentaries found on YouTube, are much more influential in this respect. Borrowing Arweck and Penny's notion of 'concentric circles' of influence (2015), it would appear that media is not usually a central ring of influence, but can still play an important, if more peripheral role, in shaping young people's attitudes.

## Young people's experiences of religious diversity in the present

Responses to the 'warm up' questionnaires reflected the diversity of the experiences that participants had of religious diversity in the present. Participants assigned very varying degrees of importance to the role that religion played in their lives (with 18.6 per cent of respondents arguing that religion was 'not important' to their lives and 22.7 per cent claiming that it was 'of great importance'). Around 41.7 per cent argued that they had observed prejudice or bias against religion in the area where they lived, 32.6 per cent claimed they had not. It is also remarkable that about a quarter of participants (25.8 per cent) were 'not sure' whether they had observed prejudice or bias against religion, which might suggest that they were unsure as to what exactly constituted such prejudice or bias. By contrast, the vast majority of participants argued that they had not (48.5 per cent) or 'hardly ever' experienced bias against their own religious or non-religious beliefs.

The open comments participants submitted as part of the questionnaire revealed that the teenagers understood and interpreted the multiple-choice questions and notions of bias and prejudice very differently. For example, students who claimed that they had 'hardly ever' experienced bias against their religious or non-religious beliefs offered a wide range of explanations in their open comments, ranging from reports of specific incidents of a relatively serious nature (including a student who explained that they had experienced verbal abuse for wearing a hijab and 'got egged' while waiting for a bus) to much broader observations (saying e.g. that 'some were surprised that I'm Catholic, but don't go to church etc., and were disappointed'). In the context of the focus group interviews, some participants also noted that they would have answered the survey questions differently had they been given the opportunity to complete the questionnaire *after* the semi-structured interviews (rather than before), arguing that the focus group discussions had prompted them to further reflect on the issues.

The focus group discussions indicated that participants largely considered religious diversity as something positive. However, this stance was not unconditional and participants had different views on the practice of multiculturalism. In many participants' opinion, people, regardless of what religion they adhered to, should accept a set of common values. Furthermore, they argued that religious extremism should not be tolerated. Moreover, at least some young people differentiated between religious diversity as an idea or concept and its (visual and concrete) materialization. Some young people in the Flemish school claimed, for instance, that they did not dispute the idea of religious diversity as such but considered visible symbols of that idea, such as wearing a headscarf or participating in Ramadan, as problematic.

It is probably not a coincidence that these young people referred to examples stemming from Islam. Almost all participating young people in the different countries observed that in society at large, intolerance particularly against Islam and against Muslims exists. At the same time, they did not always consider this intolerance from a religious perspective, rather they viewed it from an ethnic-cultural standpoint. Some also provided examples of intolerance against religions other than Islam. In their opinion, this occurs more among older people. Many participants claimed to be more tolerant and open-minded towards religious diversity and towards other religions than older people.

Throughout the focus groups, young people showed themselves capable of deconstructing stereotypes about religion and religious diversity. Also, they succeeded in not reducing people solely to their religious identity. By contrast, they acknowledged the multilayered character of identity, and seemed to take this into account when talking about religious diversity. This was all the more the case among those young people encountering a lot of religious diversity in their daily life. There appeared to be a connection between the extent of religious diversity which young people experienced in their living (and school) environment and their attitudes and opinions. The more diversity young people encountered, the more they testified to an open-minded stance; the less diversity they experienced themselves, the less they seemed to understand it, and the more they testified to fear it.

With regards to the role schools can play in relation to (the appreciation of) religious diversity, young people all acknowledged the importance of knowledge and awareness of religious diversity, both in terms of getting to know each other and about world religions more generally. They also desired to see history taught in relation to their own immediate setting and context – for example, the evidence of the religious past in local buildings, parks and street names. There was also a preference to go beyond learning historical 'facts' about religious diversity in the past, and instead relating it to religion 'as lived' in the present.

## Connections between young people's reference knowledge and beliefs of religious diversity in the past and present

Young people's attitudes towards religious diversity in the present are not informed by the past. The opposite is rather true. It appears that many participating young people 'back-project' their knowledge and opinions of religious diversity in the present on to the past. They combined this with the assumption that in the past, things were 'by definition' worse. They assumed that situations, events and mentalities that exist today existed in the past as well, but in a worse way. As a result, they built a negative social representation of religious diversity in the past. 'Societies in the past were ten thousand times more religious than nowadays,' a teenager in Flanders stated, 'And the church forced people to believe in [the Christian] God. Nowadays, you can choose whether you want to be Christian, or Muslim, or atheist; back then, you could not.' In other countries as well, young people built very biased, one-sided and simplistic representations of religion and religious diversity in the past.

The same dynamic was also evident, at least among some young people in Flanders and in Germany, on a procedural level. During the focus group interviews, young people were asked how accurate or inaccurate, fair or unfair, they thought different television programmes, shows or series are when they portray present-day religious diversity. As mentioned above, this question yielded clear answers with regards to young people perceiving the portrayal of religion as simplistic, biased, one-sided and often negative. Some of them, while discussing this, took the debate a step further, and back-projected their criticisms of current media to popular representations of religious diversity in the past, for example, in historical movies. One focus group referred, for instance, to the very stereotypical way of representing Muslims and Christians in the Hollywood movie *Kingdom of Heaven* (2005).

## Conclusion and discussion

In drawing and discussing conclusions, we need to take into account some limitations of this study. First, although 132 young people participated in the focus group interviews, this is far from a representative sample of young people across Europe, meaning we need to be careful in generalizing results and interpretations. Second, the twelve schools involved only included six European counties. We were hence not able to grasp all possible national peculiarities across Europe. Third, the results might have been influenced by a selection bias. As participation in the focus group interviews took place on a voluntary basis, perhaps only those young people interested in the topic and having already given much thought to the topics at stake decided to participate. Fourth, our focus group approach also carried limitations. While the semi-structured interviews were meant to allow students some flexibility, they still provided a structure – which meant that some important issues may have slipped through the net. Their duration was limited, and the groups were composed of young people who knew each other, making speech among them easier, yet perhaps at the same time setting invisible barriers in terms of interpersonal dynamics.

Nevertheless, some interesting conclusions can be drawn and discussed. The first concerns the narrow range of historical knowledge the participants testified to. When asked for concrete examples of religious diversity in the past, students could only name few major events or turning points, particularly stemming from the history of their own national or regional context. Previous research already showed that young people's reference knowledge with regards to various types of history is often limited. It also raised questions about the (non)sense of testing factual knowledge among young people. As far as the knowledge of religious diversity in the past is concerned, we should add that this theme does not always receive as much attention in school education and does not feature prominently in popular historical culture. Limited historical knowledge of religious diversity, therefore, should not come as a surprise. However, conceptual knowledge was also in short supply. Throughout the conversations, a conceptual confusion arose between religious and ethno-cultural diversity, in the sense that students did not differentiate between them. Either students mixed up both or they reduced experiences of religious diversity to ethnic-cultural diversity. Experiences of prejudice or bias, for example, against Muslims were seen in ethnic-cultural terms rather than in purely religious ones. In this sense, the descriptive-quantitative results of the questionnaire prior to the focus group interviews should be addressed carefully. This also points to the need of conceptual clarification when teaching about or discussing religious diversity. Are we actually talking about religious diversity, or rather about ethnic-cultural diversity? This can help in keeping debates straight and clear.

A second finding concerns the sources of knowledge young people mention with regards to religious diversity. It becomes clear that both school history and popular historical culture (audiovisual and internet sources next to conversations with family and friends) feed young people's knowledge and social representations of religious diversity in the past. This reinforces the aforementioned plea of eminent Canadian history education scholar Peter Seixas (1993) about the necessity to build bridges between school history and family/community history as sources of historical knowledge. Students entering a history classroom are not 'blank slates'; rather, they possess existing knowledge and opinions which is important to address and dialogue with. This is necessary on two levels. With regards to the content (i.e. the knowledge and understanding of the past itself) it is necessary to seek connections, in order to make this knowledge meaningful for young people and to ensure that, regardless of their ethnic and cultural heritage, they can recognize themselves in school history. In addition, a connection must be sought on a 'procedural' level, in terms of learning to deal critically with all representations of religious diversity they encounter, both in and outside school, and both in and outside their family and community circles. After all, young people are exposed to a variety of representations, but these may not be of equal value. Not all representations of religious diversity in the past are reliable and representative. This applies not only to a typical medium from school history, namely textbooks on history (see Chapter 3), but also to the audiovisual and internet sources that young people have at their disposal. Introducing young people to a critical approach to historical sources is necessary to enable them to deconstruct fake news and alternative facts and to reject misplaced (often absolute) truth claims (Wineburg 2018).

This connects closely to a third finding from this research, namely the challenges of 'presentism' in young people's thinking about religious diversity in the past. It is obviously a positive observation that young people participating in our study were well capable of deconstructing present-day representations of current religious diversity. They almost all understood the negative framing news media testified to in portraying religion, and were able to deconstruct the bias, generalization and even stereotypes that media often displayed with regards to religion and religious diversity. In that sense, the present might form a starting point for young people to engage critically with historical sources, both primary and secondary, and the biases they may reflect. However, we need to be careful in making such a suggestion, as we do not aim to encourage a presentist stance among young people, meaning they consider and judge the past from a present-day perspective, and through a present-day moral perspective. This is what we, in line with previous scholars (Borries 1994; Angvik and Borries 1997), encountered throughout the focus group interviews. Young people built very biased, one-sided and simplistic representations of religion and religious diversity in the past, based on a presentist approach. This clearly shows the necessity to foster among young people the ability to think historically, to understand the past in its own logic and to consider past events in their historical context (Wineburg 2001; Seixas and Morton 2013). At a content level, this requires that young people are provided with a rich and nuanced historical understanding of religious diversity in the past – instead of a one-sided, negatively framed social representation focusing solely on conflict and violence. On a procedural level, as mentioned earlier, this requires the fostering of skills that enable critical analysis of historical sources.

Here, our research offers insights into approaches to teaching young people to think historically, to draw on a critical perspective on religious diversity in the past which can help them to reflect in a nuanced way on religious diversity in the present (in general and in their living environment) and on the complex relationship between past and present. It became very clear throughout the focus group interviews that the young people participating were longing to attribute meaning to – and were constructing an opinion about – religious diversity. In so doing, nevertheless, they can only benefit from a good understanding of the past as a necessary starting point to reflect on religious diversity in the present. This will enable them to reflect deeply and to experience at the same time a meaningful bridge between school history and their private understanding of the past (Husbands 1996). During the focus group interviews, young people hinted at this themselves, by making pleas for more attention to local history and family history. In this respect, existing research indicates that this approach stirs the most interest in the past among young people (see e.g. Grever, Haydn and Ribbens 2008).

What the focus group interviews also revealed is that young people were very eager, and at the same time capable of discussing a sensitive issue such as religious diversity in a very respectful, sensitive and constructive manner. This is an important finding, for in both formal and in- and non-formal educational settings, teachers and educators are sometimes afraid to raise sensitive issues among young people. They fear this might cause turmoil and conflict. The focus groups we organized showed the opposite. Of course, we need to stress here that participation took place on voluntary basis. However, the most important condition was the establishment of a 'safe' environment, in which young people felt confident to express their views and to discuss them with peers who did not necessarily share those views. It may also have made a difference that the students were not being assessed. A clear framework of agreements among and established with the participants and an explicit explanation of the purpose of the conversation contributed to a respectful and sincere debate.

The focus group interviews, as already mentioned, were in preparation for starting a process of developing 'docutubes'. To end, it seems appropriate to elaborate briefly on this. Docutubes are historical accounts young people construct about an historical issue, in the shape of a short film similar in style to the popular Vlogging videos on YouTube. The methodology accompanying the process of making docutubes has a lot of potential in our opinion. First, before young people start to make docutubes, they are offered a number of so-called clippings: commented excerpts and examples stemming from historical and contemporary representations of religion and religious diversity (including historical peace treaties and arrangements). In small groups, young people read and observe these clippings. The clippings aim to provide young people with historical knowledge, and serve as sources of inspiration to think about the past, present and future forms of religious diversity and religious coexistence in an informed, nuanced, empathetic way. The clippings are accompanied by questions, in which we aim to challenge their existing opinions, while also encouraging them to draw on their own knowledge and experiences, and to invite them to think critically of the representation in the clipping. That way, we encourage them to think historically, and to enter into a dialogue with peers. Subsequently, young people are invited to express their thoughts in a docutube, a short film they make, with the help of the clippings and also by making use of their own film footage recorded with video cameras. Young people thus need to organize their ideas and shape them in a coherent way. In so doing, they deepen their knowledge, engage in historical and critical (instead of presentist) thinking, enter into a dialogue with peers on religious diversity, and construct a substantiated opinion that they can share with others and continue to discuss.

# Representing European religious diversity in textbooks for history education

Karel Van Nieuwenhuyse, Madis Maasing and Laura Galián[1]

## Introduction

When watching and listening to societal and political debates and media news coverage, one often gets the impression that religion and religious diversity are perceived in a negative way, in that they are linked to conflict, exclusion, violence, acts of aggression and even war. Recent research among 17,401 people aged between sixteen and sixty-four years, conducted via interviews in twenty-three countries worldwide, confirms this impression (Ipsos 2017). Overall, half of the participants in this study stated that they were convinced that religion does more harm than good in the world. At the same time, however, about three-quarters of them said that they felt completely comfortable being around people who had religious beliefs different from their own. These apparently contradictory positions suggest that people today have mixed opinions about (different aspects of) religious diversity.

Research shows that our perceptions of phenomena in the present are often influenced (among other factors) by social representations of the past (see e.g. Wertsch 1997, 2004; Borries 1994). It would therefore be interesting to try to gain a precise picture of how religious diversity in the past is represented today. Such research can focus on all kinds of 'carriers' of social representations: statues, historical films, popular stories, museums and so on. This chapter focuses on one specific medium: history textbooks for secondary education. These are interesting forms of social representation which are worth analysing because they are an important source of information for many (young) people who study history, a compulsory subject in many countries. History textbooks are therefore important producers of societal knowledge, and have the potential to influence many young people's ideas and perceptions, in this case on religion(s) and religious diversity in the past (Van Nieuwenhuyse 2019a: 1–15).

Using a comparative approach across various European countries, this chapter examines the social representations of religious diversity in the past that are presented in history textbooks for secondary education and disseminated among young people across Europe today. Our analysis will focus in particular on the representation of a selected number of interreligious contacts over the course of history and we will be asking the following questions: How are the contacts represented (in a positive, negative or neutral way; as peaceful or violent encounters etc.)? What particular historical events are addressed within each contact? To what extent are these contacts in the past connected to the present? To whom is agency attributed in these contacts, and from whose perspective(s) are they described? These questions offer an in-depth view of the social representations of historical interreligious contacts. The textbooks we analysed are used in a broad range of eight European countries: Austria, Belgium, Estonia, Finland, Germany, Spain, Switzerland and the UK. This research will offer insights into both the outlook and the how and why of (possibly differing) social representations, and their connection with specific religious, national, sociopolitical and cultural contexts.

With this in mind, we will begin by offering a brief introduction to existing international research. We will then go on to describe the research questions, data collection and the methodology we applied and explain how we selected the interreligious contacts and the textbooks for analysis. We also describe our diachronic and synchronic analysis of the content and narrative. The chapter ends with the presentation and discussion of the results of our research.

## Textbook analysis research on interreligious contacts in the past

A great deal of research has been done on textbooks, exploring, for example, what is a textbook? How is it best defined or classified? Without going into excessive detail, in general, researchers regard textbooks as commercial products (which must therefore take into account the expectations of their primary users, i.e. teachers), pedagogical tools (part of teaching and learning processes) and cultural artefacts. As regards the latter, many researchers regard secondary-school textbooks as concrete manifestations of the (historical) culture(s) in a society (Klerides 2010: 31–54). Three research traditions exist with regards to the analysis of (particularly history) textbooks as cultural artefacts (Van Nieuwenhuyse 2014: 79–100; Bock 2018: 57–70; Štimac 2018: 251–65): (1) 'checking scholars', who investigate history and religion textbooks in search of revanchism, polarization, superiority feelings and so on, and examine the extent to which new research results have found their way into them, (2) 'representational scholars', who concentrate their research on the representation of a specific (interreligious) event, development, or agent in the textbooks, and link it with existing collective memories and social representations within society and (3) scholars who perform 'narrative analysis' of textbooks, a method that focuses on the narrative underlying the textbook as a whole, and considers specific parts of the textbooks and specific representations (and their significance) in the light of that whole.

Scholars from all three traditions have conducted a great deal of research (mainly via content and discourse analyses) on social representations of religion(s) and their past in textbooks, particularly in the last decades, because of the growing recognition of the role of textbooks as producers of knowledge about religion(s) (Andreassen 2015: 7–9).

As Štimac (2018) explains, studies in this field tend to focus on the social representation of one religion in the past and/or present, from a national or international comparative perspective (see e.g. Douglass 2015; Gottschalk 2019: 284–95; Hock et al. 2012; Liepach and Sadowski 2014; Linkenbach 2015: 23–44). In particular, they examine, for instance, the (evolving) representation of the doctrine, practices and symbols of a specific religion, or the extent (also evolving) of generalizing and polarizing tendencies in the attributions of characteristics to specific religions and religious people. Most of them concentrate on social representations of the major world religions of Judaism, Christianity, Islam, Hinduism and Buddhism, although since the 2000s, indigenous religious beliefs and non-religious world views have also entered the frame. Another striking recent tendency is that since the 1990s – in line with societal debates worldwide – the representation of Islam and Muslims has become the subject of a large, increasing body of research (see e.g. Härenstam 2009; Spielhaus 2018; Berglund 2018; Karaca and Schmitz 2018; Kröhnert-Othman 2015).

One area of history textbooks that has been subject to much less scrutiny is the social representation of interreligious contacts, by which we mean contacts between religions and their leaders and followers. While some research focuses on how religion textbooks try to instigate interreligious dialogue, or on mutual representations of a religious 'other', the mere representation in textbooks of the what, how and why of past and present contacts between religions and religious people has been largely neglected in textbook research (Lähnemann 2013: 15–25). Such research does exist, however, with regards to the representation of intercultural contacts in the past. One example is the study by Van Nieuwenhuyse (2018) who, based on a framework proposed by the sinologist Nicolas Standaert (2002), examined the representation of intercultural contacts during the Imperial Era in Belgian history textbooks since 1945. The categories involved in this analysis were, among others, agency (Who were mentioned as agents and who appeared as passive entities?), positive or negative connotations attributed to these agents/entities (including stereotypes), any opinions or judgements expressed by the authors, the assessment of the relations between the different agents, the possible use of 'us' versus 'them' and the (origin of the) historical sources included in the textbooks. Several of these categories could also be applied in the analysis of the representation of interreligious contacts over the course of history.

This is definitely true of agency, which can be defined as 'the ability to act on decisions in order to bring about desired goals (whether those involve changing aspects of society or conserving them)' (Barton 2012: 132). The concept of agency therefore addresses the question of who has the individual or social potential to act purposefully and to effectuate change in society. This is an important question to examine in history textbooks, not only as a means of analyzing what kind of insights they offer students about the course of history, but also because of the pedagogical implications of how agency is represented. Scholars argue that teaching young people about agency could influence their civic behaviour. Reflection on the various agents in the past and how they contributed to changes in society can indeed make students aware of their own role in society today (Harris 2011; Peck, Poyntz and Seixas 2011; Wilke, Depaepe and Van Nieuwenhuyse 2019). Research on this issue shows, however, that textbooks ascribe agency mostly to non-human agents, powerful individuals ('great men') and groups.

Ordinary agents, ordinary individuals or groups of people who are not specifically in a position of power are rarely attributed agency; they are predominantly presented as passive. Women also are rarely portrayed as agents. Furthermore, previous research also shows that historical agents are often homogenized in history textbooks, with the result that the differences that exist within particular groups tend to be ignored. Another important finding was that not all the historical agents who played a role in historical events are ascribed agency. In the modern imperial context, for instance, often only Western agents are represented as active agents, while the indigenous peoples, by contrast, are depicted as passive victims of European profit-seeking and violence. This is the case in history textbooks in Belgium, England, France, Italy, Portugal and Spain, in which very little attention is paid, for example, to the indigenous groups who rebelled against European rule (Barton 2012; Van Nieuwenhuyse 2019b; Štimac 2015; see also Van Nieuwenhuyse and Pires Valentim 2018).

## Research question, data collection, methodology

The main research question addressed in this chapter is as follows: What social representations of interreligious contacts in the past are being constructed and disseminated among young people across Europe today in history textbooks for secondary education (generally from seventh till twelfth grade, aimed at young people between twelve and eighteen years old)?[2] To this end we analysed textbooks from eight countries: Austria, Belgium (Flanders), Estonia, Finland, Germany (from the states/Länder of Bavaria, Brandenburg, Hessen and Nord Rhine-Westphalia), Spain, Switzerland (German-speaking areas) and the UK (England). These countries were selected for several reasons. They are representative of all the different parts of Europe (North, East, South, West and Centre) and of a range of different religious backgrounds and traditions. Some of these countries are steeped in the Catholic tradition (e.g. Austria, Spain and Belgium), while others are characterized by (various) Protestant traditions (e.g. Finland and England), or are home to several different major religious traditions (e.g. Germany and Switzerland). One of them (Estonia) was ruled by a communist regime under which religion was at best very tacitly tolerated in the margins, or at worst actively repressed. These countries also vary in terms of the extent to which they have evolved into lay, secular states. Some of the countries involved are also home to a significant group of people who adhere to Islam or Judaism, while in others these religions are much less prominent among the population. Finally, the selected countries had different ways of dealing with interreligious contacts in the past, in terms of type, size, depth and nature. The analysis particularly seeks to identify major similarities and differences in the way these contacts are described in history textbooks from this diverse range of countries.

For each country, we analysed one secondary school history textbook per grade, although in some cases the same textbook was used over two grades. Preference was given to textbooks that were widely and frequently used in each of the countries involved. The availability of textbooks (in many cases via the library of the Georg

Eckert Institute for International Textbook Research) was also a factor in this decision. For Germany, textbooks from multiple federal states/Länder were examined.[3] All analysed textbooks date from 2010 onwards. In order to keep the analysis of some fifty textbook volumes feasible, we focused on six specific interreligious contacts in the past: (1) between Christians and Roman polytheistic believers during the Roman Empire (first–fifth century CE); (2) between Jews and Christians in Medieval Europe (sixth–fifteenth century CE); (3) between Muslims and other religions during the Middle Ages (seventh–fifteenth century CE); (4) between Catholics and Protestants in the Early Modern Period (sixteenth–eighteenth century CE); (5) between those in favour of secularism and those who wanted religion to have a strong position within society (eighteenth–nineteenth century CE); (6) between Muslims and other (non-) religious groups in the present, since 1989 (post–Cold War era). Several criteria were used to select these specific interreligious contacts. We wanted, first, for the contacts to cover different historical eras, and, second, to involve a diverse range of religions within Europe. Finally, we wanted them to constitute important, influential and significant developments in European history with long-lasting consequences. This last criterion was particularly important as it made it more likely that the contact was actually addressed in history textbooks. A preliminary check was carried out to make sure the interreligious contacts we had selected were covered in the textbooks. As a result of that check, we decided to exclude one of the contacts, namely the interreligious contact during the pre-modern and modern imperial encounter. A quick analysis of the textbooks examined here revealed that many of them addressed imperialism and colonialism in political, socio-economic and cultural terms, while glossing over their interreligious dimension. It was therefore decided to exclude the colonial encounter from our list of contacts.

In terms of operationalized and concrete (sub-)research questions, for each of these interreligious contacts in the past, we examined what kind of events are mentioned, what the geographical focus is, how they are represented (in terms of peace and violence, tolerance and intolerance, coexistence or not), from which perspective they are looked at, in what societal context they are framed (political, economic, cultural, religious, social), which groups are treated as agents, which actors are named, how the contacts are framed, what connotations (positive, negative or neutral) are attributed to them, what historical sources are mentioned and included, whether attention is paid to mutual representations of the agents involved, and to what extent and how past and present are related to each other. On the basis of these issues, and partly in line with similar (abovementioned) research into the representation of intercultural contacts during the modern imperial past, an analysis scheme was designed, establishing a system of categories and subcategories in order to carry out a fine-grained analysis of the textbook accounts. This involved diachronic and synchronic analysis of both the content and the narrative, as our main objective was to understand educational representations in context. We began by analyzing each textbook according to this procedure, and once we had acquired a precise picture of the social representations of these contacts in each book, we then performed an international comparative analysis of the textbooks from the different countries. In this way we sought to obtain a Europe-wide view of the way interreligious contacts are represented in history textbooks, as well as an assessment of the most important similarities and differences between them.

# Research results

In this section, we will begin with an international comparative perspective, instead of first reporting country per country. The various research questions will be addressed in the following order: (1) the specific content of each interreligious contact; (2) the geographical and societal focus; (3) the attribution of agency; (4) the context within which each contact is framed and (5) possible connections between past and present.

## Which events are mentioned in the different accounts of each interreligious contact?

When comparing the different accounts of each interreligious contact in history textbooks from eight countries, the first thing we observed was the remarkable similarity between them, at least in their description of the most important aspects of each contact. If we start, for example, with the interreligious contact between Christians and Roman polytheistic believers during the Roman Empire (first–fifth century CE), all the textbooks mention the birth of Christianity in the first century CE, and then go on to describe the persecution of the Christians by the Romans. They then proceed to the successful spread of Christianity, almost all mentioning the Edict of Milan issued in 313 by Constantine I, and sketching out the process through which Christianity became the state religion of the Roman Empire.

If we move on to the contact between Jews and Christians in Medieval Europe (sixth–fifteenth century CE), the specific issues mentioned by the textbooks include the fact that during the High and Late Middle Ages (particularly from the eleventh to the fifteenth century) Christians and Jews lived together in European towns where, initially, the Jews enjoyed some privileges, but were later the subject of persecution. They tend to focus on pogroms against Jews, particularly during the Crusades (the murder of Jews in Jerusalem in 1099 is often cited as an example) and the crises caused by the Black Death. Some textbooks highlight the contrast, here, with the tolerance Muslims showed towards Jews and Christians in al-Andalus during the same period.

As regards the interreligious contacts between Muslims and other religions during the Middle Ages (seventh–fifteenth century CE), all the textbooks describe the birth, spread and expansion of Islam, focusing on the Crusades, and on the cultural influence that Islam had on science (medicine, mathematics, geography etc.) and arts in Europe – most often with reference to al-Andalus, which in Spain receives its own separate chapter. The internal division of Islam between Sunnites and Shiites is not always addressed in the textbooks across Europe.

The interreligious contact between Catholics and Protestants in the Early Modern Period (sixteenth–eighteenth century CE) receives a lot of attention in most textbooks. The crisis within the Catholic Church, the reaction of Martin Luther with the publication of his Ninety-Five Theses in 1517, the spread of Protestantism and the Reformation throughout Europe (different denominations such as Calvinism, Anabaptism and Anglicanism are mentioned), religious wars, the Peace of Augsburg in 1555, the Council of Trent and the Counter-Reformation, the Thirty Years' War and sometimes also the Eighty Years' War, and the Peace of Westphalia were all mentioned and briefly described. The only markedly different account appears in the English textbook, which will be discussed in more detail below. The accounts of the contacts between those in favour of secularism and those in favour of religion having a strong position within society (eighteenth–nineteenth century CE) also show many similarities with a focus on Enlightened philosophers and their books (such as Montesquieu's *The Spirit of the Laws* from 1748, Rousseau's *Discourse on Inequality* from 1754 and *The Social Contract* from 1762, and Kant's *Critique of Pure Reason* from 1781), the translation of Enlightened ideas into a policy of religious toleration within society, and the growing opposition between scientific and religious world views (often illustrated via Charles Darwin and his theory of evolution).

Finally, as regards the interreligious contacts between Muslims and other (non-) religious groups in the present day since 1989 (post–Cold War era), the events most frequently addressed in the textbooks include the tension between Israel and Palestine (focusing on the peace talks and Oslo Accords of 1993, the assassination of Yitzhak Rabin in 1995, and the First and Second Intifada (1987–93 and 2000–5, respectively)), Islamic fundamentalism and terrorism (with the attacks of 9/11 as the most frequently cited example), the wars in Yugoslavia and Afghanistan, and the Arab Spring from 2010.

Overall, it would seem that the history textbooks across Europe offer quite similar accounts of the most important aspects of each interreligious contact and of the specific events and agents involved. To a certain extent, one could almost venture to speak of an implicit European historical canon, at least on a general level. However, certain differences were also observed between the different countries, regarding the depth and detail with which certain contacts were addressed, and also with regards to the regional, national and local focus. If we look, for instance, at the interreligious contact between Catholics and Protestants in the Early Modern Period (sixteenth–eighteenth century CE), it is striking to note how the Flemish history textbook went into great detail about the Eighty Years' War in the Low Countries, while Swiss textbooks focused mainly on events in the Holy Roman Empire and on wars on Swiss soil. English textbooks adopted an even more nationally oriented outlook on the interreligious contact between Catholics and Protestants, by focusing almost exclusively on events in England and Scotland (such as the English Revolution and Civil War), and on Anglicanism. Furthermore, while English history textbooks addressed the interreligious tensions accompanying the rise of Protestantism in the colonies of Northern America, and Spanish history textbooks emphasized the spread of Catholicism (among others via Jesuit education) into the Southern American colonies, other textbooks chose not to mention these issues. Some (like the Estonian, Flemish and German textbooks) nevertheless mentioned confessional migration flows within Europe, such as the migration of Protestants from the Southern to the Northern Netherlands during the Eighty Years' War.

### What is the geographical and societal focus in the accounts of the selected interreligious contacts?

As explained in the previous section, we observed that while history textbooks across Europe address more or less the same main themes, they each have their own particular geographical focus. The Austrian, English, Swiss and Spanish textbooks are, for instance, mainly nationally centred in that their accounts of each of the interreligious contacts being studied, except for that between Christians and Roman polytheistic believers during the Roman Empire (first–fifth century CE), were mostly (or in the English case almost exclusively) centred on events that took place on the same soil as the present-day state. History textbooks in Belgium (Flanders), Estonia, Finland and Germany, on the other hand, took a broader geographical perspective, addressing a wider (Western and Central) European situation.

As regards the societal contexts in which the interreligious encounters are situated, it is interesting to note that they are never addressed from a purely religious perspective; all the textbooks situate and analyse the various interreligious contacts in a broader societal context, and relate them with other political, cultural, social and often economic issues. In fact, the links between these different societal domains are often made explicit. If we look, for example, at their accounts of the Crusades (within the interreligious contacts between Muslims and other religions during the Middle Ages), multiple religious, economic, political, social and cultural causes are discussed, as well as the connections between them. The same applies to the Reformation. In explaining the persecution of Christians in the Roman Empire, the Flemish textbook explains that because of its monotheistic character, adherents of Christianity refused to make offerings to the traditional Roman gods or to the emperor, which made them dangerous, as by acting in this way they undermined the emperor's position and the social order (Bering 2014). In this way, the textbook interweaves political, religious and social aspects of this question, while the German textbook even added a socio-economic dimension, pointing to the divide between the poor who supported Christianity and their rich and powerful enemies, during the early centuries of Christianity (Sauer et al. 2015: 138–9).

Of course, this is not to say that the religious dimension is ignored. Religious issues and doctrines are mentioned for each of the contacts (in line with a finding in Chapter 6), but the general focus is much broader and goes beyond purely religious aspects.

### Who is attributed agency in the interreligious contacts?

In line with previous research on the attribution of agency in history textbooks, we found that, in textbooks across Europe, the agents most frequently cited in accounts of interreligious contacts in the past are powerful individuals, groups (not always powerful) and non-human agents. Powerful individuals are often religious leaders (like Pope Urban II, Ignatius of Loyola, Muhammad, Martin Luther or John Calvin), kings and emperors (like Constantine the Great, Saladin or Henry VIII), terrorist leaders (like Osama Bin Laden), intellectual leaders (like Rousseau or Voltaire as Enlightened philosophers) or political and military leaders (like Charles Martel, Yasser Arafat, Yitzhak Rabin or George Bush Jr.). Ordinary individuals are almost never mentioned, nor are women, although some ordinary social groups, such as peasants, merchants and (poor) townsmen are referred to on occasions. Powerful groups in society, such as the clerical and social elite, the knights, the Jesuit Order or the rich bourgeoisie, are mentioned more often. Non-human agents, such as the state, the church, and specific religions such as Anglicanism, Zoroastrianism, Islam or Christianity are also portrayed as agents.

As can be deduced from this overview, and in parallel with the various societal contexts within which interreligious contacts are situated, these agents are not only described in religious terms (such as a 'group of Christians') but also in national, social, political and economic terms, with references, for example, to German Lutherans, Dutch Calvinists, Bavarian Catholics, French Protestants, peasant Protestants, or poor and rich Christians; the ethnic term 'Arabs' is often used interchangeably with the religious term 'Muslims', as are national terms such as 'Turks' or 'Ottomans'.

Another striking finding is that agents are very often (except for some eleventh and twelfth grade textbooks) homogenized in the accounts about interreligious contacts. Quite different parties involved in certain historical events are often represented as one homogeneous entity. Textbook authors across Europe commonly refer, for example, to 'the Christians', 'the Muslims' and so on, disregarding the differences within these groups. As mentioned earlier, there is often no clear distinction made between Sunnites and Shiites, nor between Scandinavian and German Lutherans. In so doing, textbook authors seem to create the impression that within a certain interreligious contact everyone involved within a specific group thought and acted in the same way. Of course, in historical reality this was not the case: people belonging to one party (e.g. 'the Christians', 'the Romans', 'the Enlightened thinkers', 'the Muslims' etc.) thought differently from one another, took different stances and acted in different ways. These differences, however, are often blurred or ironed out in the textbooks. The only instance in which all textbook authors are consistent in not homogenizing these groups is when they address the contacts between Muslims and other (non-)religious groups since 1989. In these accounts, the authors emphasize the important differences between moderate and extreme Muslims (including terrorists). A clear and explicit distinction is made between Islam and Islamist religious extremists. One textbook in Flanders even goes a step further. Under the heading 'Us and Them?', it explicitly deconstructs us-them mechanisms, explaining, for instance, why representations such as 'Turkish devils' and 'Christian dogs' had been created during the Crusades and had persisted long afterwards (Berings 2016). However, this effort was not taken to a higher level in terms of the general deconstruction of stereotypes, and in terms of recognizing their own homogenizing descriptions of the agents in historical phenomena.

An important question with regards to agency is to establish which of the various parties within a specific interreligious contact are treated as active agents. Is agency attributed to various parties and agents involved in the contact or to just one? The analysis clearly shows that in almost all the textbooks studied in this research, agency is attributed to various different parties in each interreligious contact. In the interreligious contact between Christians and Roman polytheistic believers during the Roman

Empire (first–fifth century CE), for instance, both the Romans and the Christians are represented as active agents; the Romans because they persecuted the Christians, and the Christians because they refused to worship Roman gods. In the contact between Muslims and other religions during the Middle Ages (seventh–fifteenth century CE) members of both religions were considered agents, as they fought each other. The same applies to the contact between those in favour of secularism and those in favour of religion having a strong position within society (eighteenth–nineteenth century CE). Enlightened philosophers are represented as active agents because they spread new ideas, while members of the Catholic Church were also active agents in that they tried to suppress these new ideas. In the contact between Muslims and other (non-)religious groups in the present day since 1989, radicalized Islamist religious extremists are attributed agency, as they carried out terrorist attacks, while the United States is also considered an active agent, as it retaliated against the terrorist groups and their supporters.

However, the fact that different parties in an interreligious contact are attributed agency does not mean that it is attributed in a balanced way. Some parties are often attributed more agency than others. In the Spanish textbook's description of the contact between Catholics and Protestants in the Early Modern Period (sixteenth–eighteenth century CE), for instance, Catholics are attributed more agency than Protestants, while in Finnish, Estonian and many German textbooks, quite the opposite is true. In almost all the textbooks covered in this research, Enlightened philosophers and thinkers are ascribed more agency than the Catholic Church in the contact between those in favour of secularism and those in favour of religion having a strong position within society (eighteenth–nineteenth century CE).

The attribution of 'mixed' agency is also reflected in the fact that many textbooks highlight the reciprocal influence that the different parties involved in the interreligious contacts had on each other. They state, for instance, that Romans and Christians influenced each other and their cult; they also refer to the reciprocal influence in the contacts between Muslims and other religions during the Middle Ages (seventh–fifteenth century CE), stressing above all the Muslim influence on Western Christian Medieval society. The same applies to the historical sources cited by the textbooks. For each of the interreligious contacts, almost all the history textbooks present historical sources from the different parties involved in the contact, although not in a balanced way.

In one of the interreligious contacts, however, one of the parties involved is almost never treated as an agent. In the contact between Jews and Christians in Medieval Europe (sixth–fifteenth century CE), it is very striking to find that Jews are mostly portrayed as passive victims who suffered as they were assaulted, hunted, attacked and murdered. Exceptions are the Austrian and, to a lesser extent, Estonian and German, textbooks in which Jews are briefly represented as active agents who lent money, traded and worked as doctors.

### How are the interreligious contacts framed?

Although the selection of specific events and the attribution of agency within each of the interreligious contacts under study has already thrown up various clues, the question still remains as to how the history textbook authors frame these interreligious contacts: in a positive, neutral or negative way?

Our analysis suggests that the language used by textbook authors is mostly neutral. They avoid using words or terms with a specific (positive or negative) connotation. The only exception is extremist behaviour, which is described in an explicitly negative way and condemned as a serious threat to peace in the world. History textbooks in Estonia and England, for instance, openly condemn terrorist attacks executed in the past two decades by religious extremists, which are clearly described as problematic and as hostile to world peace (Nutt and Vahtre 2014: 181; Bates et al. 2015b: 120–3).

Although the language they use is generally neutral, history textbooks do not always present the interreligious contacts themselves in a neutral way. In fact, the analysis reveals that they almost always present them in a negative way, as conflict-provoking and violent. This links in well to the central thesis of theologian William Cavanaugh, who argues that religion, particularly in Western societies, is widely yet wrongly considered to be a cause or promoter of violence – an idea he believes to be one of the foundational legitimating myths of Western society (Cavanaugh 2009). The interreligious contact between Christians and Roman polytheistic believers during the Roman Empire (first–fifth century CE), for instance, is always introduced within a context of hostilities, with an emphasis on persecutions. The reign of Constantine I and especially the Edict of Milan are normally presented as bright spots, although they are immediately followed by the remark that once Christianity became the state religion, intolerance began to appear again. The contact between Jews and Christians in Medieval Europe (sixth–fifteenth century CE) is also framed within a context of intolerance leading to violence and massacres. A Flemish history textbook has this to say: 'Medieval society was very intolerant towards people who were different or behaved differently.' (Berings 2016: 101). At the same time, this textbook offers an example of religious toleration. One of the historical sources cited by this textbook tells the story of a German bishop who invited Jews to his town (Speyer) so that they could live there in peace. Some German textbooks also offer examples of toleration, mentioning toleration and protection of Jews by Holy Roman emperors and German princes. As regards the rise of Protestantism and the interreligious contact between Catholics and Protestants in the Early Modern Period (sixteenth–eighteenth century CE), English, Spanish and Flemish history textbooks explicitly state that religious differences and problems were a cause of conflict. The only events with a positive slant appear in the Swiss textbook, which discusses at length the existence of biconfessional towns in Switzerland at the time, in which peaceful coexistence was possible (Weiß et al. 2011: 216–51). The general focus in the textbook accounts is, however, on conflict, violence and wars. Even the Peace of Augsburg (1555) is mentioned in a negative way in the Austrian, Estonian and Swiss textbooks; the authors claim that this Peace did not endure and had negative consequences, as it did not include Calvinists, and it fragmented Germany and led to the Thirty Years' War. German textbooks, by contrast, tend to emphasize the positive aspects of this Peace. All the textbooks mention the Treaty of Westphalia in a positive way, while framing it in a political rather than a religious context. The same general finding applies to the contact between those in favour of secularism and those in favour of religion having a strong position within society (eighteenth–nineteenth century CE). All the textbooks state that religion and church are a source of conflict, and that the demand for religious toleration came from the non-religious side. The fact that both secularism and toleration had profound religious roots in Christianity is largely ignored by the authors of these textbooks.

Similarly, the very recent interreligious contacts between Muslims and other (non-) religious groups since 1989 (post–Cold War era) are normally framed within a context of war, conflict and terrorism. The Oslo Accords of 1993 are a brief exception. The Flemish textbook even goes so far as to state: 'Conflicts, such as the chaos in Iraq and Syria, can only be fully explained from that ethnic and religious diversity.' (Geuens et al. 2015b: 226). The implicit message seems to be that religious diversity intrinsically carries with it the seeds of conflict.

Only one interreligious contact, namely that between Muslims and other religions during the Middle Ages (seventh–fifteenth century CE), is framed in a somewhat different manner. All the textbooks address the violent side of that encounter, as manifested in the expansion of Islam and the Crusades while, at the same time, highlighting the peaceful and enriching cultural exchange that took place within this contact. One of the English textbooks focuses exclusively on this aspect of the contact with a lengthy discussion of Medieval medicine and cultural exchanges (Cloake and Wilkes 2016: 12–15). In this case, however, the focus is not so much on tolerant and peaceful interreligious coexistence, but on beneficial cultural exchange. The Estonian and Flemish textbooks, furthermore, state that this was an exception which did not last that long. In other words, in their opinion, the default situation for interreligious contacts is conflict, not peaceful exchange. The contact between Muslims and other religions in that period inspired one history textbook (from Bavaria, Germany) to reflect on how this encounter is represented, raising the question as to why Islamic-Christian interreligious contacts are mostly described through conflicts and wars, while peaceful coexistence is often neglected (Brückner et al 2011: 53). Such a reflective stance on interreligious contacts is, however, very exceptional in the textbooks we analysed, which tend to represent religion and religious encounters as sources of conflict.

### To what extent and how are the past and present related to each other in the interreligious contacts?

Very few textbooks establish connections between the past and present in their accounts of the interreligious contacts. In the very few instances in which such connections are made, it normally involves a comparison between the past and present. In the chapter on the interreligious contact between Christians and Roman polytheistic believers during the Roman Empire (first–fifth century CE) one of the German textbooks asks, for instance, whether the role of religion in society is smaller today than it was in Antiquity; it also asks students to compare the policy of Emperor Theodosius with that applied in Germany today (Gawatz et al. 2018: 181). Similar comparative questions can occasionally be found in Austrian, Flemish, Finnish and Spanish textbooks as well. A second way of connecting past to present, which is seldom applied, involves a postmodern approach in which current representations of specific interreligious contacts in the past are discussed and students are asked to reflect on them. This approach is applied in the representation of the Crusades in Estonian, Flemish and German history textbooks.

Despite the fact that few connections are made between the past and present in the history textbooks we analysed, the present nevertheless exerts a clear influence on representations of the past, particularly on those accounts about interreligious contacts in which Islam and Muslims are involved. As mentioned earlier, almost all of these textbooks make a clear and explicit distinction between Islam and Islamist religious extremists in the present, and state that the latter are problematic and hostile to world peace, while Islam is not. The authors seem to want to pass on a similar message via their account of the interreligious contact between Muslims and other religions during the Middle Ages (seventh–fifteenth century CE), almost always emphasizing the positive contribution made by Islam and Muslims to societies in the West, and state that most Muslims are peace-loving. It would seem that they are aware of the negative perception of Muslims and Islam within large parts of society, and aim to provide young people with a more positive, more nuanced picture. One Swiss history textbook does so very explicitly in its introductory text. It states that it is very important to understand the Islamic world in a peaceful way, particularly after the 9/11 events in the United States. In this respect, the textbook continues, studying the past is very important. Further references are made to al-Andalus and the Muslim contribution to the advancement of science in the Middle Ages, after which the textbook invites students to think about Islamic scientific discoveries that are still important today (Weiß et al. 2011: 78–9).

## Conclusion and discussion

The aim of this chapter was to examine the social representations of religious diversity in the past that are being constructed and disseminated among young people across Europe today, from a comparative European perspective. To this end, we selected various important interreligious contacts over the course of history and examined the way they are represented in history textbooks used in secondary schools in a broad range of eight European countries: Austria, Belgium, Estonia, Finland, Germany, Spain, Switzerland and the UK. We also sought to identify major similarities and differences between the different countries.

When discussing our findings and drawing conclusions, caution is required. This study has a number of limitations. Although we have examined textbooks from a range of European countries, many others were not included. We were also only able to analyse a limited number of textbooks per country. There are a lot more textbooks on the market in each country. The focus of the analysis was on six interreligious contacts, while obviously many more could have been chosen. The result is that the analysis presented in this chapter cannot paint a complete picture of social representations of religious diversity in the past. A more extensive analysis might perhaps reveal slightly different or more nuanced conclusions. It might also identify additional silences, on top of the interreligious dimension of the colonial encounter, for example.

Nevertheless, on the basis of our analysis of some fifty textbooks, we can draw some firm conclusions and then go on to discuss them. The first conclusion we can come to is that the accounts are actually quite similar across the range of textbooks from different countries, especially in terms of the people, events, developments and agents they choose to focus on when describing these interreligious contacts. This seems to indicate the existence of an implicit European historical canon. At the same time, however, a national emphasis could be observed in the textbook accounts from various countries (especially England). Despite this, it is clear that textbook history has evolved a great deal in recent decades, especially since the end of the Second World War, from taking a predominantly or exclusively nation-centred approach to a broader vision centred on their part of Europe (Western, Southern or Central) or on Europe as a whole (see Erdmann, Maier and Popp 2006; Cajani, Lässig and Grever 2019). This is also reflected in the geographical focus of their accounts of these contacts.

Our second main conclusion is that all the textbooks embed interreligious contacts within a broad historical and societal (political, socio-economic and cultural) context. The religious context itself is also described. This is another sign of the evolution of textbooks, again particularly since the end of the Second World War, from a predominant focus on political and military history to a broader, more diversified coverage of various societal domains.

Our third conclusion, in relation to the attribution of agency, is in itself hardly surprising in that it confirms previous research which found that those most likely to be considered as agents in historical events were above all powerful individuals and groups, and other non-human agents. Ordinary individuals are almost never mentioned; neither are women. As regards the latter, we found that none of the books apply a gender perspective in their accounts of the interreligious contacts we studied. Another interesting finding is that humbler social groups, such as peasants, merchants and (poor) townsmen are referred to on occasions in these books, while in previous research on other subjects, such as the Cold War or the colonial encounter, these groups were rarely mentioned (Van Nieuwenhuyse 2019b; Van Nieuwenhuyse and Pires Valentim 2018). Another aspect worth noting is that, even if agency is not always attributed in a balanced way, the various parties involved in the interreligious contacts are all assigned some degree of agency. This suggests that the textbook authors wanted (to some extent) to explain these events from a range of perspectives.

Fourth, and also in line with previous research, we found that a great deal of homogenization took place in the textbook accounts of interreligious contacts. This may partly be due to the particular characteristics of the textbook genre, in which the past is approached in a very abstract, structural, 'social science' way. Textbooks focus particularly on the broad outlines and the processes of change in the past, and tend to overlook the micro-history, the individual human being of flesh and blood, and the nuances and differences within the parties involved in a historical phenomenon (Van Nieuwenhuyse and Bentrovato 2017). Within this analysis it is also worth noting that the textbook authors (except for some eleventh and twelfth grade textbooks) usually pay little attention to differences within the different parties involved in interreligious contacts. Instead, they give the impression that all those within each party thought and acted in the same way. The only case in which this observation is not entirely valid is in the contacts involving Muslims, in which the authors distinguish between moderate Muslims and radical Islamists. In so doing, they seem to want to tackle the persistent, generalized, negative views and prejudices in Western society today about Muslims in general.

Fifth, the same concern for the present can also be discerned in the interreligious contact between Muslims and other religions during the Middle Ages (seventh–fifteenth century CE), where the positive contribution of Islam and Muslims to societies in the West, and the fact that most Muslims were peace-loving, tends to be emphasized. This appears to be the only instance in which the influence of the present is clearly recognizable. Other than that, the textbooks are mainly past-oriented, in the sense that the past is treated completely independently of the present (Wils et al. 2011). We found very few examples of authors relating the past with the present. When they did, this mainly involved questions of comparison, and very occasionally offered a postmodern-inspired reflection on how the present deals with the past. Likewise, there were few traces of presentism, in the sense of projecting our contemporary frames of reference and values onto the past, and judging the past according to modern-day logic, rather than trying to understand it from its own perspective. It seems as if the textbook authors wanted above all to report on the past itself.

A sixth conclusion is that most of these authors offered a one-sided, negative representation of interreligious contact in the past, as a source of conflict, violence and even war. Although many of these contacts did indeed result in conflict, this was not always the case, which means that other stories could also be told. These contacts also led to peaceful coexistence and mutual understanding. Historians have also shown, for example, that secularism (treated positively by the textbook authors) has profound religious roots in Christianity. This side of the coin, however, is largely ignored in the history textbooks. As mentioned earlier, the message young people are receiving is that interreligious contacts generally have negative outcomes. This is clearly incorrect and unacceptable on various levels. As regards, for example, students' understanding of the past, this will inevitably be limited and one-sided; Cavanaugh, as mentioned earlier, went so far as to argue that history textbooks adopt this approach as a way of maintaining the myth that religion has a dangerous tendency to promote violence (Cavanaugh 2009). The result is that young people are not shown or taught the full richness and complexity of the past, and are therefore unaware that many of the agents in these interreligious contacts could and did make choices. Instead, the impression they receive is that conflict, violence and war were somehow inevitable, unavoidable outcomes of these contacts (Bermudez 2019). This annuls people's agency and ignores the contingent nature of the past.

Another result is that young people's view of interreligious contacts in the present can be tarred by the social representation of such contacts in the past. Some textbook authors seem to be aware of this possibility when they make clear that Islam cannot be equated with Islamist religious extremists, and that not all Muslims are extremists. However, they do not extend this awareness of the need to present a nuanced picture of the past to correct their own one-sided approaches to interreligious contacts, thereby giving students the impression that these contacts are bad by definition because they are a source of conflict and violence. This does not help young people to think about and deal with their own religious beliefs and those of others, nor about (their position in) society today.

Of course, this does not mean that history textbooks should cast a veil over interreligious contacts in the past. On the contrary, as the UNESCO highlighted in a guide to intercultural education, 'it is fundamentally important that democratic societies address interreligious issues through education' (UNESCO 2006: 14). For a good understanding of interreligious contacts, it is important to understand both the past and the present, as societies become increasingly religiously diverse (Patrick, Gulayets and Peck 2017). In history education, it is more important to build a good understanding of different religions and interreligious contacts than to develop religious understanding (i.e. an initiation into a religious way of life) (Jackson 2014).

So, how can a good understanding of interreligious contacts be acquired? First of all, students should be provided with accurate, nuanced and balanced information (Patrick 2015; Patrick, Gulayets and Peck 2017). This means that the different aspects and sides of interreligious contacts need to be addressed: the positive as well as the negative, the peaceful together with the violent. It is also important to not view religion only in relation to political developments (which often mean conflict). Interreligious contacts are much broader and richer than that. The various actors and parties involved should also be portrayed in all their diversity, that is, without homogenizing them into a single uniform group. Second, when studying these issues, students' critical skills need to be sharpened. It is important that they learn to critically analyse historical sources and to recognize perspectives. They should also be able to understand mutual representations (of any kind) within their context and deconstruct them, and develop a nuanced understanding of agency. Third and finally, the ability to take an open-minded approach and to engage in honest dialogue must also be strengthened.

These three goals can be pursued in textbooks through the application of didactic methods such as the interpretive approach and the dialogical approach (Jackson 2014). The interpretive approach concentrates on the representation of religions and interreligious contacts by others and on how students interpret them. It also encourages students to reflect upon these issues amongst themselves. The dialogical approach develops students' acceptance of diversity and difference, encouraging them to explore and understand these issues, and to discuss them openly. In so doing, history education can help young people become critical and constructive, open-minded citizens. It also develops important skills, such as understanding 'the other' and problematizing the 'othering' of different religious individuals and groups, adopting an open world view, avoiding stereotyping, and the ability to situate controversial issues within their past and present contexts, and to approach them from multiple perspectives.

# Society exhibited: Museums, religions and representation

Merve Reyhan Kayikci, Tamara Sztyma-Knasiecka, Naum Trajanovski
and Marija Manasievska

## Introduction

This chapter explores the ways in which the cultural heritage of ethnic and religious minorities in Europe is represented in European museums. More precisely, we will examine museum discourses on minority issues, religious tolerance and cultural diversity in different parts of Europe in the light of various political and social developments.

Why museums? In the past thirty years, we have observed a growing social and cultural role for museums as institutions which can bring about change in public discourse and opinions. This is connected to the development of 'new museology', as a guild initiative to shift the emphasis from museums' internal practices to a wider awareness of their social role and function (Vergo 1989: 2–3). Thus, in contemporary museums, education and visitors' experiences have become just as important as collecting, preserving and documenting heritage. In this way, museums are constantly developing methods for exhibition design, storytelling and communication, and their messages are consciously and thoughtfully constructed. As a result, they are becoming attractive tools for different social and political groups who want to promote their own particular world view. This can result in the politicization of museums, although sometimes the opposite occurs and museums struggle to promote critical discourses on the prevailing societal tropes. In any case, most contemporary museums are highly sensitive to current issues and refer to them in their practices. When studying contemporary museums, it is always important to ask: Why are some particular narratives chosen? Why not others? Who constructs these narratives and why? Is there any political/social aim behind them? What does this tell us about the society or social group that launched the museum?

One of the most challenging issues in these new, reoriented, highly competent museums is how to represent religious diversity, multi-ethnicity and multiculturalism in line with the developments in European policies in recent decades. The influx of immigrants from outside Europe and the internal migrations facilitated by the fall of the Iron Curtain in the 1980s and free movement of citizens within the European Union (EU) have contributed to the creation of multicultural societies, often characterized by a conflict between traditional national discourses and the challenges of real, everyday life in the newly transformed communities, in which the question of who is included and excluded is unavoidable and must be addressed on a daily basis in all walks of life. These transformations, coupled with other developments earlier in the twentieth century – the final collapse of colonialism, the two world wars, the Cold War and the birth of the concept of European unity – have also kindled a desire to revise and rethink Europe's complex history. The homogeneous national narratives are being questioned and closely scrutinized. In the light of all this, the discussion on tolerance and coexistence – their meaning, extent and the ways to achieve them – has become unavoidable and essential.

These developments have had a significant impact on the EU's cultural policy. In order to deal with this new challenge, the EU has adopted a slogan – 'unity in diversity' – and has started to invest more funds in cultural heritage programs, exhibitions and events. The document 'A Community of Cultures: The European Union and the Arts', issued by the European Commission is an important example: 'The aims of the EU cultural policy are to bring out the common aspects of Europe's heritage, enhance the feeling of belonging to one and the same community, while recognising and respecting cultural, national and regional diversity, and helping cultures to develop and become more widely known' (European Commission 2002). As this document makes clear, the idea is to find a commonality among the different regional and local cultures and work towards a common European heritage and identity. This idea of 'being united in diversity' was a guide for the creators of the House of European History – the museum founded by the European Parliament in Brussels. It is intended to convey the outlines of European history and to enhance people's understanding of more recent events and of the present. In doing so, the exhibition does not seek to present national or regional histories and instead focuses on the key features specific to European history, on the common values and common developments. The curators attempt to highlight certain defining moments in the development of European culture and civilization, such as Greek antiquity, Ancient Rome, the spread of Christianity, the development of Humanism, colonialism, the Age of Enlightenment, the French Revolution, nineteenth-century industrialization, the development of the ideas of the nation state, capitalism and socialism, and finally, murderous totalitarianism and the two world wars. They call it a shared history, moments that have helped form the continent, while at the same time emphasizing that many different nations and social groups were involved in these events and were affected by them in different ways, and therefore associate them with different experiences, interpretations and memories (Mork 2018). It is important to note, however, that a unifying message of this kind can also be marred by ambiguity: the House of European History promotes 'common moments' of European identity and therefore avoids exploring themes which – according to the museum planners – could create 'divisions' such as religion and migration.

Apart from this 'unity in diversity' slogan, there is also a more straightforward discourse on religious diversity as a means of promoting tolerance, which dominates the European narrative today. This was exemplified in a speech by Angela Merkel on 31 December 2018:

> Tolerance is the soul of Europe and an essential basic value of the European idea … Europe is our best chance for peace, prosperity and a good future. We must not let this chance slide; we owe this to ourselves and to past and future generations. Nationalism and egoism must never have a chance to flourish again in Europe. Tolerance and solidarity are our future. And this future is worth fighting for. (European Parliament 2018)

In such circumstances, ideas about intercultural dialogue, cultural diversity, cultural exchange, solidarity and coexistence all play a part in the construction of heritage narratives in museums today, even though these ideas are approached differently, depending on the social, political and historical context and the geographical location of each one. This will be the central theme of this chapter in which we will be studying the relationship between the different contexts of museums and their many and varied approaches to religious diversity and religious pluralism. For this reason, we will be focusing on three different ethnic and religious groups: Jews, Muslims and the ethnic minorities of the Balkans as represented in various museums across Europe.

The first section is dedicated to Islam, which has been regarded as Europe's Other in terms of religion, social organization, culture and politics (Bracke and Fadil 2008). In view of the increasing Muslim population in Europe after labour migration in recent decades, museums are changing the way they represent Islamic art and culture in an attempt to be more inclusive and diverse. Some scholars have described this as an agentive approach, because it allows space for conversation about heritage. Visitors not only look at the objects but also add their own input, ask themselves questions and discuss the exhibition with others. Exhibitions also include communities to some extent and their experiences of heritage and historical knowledge. This section will explore the transition from the representative to the agentive approach in displaying Islamic heritage.

The Jewish case, presented in the second section, is different. Judaism has been Europe's 'inside Other' since the Middle Ages and despite their partial exclusion, Jews living in Europe have participated in its economic and social life. They became more integrated into society as a consequence of emancipation after the eighteenth century, a progression that was shattered by the Holocaust. The enormous trauma this caused led to various decades of silence in relation to Europe's Jewish past. The task of restoring our memory and tracing the long history of Jewish presence in Europe is today being conducted by a range of Jewish museums, often developed in co-operation with Jewish organizations or Jewish communities. These museums usually present Jewish heritage 'from within', in a bid to bring about changes in public attitudes towards Jews and Jewish culture. They are also closely involved in the wider social discourse on democracy and tolerance.

The final section discusses a small European country, North Macedonia (part of Yugoslavia until 1991) in the Southern Balkans, a region reputed for its diverse population. It analyses how changing political and social dynamics reflect on the representation of Macedonia's minorities in local museums. This section differs from the previous two sections in the sense that it focuses on one specific country that is currently immersed in the process of entering the EU. North Macedonia has a multicultural, multi-ethnic and multilingual population, which at certain times in history has given rise to tension and conflict. This section also unravels how identity is assembled and disassembled in museums in line with the prevailing political rhetoric. It questions the meaning of diversity in a post-conflict context and how this creates systems of inclusion and exclusion.

## Islam in museums: From representation to agency

Heritage institutions such as museums are actively addressing the changes taking place in European society today as a result of growing multicultural and multireligious diversity. Islamic civilizations have long inspired the curators of the great museums of Europe, and in recent decades these curators have also had to take into consideration that Muslim communities are now part of European society. The presence of Muslims in Europe is reflected not only in social and political debates, but also in discussions concerning their representation in mainstream heritage institutions (Naguib 2019: 376–7). This section explores how Muslims were represented in European museums in the past and how changing pluralistic societies are reflected in exhibitions today.

To this end we gathered data from fifteen different museums and exhibitions and their Islamic collections in Amsterdam, Brussels, Paris, Berlin and London. We visited these exhibitions, collected images and textual descriptions from them and, where possible, interviewed their curators. We were unable to interview curators in museums such as the British Museum, the Victoria and Albert Museum and the Louvre, but we did speak to the curating and outreach staff at the Museum of Islamic Art in Berlin, the Brussels Museum of Art and History, the Rijksmuseum and the Tropenmuseum in Amsterdam, and the Institut du Monde Arabe. Our ethnographic research took place between 2018 and 2020.

The question of what is Islam and Islamic heritage has been a much-debated issue in recent academic scholarship. A first set of studies argued that Islamic exhibitions in museums often accentuate the 'splendour' of Islamic civilizations as a way of counteracting contemporary prejudices towards Islam and Muslims (Shaw 2012: 1; Shatanawi 2012a). These studies suggest that while exhibitions embrace the aesthetically pleasing aspects of Islamic art, they also imply that this art belonged to a bygone era and no longer exists today (Shaw 2012: 1). Museums engage with Islamic civilization as a historical phenomenon from the distant past (Vernoit 1997). Scholars in this field also claim that there is an excessive emphasis on aesthetics and a lack of critical engagement and contextualization of the objects on display (Heath 2005: 155). Other scholars have contributed to this argument by adding that the repeated framing of Islamic art as 'glorious and splendid' has reinforced the stereotypes that Islam is a pre-modern religion that inspired pre-modern forms of art and aesthetics (Shatanawi 2012b). According to these researchers, Islamic art is an 'index of civilizations' (Scheid

2012: 93) but should be regarded as inferior to Western art, which progressed to the Enlightenment and beyond (Kamel 2019: 374).

A second line of studies has argued that the representation of Islam in museums has become 'decaffeinated' (Peter, Dornhof and Arigita 2013). Building upon Zizek's concept of a 'decaffeinated Other' (2010), an 'Other' that is deprived of its otherness for the sake of political gain, scholars have sought to identify the 'decaffeinated Muslim', the Muslim who is integrated into the cultural and the artistic sphere as a means of displaying the 'refined aspects' of Islam and Muslims (Peter, Dornhof and Arigita 2013). These studies point out that most museums refrain from making explicit political statements and seek only to draw attention to the artistic qualities of Islamic or Middle Eastern artwork (Shatanawi 2012b). Referring to this as a deliberate strategy, Mirjam Shatanawi says that the aim is to 'focus on a universal love of aesthetic; substituting beauty for violence and artistic skill for backwardness' (2012b: 177). Shatanawi argues that this approach does not stop visitors from establishing a connection with what is displayed in the museum (in an apolitical context) within the context of 'a clash of civilizations' (Shatanawi 2012b: 177; Huntington 2000). Visitors approach the exhibitions with some previous knowledge of Islam and Muslim societies, often based on what they see in the media or hear from politicians. In turn, the decaffeinated representation of Islamic art and culture becomes the museum's way of defending Islam as a tradition that has elements with which European cultures can relate (Flood 2012). According to scholars, decaffeinating the Muslim creates a binary: on the one hand there is the Muslim who is able to communicate through an artistic, eloquent medium (Khabeer 2016; Winegar 2008), and on the Other the Muslim who is 'stuck' in their tradition, unable to move forward and unable to communicate with wider society (Peter, Dornhof and Arigita 2013; Kamel 2019). Scholars have highlighted that the rearticulation of these discursive binaries can further reinforce the stereotypes that are projected on Muslims (Peter, Dornhof and Arigita 2013).

The two lines of study run parallel to one another in that they draw our attention to how heritage discourses can create binaries between refined and unrefined Islam. This is why in the last few years curators have been working to develop better techniques and narratives to convey the diversity within the Islamic tradition and among Muslim populations without falling into the trap of essentialization (Weber 2018). In the past few years the discussion has shifted from representation to agency, and to including the communities in question in the deliberations on the representation process (Sternfeld 2016).

Exhibitions in which art, culture and aesthetics are brought to the forefront and politics and conflict are left to one side have been pivotal in creating spaces for public discussion. Museum directors and curators have clearly stated that they aim to promote tolerance, mutual respect and open-minded thinking through exhibitions (Arab 2020). When the Dutch minister of social affairs and employment, Wouter Koolmees, opened the *Longing for Mecca* exhibition in February 2019, he stressed the importance of such exhibitions as a form of soft power (Arab 2020). According to Koolmees, these exhibitions helped to promote integration without being too political. In this regard the museum provides an apolitical space in which normally uncomfortable subjects – such as the integration of Muslims – can be discussed.

As part of our fieldwork we visited several permanent and temporary exhibitions about Islam in ethnographic and art museums in Europe. On the basis of our findings, we discuss how museums in pluralistic societies are gradually moving towards a more agentive approach in their exhibitions. We reveal how this approach is embedded in political discourses of integration, tolerance and coexistence.

In 2018, the Den Haag City Museum (Gemeentemuseum Den Haag) organized a temporary exhibition called *Splendor and Bliss: Arts of the Islamic World*. The exhibition focused on the ornamental character of Islamic art and on material manifestations of culture, tradition and craft. Writers, musicians and cooks paid tribute to the objects in the exhibition. They wrote texts, recipes and played pieces of music, which they felt were related to the exhibition. The exhibition catalogue said that it paid tribute to the use of highly detailed ornamentation in Islamic art: 'the decorations have a religious character, reminding the faithful of all the wonderful things that await them in the afterlife' (Gemeentemuseum Den Haag 2018). One of the main criticisms that such exhibitions receive is that they focus more on technique and decoration and less on cultural life in the Muslim world (Heath 2005). In this regard the exhibition reflects the critical argument put forward by scholars such as Shaw and Shatanawi. Indeed, many famous museums, such as the Louvre, the British Museum, and the Victoria and Albert Museum, follow the same line of conventional representation. The problem with conventional representations of Islam in museums is that they do not provide a better insight into Muslim societies and daily life (Shatanawi 2012b: 178; Heath 2005). However, the *Splendor and Bliss* exhibition also included the input of contemporary creative actors and interactive audiovisual material for youngsters. Unlike previous Islamic exhibitions, newly emerging contemporary exhibitions are careful to include elements that reflect on contemporary society and the development of culture. They also reflect on how cultural heritage – including food, music, art – is passed down to the younger generations, and on what is forgotten and what is remembered in the process.

Nevertheless, the *Splendor and Bliss* exhibition provides a notable contrast to the Islamic exhibitions held at the Louvre and the Victoria and Albert Museum, whose collections cover the period between the seventh and nineteenth centuries. The exhibition at the Louvre, like many recent exhibitions on Muslims and other minorities, sought to incorporate community perspectives and voices, not only by reaching out to creative actors from the community but also by providing space for youngsters and everyday individuals to engage with the public and talk about their heritage.

Another significant example is the Amsterdam City Museum in the Netherlands and its *New Narrative Tours* in 2019. Every month an individual from a minority community was invited to the museum to talk about issues pertaining to identity, religion, gender and so on. In June, a young Muslim PhD student took the floor to testify about her daily experiences as a Muslim woman in a pluralistic society. She talked about what it meant to be Dutch, Muslim, Black and female, and how these different heritages came together in a single body – hers. This is another example of how museums are increasingly departing from the passive display of objects, in which the role of visitors is simply to view material heritage. Instead, visitors are actively engaged by having to listen and ask questions, thereby making exhibitions more than just an aesthetic spectacle to enjoy but also a space for learning, understanding and, in some cases, responding.

In 2018, we attended an event entitled *Muslim Cool, What Does It Mean to Be Muslim within Popular and Digital Culture*, which was held at the Tropenmuseum, an ethnographic museum in Amsterdam. The event involved various performances from Dutch Muslim musicians, and speeches from (Islamic exhibition) curators, museum directors and academics. The general aim of the event was to discuss how museums could become more inclusive, especially in the way they represent Muslim communities and cultures. One aspect of the event that was heavily criticized by the audience, composed of mainly Dutch-Muslim youngsters, was the choice of the name, Muslim Cool, which they claimed reinforced the idea that there were cool, refined, civilized Muslims and uncool, unruly, non-civilized Muslims. They said that although the event was a step forward in creating a platform for mutual understanding it also risked confirming public discourses about 'good' and 'bad' Muslims (Mamdani 2002).

Similar comments were made about the *Longing for Mecca* exhibition, which was held in the same museum. The exhibition showcased many objects related to the Muslim pilgrimage experience, the *hajj*. There were several prayer objects and tokens from Mecca, which had been loaned to the exhibition by people who had made the pilgrimage. There were also interesting facts, figures and maps that described the flow of people to Mecca from different countries around the world. The exhibition included video recordings of Dutch Muslims who had done the *hajj* and who talked about their experiences. Most of the short video clips referred to the *hajj* as a life-changing experience that touched the heart and soul. The participants extensively expressed their feelings of community, family, love and tolerance. Many saw the *hajj* as a way to move forward as people. It was a road to becoming a better person, not only as an individual but also as a community.

While these aspects of the *hajj* were emphasized throughout the exhibition, other aspects were visibly toned down. One of the exhibits was a painting of a Dutch ship that sailed from the Dutch Antilles to Mecca, carrying Antillean pilgrims. However, the colonial connection between the Dutch Empire and Muslims stopped there and the exhibition did not delve any further into colonial history (Arab 2020). Likewise, although there were historical pictures of Black servants, visitors were not told their stories (Arab 2020). Pooyan Tamimi Arab, an anthropologist and one of the curators of the Islamic exhibition at the Tropenmuseum, emphasized this point: 'the museum collection contains, for example, a nineteenth century lithograph of black slaves, musicians, who performed in Jeddah … which could have been shown' (2020).

The *Longing for Mecca* exhibition, much like the *New Narrative Tours* and to some extent the *Splendor and Bliss* exhibition, conveys a sense of moving forward as a society. These exhibitions acknowledge that contemporary societies are pluralistic and that there is a great deal of cultural exchange between the different communities. It is also important to realize that these communities are themselves internally heterogeneous. Exhibitions in recent years have engaged with how society can make the best of this multiplicity. This issue becomes more pressing when the subject concerns Islamic heritage and Muslim populations, whose identities lie at the interface between the hackneyed binary of Western and non-Western (Hall 1992).

There have been many studies that have explored how images of the Muslim as the Other in post-Enlightenment Europe have been recovered, in a bid to portray Muslims as incompatible with European values (Fadil 2011). If we were to cite once again the words of Dutch Minister Koolmees (Arab 2020), recent exhibitions aim to tackle these discourses in a less political space and by using art as a medium.

In doing so, the gaze is no longer fixed on the object on display, as is still the case in the Louvre and the Brussels Museum of Art and History. The agentive approach requires more nuances, discussion and critique. However, giving more agency to the subjects of the exhibitions does not necessarily result in a more diverse representation of the Muslim world (Shatanawi 2012b). According to Shatanawi, some museums, such as the Tropenmuseum, have revised their Islamic exhibitions and taken a more agentive approach. This has led to some Muslim communities being given more prominence than others and to emphasizing certain great moments in the history of Islam such as the Ottoman Empire or al-Andalus (Shatanawi 2012b). In some cases, religion has also been a problematic issue with some museums wanting to distance themselves from the idea that religion is the only dynamic in Muslim lives, while others seek to highlight the connection between Islam and cultural progress.

In 2019 we visited the Institut du Monde Arabe, an organization founded in Paris in 1980 by the Arab League to research and disseminate information about the Arab world, and its cultural and spiritual values. The institution has large exhibition halls with permanent and temporary exhibitions displaying contemporary art by Arab artists as well as historical ethnographic pieces. During our visit, we were told very clearly by museum administrators that this was not a 'religious exhibition' – it was a secular exhibition with religious objects on display. The ethnographic exhibition did indeed contain religious objects, not only Islamic but also pre-Islamic, Christian and Jewish objects. According to the exhibition description, which was displayed on glass panels at the entrance, the aim was to explain the religious diversity of the Arab world and to challenge the conception that Arab meant Islam (see Figure 4.1).

Other exhibitions focused directly on the religious traditions of the Muslim world. The exhibition *Islam, It's Also Our History*, for example, organized by Tempora, an exhibition design company in Brussels, with the support of the European Union Culture Program, explored the historical interaction between Europe and the Muslim world. Unlike the Institut du Monde Arabe, it took Islam as a cultural defining point. Both Tempora and the Institut du Monde Arabe are well-known institutes that attract hundreds of visitors. Smaller, more peripheral, institutions offer a less visible platform. The problem with the agentive approach employed by these museums is that heritage has a complex relationship with the audience and the subject.

There are many layers to heritage and, especially, to one as geographically broad as Islamic heritage. Different ethnicities, nations, cultures, languages and even religious ways of life have contributed to what we refer to as Islamic heritage. The main aim of most exhibitions today is to acknowledge the many complexities and the interweaving between these different strands.

In the process, both peripheral and mainstream institutions (museums, exhibition spaces) are faced with a difficult mission in which they have to challenge these

**Figure 4.1** Institut du Monde Arabe
*Source*: Photo by Merve Reyhan Kayikci, 2019.

pre-existing knowledges, without 'politicizing' their exhibitions and without singling out communities that are less visible (Shatanawi 2007). Museums that are pushing for a more agentive approach in their exhibitions rather than a passive display are also grappling with these issues. The trajectory of museums towards a more inclusive, more conversational, outlook is deeply engrained within social, political and global dynamics (Rey 2019), but the question remains as to how effectively museums can embrace this complexity.

## Jewish museums in Europe: reviving memory and transforming national narratives

Jewish museums present the history of the Jewish community, which throughout the centuries has been an important element of religious diversity in Europe. Although Jews in Europe also lived in Muslim-ruled areas (in parts of the Iberian Peninsula until the fifteenth century and in the Balkans between the fifteenth and the nineteenth centuries), since the eleventh or twelfth century the majority of European Jews have lived in Christendom. Although their situation varied from one region or period to the next, in general they were regarded as 'the Other' because of their different religion and customs and they were partly excluded from the societies in which they lived. Their life was regulated by a separate set of laws (in Christendom the hostility towards the Jews was reinforced by the theological anti-Judaism of the church). At the same time, however, they participated in economic and social life, and multicultural exchange was commonplace (Nirenberg 2014). The gradual emancipation of European Jews helped integrate them into their respective societies, but it did not completely deprive them of the 'Other' status. This eventually resulted in the development of modern anti-Semitism based on a combination of old theological and social stereotypes and new ideas about race, which contributed to the mass annihilation of most European Jews during the Second World War (Polonsky 2013). For several decades afterwards, the trauma caused by the Holocaust, as well as the unsettled issues of guilt and responsibility, prevented the subject of Jewish heritage in Europe from being addressed honestly and openly. The annihilation of the European Jewry and the destruction of their heritage were veiled in silence and dealing with this topic was considered uncomfortable and therefore avoided. The 'Jewish issue' aroused controversies, disputes and emotions, and the creation of Israel and the conflict between Israelis and Palestinians only made the subject thornier.

So, in contrast to Islam and Muslims and other immigrants and newcomers to European countries, when dealing with Jews and Judaism, the European idea of opening up to diversity does not materialize in 'integrating them into the society', and instead involves rethinking and integrating Jewish history and culture into the European mould. It is more a question of 'rethinking and better understanding the past' in order to shape the present and the future according to the new values, based on European ideals of human dignity, freedom, equality, solidarity, democracy.

The breaking of this silence around the Holocaust and Jewish heritage in Europe was a slow process that took decades. The change began in the 1970s and finally gathered pace after the collapse of communism in Eastern Europe in 1989. The growing democratization of life and increasing European integration (in which the idea of diversity began to take on great importance), especially after the fall of the Iron Curtain, made it possible for a more open debate – first on the Holocaust, and then on the role and place of Jewish heritage in European culture. There was a need to create a space for open and critical debate and for recovering the Jewish past neglected by many European societies. Confronting 'Jewish themes' became part of democratic changes and the development of open civil societies. Many books on the topic began to be published and Departments of Jewish Studies were opened in various university faculties. This also paved the way for establishing new museums devoted to Jewish heritage.

Jewish museums are not a new phenomenon in Europe – the first museums presenting Jewish heritage were established by Jewish communities at the end of the nineteenth century and in the interwar period (Vienna, Frankfurt, Hamburg, Prague, Budapest, Prague, Warsaw) and sought to preserve the Jewish tradition, reinforce Jewish identity in the modern world and present Jewish culture to non-Jews (Cohen 1998). The Holocaust of European Jews destroyed most of the Jewish communities and their museums. A few of these institutions managed to continue their activities after the war, mostly on the initiative of those who had survived. They were depositaries of memory in the initial post-war decades of silence that settled over the Shoah and pre-war Jewish life. They operated on the sidelines of national cultural life; in the main national museums, and in both Eastern and Western Europe, Jewish culture and history was perceived as unimportant and was only represented in exhibitions on a very limited scale.

This situation started changing from the 1980s onwards when Europe witnessed a real boom in Jewish museums. Since then new Jewish museums have been established in most European countries or existing ones have been renovated and given more prominence. The newly established museums include the Frankfurt Jewish Museum (1987), the Jewish Museum in Stockholm (1987), the Vienna Jewish Museum (1986), the Museum of Art and History of Judaism in Paris (1998), the Jewish Museum Berlin (the project started in 1989 and the museum opened in 2001), the POLIN Museum of the History of Polish Jews in Warsaw (initiated in 1994 and opened in 2013), the Museum of Italian Judaism and Shoah in Ferrara (initiated in 2003 and opened in 2018), the Jewish Museum in Copenhagen (2004), the Jewish Museum in Munich (2007), the Jewish Museum in Oslo (2008), the Jewish Museum in Erfurt (2009), the Jewish Museum in Spire (2010), the Holocaust Memorial Center for the Jews of Macedonia (2011) and the Tolerance Center in Moscow (2015). The existing museums that have been renovated and expanded to a more national scale include the Jewish Museum of Greece in Athens (1993), London Jewish Museum (1995), the Jewish Museum in Prague (1994), the Jewish Museum in Amsterdam (first modernized in 1989 and then again in 2007) and the Jewish Museum and Archives in Budapest (2018). These museums are usually very receptive to new trends in museology, which focus on conscious constructing of the narrative and achieving the best possible visitor experience, deploying to this end the most appropriate exhibition resources for achieving these goals.

Although these museums are mostly established and run by non-Jews, in many cases they are initiated by the local Jewish community or by non-profit organizations (Jewish or non-Jewish) interested in preserving Jewish heritage. In some rare cases, Jewish museums are run by or are directly connected to the Jewish community, for example, in Rome, Venice, Budapest, Athens, Thessalonica, Trondheim and Bratislava. Most of these museums are national or municipal institutions and are targeted at a wide audience: citizens (from the city itself or from the rest of the country) and tourists many of whom will be non-Jews. Members of local Jewish communities and Jewish tourists are only part of the audience.

The 'nationalizing' of Jewish museums should be perceived as an expression of the need felt by European societies to come to terms with their difficult Jewish histories, and to break the silence that surrounded the Shoah for several decades after the war. The main mission of contemporary Jewish museums in Europe is to recover the history of Jewish life in a particular country, region or city. They aim to include Jewish history in the national narratives, while at the same time questioning the idea of homogeneity of nation-centred narratives, basing their discourse on the European idea of cultural diversity and pluralism. Many of these museums in their mission statements refer to the 'ages of Jewish history' in a particular region (e.g. POLIN – one thousand years; Berlin and Ferrara – two thousand years; Copenhagen – four hundred years, etc.), in this way reminding visitors of the continuous Jewish presence and the multi-ethnic past of a city, region or country (Kirshenblatt-Gimblett 2013: 84). Although they differ in many details, the historical exhibitions of Jewish museums share a general meta-historical approach – presenting local history as something shared by the different groups that lived in the area. Jews are introduced as 'locals' not as 'strangers'. What is especially important is the way they deal with diversity and pluralism, based on the idea of 'coexistence' – a very appropriate term that can encompass both co-operation and mutual influences as well as moments of crises.

An example of such a narrative is the core exhibition at the POLIN Museum of the History of Polish Jews located in Warsaw. It is dedicated to the age-long history of Jews in Poland, which from the late Middle Ages had been home to the world's largest Jewish community and was an important cradle of Jewish Ashkenazi culture. However Polish Jews made up the highest proportion of the Jewish victims of the Holocaust and their destruction meant that their heritage was also highly marginalized and obliterated in post-war decades. The creation of the POLIN Museum of the History of Polish Jews began in the 1990s, coinciding with the fall of communism and the process of democratization. The project was originally proposed by the Association of the Jewish Historical Institute, which managed to gain support from both municipal and national authorities, as well as from the world Jewish community, many of whom had roots in Poland. The core exhibition of this museum, designed by a wide team of scholars, curators and designers over many years, finally opened in 2014. It presents a history of one thousand years of continuous presence of Jews on Polish soil and aims to show that the history of Polish Jews is an integral part of the history of Poland, which would not be complete without the history of Polish Jews. Barbara Kirshenblatt-Gimblett, the chief curator of the exhibition (and one of the leading experts in the field of Jewish museums), wrote in her introduction to the exhibition catalogue:

> A relational history starts from a different premise, namely, that Polish Jews were not only in Poland but also of Poland. They were subjects and agents of history, and not only objects into which others projected their fantasies and fears. The result is a history 'in common', a story of coexistence, competition, conflict and cooperation. Indeed, a multi-perspective on events became central to the historical narrative. The exhibition presents the broad spectrum of relations, from the best to the worst. (2014: 32)

An important element of the narrative strategy of the POLIN Museum is also the emphasis on the unique character of the Jewish culture that developed in Poland and was shaped by local conditions. This idea transmits the message that (not only) Polish history is incomplete without its Jewish history and that Jews played a significant role in the historical events of these lands. It also stresses that the Jewish culture that developed on Polish soil survives today in many Jewish communities around the world, where it left its own specific imprint due to the particular local conditions – local history, culture, geography. Moshe Rossman (n.d.), one of the historians working on the exhibition, described it as 'categorically Jewish but distinctively – Polish'. This idea is especially symbolized by the reconstruction of the painted wooden roof of the Gwoździec synagogue, which dates from the first half of the seventeenth century, and is the central feature of the seventeenth- and eighteenth-century gallery called 'The Town' (see Figure 4.2). Such wooden synagogues with a baroque appearance, elements of folk art and rich painted decorations full of Jewish symbols were unique architectural forms in seventeenth- and eighteenth-century Poland.

The long-enduring history of local Jewish presence and the idea of diversity and pluralism is not only expressed in the exhibitions held at these different museums, but is also enhanced by their locations and their architecture. Many of these museums are located in places once inhabited by the local Jewish population. They are often established in former synagogues, many of which had been neglected for centuries (Erfurt, Prague, Budapest, Toledo, Rome, Venice, Amsterdam) or in other buildings connected to the history of the local Jewish community (Frankfurt, Spire, Hohenems). Telling the story of the Jewish community in the restored architecture in which some of the events took place makes the story more credible and authentic. It helps to recover their history, hitherto forgotten or neglected, and links the past with the present.

A good example here is the Museum Judengasse in Frankfurt, a department of the Jewish Museum in Frankfurt, that tells the story of the Jewish community in Medieval Frankfurt. The Museum is located on the excavated ruins of five houses from the former ghetto. The *Judengasse* existed as an enclosed area from the end of the fifteenth

**Figure 4.2** Reconstruction of the roof of the synagogue in Gwoździec at the core exhibition of the Museum of the History of Polish Jews POLIN

*Source*: Photo by Magda Starowieyska, POLIN Museum.

century until around 1800 and was eventually demolished at the end of the nineteenth century. The discovery of the foundations of several houses of the former *Judengasse* in 1987 by workers constructing a building for the Frankfurt Utility Company aroused considerable public debate, and some Frankfurt residents protested and demanded an end to the construction works. This was the first time in post-war German history that the issue of Jewish heritage had appeared in public debate. Eventually the foundations were reconstructed and became the heart of the exhibition, which tells the story of the Jews in Medieval and pre-modern Frankfurt (Backhaus 2016).

Another museum with historical architecture at its heart is the Sephardic Museum in Toledo, located in a Medieval synagogue that was founded by the local Jew Samuel ha-Levi, the treasurer of King Pedro I of Castile in the first half of the fourteenth century (Catlos 2014). The impressive Mudejar-style synagogue was constructed at a time when Jews were an integral part of Medieval society and some of them even held high positions in the courts of both Muslim and Christian kings. Following the Edict ordering the expulsion of the Jews from Spain in 1492, the synagogue was transformed into a church and served as such until the nineteenth century. In 1964, the building that attested both to the role played by the Jews in Medieval Spain as well as to the ages of oblivion that followed their expulsion became the site of the Sephardic Museum, which opened to the public in 1971. This was part of the process of recovering the memory of the Sephardic Jewish community and their contribution to Spanish culture.[1]

Apart from revitalizing historical buildings, the complex history of Jews in different European countries is also strongly addressed in the architectural design of the new museums. Contemporary architecture, with its abstract yet expressive forms, can capture the very essence of the historical and social context of an institution. It can convey some of the complex issues of memory and the Shoah, and link these issues to the transformations taking place in the present and the idea of renewal, reparation and continuity of Jewish life that they wish to promote (Kirshenblatt-Gimblett 2013: 85–6).

Perhaps the best example is the Jewish Museum Berlin, designed by Daniel Libeskind and opened to the public in 2001. This building is a metaphor for the difficult German-Jewish history. The entrance is located in what was once the Prussian Court of Appeal in the eighteenth century. The main exhibition is situated in a new expressive, monumental building designed in Libeskind's 'deconstructivist' style that breaks with architectural canons and traditional engineering. Although the two structures at first appear to be separate entities, they are in fact connected thereby creating a metaphor for German-Jewish history. The elegant Prussian Baroque palace indicates that German-Jewish history is anchored in Germany's past. The expressive contemporary building, with a metallic, anti-classical facade and slanted walls dominated by skylines that pierce the building at an angle, expresses the difficult, emotional dimension of German-Jewish history. Inside the building, the exhibition spaces are disrupted by empty, mostly inaccessible voids made of bare concrete, which symbolize 'the emptiness that is created when an entire community is eliminated or when individual freedom is suppressed'. Just passing through the building is an emotional experience for visitors. Before entering the main exhibition, they are forced to 'descend' and walk down the underground passage composed of three corridors that symbolize the fate of the Jewish population in Nazi Germany: the Axis of Continuity, the Axis of Exile and the Axis of the Holocaust. The Axis of the Holocaust ends in the so-called Holocaust Tower, which is accessed by a heavy door that opens onto a 24-meter-high hollow space made of concrete (once inside visitors have the feeling of being cut off from daily life, just as the Jews were during the Nazi dictatorship). The whole ensemble refers to the Holocaust as a most dramatic, unprecedented event, and at the same time attempts to integrate it into the city's consciousness and memory. According to the architect, it is 'only by recognizing and dealing with the obliteration of Jewish life in Berlin and the ensuing void this left behind that Berlin and Europe can have a humane future'. In this sense, however, the building also expresses hope for reparation and renewal. This message is especially evoked by the monumental glass courtyard added to the Old Building, which houses the museum restaurant. The courtyard resembles a Sukka, a traditional Jewish tent built on the occasion of a holiday that celebrated the story of the Israelites escaping from slavery in Egypt (Beeck 2011; Kamczycki 2015).

A similar complex message and the interplay of the difficult past and present renewal is encapsulated in the building of the POLIN Museum in Warsaw designed by Finnish architect Rainer Mahlamäki. Its modest cubic facade covered with glass panels and shining with light enters a dialogue with the monument standing opposite to the Warsaw Ghetto Uprising and with the neighbouring residential buildings erected after the war on the unexcavated rubble of the ghetto. Whereas the Monument is dedicated to the victims of the Shoah, and the communist apartment blocks symbolize the post-war silence and eradication of memory, the shining building of the museum conveys the idea of life and hope. Although modest from the outside, it has a unique interior that is flooded with light from the huge window. The whole space is full of curved surfaces, bridges and skylights. It expresses the drama of history while also communicating the idea of change and transformation (Ark 2014).

Given their aim to transform homogenous national narratives and the fact that they are approached in this way within the contemporary discourse of diversity, the Jewish museums naturally tend to reach beyond Jewish topics to encompass wider issues of human rights, equality, democracy, inclusion, as promoted by the European discourse in recent decades. By examining the mechanisms of the historical stereotypes that led to the exclusion of Jews, they present the highly negative consequences of all kinds of religious intolerance, nationalism and racism. For some museums, this universal dimension is especially important and, through their exhibitions and activities, they give voice to excluded minorities and take action against all forms of discrimination or exclusion – be they related to race, religion, gender, nationality and so on. They promote the idea of civic society and cultural pluralism and seek to provide an arena for social dialogue.

This mission has been particularly important in recent years, when, with the influx of immigrants and refugees from Muslim countries and Eastern Europe and the associated changes in the population of Europe, the issue of multiculturalism and interreligious dialogue has come to the fore. The new civilizational conflicts that emerged after the relatively calm 1990s established a new framework for the activity of Jewish museums, which more and more often go beyond the specifically Jewish experience to adopt a universal outlook – in a bid to promote pluralism and multiculturalism, shape inclusive, civic attitudes, provide a voice for minorities, and speak out against various manifestations of discrimination, exclusion and hate speech. For example, the Belgian Jewish Museum in Brussels held an exhibition entitled *Brussels – a Safe Port?* (13 October 2017–18 March 2018) dedicated to the various waves of emigrants arriving in the city. The exhibition analysed why people left their countries and how they ended up and were received in Brussels; it also presented works by contemporary artists dealing with migration and cultural diversity in Brussels today. In this context, it seems symbolic that in addition to the works of Jewish artists, the London Ben Uri Gallery and Museum has, for several years, also been collecting the works of other artists who came to Britain as emigrants.

A multicultural perspective can also be introduced by presenting the common roots of the three main religions – Judaism, Christianity and Islam (so reaching beyond the Judeo-Christian idea and even Muslim culture, which has the same monotheistic and ethical roots as Judaism and Christianity). In the last two decades this has been especially true of the Jewish Museum Berlin, which has organized several such exhibitions, for example, *Cherchez la femme* (on the ideas surrounding ritual head and body coverings) (Jewish Museum Berlin 2007), *Snip It! Stances on Ritual Circumcision* (on the ritual of male circumcision) (Jewish Museum Berlin 2013) and *Kosher & Co.: On Food and Religion*, which deals with religiously motivated dietary laws and Judaism's broader relationship with food. It also includes comparisons with other world religions, primarily Christianity, Islam and Hinduism (Jewish Museum Berlin 2009).

However, the involvement of Jewish museums in contemporary social and political discourse has also led to conflict and controversy, with some of their actions receiving harsh criticisms from groups representing different world views. This has become more and more evident in recent years with the growth of nationalism and populism, particularly in countries such as Hungary, Poland and Slovakia. One very recent, very evident, example of this was the POLIN Museum in Warsaw, which, after the rise of the right-wing nationalist and populist government, has been strongly criticized by the authorities. The flashpoint in this conflict was an exhibition titled *Stranger in the House: March'68* organized by POLIN to mark the fiftieth anniversary of the anti-Semitic campaign launched by the communist authorities in 1968. The exhibition was perceived by the government as 'anti-Polish', as it did not propagate the view promoted by the government – which simplified the interpretation of the March 1968 events as launched by 'communist authorities'. Instead, the curators focused on the complex social and political mechanisms that led to the growing exclusion and expulsion of 16,000 Jewish citizens from Poland, deconstructing the mechanisms of political propaganda and the complexity of sensitive issues in Polish-Jewish relations (Koszarska-Szulc and Romik 2017). As a final outcome of this conflict, the minister of culture refused to extend the contract of the director, Dariusz Stola, causing more than a year of uncertainty and upheaval in the functioning of the institution. He also limited funding and attempted to gain more control over the institution. Another recent case of political controversy in relation to a Jewish museum was the controversy surrounding Peter Schäfer, the director of the Jewish Museum Berlin, whose criticisms of Israel's anti-Palestinian policies were rejected by the German authorities, who for historical reasons try to avoid excessive criticism of Israel. Schäfer was accused of taking stances that were incompatible with his post and this led to his eventual resignation (DW 2019).

## The Macedonian museum scene and museology

While the first two sections of this chapter discussed the representations of Muslims and Jews in European museums, we will now move on to look at the representation of religious diversity in North Macedonia. This section aims to provide a comprehensive national case study of museums in North Macedonia in order to discover how cultural representation deals with the complexity of religious difference after an armed conflict in which ethnic and religious divisions were mobilized.[2]

The sociopolitical context within which museums have been established in Macedonia is quite different from the contexts in which national museums were established across Europe. This special context has also conditioned the subsequent development of museums in today's North Macedonia. The initial efforts to institutionalize museum collections in the state known today as North Macedonia can be traced back to the early twentieth century, in the aftermath of the First World War, when the new Serbian authorities launched a project for the Museum of South Serbia in Skopje (see Aleksoska-Bačeva, Mihajlova and Bogoeski 2015). The museum was said to be part of the policy of promoting Skopje as a 'role-model city' for the pro-Serbian regime (Boškovska 2017: 160) – and the interwar Kingdom of Serbs, Croats and Slovenes (as of October 1929, the Kingdom of Yugoslavia) did not recognize the national particularity and the national programme of ethnic Macedonians, or the multi-confessional and multicultural population structure of one of the last Ottoman provinces in the Balkans – Macedonia.

However, even though the first state-sponsored museums appeared in the interwar period, it was not until after the First World War when the 'true and systematic formation of museal institutions in the territory of Republic of Macedonia' began to take place (Bogoeski 2011: 34). In the first post-war decade, the number of museums in Yugoslav Macedonia rose from three in 1945 to nine in the 1950s, seventeen in the late 1960s and forty-seven 'museums, independent collections and memorial rooms' in the 1970s (Petkovski 1976). This 'museum boom' mirrored the post-war 'finalization' of Macedonian nation-building (Spaskovska 2010), or in other words, the process of establishing key 'transmission belts' for disseminating the national-historical canon (see Troebst 1997). The codification of the Macedonian language (1945), the establishment of the Macedonian Orthodox Church, the Macedonian Academy of Sciences, Skopje University and the Institute for National History – all of which began in the two initial post-war decades – were just a part of the institution-building process that dominated the politics of the day.

Transnational knowledge-transfer also played a formative role in the construction of the post-war Macedonian museum scene. The serious shortage of museum employees, together with the catastrophic 1963 Skopje earthquake, led to appeals from the Macedonian museum guild for foreign help (more in Trajanovski 2020b). This was materialized in the post-earthquake reconstruction of the Museum of Skopje and the establishment of the Museum of Contemporary Arts in Skopje, both of which were carried out with significant foreign logistical and expert assistance (More in Vasev Dimeska 1983 and Korobar 1989). The Museum of Contemporary Arts was solemnly erected as part of the Polish programme of solidarity with post-earthquake Skopje and it still holds a large collection of international artworks donated to the city in the 1960s. The international developments in the museum field in the 1950s and the 1960s, inter alia – the new museology movement – also set the tone for the development of Macedonian museology.[3]

Even though the religious communities of Orthodox Christians, Muslims and Jews were only recognized by the state after the First World War, in addition to the prevailing transnational paradigm of new museology, it could be argued that the history museums in Yugoslav Macedonia presented a rather ethnocentric narrative about the past. In Kuculovska's words, museum workers placed 'special emphasis' (Kuculovska 1986: 31) on Yugoslavia's lifelong President Tito and affirmed the role of the Communist Party of Yugoslavia and the Communist Party of Macedonia, as a framework within which to interpret recent Macedonian history and nation-building. In fact, Tito's personality cult was not only recreated in museums dedicated to the recent history across the state, but also in Skopje's Archaeological Museum – where the permanent exhibition started with an extract from a speech made by Tito on a visit to Skopje in 1970 (Zdravkovski 1983: 26). This trend was also evident in the permanent exhibition at the Old Bazaar Museum in Skopje, which opened in 1982 and contained photos of Tito on a visit to the Bazaar in 1975.

The demise of Yugoslavia and the formation of the sovereign Macedonian state in 1991 did not fundamentally alter the state of play in the museum field. The pressing issues affecting the state since the early 1990s pushed debates on transitional justice, the treatment of the recent past and memory politics to one side for almost a decade (Trajanovski 2020a). The seven-month conflict in 2001 between Macedonian forces and ethnic Albanian radicals, which was settled with the Ohrid Framework Agreement (mk. *Ohridski ramkoven dogovor*), contributed to this generalized neglect of questions relating to public memory (see Chapter 7 by Georgieva, Wolffe and Trajanovski dedicated to the memory of the Ohrid Framework Agreement in this book). In the museum sphere, in particular, 'after gaining independence, the anticipated changes in museum work failed to appear' (Bogoeski 2011: 35). A legislative infrastructure for museum work was eventually established in 2004 in the form of a new Museums Law (mk. *Zakon za muzei*), which was strongly criticized at the time for offering legal solutions similar to the previous Yugoslav law on museum work.

Two opposing tendencies can be observed which are crucial for a better understanding of the discourse on religion as recreated in post-2001 Macedonian museums. On the one hand, there was a strong nationalizing tendency, which increased the representation of the ethno-Macedonian past in museum spaces, and which often, at a narrative level, downplayed the state's multi-confessional 'character' by presenting Orthodox Christianity as an identity-marker for Macedonians. On the other hand, in some museums it is possible to observe (from the late 1990s onwards) a reinvention of a museum narrative that highlighted Macedonia's multicultural and multi-confessional dimension.

The initial tendency was first observed in the late 1990s and the early 2000s. This critical discourse was initiated by Zoran Todorovski, one of the leading Macedonian revisionist historians in the first two post-Yugoslav decades, who noted that its proclamation as a new sovereign state had not contributed to a significant change in the predominantly socialist narrative of Macedonian history – a criticism that could also be levelled at museums (2008, 2009).[4] This argument materialized after the general elections of 1998, which brought the right-wing VMRO-DPMNE party to power. The party brought in new management in most of the state's museums, a move that was criticized by experts as yet another 'exaggerated ideologization' of the museum sector (Bogoeski 2011: 36). On a narrative level, the key museum event from this particular period was an exhibition entitled *Macedonian Iconostasis – 12 apostles of IMRO* (mk. *Makedonski ikonostas – 12 apostoli na VMRO*). This exhibition was dedicated to Macedonian revolutionaries from the late nineteenth century and suggested possible links with the modern-day VMRO-DPMNE – provoking a massive round of public criticism (see e.g. Blaževska 2001; Georgievski 2001).

It was not until the 2010s and the second VMRO-DPMNE government in North Macedonia that the so-called 'Macedonian museum renaissance' (more in Trajanovski 2020b) took place. The most evident example of this transformation was the 'Skopje project 2014' (mk. *proekt Skopje 2014*), an umbrella term covering the 137 monuments and memorials erected in the city. One of the most significant outcomes of this project was the new Museum of the Macedonian Struggle (mk. *Muzej na makedonskata borba za državnost i samostojnost*; see Figure 4.3) and the new building for the Archaeological Museum (mk. *Arheološki muzej*) in Skopje. 'Skopje 2014' was itself inspired by a series of new museum institutions and objects, such as the 'Bay of Bones', an open-air Archaeological Museum on Water (mk. *Zalivot na koskite*) in Gradište, Ohrid, and the Memorial House of Mother Teresa, the Catholic nun and missionary who was born in Skopje and was famous for her work among the poor of India (mk. *Spomen kuḱa na Majka Tereza*). Both of these museums opened to the public in 2009, together with the aforementioned Museum of the Macedonian Struggle and the Memorial House of the late pop-singer Toše Proeski (mk. *Spomen kuḱa Toše Proeski*, 2011).

The Museum of the Macedonian Struggle is also significant in that it set the standard for the subsequent trend of Macedonian Revolutionary Organization (MRO)-centred narrative museums that were built across the state – the Museum of the Activists of VMRO from Štip and the Štip region (1893–1934) (mk. *Muzej na dejcite na VMRO od Štip i Štipsko*) opened in 2014 in Novo Selo, Štip, and the memorial house dedicated to the Tatarčev family (mk. *Spomen kuḱa na Tatarčevi*) opened in Resen in 2016, among others. Both these museums, similar to the Museum of the Macedonian Struggle in Skopje, host permanent exhibitions that narrate recent history. The thematic structure of 'Skopje 2014' was also reflected in a state-sponsored documentary series, which was launched in the early 2010s and continued until the government left office. Finally, the political initiative to 'give the town a new face' (Popovska 2015: 97), in the words of the former Mayor of Skopje, was extended right across Macedonia, even though it did not manifest itself in full, Skopje-like form. New memorial objects were constructed across the country (Dimova 2013; Reef 2018), while the socialist heritage was abandoned in 'chronic neglect and silent destruction' and is now 'largely unprotected and forgotten'

**Figure 4.3** The Museum of the Macedonian Struggle and the Archaeological Museum in Skopje

*Source*: Courtesy Wikicommons.

(Janev 2017: 160). In Chapter 7 of this book, which deals with the Ohrid Framework Agreement and the Good Friday Agreement, it is argued that the launch of the ethnocentric memory culture trapped the different religious affiliations within their ethnic-identity domains – with Orthodox Christians being identified as Macedonian and, later on, Muslims as Albanian.

The second trend relates to the attempts by museums to recreate the history of Macedonian multi-confessionalism and multiculturalism. This revolved around two essential developments: (1) the agency of minority groups as memory activists, with their particular outlook on multi-confessional Macedonian history and the consideration of the museum space as a platform for expressing these views, (2) and the agency of museum institutions and workers in the Macedonian periphery. In both cases, multi-confessionality was recreated through the prism of Ottoman multiculturality and the late Ottoman past was held up as a formative period for the establishment of good interethnic relations in Macedonia.

The best illustration for the first point is the story behind the setting up of the Holocaust Memorial Center for the Jews of Macedonia (HMC) in Skopje – which was proposed by several predominantly Macedonian Jewish stakeholders. The initial idea for establishing the HMC came after the Denationalisation Law (mk. *Zakon za denacionalizacija*) was passed in 2002, thereby providing a legal basis for the creation of an institutional body that would safeguard the property rights of deported Jews who had no living heirs. The HMC was finally inaugurated on 10 March 2011, the annual day of mourning for the 7,144 Macedonian Jews deported to the Treblinka extermination camp in 1943, and the content for the first permanent exhibition was developed by a team of internationally renowned experts, including Michael Berenbaum and Edward Jacobs.[5] Even though it was devoted to the 'cultivation of the Jewish culture and tradition', the initial HMC program was, as observed by James E. Young in other similar cases across the globe, far from being 'shaped in a [sociopolitical] vacuum' (1993: 2–3). Its main mission involved 'presenting, educating and researching multi-ethnic societies, freeing them from any kind of danger from various intolerances, chauvinism, anti-Semitism' and it therefore aimed 'to build a society in which ethnic and religious diversity will become a civilisational asset and a basis for further prosperity'. This shows that HMC clearly recognized the need for post-conflict reconciliation in North Macedonia.

The history of the Macedonian Jews was also reinterpreted in the early 2000s by several other museums, which opted for a broader, more inclusive understanding of Macedonian multi-confessionality prior to the First World War. One example was an ethnographic exhibition organized by the Museum of the City of Skopje in 2005, which was titled *The Ethnic Colorfulness of Skopje from the Late 19th to the Beginning of the WWII* (mk. *Etničkoto šarenilo na Skopje od krajot na 19. do početokot na Vtorata svetska vojna*). One of its main themes was the history of peaceful coexistence of the multicultural and multi-confessional population of Skopje (Sazdova Kondijanova 2011). This trend could also be observed in two other exhibitions organized on the occasion of the sixtieth anniversary of the deportation of the Macedonian Jews. The first exhibition titled *The Echo of Macedonian Sephardis* (mk. *Ehoto na makedonskite Sefardi*) was held at the Museum of Macedonia, while the second *The Phoenix Trail* (mk. *Po tragite na Feniksot*) was organized by the Museum of the City of Skopje. Both exhibitions described the long history of Macedonian Jews and the common suffering of the various ethnic groups in Macedonian territory.

Finally, we should analyse the developments in the Macedonian periphery to better understand museum politics *in toto*. The southwest part of North Macedonia, for instance, followed the nationalizing tendency from its symbolic centre – culminating in the opening of the Memorial House dedicated to the Tatarčev family in 2016. This museum tells the story of the Tatarčev family and is located in their house, which played an instrumental role in the operations of the Macedonian Revolutionary Organization in its early years. The memorial house also hosts an ethnographic room, which largely ignores the multicultural and multi-confessional history of the region of Prespa and presents it from a predominantly Orthodox Christian perspective. It is important to mention that when asked what they thought about the new museum, many locals complained about the museum's slant on history accusing it of resurrecting 'phantoms' (Alon 2016), while Velika Ivkovska identified this same trend towards nationalizing the country's ethnographic heritage in the 'Macedonian village' project, a political endeavour recreating twelve 'traditional Macedonian houses' in 2016 in what she described as a process of 'validating Macedonian identity' (2016: 81–2).

Some regional institutions, however, followed their own particular course in opposition to this dominant narrative, which shows that local and regional administrations are not always a fertile ground for applying the core ideas emanating from central government and often construct their own individual narrative based on the historical and cultural particularities of their region. The Museum of the City of Bitola is an excellent example. The main collection follows a linear timeline, starting from the prehistoric period, and as the visitor progresses through the museum, the exhibition extends into several thematically arranged side-rooms. The core exhibition presents the three main religions in the history of the city and the region – Christianity, Islam and Judaism – with related religious artefacts and objects recreating religious rituals. The museum also portrays the 'joint coexistence' in the local region using artefacts, historical texts, documents, chronicles and maps.

The Museum of the City of Bitola also hosts a memorial room dedicated to Mustafa Kemal – Atatürk, the founder of the modern Turkish republic, who spent part of his formative years in Bitola. In fact, the Museum building once housed the Monastery Military School, which was attended by the Turkish statesman. The Museum of the City of Bitola is also responsible in administrative terms for the Resen-based Tatarčev family memorial house, and for the management of the memorial house in honour of the foundation of the Albanian alphabet, which was opened in 2012 in Bitola. Even though this memorial house celebrates a key event in Albanian history and in the history of Macedonian Albanians, it faces serious challenges in its day-to-day activities due to financial problems and cuts in governmental support. This leads us to conclude that the history of minority groups is also subject to instrumentalization.

## Concluding remarks

The different sections of this chapter explored the dynamics of representation of the cultural and religious heritage of minorities in different museums in European countries. We share the idea that the internal practices of museums can have an impact on wider society. Contemporary museums are not curated to be observed, but to be engaged with. Visitors experience the museum by thinking through its content in relation to their existing knowledge and experiences. Museums are not only spaces for representation but also for education, critique and discussion. This role is becoming even more significant as museums seek to represent the diversity and heterogeneity of modern societies. Today, there is much discussion on what it means to be a nation, a united society and a united Europe after the changes brought by several decades of migration, and museums are contributing to these debates.

In public discussions about diversity and society, Muslim communities often come under the lens. Many studies have explored how Muslims have been the cultural and religious 'Others' of Europe, while the artistic repertoire of Islamic civilizations has been a widely admired source of inspiration for many European art museums. This leads to a contradictory situation in which Islam is seen as a pre-modern religion with pre-modern norms and customs, while at the same time being hailed as an inspiration for glorious art. This duality has been a point of reflection for many contemporary museums, which have tackled it by adopting a more agentive approach in their exhibitions. Bearing in mind public debate about the Muslim communities who live in and form part of Europe today, museums aim to create an apolitical space for further discussion of issues that are highly political and sensitive.

The Jewish museums, which are a distinctive phenomenon of late-twentieth- and twenty-first-century Europe, also offer a wide platform for rethinking national narratives and for discussion on tolerance, diversity and inclusions versus exclusions. Quite separate from art, ethnographic and national museums, Jewish museums represent the diversity inherent to Europe, and support the narrative that although Jews have their own distinctive culture and religion, their history is also part of European, national and local, history. These museums were originally founded to preserve Jewish culture and tradition, but they have since evolved and now also explore matters that transcend purely Jewish issues. Contemporary Jewish museums bring subjects such as human rights, equality, democracy and inclusion to their galleries and aim to include different minority groups in addition to Jews.

On a final note, we should point out that museum practices vary greatly depending on the fabric of the society in which they are established and operate. This is well exemplified by the last case discussed in this essay – Macedonian museums – which demonstrates how nation- and state-building processes can influence the way museums represent the intra- and interethnic 'Other'. In the case of North Macedonia, this process could be observed both during the state-sponsored boom in museums after the Second World War and in the aftermath of the breakup of Yugoslavia.

# Religious diversity and generation Z: TV series and YouTube as instruments to promote religious toleration and peace

Mikko Ketola, Ivan Stefanovski, Kaarel Kuurmaa and Riho Altnurme

## Introduction

In this chapter we will be analysing the role played by TV Series and YouTube as instruments for promoting religious toleration and peace. Our analysis will be based on research into the representations of religious toleration in different media and their influence on young people. Fresh results of such research can be found in the conclusions obtained from the focus groups organized within the framework of the RETOPEA project, as published in Chapter 2 of this book. These include the following findings:

> The ability of some young people to freely cite examples of representations of religion, and also articulate generalizations and biases suggests that popular culture may have a greater influence than previously thought.
>
> In all focus groups, young people stated that their beliefs and representations were not influenced primarily by television series and films, and media in general. According to them, (conversations with) family and friends, and in some cases, documentaries found on YouTube, are much more influential in this respect.

If we think about where young people (thirteen to eighteen year olds as defined in the RETOPEA project) in Europe today are most likely to obtain information and ideas about religion and religious coexistence, the most obvious sources that spring to mind are friends, school, neighbourhood, sports groups and family (although in some families religion is rarely discussed). However, these ideas are also increasingly acquired through popular mass media (films, TV series), the internet and social networks. From the comments made during the focus groups cited above, we can conclude that although popular culture in general influences young people's views to a significant extent, the influence exerted by its different components varies considerably. In ascending order, the sources that have the greatest influence are: media in general, television series and films, and YouTube. A study from 2016 shows that the young people who spend longest on social networking sites and online media believe that it is acceptable to freely pick and choose their religion, and to practice multiple religions, contrary to the teaching of the established religion in their countries (McClure 2016).

Popular culture could be defined as a set of beliefs, practices and objects which prevail and dominate in society at a given moment in time. The concept of popular culture also entails feelings and activities that are created as a result of the interaction of said objects on the base provided by said practices and beliefs. Dustin Kidd (2017: 1) defines popular culture as a 'set of practices, beliefs, and objects that embody the most broadly shared meanings of a social system. It includes media objects, entertainment and leisure, fashion and trends, and linguistic conventions, among other things'. The modern world we live in today is heavily influenced by the media, and in particular by mass and social media, and this enables popular culture to be even more present and influential, as it permeates the everyday lives of people in societies across the planet. When studying this relationship between popular culture and media, perhaps the first port of call should be the work of Julie McGaha (2015: 33), who reflects on the growing body of literature dealing with popular culture in the mass media and its potential to shape people's attitudes towards different issues, in particular religion. For his part, the anthropologist Marcel Danesi (2012: 5) refers to a broader study of popular culture 'organized around specific media formats such as radio, television, film, and music'.

The birth of the internet and the dynamic development of social media has fundamentally changed everyone's lives, for better or for worse. It has also dramatically transformed popular culture. The rapid penetration of the internet into all walks of life together with the wildfire spread of social media has further extended the transformation and the development of popular culture. When Jackie Marsh spoke about the interaction between new media and popular culture in 2005, she described new media as a 'wide range of technologies and communication media which have developed more recently', even though at that stage Facebook and YouTube were probably still being tested (2). One thing that must be borne in mind is that new media and the internet sometimes also open a Pandora's Box with problems such as excessive use, superficiality and forced digitalization. However, one of the primary goals of the project which inspired this book is to discover the best ways to use the internet, social media and new technologies in order to promote religious tolerance and peace, and to reshape the representation of religious diversity so that it can serve good and noble purposes. The positive and negative examples that are provided in the empirical section of this chapter stem from TV and documentary shows that have been widely disseminated and watched, primarily because of the growing interest of young people in internet, social media and online networks. This is a strong point of departure when seeking to use new media for the promotion of religious diversity, tolerance and peace.

The beliefs, practices and values of popular culture are channelled into the public sphere through numerous communication channels: face to face, printed media, the TV, as well as via new media and, in particular, social networks. TV is still considered to be the traditional mainstream carrier of information and the most important, most widely watched, medium. This chapter assesses the role that TV series and YouTube videos could play in promoting mutual understanding and religious tolerance. As regards TV, over the years it has evolved from a 'popular culture' into a 'creative industry'. In the words of John Hartley (2008: 11), 'these developments are welcome because they allow for some long-standing problems of cultural communication to be addressed more directly, most importantly that of a continuing structural tension in the relations between "addresser" and "addressee" in popular culture, between professional/managerial expertise and control on the one side and consumer/network creativity and activism on the other'. Some argue that this has enabled television to hold on to its position as the most influential medium in the world despite increasing competition from online media (Gulick 2018). It is fair to say, however, that television is more popular among adults than young people. It is also important to bear in mind the emerging influence of services like Netflix (Jenner 2018), HBO, HBO-go and similar providers of content that have fundamentally reinvented television.

Nevertheless, the majority of younger people gain information on social networks and other online services (see Chapter 2). It is therefore interesting to analyse the role of YouTube as a channel that could influence or shape the ideas of its millions of viewers. This digital media platform, which first appeared in 2005, has dramatically changed the digital media environment. YouTube has an important dual function 'as both a "top-down" platform for the distribution of popular culture and a "bottom-up" platform for vernacular creativity; and the ongoing blurring of the boundaries between the two' (Burgess and Green 2018: 18). Bearing this duality in mind, it is important to recognize YouTube's role in shaping the views and attitudes of people around the world. YouTube functions all at once as a social network, a search engine and a video platform. This makes it a very interesting, popular postmodern hybrid where creation, consumption and distribution are all happening at the same time. YouTube has become the second most trafficked website and is the second largest search engine in the world. In Europe as of January 2019, 86 per cent of the population use the internet and 55 per cent (462.5 million) are active social media users (We Are Social and Hootsuite 2019: 18). According to a recent Pew study, 85 per cent of teenagers use YouTube, making it the most popular platform amongst this age group (Pew Research Center 2018).

More research is therefore required to better understand how we could use YouTube as a tool for developing knowledge about religion and religious coexistence. An important and encouraging discovery was that 80 per cent of Generation Z teenagers claimed that YouTube had helped them become more knowledgeable about something and 68 per cent said it had helped them improve or gain skills that would help them prepare for the future (Duffy et al. 2018). This drive for self-improvement is taking shape in unexpected ways such as in 'study-with-me' videos, a growing genre in which people film themselves studying to encourage good study habits. In this way, this generation is introducing a new video format that brings together a desire to learn with a need for togetherness and human connection (Anderson 2018).

Since approximately five hundred hours of fresh video are uploaded to YouTube every minute by 50 million different users who create content (a lot of those videos violate YouTube's guidelines and subsequently get taken down), it is impossible to determine the exact number of videos hosted on the platform. One person could spend an entire lifetime trying to watch all the content uploaded to YouTube in just one day (Hale 2019). We have nevertheless decided to try to make a relevant selection of YouTube videos dealing with religious history and religious coexistence. The first selection was made by searching for 'religion' in the YouTube search function. Through further observatory work (basically watching possible selections) we selected what seemed to be the most suitable videos to meet the research objectives of this project. It is possible that the selection may be restricted to some extent by the researcher's personal and subjective choices but it does seem to include a variety of different types of videos that cover the range offered by the YouTube collection. Our search focused exclusively on videos in English, which is by far the most popular language for videos uploaded to YouTube.

Popular culture can help to bridge the gap between different religious communities in order to overcome conflicts between people with different confessional backgrounds. Television and new media can provide useful platforms from which to address divisions between different groups. Religious tolerance and peaceful coexistence are in essence defined by a plethora of authors as 'understanding the nature of conflict at various levels from personal to global, studying the causes of war and human aggression, and exploring a range of awareness of the rights and responsibilities of individuals and groups in the world' (Yusuf 2013: 224; see also Afdal 2006).

In this chapter, we will be analysing both television series and YouTube videos in order to determine how religion and religious diversity is treated in different contexts and whether these depictions and portrayals can be seen as influential among the viewers of these shows and videos. The term 'viewer' here refers not just to young people but to viewers in general, although young people are probably the most avid consumers of the mass media and YouTube videos.

To this end, we will be analysing the contents of four television series from opposite ends of Europe: the Balkans and Britain. From the Balkans, we analyse two fictional (*Prespav*, *Koreni*) and one documentary (*On the Same Side*) series. *Prespav* and *On the Same Side* were made in North Macedonia, while *Koreni* was made in Serbia. All of them tackle the subject of religious coexistence of Christians and Muslims in the region. We then look at *Citizen Khan*, a sitcom about a British Pakistani Muslim family in Birmingham. In our analysis of the programmes from the Balkans, we focus on how they portray the relations between the members of different religions. In the case of *Citizen Khan*, we also look at how the series was received in Britain, about which there are plenty of sources, unlike in the Balkans where this question is more difficult to assess. One of the main ideas behind this approach is to find out more about the mechanism for transposing good practices of religious diversity and tolerance from one region to another. Another important objective is to learn from the negative examples of misrepresentation of the same concepts in the two regions and try to eliminate or minimize them as far as possible.

We will now analyse each of these television series in more detail before moving on to the wider, more varied field of YouTube channels.

## TV series in the Balkans

The TV landscape in the Balkans is rather peculiar, and quite unlike that in Western Europe. One of its most striking features is that it operates within a specific environment that is religiously and ethnically diverse. At certain times in the past, this variety of religions and cultures has coalesced to produce glorious music, arts and architecture, while at others it has proved divisive, triggering conflicts and even civil wars. Nowadays, following the formal completion of the reconciliation processes, the TV stations are predominantly ethnocentric and monolingual, a pattern that can also be observed online. In this chapter, however, we will be looking at some of the positive examples promoting religious diversity and peaceful coexistence.

As regards the main ways of appealing to the wider general public in terms of religious diversity and tolerance, producers in the Balkans frequently use two contrasting approaches: either humour and satire, or historical memory presented mainly through painful religious cohabitation. This has much to do with the historical and cultural background of the region. The painful history of the region, as played out in the many violent conflicts that have taken place in the last two centuries, consistently impregnates the mantle of sadness and sorrow that continues to cloud many people's attitudes. Indeed, the Balkans, and in particular Bosnia and Herzegovina, were the site of the largest genocide on European soil since the Second World War – the Srebrenica massacre in 1995. Given this background, it is hardly surprising that the series analysed here mainly rely on the two approaches described above (humour and painful religious cohabitation) to tell their stories.

These approaches are evident in the narratives created by the screenwriters, producers and directors of the series made in the West Balkans. This is why in this research we tried to strike a balance between a popular TV sitcom (*Prespav*) with plenty of satire, a historical drama (*Koreni* – 'Roots') that is based above all on tragedy, sorrow and broken family relationships in the politically contentious environment of nineteenth-century Serbia, and a documentary series called *Na ista strana* (On the Same Side), which describes the traditionally good interethnic and interconfessional relationships between different communities in North Macedonia, in the light of the violent conflict that erupted in 2001 and the sporadic tensions which tend to flare up due to the provocative statements made during election campaigns.

In order to be able to comprehend the context within which these different narratives operate (humour and satire, grave historical tragedy and a more documentary approach to religious tolerance), we will now describe each show in more detail:

### Prespav

Presented as a real-time story located in North Macedonia somewhere after 2015, *Prespav* showcases the adventures of a family that sets up a local business – a small hotel near Lake Prespa – which aims to offer a fresh approach to tourism in the area, boost the local economy and create jobs. Set amongst the local traditions and some of the more negative aspects of Macedonian society such as corruption, nepotism and the politicization of state institutions, this sitcom tries to promote religious tolerance and coexistence, gender equality, the rights and freedoms of marginalized groups, and multiculturalism. As regards religious tolerance and peace, *Prespav*, which is set in a dominantly Orthodox Christian environment, shows how many religions can cohabitate both intimately and professionally. Kosta (Orthodox Christian) is married to Ula (Catholic Christian), while his brother Toni (Orthodox Christian) is having an intimate relationship with Mario (Catholic Christian). The hotel reception is manned by one of the most likeable employees Talat (Muslim). The family have a partner in the running and ownership of the hotel, Naim (Muslim), who works in neighbouring Albania but frequently visits the hotel and helps with the daily management. In this way, the series presents varied examples of tolerance and coexistence, especially in terms of religion, thereby transmitting a positive message in an often contentious, intolerant Balkan region.

### Koreni

Following independence in 1878, and the proclamation of the Serbian Kingdom under King Milan I, Serbia was mostly inhabited by Orthodox Christians who adhered to the Serbian Orthodox Church. This series is set in the small village of Prerovo, located somewhere in Central Serbia, which is a stronghold of the People's Radical Party, the largest political party at that time. The main divisions depicted are political – between members of the People's Radical Party and the Liberals who strongly support King Milan I. Within this small political arena, we are introduced to a Muslim family composed of Ika, the owner of the small local restaurant/café bar and his wife Bula, together with their children, who live peacefully together with the dominant Orthodox Christian majority. In addition to being free to practise their religion, their restaurant is also the most popular meeting point in the village, where neighbours congregate to discuss local politics, the economy and their personal daily happenings.

### On the Same Side

The main goal of the documentary *On the Same Side* is to promote and encourage communication between the different religious communities in North Macedonia. Shot in the field, various speakers from different religious backgrounds debate about the positive values of religion. They also discuss prejudices and the best ways to combat them. The central goal of the show is to send out a message of peace, tolerance and reconciliation, so that a situation in which a priest and an imam talk to each other in the street is not worthy of a news headline and instead is considered an everyday event. The documentary conveys a message of universalism where every faith and religion in its original, pure form means love of God, righteousness and respect towards the other'. Macedonia, the documentary argues, provides numerous examples in which communication, respect and close ties between different religions have managed to nurture positive values throughout history. It also emphasizes that the experience of Macedonia today demonstrates that different religions can be unifying elements of coexistence.

## Religious diversity in popular culture in the Western Balkans

The three aforementioned TV shows were selected in order to present three different contexts or frameworks within which religious diversity in the Balkans is presented: the positive/happy frame, the negative/sad frame and the neutral/objective frame. But what is a frame? Frames and frame alignment are discussed in seminal research by Snow et al. (1986: 464), which is based on Goffman's conceptualization of 'frame'/'framework' (1974), in which frames are said to 'denote "schemata of interpretation" that enable individuals "to locate, perceive, identify, and label" occurrences within their life space and the world at large. By rendering events or occurrences meaningful, frames function to organise experience and guide action, whether individual or collective'.

Our exploration of the three Balkan TV series was based on two main hypotheses/ assumptions: (1) Popular culture can help bridge the gap between different religious communities in order to overcome persistent conflicts between people with different confessional backgrounds and (2) Television and social media are excellent forums for addressing religious divisions between different groups, especially among the members of Generation Z.

The frame analysis applied here stems from the theoretical and conceptual notions described in the previous paragraphs, as well as from the context within which the producers of popular TV shows in the Balkans operate.

## The positive frame

There are various examples of the positive context in which religious diversity is presented in the TV show, *Prespav*. The first example shows how Jelena and Talat, both receptionists at the Prespav guesthouse, work together at the reception, joking and having fun. Jelena is an Orthodox Christian from Skopje, while Talat is a Muslim who is originally from the village of Djepchishte, near Tetovo. In this specific frame, he is dressed in traditional Albanian clothing while Jelena is dressed, as always, in the latest modern fashion (A1on 2019).

In another scene we see the humorous flirting between Ula, Kosta's wife, and Naim, one of the co-owners of the hotel. Ula, a Protestant Christian from Germany, fell in love with Kosta, an Orthodox Christian and one of three brothers who started the hotel business in the small tourist region of Prespa. Naim is an ethnic Albanian from a nearby border region of Albania, who runs other businesses in his home country. He is also one of the junior partners in the hotel and is often there helping out. He is always smiling and joking with his partners, and flirts with Ula whenever he gets the chance. This frame provides the public with colourful examples of religious diversity and presents them in a positive, attractive context.

The third example from this TV series shows the intolerant behaviour of Mile, the eldest of the three brothers who co-founded Prespav Hotel. Mile is presented as a typical old-fashioned Orthodox Christian from the Balkans, who has no time for diversity or difference and no sensitivity towards other religions or cultures. He is always insulting Mario, Talat, Ula and Naim, and uses rude, inappropriate language in his claims of ethno-nationalist Macedonian and Orthodox Christian superiority. However, this is done in quite a humorous manner, and the message being sent to the viewers is that this is an example of 'how not to behave' in modern twenty-first-century North Macedonia.

## The negative frame

The negative (sad) framing examples are taken from the TV show, *Koreni*. The first example of a negative frame shows three characters: Djordje, Ika and Bula. Djordje is an Orthodox Christian, the son of a rich and powerful businessmen and politician from Prerovo called Achim Katich, who is also the frontman of the Radical Party in the region. Djordje is respected in the community mainly because of his father's position and wealth, while his father sees him as incapable and spoilt. The fact that Djordje and his wife Simka cannot conceive a child only adds to the pressure from family and society. This creates a serious, tense atmosphere, which seems to exacerbate the situation even more. Djordje is filled with grief and sorrow and cannot cope. He turns to drinking, spending most of his time in Ika and Bula's *kafana* (small family-owned restaurant), where most of the social interactions in Prerovo take place. Ika and Bula are Muslims, as can quickly be deduced from their clothing. Apart from being her name, 'Bula' is also a Serbian word meaning 'woman wearing a headscarf'. Ika also occasionally wears clothing that was typically worn by Muslim men in the late nineteenth or early twentieth century. This frame offers another example of religious toleration and diversity, but in a very difficult setting in which many of the characters are overwhelmed by pain and sorrow. In the second example, Simka is in an Orthodox Church near Prerovo, praying to God to conceive a child. Although she is ready and willing to sacrifice everything to become pregnant, God is not answering her prayers. The atmosphere in the typical Medieval church is peaceful, but there is also a sense that the weight of society is bearing down upon her, and her feelings of worry and unease are evident to the viewers. On a more positive note, this frame from *Koreni* also highlights the importance of the church in fostering peaceful coexistence and toleration. As a profound believer, Simka is tolerant, very pleasant to members of the small Muslim community and very communicative. However, her deep underlying sorrow strikes a strong chord with the viewers.

The third example from *Koreni* illustrates some of the Orthodox Christian customs performed during the baptism of children. Djordje is seen holding his newborn son Adam in his arms while the priests are preparing to baptize him. The baby is wrapped in a typical white robe often used during the baptism ceremony. However, Djordje's eyes reveal unease and sadness because deep inside he knows that Adam is not his son, and in fact was fathered by Tolo, a labourer who does odd jobs for the family.

## The neutral frame

The third set of examples are presented within an atmosphere of perceived objectivity and neutrality, mainly because they are taken from *On the Same Side*, a TV documentary that is almost entirely devoted to promoting religious coexistence and toleration, and which was created in a post-conflict, mainly reconciled, Macedonian society. The first example of this more neutral framing of religious toleration and peace shows two representatives of the majority religions in Macedonia – an Orthodox Christian priest and a Muslim imam. The two men explain how the two largest religious communities in Macedonia peacefully coexist in the local environment where they work and preach.

The second example from this documentary TV series was filmed at an Orthodox Christian convent in Rajchica in the western part of North Macedonia. A nun from the convent is talking about interconfessional toleration and co-operation between the Orthodox Christians and the Muslims in the western part of the country and sends positive messages about peace following the worsening of relations in the aftermath of the armed conflict of 2001.

The third and last example of how religious toleration and peace in the Balkans is represented in this series comes in an interview with a Muslim cleric who works at the famous mosque in Tetovo. In this apparently neutral, objective frame, he discusses the relations between the two main religious groups in the country, the Muslims and the Orthodox Christians. In Tetovo, Muslims are the dominant religious group and Orthodox Christians are a minority. Although there are sporadic interethnic tensions, in general interconfessional relations are stable and provide a positive example of how they should be fostered beyond the Balkans.

## *Citizen Khan*: A ground-breaking comedy about British Pakistani Muslims

### The funny frame

It would be difficult to classify *Citizen Khan* within any of the frameworks (positive, negative or neutral) applied to TV shows in the previous section of this chapter. It has a different approach and a different frame: humour. *Citizen Khan* aims to be funny all the time. While it is ground-breaking in setting the story within the British Pakistani Muslim community, it remains true to the style of a traditional British family sitcom or situation comedy. It is perhaps difficult to imagine any other country where a similar comedy show about Muslims would be possible. A recent book on religious diversity in the Nordic countries focuses, among other things, on the visibility of religion in the Nordic media, including cinema, and one section analyses how Islam is depicted in Nordic films. The word 'comedy' is never mentioned, but violence, hatred and revenge are (Furseth 2018).

### Immigrants in Britain

After the Second World War, the increasing numbers of immigrants gradually turned Britain into a multicultural society. In his study of British immigration policy since 1939, Ian Spencer (1997: 161) described this phenomenon as follows:

> Asian and black immigration to Britain since 1945 was the migration of a complex mosaic of communities of highly diverse backgrounds and qualifications.

The first comers were West Indians, but the important Commonwealth Immigrants Act of 1962 led to large-scale immigration from the Indian subcontinent (India,

Pakistan, Bangladesh) and by the 1980s they were by far the biggest group (Spencer 1997: 129–33). In the 2000s, there were new sources of immigration to Britain, especially from Eastern European countries such as Ukraine and Poland. In the census of 2001, Muslims made up 2.7 per cent of the UK population, thereby forming the second-largest religious community after Christians (Peach 2005: 19).

The assimilation of immigrants into British society has been a recurring concern in the immigration policy debate. However, studies by Manning and Roy (2010) and Kabir (2010) appear to show that the younger generations of South Asian immigrants in particular have largely adopted the British national identity or, more accurately, the English, Welsh or Scottish identity. *Citizen Khan* offers a funny, illustrative example of the way the 'older' immigrants view the newcomers. Mr Khan is conversing with daughter Shazia:

Mr Khan:    Too many bloody immigrants coming to this country!
Shazia:      You're an immigrant, dad.
Mr Khan:    I'm not an immigrant sweetie. I've been here 30 years. Immigrants are the Eastern Europeans, coming over here, taking our jobs, jobs meant for us Pakistanis! (*Citizen Khan* 2012)

Although there have been many success stories among the ethnic minorities, Spencer (1997: 160) points out, 'the common experience of Asian and black employees in Britain is of racial discrimination and the undervaluing of … their qualifications'.

The representation of ethnic minorities on television in Britain started quite early, although in the beginning this often meant the audience laughing at them instead of laughing with them. The first Black or coloured characters in British television series were seen in the 1970s (Malik 2002: 91–107). The first television show with an almost entirely British Indian cast was the comedy series *Goodness Gracious Me* (BBC Radio 4 1996–8, BBC Two 1998–2001). The sketches delved into British Asian culture and poked fun at the points of friction between traditional South Asian culture and modern British life. Sometimes the British were viewed from a South Asian point of view, and sometimes the show explored British stereotypes of South Asians. Anil Gupta, the producer of the series, said in an interview that he had had trouble convincing the commissioning editors at the BBC that Asians could be funny enough to carry a comedy series (Huq 2013: 78).

### *Citizen Khan* arrives

On 27 August 2012, a new family sitcom, *Citizen Khan*, was premiered on BBC One. It was the first BBC sitcom where the action centred around British Pakistani Muslims. The timing was perhaps especially propitious in the afterglow of the London Olympics, deemed a resounding success, which had finished just a fortnight earlier. The biggest hero of the Games – at least for the British – was perhaps the distance runner Mohammed (Mo) Farah, who won both the ten thousand metre and five thousand metre races. Farah is a British Somali Muslim. One can only assume that Farah's popularity reflected well on British Muslims in general and perhaps increased goodwill towards them. A few years later, another Muslim sportsman, the Liverpool footballer Mohamed Salah, also became hugely popular in Britain. His story and influence are explained in the next section of this chapter.

*Citizen Khan*'s title is a playful reference to Orson Welles's famous movie, Citizen Kane (1941). Khan as a Muslim name is also very representative. There are well over 23 million Khans on the planet, making it the seventeenth most common surname in the world. Khan is most common in Pakistan (forebears n.d.). In the opening episode of the fifth series, a very famous Khan, Sadiq Khan, the mayor of London, makes an appearance.

*Citizen Khan* was created by actor and comedian Adil Ray (born 1974), a British Pakistani Muslim. His father was a Pakistani Punjabi bus driver and his mother a Kenyan Asian civil servant. The character Mr Khan did not appear out of nowhere. Adil Ray had portrayed him first in the comedy series *Bellamy's People* (BBC Two, 2010), on BBC Radio 4's comedy series *Down the Line* and on his own online series on the BBC Comedy website. Outside the UK, the show has been shown on TV in Australia, Belgium, Bulgaria, India, New Zealand, Russia, South Africa and New Zealand. There have been plans to make a new version in Germany, based around an immigrant Turkish family. *Citizen Khan* was a hit with the viewing public, with each episode garnering up to 5 million viewers in the UK (Laws 2015). The show ran for five series from 2012 to 2016 (Internet Movie Database (IMDb n.d.)). All the series are also available on subtitled DVDs.

*Citizen Khan* is set in Sparkhill, in Birmingham. In the series, Mr Khan describes Birmingham as 'the capital of British Pakistan'. In fact, Birmingham has the second-largest Pakistani community in the UK, behind London, and within Birmingham, Sparkhill has one of the largest concentrations of Pakistanis. According to the 2011 census, there were around 1.1 million Pakistanis in the UK (2.0 per cent of the population), making them the second-largest ethnic group in the UK. The largest immigrant ethnic group in the country are from India with a population of 1.45 million (Gov.uk 2020).

Although *Citizen Khan* and especially the character Mr Khan was developed above all by Adil Ray, at the stage when the show was beginning to take shape as a sitcom, Ray started working with Anil Gupta and Richard Pinto whose earlier credits included *Goodness Gracious Me* and *The Kumars at No. 42*.

## The premise of *Citizen Khan*

In one sense, *Citizen Khan* is quite a traditional sitcom with a family set-up. The main characters are Mr Khan, who proudly describes himself as 'a community leader' whom 'everybody knows', his wife Mrs Khan, their two daughters Shazia and Alia, son-in-law Amjad and Mr Khan's mother-in-law Naani. Assorted other characters also appear, such as Dave, the local mosque leader, and Mr Khan's friends Riaz and Omar.

A lot of the action takes place in just two settings: the family home and the mosque office. *Citizen Khan* plays with common prejudices and stereotypical ideas about British Muslims. 'Here we have a British Muslim family on television that aren't terrorists or paedophiles or on-street groomers, which is how the Pakistani community has been tarnished,' Adil Ray pointed out in an interview (Sturgis 2015). These stereotypes were confirmed by the fact that when a TV station needed a spokesperson from the Muslim community in Britain to comment on any particular subject, they would often choose a bearded, older man who made angry noises about whatever he was asked to comment on (Akbar 2012).

In the series, Mr Khan, the father, played by Adil Ray himself, is also a bearded, older man who considers himself the epitome of a successful Muslim businessman. He is sometimes angry, but often for fairly foolish reasons. It is often his wife who makes him see sense. Another skilful handling of a stereotype is the depiction of Mr Khan's younger daughter. In reality she is just the same as other teenagers of her age, in that she is interested in partying and boys and inseparable from her smartphone. But when Mr Khan is at home, she puts on her hijab, she pretends to read the Quran or another religious book and talks about going to the mosque for prayers. Mr Khan is convinced that she is a very pious girl who is not at all interested in boys. This aspect angered many Muslim viewers who claimed that Ray was being blasphemous. On the other hand, many others found these depictions to be spot-on and something that made the series worth watching. The big service that the series does for the wider public is to 'demystify' the status and character of British Muslims as some sort of sinister alien presence. Mr Khan is proud of both his Pakistani heritage and his Britishness. He is in a sense a rather secular Muslim. He views more recent immigrants to Britain with prejudice and stereotypes them. When his home mosque gets a new director, who is a ginger-haired Scottish convert to Islam, Mr Khan treats him with suspicion because he is 'not brown' like real Muslims. He also claims that all Scots tend to be alcoholics. However, they later become quite good friends.

Adil Ray has said that Mr Khan is an 'amalgamation of many people' whom he observed and 'did impressions of' while growing up in 1970s Birmingham. The show was intended to have 'a universal appeal':

> This could be an Irish family, or a Jewish family or an Italian family. ... It doesn't matter what religion you are or what background, we all have the same comedy mishap. (Adewunmi 2012)

Ray told another interviewer that he aimed to make *Citizen Khan* 'family-friendly viewing' and that one of the things that motivated him to do comedy was the joy you could bring to families. He hoped his comedy would cross ethnic and religious boundaries. He believed there were plenty of Mr Khans in English families too. His own comedy favourites included *Fawlty Towers* and *Only Fools and Horses*. Ray said that his way to deal with criticism was to use Islamic teachings to ask himself what his intentions were (Conlan 2013).

## Complaints and praise

Although *Citizen Khan* poked occasional fun at Christians and Christianity, the feedback it received was almost all about the way it portrayed Muslims and Islam. After the first episode in August 2012, BBC received both complaints and praise about the show. Many of those who complained found the show either dated and unfunny, or blasphemous and racist and felt that it used stereotypical images and ideas about Pakistanis. The Labour MP Rupa Huq (Ealing Central and Acton) felt the show contained 'little to suggest we are in 2012'. In her view, *Citizen Khan* was

> like an old-fashioned sitcom from the politically incorrect 1970s where the set design comes across as if in 50 shades of beige and Asians were presented as figures of fun – right down to the omnipresent canned laughter. (Huq 2013: 79)

Huq wished *Citizen Khan* would offer 'humorous treatments' of the complexities in the events of daily life rather than portray Asian Muslims as 'backward Philistines'. That would be something that 'the second-generation Asian viewers' and the viewing public at large could better identify with (Huq 2013: 82).

Some of those who objected to *Citizen Khan* said it insulted Islam and was disrespectful to the Quran. They were especially incensed about how the younger daughter was portrayed. In a typical scene, when Mr Khan comes home, his glamorous daughter pulls on her headscarf to hide her fully made-up face and starts to read the Quran to please her father. By contrast, there were many other viewers and commentators who recognized this kind of behaviour from their own experience and said it rang very true. Journalist Saira Khan (2012), for example, writing in the *Daily Mail*, said that in her experience, Asian girls who behaved like that could be found in any big city in Britain:

> Such girls realized that as long as their father saw them going through the dutiful motions, he would be happy that they had remained loyal to their family traditions. It was this understanding that made the scene so funny. It was so true to real life.

Khan (2012) also thought that accusing *Citizen Khan* of perpetuating racial and religious stereotypes was not only ridiculous but also implied a failure to comprehend what lay at the heart of much of British humour: 'The best nationality-based jokes are firmly rooted in cultural and, often, religious stereotypes. This is the basis of the best Jewish jokes.'

Muslim journalist and academic Hasnet Lais (2012) corroborated what Arifa Akbar (2012) had said about Alia-like Muslim girls:

> Even in my circles, there are girls who see the hijab as a bartering chip and win favour with their fathers through flattery, only to later fly in the face of tradition and jettison Islamic morals for a slightly more seductive gospel. Feigning obedience and working their way into daddy's good books through a mixture of bluff and charm is a survival strategy for the Alias of this world. I'm certain director Adil Ray knows all too well those Muslim fathers, heaping praise on their daughters' covenant with the Almighty but ultimately unsuspecting of their double shuffle.

Conspiracy theories also surfaced. Some Pakistani viewers were suspicious of the number of Indians in the cast. Some of them thought the Indian actors had an agenda, which evidently was to cast Pakistanis in a bad light. Someone even claimed the show was 'masterminded' by Hindus (Brown 2012).

Some of the ire was inevitably directed towards Adil Ray himself, and he even received death threats. However, as a British Pakistani Muslim himself, he could not be accused of getting things wrong because he was an outsider. Professor Tahir Abbas (Fatih University in Istanbul), who was otherwise rather critical of *Citizen Khan*, admitted that Ray had 'excellent comedy timing' and was 'generally in tune with the pulsating rhythms and colours, sights and sounds, as well as the changing fortunes of the city' (2013: 85, 90).

Abbas made interesting observations about the representation of Pakistan masculinity and femininity in the show. Mr Khan was the patriarch who overestimated his abilities and prowess. The daughters were represented as 'submissive' to the patriarch while Mrs Khan, the matriarch, was misunderstood by her husband. In Abbas's view, the daughters were represented as poles apart, Alia being portrayed as 'duplicitous' and overly sexualized while Shazia was 'plain, insignificant and almost invisible'. Abbas (2013: 87) equated this with the 'classic juxtaposition found in the historical representation of the Orient in European literature':

> Asian men are sly and slippery while Asian women are imprisoned by the men but when they are given the sight of freedom, they are full of sexual allure and promise. While this exposes aspects of gender inequality found among certain Pakistani households, it does so by exaggerating the polar extremes, which, arguably, is a function of comedy.

The BBC received a fair share of the blame. Tahir Abbas thought the BBC and its commissioners were the ultimate problem because they were locked in the past but still wielded power. Abbas claimed that the BBC had put too little effort into making the show about 'genuinely important contemporary developments' in the British Pakistani community and instead portrayed them in a comical manner. He thought the real nature of the BBC was thus revealed: 'an overly large, unwieldy, hierarchical, patriarchal, and increasingly out of touch organization' (Abbas 2013: 89).

Other critics claimed that *Citizen Khan* was not particularly funny, although this judgement was far from universal. In Anamik Saha's view, the critics of *Citizen Khan* failed to appreciate the show in the right context, the traditional British family sitcom, and had not grasped the novelty it brought to the genre:

> Such is the rarity of Muslims portraying themselves on British television, such is the ubiquitousness of the dominant discourse of the 'angry Muslim' protesting against the latest book or film that insults Islam, that when we have a situation where Muslims are satirizing their own communities it is genuinely unsettling. (2013: 100)

Saha (2013: 97) thought that those who criticized the show 'would never watch a BBC One family sitcom in the first place and did not realise that *Citizen Khan* captured people's imagination because it was the first ever sitcom about British Muslims and much more potentially subversive than the reviews give it credit for'.

The fact that *Citizen Khan* gained a viewing slot on British television's most prestigious channel, BBC One, and that it continued to be popular over the years, signalled that there was a large viewing public that enjoyed a comedic take on Muslim family life. The show was watched in several countries all over the world, testifying to its global appeal. The prominent roles played by the Khan children, and especially the teenage daughter Alia, probably increased its appeal to the younger generation. Presumably a large part of the viewers were Muslims themselves. Seeing Muslims satirizing themselves may have been an opportunity for many non-Muslims to rethink their earlier views of Muslims as overly pious, angry critics of British society and to realize that the everyday problems of a Muslim family were not that different from those of any other family. Increasing religious toleration in this way may not have been a priority objective of the show's producers but it may well have had that effect.

## Religious tolerance in online media: YouTube channels

As early as 2009, the then European commissioner for consumer protection, Meglena Kuneva stated: 'Personal data is the new oil of the Internet and the new currency of the digital world'. In 2017, *The Economist* also stressed that data had replaced oil as the world's most valuable resource. Unfortunately, this means that big companies such as Google, which also owns YouTube, very rarely share with outsiders the precise statistical data they gather. YouTube channels do share information about the number of subscribers, the total number of views and the number of views for each video, but do not provide demographic or geographic data which is 'in there somewhere', but unfortunately is not available for everyone to use. So closer sociological country-specific surveys are needed to get better data as to how widely different YouTube videos actually travel.

Roughly speaking, YouTube divides its videos into two types of content: UGC (user-generated content) and PGC (professionally generated content). The amount of UGC far exceeds that of PGC but Google has announced that it wants to expand the PGC side and promote its usage, which means it will be harder to get people to visit single uploaded videos compared to established channel videos with higher view numbers and a bigger fan base (Kim 2012).

The RETOPEA project aims to teach religious tolerance by making films that compare past and present situations and offer examples of religious tolerance in history. The technical process is the same as when somebody makes a YouTube video. Several authors have stressed the value of expressing one's creativity by making videos for YouTube, even if the results are not perfect (Gauntlett 2011; Strangelove 2010). Still the reasons why people decide to make certain videos and the ideological background behind some of the ideas they express can vary enormously. Similarly, a theoretical explanation based on solid research may not be the ideal ingredient for entertaining or amusing vlogs. Below we propose one possible systematization of YouTube channels as a provider of religious diversity content to teenagers in order to show the possibilities it offers – and perhaps also some positive and negative examples. It is often difficult to know how and why certain seemingly simple videos are made – another problem is that their influence can only be evaluated on the basis of group interviews in which the target group can express their opinions. This has already been done in part in Chapter 2 of this book.

## TV/online news and coverage in the form of a short documentary

Almost all the members of the European Broadcasting Union (EBU) and all bigger news channels are currently investing more in short visual news/documentary content and uploading it onto online platforms. Many of these have well-curated YouTube Channels like DW Documentary, Guardian Culture, BBC Documentary, ARTE and so on. Teachers should encourage their students to visit these channels, as they include many short films that deal with religious diversity in Europe. One good example is a short documentary by Guardian Culture in which Muslim women discuss removing their hijab at work, following the ruling by the European Court of Justice which allows employers to ban religious symbols in the workplace. This film takes us to Spain, The Netherlands and the UK, where three women share their experiences of looking for work while wearing a hijab (Guardian Culture 2017). A woman from Valencia complains that 'wherever I apply for a job, they say, "You need to take off your hijab"'. Another woman in Amsterdam whose face has been blurred confesses: 'It was like a wall separating me from Dutch society.' A woman from London who was clearly a native English speaker encountered a similar problem: 'As soon as they see you, they think they know you. Like, right, hijab. OK. Illiterate, uneducated, probably can't speak the language.' This video shows how complex the legal issues regarding religious symbols can be in our diverse Europe and how one decision can have a life-changing effect on many people around the continent. It is a timely topic and watching clips from this video could serve as a basis for a good debate in classrooms around Europe.

Another excellent source for teaching how religion functions in our society is a Channel 4 short documentary about Liverpool FC striker Mohamed Salah, a football superstar who serves as a positive role model for kids around the world. As an openly Muslim athlete he is helping to change the negative perception of Islam in the UK and around the globe. This clip includes manager Jürgen Klopp's comments on Salah's prematch religious rituals in the dressing room and remarks by the chief executive of Liverpool Mosque and other Muslim and non-Muslim commentators, who stress the positive contribution made by Mo Salah to the image of Islam in the local community with his popularity as a footballer (Channel 4 2018). It is also well worth noting how videos of two football fan chants have gone viral. These highlight the positivity of Mo Salah's faith with a clear twist of British humour. It is hard to describe the lyrics (which also appear in this documentary) any other way: 'If he's good enough for you, he's good enough for me. If he scores another few, then I'll be Muslim too. If he's good enough for you, he's good enough for me. Sitting in the mosque, that's where I wanna be!' One of the first videos of this song recorded in February 2018 went quickly viral and now has over 2 million views via the Liverpool FC fan site The Redmen TV, making it by far the most viewed video on this YouTube channel (The Redmen TV 2018). Another popular chant is a new version of an old American country song called 'You Are My Sunshine' with lyrics like: 'Mohamed Salah. A gift from ALLAH. He come from Roma To Liverpool. He's always scoring, It's almost boring. So please don't take ... Mohamed away' (LFC Leader 2018). In these YouTube videos we can see that these songs are being sung by predominantly white football fans in a country that is supposed to have alarming rates of Islamophobia (Aljazeera 2018).

This is a clear sign of how religion can pop up in really unexpected places and how one person can make a difference, with the help of global social media and their enormous capacity to share and spread content. This can even have a proselytizing effect as explained by an ex-Islamophobe white English national who declares that he was converted to Islam with the help of these viral songs (Bird 2019). A recent study by Stanford University Immigration Policy Lab asked whether celebrities can reduce prejudice and whether the Mohamed Salah effect had had any clear impact on Islamophobia? By analysing 15 million tweets, it was found that the number of anti-Muslim tweets posted by Liverpool fans against fans of other top-flight clubs had halved and that there had been a 16 per cent drop in the hate-crime rate in the Merseyside region after Salah signed for the club relative to the expected rate had he not done so (Alrababa'h et al. 2019). Explicit proof that Mo Salah's open religiosity has an effect not only on grown-up football fans but also on the next generation can also be seen in a video where a small boy mimics Mohamed Salah's prostration after scoring (DawahCallIslam 2018). Even though this young child is probably unaware that this form of bowing, called *sujūd* in Arabic, where you touch the ground with your forehead, knees and hands while reciting phrases to glorify God, is part of the standard daily prayers of millions of Muslims around the world, it is a very strong symbolic act. A sceptic might even wonder: was this video actually staged in order to promote Islam?

## Feature films and TV series

Film trailers serve initially as a short advertisement for a full-length film, but by themselves can also provide surprisingly good educational tools for religious tolerance. These include, for example, award-winning films such as *In the Fade, Tangerines, Dancing in Jaffa* or *What Will People Say* (further information about these films is available in the IMDb), which in addition to various humanistic values also deal with religious conflict, a subject that is mentioned in their trailers as well. Of course, the full-length film tackles this subject in a much deeper, more nuanced way, but with clever editing even a few minutes of these trailers can tell a story in which religious tension is happening on screen.

## Educational channels

There are many channels that create content for schoolchildren, and many of them are surprisingly good. In a Nutshell, Ted ED, Crash Course or AsapSCIENCE all have over or around 10 million views. Given the general lack of civility elsewhere on YouTube, the academic approach taken by these sites is a real breath of fresh air. Interconvictional associations also sometimes produce similar types of videos (see Chapter 9 of this book). Of course, information in these channels is extremely compressed in terms of its verbal context, and it is made more appealing and informative using animation, music, colourful flashy effects and so on. It seems that fast-paced, dynamic content, with compressed information and a twist of humour is the best way to attract large audiences. Videos uploaded by these channels clearly have a strong production team of scientists, animators and film-makers on board. The videos are well scripted and worth watching. One very good example is a short video story from the Ted ED channel called *It's a Church. It's a Mosque. It's Hagia Sophia* (TED-Ed 2014) about Hagia Sophia in Istanbul – a highly symbolic building that has served a variety of purposes over the centuries all of which are discussed in a clear and simple way that can then give rise to a discussion in the classroom. This video was made before Turkish President Recep Tayyip Erdogan signed a reclassification order in July 2020 by which Hagia Sophia would once again be used as a mosque, but that could actually make the video even more timely for educational use. This five-minute video shows how to tell a complex story filled with religious and political tensions with the help of creative animation, film-makers and historians in a way that is both aesthetically attractive and historically accurate.

Although they are significantly smaller, channels such as Smarthistory or Religion for Breakfast also provide interesting content on questions of religion and religious coexistence. These two YouTube channels are not aimed at schoolchildren and have a more grown-up academic approach, although this means that they have total view-counts of less than two hundred thousand. A good example is a video titled *Judaism, Islam and the Survival of Ancient Greek Texts* (Smarthistory 2017), which has less than ten thousand views but offers a great introduction to a fourteenth-century book on display at the Metropolitan Museum of Art. This book titled *Sefer Musre Hafilosofim* (Book of Morals of Philosophers) is an anthology of philosophy in Hebrew. It is a copy of a book originally written in Arabic that was itself a translation of works from Ancient Greece, thus illustrating how the respective histories of Christianity, Judaism and Islam in Europe are closely intertwined.

**Popular YouTubers/influencers**

There are countless numbers of YouTubers. As of 2019, there are over eight thousand YouTube channels with over 1 million subscribers and this number is growing fast (in 2016, there were only two thousand such channels). A good example is the viral hit *History of the Entire World, I Guess* by singer-songwriter (and now also online video creator) Bill Wurtz (2017), which was uploaded on 10 May 2017 and has received more than 130 million views in five years. Wurtz is perhaps not the most typical example of a YouTuber, as he is not a regular or 'permanent' contributor, with just a few 'hits' that are in fact carefully prepared films, but he is very popular. This twenty-minute video, which covers everything from the Big Bang to the near future, is still receiving new viewers and there is also a special version without swearing which is popular in classrooms (Andy Does Stuff 2017). Religion is portrayed here in a humorous way as an invention that pops up from time to time. The following extract explains how Buddhism, Christianity and Islam came to life according to Bill Wurtz.

The year is now −500.

Narrator: Ah, the Buddha was just enlightened!

Other Voice: Who's the Buddha?

Narrator: This guy, who sat under a tree for so long that he figured out how to ignore the fact that we're all dying. You could make a religion out of this.

The year is now 30 CE.

Jesus Christ: Hi, everything's great.

Narrator: ... said some guy, who seems to be getting very popular, and is then arrested and killed for being too popular, which only makes him more popular. You could make a religion out of this.

The year is now 622.

Narrator: ... and everyone got so mad at him that he had to leave town and go to a different town. You can make a religion out of this ...

Different denominations within Christianity are also addressed with an emphasis on conflict rather than on an ecumenical drive to reunite. The first example takes place around the year 1000.

Narrator: The Pope is ready to make some more emperors of the Roman Empire, the Holy Roman Empire. It's actually Germany, but don't worry about it! New kingdoms!

Distorted Voice: Christianize all the Kingdoms!

Narrator: Which brand would you like?

Roman Catholic Church: Mine's better.

Eastern Orthodox Church: Mine's better.

Roman Catholic Church: Mine's better.

The second time is just before the Reformation when the author also mentions the Shia-Sunni split inside Islam.

The year is now 1501.

Narrator: Persia just made Persia Persian again. Let's make it the other kind of Islam, the one where we thought the first guy should have been the other guy.

Roman Catholic Church: Hey, Christians! Do you sin? Now you can buy your way out of Hell.

Martin Luther: That's bullshit, this whole thing is bullshit, that's a scam, fuck the church. Here's 95 reasons why.

Narrator: ... said Martin Luther, in his new book which might have accidentally started the Protestant Reformation.

Despite their huge popularity, one should perhaps question the reliability of history-based videos made by enthusiasts who may not be expert historians. Communicating the results of historical research in a simplified and compelling way does however make it more likely that the reader, or in this case the viewer, can empathize with them. On the other hand, there is a risk of oversimplifying things to such an extent that the diversity of historical processes remains inaccessible to the viewer. The positive side of this approach is that it arouses interest through provocation, although it should not, however, remain the 'ultimate truth' for the viewer. It is important to start the dialogue on the basis of a historical event and to provide opportunities for reflection and access to other sources in order to complement the simplified scheme offered to the viewer. It is also important to realize that the mindset is quite different from that of a museum or textbook, in that the viewer does not have to assume that a video made by a YouTube enthusiast has an objective, universal approach. Subjectivity is self-evident. Through formal education in schools, young people can be given the tools they require to critically analyse and understand what is being offered to them on social media, rather than relying on them as a source of information.

The main genre amongst popular YouTubers who include religious content in their videos are pranks and (social) experiments. Popular Muslim YouTubers, who deal with religious topics, include, for example, Adam Saleh whose *Pulling Hijab Off Experiment!* (2016) has over 22 million views while *Praying in Public!* (2013) has 16 million views. Karim Jovian with 1.9 million subscribers creates parodies and videos about Muslims and many of his videos have gone viral. His video *10 Hours of Walking in NYC as a Woman in Hijab* (2014) has over 18 million views and he has many other videos with over 10 million views that include religious content. These types of experiments tend to travel from country to country, and one excellent example is a practically identical experiment carried out in different European Union (EU) countries, such as Italy, Norway and Sweden, in which a Muslim girl who is wearing a hijab stands on a street with an empty poster with a sign saying: 'I am Muslim … and that makes me …' (in Sweden, Othman, Jara 2016; in Italy, Fly with Haifa 2016; in Norway, It's Soso 2016). The purpose of the experiment is to find out people's reactions by asking them to write something on the empty board to complete the sentence. These three videos of the same experiment are clearly campaigning for greater tolerance in their respective societies and all are made in a simple style with no help from professional film-makers, making this type of grassroot activism a great tool to enable teenagers to teach each other about religion.

## Conclusion: Educate the educators?

When we look at the media, and how they influence young people as mediators of popular culture, one has to admit that the current form of education provided in schools today needs to be updated to take into account new forms of communication that can have an enormous influence on young people.

Substantially increased investment in media literacy is of the utmost importance for promoting media intelligence and critical thinking among young people, as they are extremely vulnerable to propaganda and fake news. The most efficient interventions could be initiated both at teacher-training institutions and also as a part of the curriculum from elementary school onwards. We should not underestimate the importance of policies at European and national levels to implement within the official curricula a comprehensive strategy to help children identify fake news and prevent it from spreading, and to promote truly critical thinking.

Greater investment in visual literacy gives educators a chance to improve the quality of their teaching and to connect with young people in a more engaging way. This could be done by supporting different film literacy programmes, for example, through the MEDIA subprogramme of Creative Europe (supported by the European Commission). This would mean investing more in audiovisual studies to enable the next generation to 'read' visual material more critically.

There are already many surprisingly good online educational programmes with audiovisual input at their core with fantastic content and a huge fan base like Crash Course, Ted-Ed, In a Nutshell and so on. The EU could create similar high-quality learning sites which could use a shared animation/video script as a base, which could be then translated into different languages through local partners. Quality subtitles would of course be a cheaper option, but local language voiceover or presenter would be more engaging.

It is easy to agree with TED founder Chris Anderson, who said that 'face-to-face communication has been fine-tuned by millions of years of evolution … It's not too much to say that what Gutenberg did for writing, online video can now do for face-to-face communication' (TED 2010). He also believes that online video will significantly affect both scientific progress and the learning process. YouTube is really on its way to becoming the biggest informal classroom in the world, and teachers and the academic community should also embrace it and create better content for it instead of fighting against it.

Television series, which are perhaps even more popular now that many are broadcast directly on internet platforms rather than on traditional TV, offer another means of communicating with young people. In this case, the media companies involved (such as the EBU) could create programmes that are based on real historical stories about religious tolerance, which might compete with the dominant narrative equating religion with conflict. Comedy series could also be created to ease the tensions between different ethnic and religious groups in society – using authors from minority groups who are recognized within their communities.

*Citizen Khan* was a pioneering project in the British entertainment industry. It was the first television (BBC One) family situation comedy to feature a British Muslim family. The Khans are a British Pakistani Muslim family, and the show is situated in Sparkhill, a suburb of Birmingham which has the second-largest concentration of Muslims in Britain. The show's creator, Adil Ray, is himself a member of a British Muslim family.

The show caused a great deal of controversy when it first went on the air in 2012. Viewers sent both angry and laudatory feedback to the BBC and the newspapers, and the show was analysed in academic journals specializing in South East Asian popular culture and comedy studies. Those critical of the show thought it insulted the Quran and Muslims and was not even funny, whereas those who liked it praised its sharp-sightedness and viewed it as a successful example of the traditional British television family sitcom. Because of Adil Ray's ethnic background, the critics could not claim that the show was the product of an outsider's ignorance and prejudice.

The fact that *Citizen Khan* gained a viewing slot on Britain's most prestigious TV channel, BBC One, and that it remained popular over the years, signalled that there was considerable demand for this comedic take on Muslim family life. Presumably, a large part of the viewers were Muslim themselves. For the larger viewing public, the sight of Muslims satirizing themselves may have changed their previous perspective of Muslims as overly pious, angry critics of British society, as many realized that the everyday problems of this Muslim family were very similar to those of any other British family. Increasing religious toleration in this way may not have been a priority objective of the show's producers but it may well have had this effect.

TV series, as well as other media influencing contemporary popular culture, normally try to convey a positive message, as can be seen from selected frames from the Balkan TV series, which paint a generally optimistic picture in their representation of religious toleration and peace in the region. This is also the result of more than two decades of replication of good examples from consolidated democracies in the West. However, as religious tolerance and peace are, like religious and political radicalization, highly dynamic concepts that can change very quickly, in the current context of strong political polarization throughout Europe, one could argue that in the near future the Balkans could perhaps start exporting good practices of religious tolerance and peace to Western Europe.

# Refugees and the politics of memory: Political discourses of religious toleration and peace

Laura Galián, John Maiden, Stefanie Sinclair and Árpád Welker

## Introduction

This chapter tackles one of the key research questions that the RETOPEA project set out to address: How are key issues of religious coexistence presented in contemporary culture and media? While this is a very wide-ranging question, this chapter focuses on representations of these issues in the specific context of political discourses. In particular, it explores how political discourses draw on history and mobilize national and transnational memories when presenting issues related to religious diversity and migration in contemporary society.

While the fact that political discourses aim to shape public opinion cannot be denied, there are ongoing debates around the extent to which political discourses actually influence public opinion (Leruth and Taylor-Gooby 2019), including the views of young people, especially since these discourses are often filtered through media coverage. When the RETOPEA team conducted focus group interviews with teenagers across Europe (see Chapter 2 in this volume), it became apparent that there are a wide range of factors at play that can influence the views of young people, such as not only different kinds of media (including social media) but also peers, parents and school. This corroborates findings of various other research in this field (see e.g. Middaugh et al. 2016; Weiss 2020). Many of the young people we interviewed as part of the RETOPEA focus groups demonstrated considerable awareness of bias, particularly in news coverage within mainstream TV news. They frequently mentioned how often they consulted social media and other internet sources for information. To encourage and develop young peoples' critical engagement with political discourses, the RETOPEA team included extracts from political speeches in the educational materials we developed for the RETOPEA project, that is, the selection of curated primary sources presented on the project website that young people use for the production of short documentary films, or 'docutubes' (see https://retopea.eu/s/en/page/clippings).

This chapter is based on background research conducted for the RETOPEA project. In particular, it considers how contemporary political discourses on religious toleration and peace draw on the past. It focuses on political discourses used in the specific context of the 'refugee crisis' between 2013 and 2017, when large numbers of refugees, predominantly from Syria, Iraq and Afghanistan started arriving in member states of the European Union (EU). We chose this focus as these debates offer good examples of how notions of history and transnational memory have been utilized to discursively frame contemporary understandings of toleration and peace. While *religious* toleration was not always explicitly at the forefront of these debates, the fact that the vast majority of these refugees came from Muslim backgrounds was frequently perceived and presented as a source of controversy within these discourses. These debates also highlight differences in perceptions of Europe's cultural and religious history and of its perceived relevance to contemporary society.

We chose to draw on examples of political discourses employed in Hungary, Germany, Spain and the UK, given that these four national contexts offer important contrasting perspectives within different parts of Europe. This chapter explores how the past and notions of a collective, shared memory have been interpreted, framed and deployed in these debates. First, we will set out our understanding of notions of 'transnational memory', followed by the provision of some contextual background about how the refugee crisis unfolded in Hungary, Germany, Spain and the UK. Drawing on examples from each of these four countries, our chapter then goes on to identify similarities, specificities and divergences in approaches to the politics of memory and considers how notions of national, European as well as religious history and identity have been discursively constructed and mobilized in these debates.

## Theoretical framework and methodology

Our chapter is embedded within the framework of memory studies. We are drawing on notions of 'collective memory' as coined by Maurice Halbwachs ([1925] 1992) in that we understand collective memory as shaped through 'narratives, recall, and communicative exchange' (Assmann 2016: 16) and in terms of shared memories mediated through many different spaces and means of communications, including the media, institutions of the state, politicians and other social actors (Rothberg 2009: 15). However, our study goes beyond the 'methodological nationalism' (De Cesari and Rigney 2014: 1) that has tended to dominate the study of collective memory in previous decades. Traditionally, approaches to memory studies have predominantly associated collective memory with the nation state. However, processes of globalization, colonialization and migration have highlighted the transnational reality of mnemonic processes. As far as people move, so do memories. So, in order to understand mnemonic processes that have been discursively mobilized during the 'refugee crisis' in Europe, we draw on the notion of 'transnational memory' as a concept that transcends the perceived static, self-contained framework of national memories (De Cesari and Rigney 2014; Erll 2011).

Discursive constructions of collective and transnational memories have undoubtedly shaped understandings of Europe and of its religious history and have played an important role in supporting the development of a sense of European identity, unity and homogeneity. However, there are also many different and conflicting understandings of European memory (Trimçev et al. 2020). Scholars, such as Macdonald (2013), Karlsson (2010) or Pérez Baquero (2021), claim that the idea of Europe has been discursively shaped by transnational memories and argue that the European project relies on transnational memories of different historical events, including the Holocaust, which is identified as the event of greatest significance.

As Astrid Erll (2011) points out, the production of cultural memory is a fluid, continually evolving process that is in perpetual motion and involves the dynamic interplay between people, media, mnemonic contents and practices. Given the wide range of countries included in our analysis and their different positionalities within the history of Europe, we believe it is necessary to go beyond the idea of the 'national' in order to understand how the different memories mobilized during the 'refugee crisis' have been encountered, negotiated, cross-referenced and have borrowed from each other in the public sphere, within national and trans-European spaces and contexts. 'Transnational memories' have, however, not yet silenced national collective memories. Memories – whether local, national or transnational – coexist and adapt to each other in a fluid and hybrid way.

The main goal of our study is to highlight complexities, similarities and differences of the discursive construction of memories in relation to notions of religious toleration and peace in the context of political debates about the 'refugee crisis' (2013–17) in these four European countries. For that purpose, we will be adopting a multidisciplinary perspective, drawing on Cultural Studies, History, Religious Studies and Memory Studies. We 'approach "memory" as a discursive phenomenon: as acts of interpretation which repeat, alter or contest a shared meaning of something understood "as past"' (Trimçev et al. 2020: 52) and are inspired by a discursive-historical approach (as developed by Wodak 2015) in that we consider broader sociopolitical and historical contexts in which discursive practices are embedded. We understand that a comparative, critical discourse analysis would require a more subtle, detailed and multifocal perspective than we are adopting in this chapter. However, an in-depth analysis of specific 'speech acts' would go well beyond the scope of this chapter. Instead, we aim to establish common themes and broad trends of ways in which national and transnational memories have been discursively constructed in the context of debates about this 'crisis', which captured 'worldwide political attention and [produced] diverse and contradictory discourses and responses' (Holmes and Castañeda 2016: 13).

## Background: The refugee crisis in the different national contexts

In the broadest terms, the refugee crisis can be regarded as *transnational* – in terms of the movement of refugees; *international* – in view of some humanitarian and political responses (e.g. UNICEF and the EU); but also *national* – as we shall see in the specificities of political discourses within each national context. These different dimensions need to be considered in an assessment of the historical background and development of the crisis.

As a transnational event, the Syrian refugee crisis needs to be set against the backdrop of multiple geopolitical 'crises' involving the forced displacement of people due to war and organized violence: the United Nations High Commissioner for Refugees (UNHCR) calculated that in 2014 there were 60 million individuals displaced from their homes worldwide (Ferris and Kirişci 2016: 2). The immediate origin of the displacement of refugees was the violence aimed at anti-government protesters in Syria from March 2011 onwards. In the same year the first temporary camps were established in Turkey, with refugees initially called 'guests' on the assumption their presence would only be temporary. The civil war in Syria rapidly developed dimensions of proxy and sectarian warfare, with the threat of death and sexual violence. The intensification of violence led to the increasing displacement of refugees, mostly Sunni Muslims, but increasingly also Shia Alwites, Kurds, Turkomans, Yazidis, Iraqi Christians and others. These people fled to Turkey, where there were over 2.5 million Syrian refugees by December 2015, and Lebanon, Jordan, Egypt and Iraq, as well as some other North African countries. According to the UN Refugee Agency (UNHCR), the number of Syrian refugees increased from around 8,000 in 2011 to about 4.6 million in 2015 (Ferris and Kirişci 2016: 29). Turkey became the main gateway of refugees into Europe. Many of these took the 'Balkan corridor' towards Western Europe through Macedonia, Hungary, Serbia, Slovenia and Croatia. The attempts of refugees to enter Europe also resulted in over three thousand deaths in the Aegean and the Mediterranean, with many relying on the operations of illegal people smugglers and traffickers.

The arrival of large numbers of refugees triggered various international responses. The United Nations established a Syrian Regional Response Plan (UNHCR 2014) and was able to raise funds. This allowed the UNHCR to manage and finance humanitarian camps in Lebanon and Jordan. In 2015 the European Commission referred to the situation as 'the largest global humanitarian crisis' of our time (cited in Holmes and Castañeda 2016: 12). Many European leaders spoke of a 'crisis', though critics have argued that this crisis was actually 'not so much a crisis of refugees, but more a crisis of the EU itself' (Freedman 2019: 705). The arrival of large numbers of refugees raised many questions about European identity, the role of the EU, national sovereignty, the permeability of national borders and the need to distribute the care and responsibility for refugees between different member states of the EU. The sociologist and international relations scholar Jane Freedman, like various other experts, argues that the use of the term 'crisis' by European politicians in this context served a 'powerful political and symbolic purpose' as it implied that political leaders faced a situation beyond their control for which political solutions were not available (Freedman 2019: 705). The EU's main intervention was in negotiations with Turkey (in the context of ongoing discussions over the country joining the EU) to reduce transit of refugees into the EU, following a year of mass migration in 2015. In March 2016, a deal was made which involved Turkey agreeing that every Syrian refugee arriving 'irregularly' in Greece would be returned to Turkey, with the EU also agreeing to accept one Syrian refugee for every individual returned. Turkey would receive 6 billion Euros for assisting refugees. It has been argued that this deal 'appeased European anxieties about a possible refugee influx but it consequentially crippled on political, ideological, and moral grounds the EU's capacity and legitimacy to exert pressure over Turkey's compliance with the EU's standards regarding human rights and democracy' (Bélanger and Saracoglu 2019: 288).

The historical specificities and contexts of the responses of the four individual nation states in this chapter require close attention. During the refugee crisis, Hungary became a particularly sought-after transit country for refugees in the 'Balkan corridor' because it was part of the Schengen Zone. When, in the summer of 2015, large amounts of predominantly Muslim refugees arrived in Hungary, discourses employed by the Fidesz government – led by Victor Orbán – presented the situation not as a humanitarian crisis but as a Muslim invasion threatening Hungary's national security and Christian identity. These discourses, practices and policies became part of a hostile campaign on 'immigration and terrorism' (Bocskor 2018; Kallius 2017; Melegh 2020).

The Fidesz government made anti-immigration a central topic of its propaganda and politics in 2015, even before the 'Balkan route' became a focus of attention. Prime Minister Orbán used the tragic events connected to the terrorist attack on the journalists of *Charlie Hebdo* to launch his warfare on immigration. In the direct aftermath of the rally of unity in Paris, he gave an interview to the Hungarian state news agency, in which he connected terrorism with migration, called for a European policy to prevent further immigration and stressed that his government would not accept newcomers (*index* 2015). Throughout the following months, as the number of asylum seekers steadily grew, several waves of carefully planned propaganda took place.

While hundreds of thousands of asylum seekers transited from Hungary to the West, in September 2015 the Hungarian government adopted strict measures to minimize the number of asylum seekers in Hungary and built a fence on the southern border. In the beginning of 2016, the Fidesz government announced that a referendum on a possible quota system within the EU would be held in Hungary,[1] followed by a 10 million Euro communication campaign that included billboards and a national consultation. Even though this referendum, which was held in October 2016, had to be declared invalid due to insufficient electoral turnout (Kingsley 2016), it served its purpose of keeping the question of migration on the agenda, despite a radical reduction of the numbers of refugees seeking asylum in Hungary. As part of the new legislation on migration, the Fidesz government announced a state of emergency in 2016, which gave it various extraordinary powers. The state of emergency has been renewed year by year, despite the fact that the arrival of Syrian refugees in Hungary virtually stopped by the end of 2015.

In September 2015, Germany, along with Austria, opened their borders to refugees who had arrived in Hungary and were trying to reach Northern Europe via the Balkan route. Chancellor Angela Merkel appealed to the German population claiming that it was Germany's 'national duty' to support refugees. Merkel argued that Germany was in a position to cope with the arrival of large numbers of refugees and made the now famous assertion '*Wir schaffen das!*' (We can do this!) (Merkel 2015). However, when more than 1 million refugees registered in Germany in 2016, Merkel's approach became subject to a lot of criticism. Between 2015 and 2019, 1.7 million people applied for asylum in Germany (Ottermann 2020; UNHCR 2020). Merkel was accused of being naively optimistic and of encouraging too many refugees to come to Germany, allowing them to take advantage of Germany's infrastructure and welfare system (Deutsche Welle 2019; Winkel 2019).

The treatment of refugees became a hotly contested topic in political debates in Germany, reflecting 'Germany's historical struggle between xenophobic tendencies and liberal aspirations' (Holmes and Castañeda 2016: 15). Responses ranged from the endorsement of a *Willkommenskultur* (welcome culture), mobilizing large numbers of volunteers supporting the establishment of refugee shelters (Herrmann 2020), to strong condemnation and concerns about the social, cultural and economic impact, including a perceived 'threat' of an increasing Islamization of Germany and Europe. In some cases, this led to physical attacks on accommodation intended for asylum seekers by far-right groups (BBC News 2015a). When in the city centre of Cologne on New Year's Eve 2015, sexual assaults on women by groups of young men, allegedly including asylum seekers primarily from Arab or North African backgrounds, were reported (Büscher et al. 2016), critics of the *Willkommenskultur* highlighted this event as a sign of the cultural incompatibility of Muslim refugees and of their disrespect for German and European values. This incident was used to justify Islamophobic protest led by far-right populist movements, such as PEGIDA,[2] which claimed that the incidents at New Year's Eve in Cologne showed that Muslim refugees could not be integrated into German society and posed a threat (Dearden 2016; News Wires 2016).

In Spain, it could be argued that the 'refugee crisis' has had much more to do with the situation in Spain – its values, identity and history – than with the situation of the refugees and asylum seekers. Compared to other European countries, such as Germany, Spain barely received any Syrian refugees, in spite of a vast amount of applications from asylum seekers in 2015. In fact, for the period between 2015 and 2017, Spain had agreed to host 19,449 Syrian refugees, arriving in Europe via Greece and Italy. However, at the end of the specified time period, the country had hosted just 2,500 people, around 12.8 per cent of the total number agreed. This was because the right-wing *Partido Popular* (People's Party), the leading party in government at the time, had informally boycotted the EU decision on the quota distribution of refugees. In fact, the country was accused, by its own judiciary system, of breaching the contract. Despite the unwillingness of the Spanish cabinet to host Syrian refugees in the context of the biggest refugee crisis in Europe since the Second World War, Spain still received migrants mainly from North Africa and Latin America as it had historically done. In 2015 Spain received the largest number of asylum applications in its recent history. According to Eurostat, 14,780 people applied for international protection in Spain, 8,934 more than in 2014, which was an increase of more than 150 per cent (CEAR 2016).

Given that the Syrian refugee crisis coincided with the national institutional and financial crisis under Rajoy's government (2011–17), political discourses employed by the Spanish government were at the time preoccupied by domestic issues rather than the international refugee crisis. There is still relatively little literature on how political or media discourses in Spain have constructed migratory phenomena, in comparison with other national or international contexts, possibly because immigration was not picked up as a significant social problem in political or media discourses until the mid-1990s (Montagut and Moragas-Fernández 2020).

In Britain, the initial political discussion concerned the offering of humanitarian support to regional responses to the refugee crisis, notably the camps in Iraq, Jordan, Lebanon and Turkey. In January 2014, the focus of discussions shifted to the resettlement of vulnerable refugees, with the Conservative (centre-right) UK government at first declining to be involved in UNHCR's attempts to mobilize nation states, but then, by the end of the month, announcing a Syrian Vulnerable Persons Relocation Programme. This was intended to allow only a few hundred Syrians into the country. Indeed, as of September 2014, while 941 refugees had been resettled in Germany, the number for the UK was a mere 38 individuals. As the numbers of refugees crossing the Mediterranean increased, in September 2015 the government announced plans to allow twenty thousand refugees to be resettled from camps in the Middle East – but not from Europe. These numbers were roundly criticized, in particular by the political opposition in the UK Parliament, including the Labour and Liberal (centre-left) parties and the (centre-left) Scottish National Party. An important aspect of criticism was the fate of children, especially in the refugee camps in Calais, France. In May 2016, the 'Dubs Amendment' to the Immigration Bill was passed in order to bring unaccompanied children to the UK from France, as well as from Greece and Italy. By early 2017, around two hundred children had been resettled in the UK, in the care of the local authorities (for the overall UK response see Ostrand 2015; McGuiness 2017).

Three main aspects of the UK response to the refugee crisis are worth a particular mention. First were the discourses around humanitarianism during the crisis. With the image of Alan Kurdi, the young boy whose body was washed onto a beach in Turkey, having a significant public impact, it has been argued that both government policy – which was to offer resettlement only to those seen as most in need – and media reporting around the Syrian Vulnerable Persons Resettlement programme focused on an ethic of 'vulnerability'. This, however, also exceptionalized the vulnerable, as 'deserving' subjects, and simultaneously tended to exclude others as 'undeserving' (Armbruster 2019). Second was the association between many of the refugees in Calais – the majority of whom were men – and the threat of Islamic terrorism (Armbruster 2019). This was in a context of years of political 'backlash' against multiculturalism, in which both 'muscular liberal' and right-wing concerns over security and the undermining of 'British values' had been paramount (Vertovec and Wessendorf 2009). Third was the distinctive political backdrop to the crisis: an economics of austerity and public debate over the 'in/out' referendum on the status of the UK in the EU, which culminated in the BREXIT vote of 2016. Anti-immigration – a constant, shrill voice in the UK response to the Syrian refugee crisis – was bound up with both these political issues.

## Politics of memory: Political discourses employed in the context of the refugee crisis

Our analysis identified three main themes in the discursive construction of national and transnational memories in the context of political debates about the Syrian refugee crisis:

1. The negotiation of disputed and difficult memories in the discursive construction of national and religious identities,
2. Mobilizations of memories of migration and displacement, and
3. The mobilization of discourses of European identity and anti-European sentiment.

### Disputed and difficult memories and the discursive construction of national and religious identities

Discourses employed in the context of political debates about the Syrian refugee crisis often drew on notions of collective memories of historical events to justify national responses to this crisis and negotiate rising tensions between expectations of the international community, humanitarian obligations and domestic pressures (Brownlie 2020). This included discursive constructions of national and transnational memory and identity, which were heavily disputed and employed with very contrasting agendas, that is, either to present refugees as 'foreign' and 'other', or to create a sense of compassion or ethical responsibility towards refugees.

In Spain, different disputed memories, mainly those of al-Andalus and that of its colonial past, constantly play out in the configuration of contemporary understandings of national history and identity, above all when dealing with its religious identity and its relationship with Islam. These memories place Spain in a unique and exceptional position in Europe. Its geographical location, historical background as well as its linguistic and social composition are among the narratives that advocate for its 'exceptionalism' in its relationship with Islam and Arab-Islamic culture (Arigita 2011; Fernández Parrilla and Cañete 2018).

These historical correspondences (the fall of Granada in 1492, the expulsion of the Jews and later the Moriscos in 1609) and the contemporary flows of immigration from North Africa are connected, as if 'they had been experienced by the same people' (Fernández Parrilla and Cañete 2018: 112). The recent phenomenon of migration and, crucially, the refugee crisis, have been understood by many as the return of the 'Moors' and have been discursively situated within a narrative of a new 'invasion' appealing to the history of al-Andalus.

The disputed memories of al-Andalus have been reflected in the ongoing search for Spanish identity in narratives of cultural and historical entanglements between Spain and Islam. In fact, 'it is impossible to understand the construction of modern Spanish national identity and its historical narratives without considering the problematic presence (or absence) of the Arab/Muslim component' (Fernández Parrilla and Cañete 2018: 112). Two competing discursive constructions of history, the 'myth of *convivencia*' (coexistence) among the three Abrahmanic religions – Christianity, Islam and Judaism – and the 'myth of invasion' as a return of Islam and the 'Moors' have been instrumentalized within contemporary political discourses. These memories and narratives, understood as a continuation or as a disruption of Spanish history, have been used to either unite and bring together or to divide, separate and isolate.

Elena Arigita (2011: 223) divides contemporary approaches to the disputed memories of al-Andalus into (1) jihadists claims of al-Andalus as Islamist territory, (2) political discourses that present Spain as a border zone that protects Christendom from Islamic threats and (3) representations of al-Andalus as a fruitful crossroad of civilizations where coexistence among religions/cultures is possible. In the context of political debates about the Syrian refugee crisis, narratives and memories of Spain as a territory of coexistence and as the fortress of Christian Europe have competed with each other. In neither of them, Islam is considered to be part of the historical or contemporary identity of Spain, nor of Europe. Both memories of the Spanish political discourses share a civilizational logic that perfectly coheres the stereotypes of the historical other for the Spanish imagination (Arigita 2011: 233).

The emotional evocation of religious history, and the mobilization of memories of al-Andalus in particular, work at different levels and still permeate political, cultural and social life in Spain (Arigita 2011; Fernández Parrilla and Cañete 2018). However, rather than emphasizing a strong Christian or Catholic religious identity, political discourses have predominantly focused on the amplification of a fear of Islam, which has led to an increasing institutionalization of Islamophobia and a greater emphasis on a security agenda.

In Germany, political discourses used in debates about the Syrian refugee crisis frequently referred to notions of Germany's historic guilt related to a need to deal with its Nazi past. Notions of historic guilt refer to Germany's responsibility for atrocities committed by the Nazi regime, its responsibility towards the victims of the Holocaust and Germany's subsequent duty to help anyone fleeing from political violence. Particularly since 1980, political discourses in the Federal Republic of Germany have demonstrated a 'great interest in the politics of memory' (Winkel 2019: 18) and reflected efforts to 'come to terms' with historical wrongdoings (*Vergangenheitsbewältigung*). These efforts largely focused on finding ways of dealing with its Nazi past, its anti-Semitic policies in particular, which led to the murder of 6 million Jews during the Holocaust (Neiman 2019). As Holmes and Castañeda put it (2016: 14), 'Germany has responded [to the Syrian refugee crisis] with an ambivalent hospitality that is uniquely nuanced and conditioned by memories (and some present-day realities) of xenophobia and fascism'.

An example of political discourse framing the refugee crisis in terms of Germany's historical responsibility (i.e. defining itself in contrast to atrocities committed by the Nazi regime) is Valerie Wilms's (Alliance 90/The Greens) contribution to a debate in the German national parliament on 15 October 2015:

After the Second World War, Germany took on a historic duty and sensibly included the right to seek asylum as a basic right in its constitution. That is because German history in particular has shown us very clearly that people who are persecuted need shelter. Many people come to us because life in their home countries has become impossible. They seek protection and we have to help them – not only to follow the constitution, but above all as compassionate people. (Wilms 2015: 12727 C, trans. from the German original)

However, these notions of Germany's historic duty have also been controversially received. Members of far-right populist parties, like Björn Höcke from the German nationalist Eurosceptic *Alternative für Deutschland* (*AfD* – Alternative for Germany), have used people's fears about the impact of large numbers of refugees arriving in Germany to promote the idea that Germany needs to 'free' itself from discourses of shame and 'obsession' with feelings of guilt around Germany's Nazi past and instead emphasize discourses of Germany's historical 'greatness' as a country of poets and thinkers (Höcke 2017). Far-right populist movements like the *AfD*, which have been attracting a growing number of followers, have claimed that the arrival of large numbers of Muslims from the Middle East and Northern Africa in particular is posing a 'threat' to German culture and values. For example, in the run-up to the national election in September 2017, the *AfD* used the slogan 'Islam does not belong to Germany!' as part of their election campaign (*Alternative für Deutschland* 2017a; 2017b; trans from the German original).

However, references to notions of religious identities and traditions in political discourses in Germany about the Syrian refugee crisis have not only included concerns about the potential impact of the arrival of large numbers of predominantly Muslim young men on Christian values and traditions in Germany (and Europe). They also included political discourses appealing to Christian values (such as the value of loving your neighbour) as values that could or should inspire compassion towards refugees (see e.g. Sarrazin 2015). Chancellor Angela Merkel, who is a member of the centre-right Christian Democratic Union (CDU), openly identifies herself as a Christian and has repeatedly highlighted Christian values as a source of inspiration to her and of the policies she stands for, including her support of the pro-refugee *Willkommenskultur* (Mueller 2016; Spencer 2016). Merkel has argued that the best path towards community cohesion and peaceful coexistence was to strengthen 'Christian values' and talk about the 'Judeo-Christian tradition', rather than the dangers of Islam. As Merkel put it, 'it is not the case that we have too much of Islam, but that we have not enough of Christianity' (Merkel 2011, trans. from the German original).

However, members of the CDU have also argued that immigrants should be expected to integrate into German society and conform to the *Leitkultur* (guiding culture). The concept of a *Leitkultur* is based on notions of Europe's 'Judeo-Christian heritage', but is also linked to secular values of the Enlightenment (Goździak and Suter 2020: 286).

In the UK, religion as a category was not a central feature in political debates about the refugee crisis. However, where 'ethnicity' and 'race' were the focus of discourse, religion and religious identity may be elided with these categories. Furthermore, specifically historicized understandings of migration were embedded in different ways in political discourses. The 'politics of memory' undoubtedly informed debates about political policy.

Debates in the UK parliament about the Syrian refugee crisis reflected a wider rhetorical emphasis on a 'tradition' of British tolerance, one which is shaped by a particular sense of historical consciousness. For example, during a debate in the House of Commons ('Unaccompanied Child Refugees') in November 2017, Labour MP Stella Creasy asserted:

Actually we have had a proud tradition of taking and supporting refugees in this country. I am mindful that Creasy, like Farage, is a Huguenot surname, and that all of us come from communities that have benefited from the input of refugees in this country. That is the true British, patriotic tradition that we should be supporting. (*Hansard* 2016: col. 549)

Various scholars have pointed out that a 'myth' of toleration is evident in discourse concerning multiculturalism. The historian David Feldman even suggests that there is a significant vein of 'conservative pluralism' on the right in British politics, informed by historical consciousness. Feldman uses this argument in relation to debates around religious accommodation in the public sphere (e.g. concerning food, clothing, religious schools). He showed how political discourse, for example, concerning legislation on Sikh turbans and motorbike helmets in the 1960s, was informed by a historical narrative of religious and ethnic toleration – for example, towards Nonconformists and French Huguenots (Feldman 2011). Some of the discourse he describes seems to assume a 'whiggish' sense of British history – one which presents a historical narrative of continuous progress towards toleration and freedoms. However, this 'tradition' is understood in different ways, with varying understandings of the implications of this tradition, what the 'limits' of inclusivity should be and how it relates to notions of Christian 'heritage'. This was evident in an exchange in the House of Commons in 2015. The Conservative MP Sir Gerald Howarth, for example, asked the prime minister, David Cameron, the following:

As we approach the festival marking the birth of Jesus Christ, may I invite the Prime Minister to send a message of support to the millions of fellow Christians around the world who are suffering persecution? May I also invite him once again to remind the British people that we are a country fashioned by our Christian heritage, and which has resulted in our giving refuge to so many of other faiths over so many centuries, but that we will not tolerate those who abuse our freedom to try to inflict their alien and violent fashions upon us, particularly in the name of Islam? (*Hansard* 2015a: col 1552)

Cameron's response was as follows:

I join my hon. Friend in saying that we should do everything we can to defend and protect the right of Christians to practise their faith the world over. That is an important part of our foreign policy. ... Yes, Britain is a Christian country. I believe that the fact that we have an established faith and that we understand the place of faith in our national life makes us a more tolerant nation and better able to accommodate other faith groups in our country. That is why, as I said earlier, we should be proud that this is one of the most successful multi-ethnic, multi-faith, multi-religion democracies anywhere in the world. That is not in conflict with our status as a predominantly Christian country; that status is one of the reasons why we have done it. (*Hansard* 2015a: col 1553)

This was against the context of debates over whether persecuted Christian minorities from Syria and Northern Iraq should be prioritized by the UK Government.

On the eve of the refugee crisis, Hungary differed from most non-post-Soviet parts of the EU in number of ways. In recent history, Hungary's experience of migrants or refugees, particularly from non-European countries, was relatively scarce. In the twentieth century, this included groups of Greek left-wing refugees arriving in the 1950s as well as members of Hungarian-speaking minorities from neighbouring countries and about fifteen thousand largely self-employed migrants from China, who settled in Hungary in the 1980s and 1990s (Melegh 2020). However, the most significant experience of larger-scale migration was the arrival of Jewish migrants in the nineteenth century. Before the arrival of Syrian refugees, political discourses associated with topics such as the non-Christian population in Hungary or issues of religious tolerance other than between Christian communities were therefore associated with the Jewish population and heavily traumatized by historical anti-Semitism. The prior lack of domestic discourse on immigration in Hungary meant that concepts like 'multiculturalism' that are part of Western European discursive traditions on immigration were empty signifiers in the political context of Hungary. They could therefore be used and misused freely in political propaganda in a media space where no such prior discursive tradition existed. Furthermore, the Fidesz government, led by Prime Minister Viktor Orbán – which can be described as a hybrid or semi-authoritarian regime – developed a monopolistic capacity to set the agenda and drive home messages uncontested (Kovács and Trencsényi 2020).

## Mobilizations of memories of migration and displacement

The refugee crisis has often brought into sharp relief understandings, sometimes contested, of national memories of migration and displacement. In contrast to Western European countries' perception as 'immigration countries', Hungary has been an 'emigrant nation' in its recent history. This perception has played an important role in political discourses used by Hungary's prime minister, Viktor Orbán, in relation to the Syrian refugee crisis. Mass emigration is a distinctive feature of the modern history of Hungary, dating back to the turn of the nineteenth and twentieth centuries. Hungarians, thus, appear to be on the side of those who were helped in and by Western Europe. This is especially the case with the memory of emigration following the October 1956 uprising against the communist regime. The 1956 uprising has been largely perceived as a pivotal moment of history on which the legitimacy of the post-1990 political system has been based. One of the longest-lasting rhetorical elements of Fidesz, the right-wing national-conservative party in Hungary led by Orbán, has been anti-communism, and the mythical significance of the 1956 uprising has only strengthened over time.

The arrival of Hungarian refugees in Austria in 1956 marked a turning point in Europe's history of migration. The sheer numbers of Hungarian refugees and the fact they did not flee open warfare posed great challenges to the newly established system of international asylum. Hungary was also a scene for another significant moment in

European history, when it opened its borders to East Germans in 1989, facilitating a route to West Germany through Austria (the 'Pan-European Picnic'). No wonder that references to these refugee-friendly instances of Hungarian history were used even in the international press (Szirtes 2016; BBC News 2015b). The main problem for governmental communication in Hungary was the fact that reality did not fit its binary representations of Hungarians as 'good' and 'strong', of immigrants as 'evil' and of the West/the EU as 'weak'. This became particularly problematic in the context of political discourses employed against the backdrop of the anniversary celebrations of the 1956 uprising on 23 October, when anti-immigration became the central topic of government communications.

At a ceremony in 2015 commemorating the 1956 uprising, Lajos Kósa, then executive vice president of the Fidesz party, vehemently denied that the fence that Hungary had erected to repel migrants at its borders was reminiscent of the Iron Curtain. He claimed that 'as Hungarians did not hesitate to defend their country we cannot hesitate today: we have to defend Hungary, Europe and European values' (Kósa cited in *Propeller* 2015, trans. from the Hungarian original). Speaking at the commemoration organized by the Fidesz party, Minister Varga saw a similar parallel: 'The Hungarians' answer is the same as it was in 1956. Hungary protects itself, its borders and its liberty' (Varga cited in MTI 2015, trans. from the Hungarian original).

In the following year, Prime Minister Orbán's speech commemorating the sixtieth anniversary of the 1956 uprising centred on the notion of 'courage', presenting it as a black-and-white concept. Orbán argued that courage 'is not a virtue which can be measured and shared out with precision: people are either brave, or they are cowards' (Orbán 2016, trans. from the Hungarian original). He also made connections between the past and present by drawing parallels between the Hungarian government's contemporary response to the refugee crisis and historical events in 1956 and 1989 and referring to notions of national memory, history and fate:

> In 1956, after the Soviets pulled out of Austria, we sought to push the Iron Curtain back beyond our eastern border. We were brave and attacked the Soviet tanks with mere Molotov cocktails. In 1989 it was we who had to open our border, to let Germans find their way to other Germans. We were courageous and did this, despite the fact that Soviet forces were stationed here. And now, in 2015–2016, it is we who have had to close our border to stop the flood of migration from the South. Not once did we request the task – it was the work of history, and was brought on us by fate. All we have done is not run away and not back down – we have simply done our duty. We have continued to do our duty, even while being attacked from behind by those who we have in fact been protecting. (Orbán 2016, trans. from the Hungarian original)

The anti-immigration policy, thus, is not only presented as a binary choice but also as inevitable, predestined by fate.

In 2017 the Hungarian prime minister selected a most radical mix of conspiracy theories to connect 1956 with the Syrian refugee crisis, which was promoted by government-controlled media. He argued:

We wanted and continue to want the European Union to be a guarantee and a vehicle with which the European nations protect their shared ideas of civilisation. In reality, however, we have made ourselves more vulnerable than we used to be. In every crisis situation they cry 'Europe!', as if it was a magic word that on its own is capable of turning around our fate. Europe has found itself in a dead-end. We Hungarians know why, and we see this most clearly at times like this, on the twenty-third of October. In the twentieth century the trouble was caused by military empires, but now, in the slipstream of globalisation, it is financial empires that have risen up. They have no borders, but they have global media, and they have bought tens of thousands of people. They have no fixed structure, but they have extensive networks. They are fast, strong and brutal. It is this empire of financial speculation that has captured Brussels and several Member States. Until it regains its sovereignty, it will be impossible to turn Europe in the right direction. It is this empire that saddled us with modern-day mass population movement, with millions of migrants, and with a new migrant invasion. They developed a plan with which they now seek to turn Europe into a continent with a mixed population. We alone resist them now. We have reached the point at which Central Europe is the last migrant-free region in Europe. This is why the struggle for the future of Europe is being concentrated here. (Orbán 2017, trans. from the Hungarian original)

The fact, however, remained that at a very memorable point of European history, Hungarian refugees were welcomed by Western Europe, and this shaped Europe's current understanding of asylum and its humanitarian approach to migration in important ways. This fact did not remain unnoticed by foreign critics of the Hungarian governments' stance on migration. The Regional Representative of the UN Refugee Agency based in Budapest noted in an interview that the first Hungarians she met were refugees, referring to the two hundred thousand Hungarians who left the country in 1956 (Toth 2015). Furthermore, Frans Timmermans, vice president of the European Commission, asked the European Parliament, 'What would Europe have looked like if, in 1956, other Europeans had said "I do not mind where those Hungarians go, so long as they do not come to us"?' (Timmermans 2015).

It was the latter that prompted a government response highlighting some of the basic assumptions of the thinking behind anti-immigration policies. László Surján, a former vice president of the European Parliament, wrote an opinion piece in a Hungarian newspaper, which turned into a tirade against Western Europe in general. He presented the Hungarian asylum-seekers as good people ('you were enriched by two hundred thousand people capable of outstanding performance'), while he argued that the West had always been dishonest ('disgraceful', 'hypocritical' and 'self-righteous') – now as in 1956. He established a narrative distinguishing between 'good' and 'evil' refugees, contrasting present-day asylum-seekers with 'good' refugees fleeing Hungary in 1956: 'I do not know either, if you, Mr. Commissioner, really do not know the amount of cultural distance between two European nations, and you really do not see the amplitude of difference in thinking, culture and religion between Europeans and present-day asylum seekers, or you mix these up consciously.' He argued that there were no 'fake refugees' among the Hungarians in 1956 (László 2017).

In the UK, a key historical reference point during the Syrian refugee crisis was the *Kindertransport*, the rescue operation in 1938 and 1939 in which Jewish children were brought from Central Europe to remove them from the danger of the Nazis. The *Kindertransport* has been described by Sharples (2012: 16) as 'occupying a crucial place within Britain's historical consciousness' and 'one of the most written about refugee movements'. This position of the *Kindertransport* in the British historical imagination has been fixed in part because of the oral and written primary sources of those involved. However, as various scholars have noted, the representation of the *Kindertransport* in the British national narrative has been somewhat partial, 'perpetuating uncomplicated, celebratory and heroic accounts of the programme while ignoring some of its complexities and limitations' (Sharples 2012: 23). During the Syrian refugee crisis, the political rhetoric of both the 'right' and the 'left' tended to present the *Kindertransport* uncritically as evidence of a tradition of British toleration and welcome for refugees. Nevertheless, the *meaning* of the *Kindertransport* within the context of the crisis was contested. In a House of Commons debate on 'Refugees and Counter-Terrorism' in September 2015, the government policy of taking in twenty thousand refugees was criticized by the Labour (centre-left) Member of Parliament Gerald Kaufman as insufficient when contrasted with the *Kindertransport* as well as the German response:

> In the summer of 1939, my parents took into our home a young Jewish girl, Johanna, who had arrived in Leeds on the Kindertransport. Her sister and others had arrived on the same Kindertransport, and Neville Chamberlain facilitated the arrival of these young children more than this Government are facilitating such things now. It is sad that this Government are doing less than Neville Chamberlain did. The right hon. Gentleman says that he is going to take in 20,000 refugees over five years. The Germans took in 10,000 on one day. What kind of comparison is that? I recognise the financial problems and the assimilation problems, but if we do not do it now, we will live to regret it for the rest of our lives. (*Hansard* 2015b: col. 33)

In response, though, the Conservative (centre-right) prime minister, David Cameron, asserted:

> I believe that the 20,000 Syrian refugees – many of whom will be children – that we will take directly from the Syrian refugee camps are the modern equivalent of the Kindertransport, and this country should be proud of that. (*Hansard* 2015b: col. 33–4)

For Cameron, then, the response of the government was comparable with the *Kindertransport*, and therefore reflected a wider British history of welcome and toleration for refugees.

Population displacement was also a historical reference point in Germany during the Syrian refugee crisis in 2015, when comparisons were made with the experiences of millions of Germans who had lived in Eastern Europe and were fleeing or expelled from East Russia, Silesia, Czechoslovakia, Poland and Hungary after the Second World War. An example of this comparison is the banner that Leipzig city council put across their city hall in autumn 2015. This displayed two photographs next to each other. One showed a group of German refugees (three women and a child) leaving the Eastern European city of Gdansk at the end of the Second World War in 1945. The other showed a woman and a child walking through the ruins of the bombed city of Kobane in Syria in 2015. According to Leipzig city council, this banner 'documents what being a refugee means: hardship, distress, hopelessness, homelessness – regardless of centuries or continents' (*Leipziger Städtische Bibliotheken* 2015, trans. from the German original). Burkhard Jung (Social Democratic Party, SPD), who was the mayor of the city of Leipzig at the time stated:

> Just 70 years ago, tens of thousands of our parents and grandparents experienced first-hand what it means to lose your home. Practically every German family has some refugee experience – as displaced persons themselves or as people who took refugees in, who worked with them and lived with them after World War II. We then mastered this situation at a much worse time. Today we must succeed in managing and organising immigration. In that process we must not ask too much of either the refugees or the local population. (Jung cited in *Leipziger Städtische Bibliotheken* 2015, trans. from the German original)

This historical analogy was also picked up by President Joachim Gauck, who argued thus in a speech delivered in August 2015:

> And I would also like to remind you that in terrible times, when Germany was desperately poor and destroyed, it had to manage much greater challenges with large streams of refugees. Of course, people living in Germany today have forgotten this. But these were extreme challenges that this country managed to overcome. (Gauck cited in Welt 2015 trans. from the German original)

Another example of this is a parliamentary speech by Carsten Körber in September 2015. Körber is a member of the German national parliament, where he represents the Christian Democratic Union (CDU):

> As a nation we have experienced many big waves of refugees before. How many refugees from East Russia and Silesia did Germany integrate successfully after the Second World War at a time when it was extremely poor? Of course, the situation isn't entirely comparable as the people concerned were displaced persons from the Eastern German territories then, and they belonged to our country and our culture. How many people in the GDR [the former German Democratic Republic in East Germany] were refugees themselves or would have become refugees had the [Berlin] Wall not fallen so suddenly? We shouldn't forget all this. And we should talk about this, especially to those who have been out on the streets, already

shouting about the downfall of the Christian West. (Körber 2015: 11874D, trans. from the German original)

It is notable that Körber, Gauck and Jung use this historical analogy to promote solidarity and empathy and try to create a positive climate for the reception of contemporary refugees, a *Willkommenskultur* (welcoming culture). Körber not only refers to the experience of flight and expulsion in the immediate period following the Second World War but also to the experiences of people who fled the GDR across the border between East and West Germany during the decades when Germany was divided. However, Körber's reference to 'our country and culture' and to people 'shouting about the downfall of the Christian West' also emphasizes difference, refers to processes of othering (of predominantly Muslim refugees). It also hints at controversies around this comparison. Indeed, questions have been raised around the extent to which generalizations can be made about these different forms of migration experiences, and whether recent representations of the integration of 13 million displaced people after the war might be more 'rosy' than the lived reality at the time. The historian Carmen Winkel, for example, argues that the 'approximation of forced migration from Syria with Flucht und Vertreibung (flight and expulsion) of Germans after WWII' has been 'decontextualized' and instrumentalized in political discourses and, in her view, this is 'not suitable as a standard of comparison' (Winkel 2019: 23).

While the Spanish central government did not pursue a national hosting policy comparable to that of Germany (as the country that has received the most asylum applications in recent years), regional governments have criticized the central government's lack of solidarity towards refugees (Villaverde Ferreño and Cruz Pérez 2019). Associations of Spanish national memory drew parallels between the experiences of Syrian refugees and those of Spanish refugees from the Civil War (1936–9) and the Franco regime (Pérez Baquero 2020: 241).

An Association of Former Members of Parliament and Ex-Senators of the General Courts also demanded the approval of a specific protocol to cater for the needs of Syrian refugees arriving in Spain, reminding the government of the fact that there were people who had to leave Spain because of the Spanish Civil War. In their opinion, 'it is a duty of humanitarian and political solidarity' to act in support of these refugees (Europa Press 2015).

However, the most important social actors that mobilized the memories of the Spanish Civil War were the cultural and civil society associations who expressed their solidarity with the Syrian refugees at a local level by drawing parallels between their experiences and those of the refugees from the Spanish Civil War. This also coincided with events commemorating the eightieth anniversary of the end of the Spanish Civil War and the exile of thousands of Spaniards in France, North Africa and Latin America. While both cities were governed by left-wing independent coalitions, the mayors of Barcelona and Madrid adopted the 'Refugees Welcome' campaign which was explained as follows:

The aim of Refugees Welcome is to create a Culture of Welcome among the citizens and to promote a real integration of the refugees who live in our house and who have many problems to access housing. The non-profit organization puts displaced people / refugees in contact with local citizens who are willing to share housing in conditions of horizontality and mutual respect. Refugees Welcome is an international initiative that was born in Germany 3 years ago and has achieved more than 1,100 coexistence in the 12 countries of the European Union, Canada and Australia where the project has been developed. The entity has been present in Catalonia (Barcelona) since May 2017. (Ajuntament de Barcelona 2015, trans. from the Spanish original)

The campaign adopted by the mayors of Madrid and Barcelona had the intention of providing housing to refugees by connecting locals with refugees. On a local level, exhibitions, documentary films, graphic novels and theatre plays drawing parallels between the experience of Spanish Civil War exiles and the current situation of Syrian refugees were used to show and encourage solidarity with Syrian refugees. Although these local initiatives did not receive as much media attention as political speeches at the national level, the support these initiatives received by the local population is worth mentioning. Despite their transnational scope, according to Javier Alcalde y Martín Portos (2018), citizens' mobilizations are deeply rooted at the local level. Furthermore, the absence of anti-refugee protests in Spain led by racist countermovements is also a sign that the majority of the local population supported the hosting of refugees in Spain.

Parallels between the experiences of the Spanish and Syrian Civil Wars were also used by politicians at national and international levels. When visiting an integration project for refugees in Berlin, Pedro Sánchez, general secretary of the Spanish Socialist Party, told a young Syrian that Spain, because of its own history, understands the drama of a civil war very well:

We suffered a long time ago from a civil war and many Spaniards left, especially to Germany and France, and we feel very closely what you are suffering now. (EFE 2016, trans. from the Spanish original)

Also, in the Spanish parliament, several interventions by different members of the parliament have drawn on historical narratives and memories. Discussions around the proposal of the Parliamentary Socialist Group on the situation of the Syrian refugees on 29 September 2015 is one of these examples. In her contribution to this debate, Esperanza Esteve, member of the Socialist Group at the Congress of Representatives, recalled the images of Spanish people fleeing to France and Latin America and appealed to the memory of the Spanish exiles and their trauma:

Today it's Syria, it's Eritrea, it's all those countries where every day we see images of horror, but before it was us. Let's remember the images after our Civil War, fleeing to France and Latin America: 800,000 people were displaced. The memory is sometimes short and it is a matter of not losing it and of understanding that there are dynamics in this global world that generate injustice and defenselessness of human beings and that sometimes the very countries that we welcome are the cause of them; it is cause, response, responsibility, where it begins and where it ends. (Esteve cited in Propuesta de No Ley 2015: 32, trans. from the Spanish original)

Carlos Martínez Gorriarán, of the group Union, Progress and Democracy, was harsher in his criticism of the 'Spanish amnesia' towards its own 'expelled people'. He goes back to the history of the Jews and the Moriscos and the twentieth-century Civil War. This is a recurrent narrative, that of al-Andalus and later the history of Moriscos, which again appeared when dealing with the Syrian refugees:

> Spain is a country that has a terrible historical tradition of producing refugees. We have been a country that has expelled large masses of people. In 1492 it expelled the Jews, in 1609 the Moors and during the Civil War there were hundreds of thousands of people who moved within the territory itself from one area to another and hundreds of thousands more who left as a result of Franco's victory. Therefore, we should be a country with a special sensibility to realise that whenever a tide of refugees is provoked, what is absent is democracy, and not only democracy, but the consideration of our fellow human beings as equals in the democratic sense of the term. (Martínez Gorriarán cited in Propuesta de No Ley 2015: 36, trans. from the Spanish original)

The utilization and contestation of examples of migration and population displacement has been evident in political discourses in Hungary, the UK, Germany and Spain. In the UK, the underlying issue was whether or not contemporary political policies were living up to the imagined tradition and standards of British welcome and whether tolerance was evident in the *Kindertransport*. In comparison, in German and Spain, the relationship between history and the present day was often presented in terms of empathy, arising from the experience of the historic past. In Spain, furthermore, as we saw in the arguments by Carlos Martínez Gorriarán, history was also referenced with a sense of shame – in the case of the expulsion of Muslims and Jews – and also with the caution that the treatment of migrants reflects on the vitality of democracy. By contrast, in Hungary, political discourses employed by the national conservative Fidesz government mobilized memories of migration and displacement in order to justify anti-immigration policies.

## The mobilization of discourses of European identity and anti-European sentiment

Europe is an ideological structure of fluid borders and definitions, given that it is predominantly a political and epistemological, rather than geographical, category. From Hegel to the most contemporary postcolonial thinkers, the majority of scholars agree that, as an epistemological category, Europe is often defined and shaped by its 'Others', that is, formed as an antithesis to its opposites or outsiders. This has also been the case with discursive constructions of the concept of Europe and European identity in political discourses employed in Hungary, Germany, the UK and Spain in the context of the Syrian refugee crisis, which have drawn on narratives about the Christians roots of Europe or a 'Clash of Civilizations' (Huntington 1997) between the East and the West. Some discourses have inflamed fears of the Islamization of Europe, presenting Muslim migrants as posing a threat to Europe's Christian and secular roots, values and identity. These discourses often perpetuate negative stereotypes of refugees; for example, by associating refugees with abuse of the social welfare system or with crime. They can also present NGOs, individuals and civil society organizations who try to defend the rights of refugees in extremely negative terms. For example, during the electoral campaign for the Andalusian Parliament, Santiago Abascal, the leader of VOX, a recently emerged right-wing party in Spain, argued that by 2050 '50% of French population would be Muslim'. Furthermore, just after entering the Andalusian Parliament for the first time, Iván Espinosa de los Monteros, the vice-secretary of the party, stated that 'Spain does not have the duty to attend to 400 millions of migrants' (Monzón et al. 2019).

On numerous occasions, these discourses are modelled on those who have been employed by extreme right-wing leaders and populist movements in countries like the United States, Hungary, France, Germany, Italy and Brazil. In Spain, Santiago Abascal insists on expanding the idea of a supposed 'invasion of Europe', warning of a risk of 'an Islamized Europe', like the right-wing populist *AfD* in Germany. Far-right Eurosceptic populist parties – like UKIP (the United Kingdom Independence Party) or the Brexit Party in the UK or the *AfD* in Germany – have also capitalized on people's fears and anxieties about the potential impact of the arrival of large numbers of refugees from different countries.

In the UK, Nigel Farage, leader of the right-wing populist UKIP which argued for a BREXIT referendum, suggested support for giving 'some Christians refugee status' in April 2015 in the run-up to the UK election. Part of the context was that UKIP had been making a case for the UK as a 'fundamentally Christian nation' and published a Christian manifesto titled *Valuing Our Christian Heritage* (UKIP 2015), which argued for full consideration of 'our Judeo-Christian heritage', whilst claiming that 'other parties have deliberately marginalised our nation's faith' (for overview see Roose 2021: 121). As Strømmen and Schmiedel (2020) argue, the implications of these claims are evident:

> If Christianity or Judaeo-Christianity is central to the Constitution, the culture and the character of the country, what is it that's unconstitutional, uncultured and uncharacteristic? The answer is, of course: the Muslim migrant. There's no need for the manifesto to name Islam. The claim to Christianity as Judaeo-Christianity does the trick. The resonances to wider trends in Europe are loud and clear.

In the case of Spain, these newly emerged right-wing actors have once again reappropriated the concept of 'Reconquista' in a new manner not seen since the Francoist dictatorship when it was used to attack leftists, atheists and those who were on the margins of the Franco regime's national-Catholic imagination. This notion of the 'Reconquista' as studied by García Sanjuán bears the idea that there is a recovery of something previously lost (García Sanjuán 2020: 139). This notion relies on the idea that Muslims took over the Iberian Peninsula illegitimately and aims to delegitimize the Muslim presence on the Medieval Iberian Peninsula and emphasize the right of Christians to take it over (García Sanjuán 2020: 140). In the context of the celebrations of the *Toma de Granada* (Conquest of Granada), a yearly event that has been largely criticized because it commemorates the end of Islamic Spain and later expulsion of the Jews and Moriscos, Santiago Abascal vindicated this event by saying that 'Centuries later, the indelible pride of a seven-century achievement remains. And there remains the determination not to submit to Islam' (Barreira 2019).

Existing literature on political discourse and the refugee crisis positions Spain as an exceptional case due to the absence of an extreme right-wing party in the decades following the end of the Franco regime (Zapata-Barrero, González and Montiijano 2008). However, since the far-right party VOX gained visibility and won parliamentary seats in 2019, VOX has been setting the social and political agenda on the issue of immigration, drawing on national and transnational memories. Discourses used by VOX in the Spanish context of debates about refugees share many similarities with discourses used by other far-right populist parties in Europe, such as the German *AfD* or UKIP in the UK (Monzón et al. 2019). Paradoxically, it has been right-wing populist Eurosceptic parties that often emphasize the existence of a common European heritage to justify their anti-immigration policies. As De Cesari, Bosilkov and Piacentini (2020: 27–8) argue:

> In this discourse, Islam and the figure of the Muslim are placed in the position of the other. Such deep preoccupation with an alleged Islamic civilization threat ('Islamization' is the code word for stoking fears of Europe's disappearance) drives a paradoxical stance: the combination of 'identitarian Christianism' with a fervent defence of secularism and liberal values such as gender equality, gay rights and freedom of speech – which coexist with the traditional social conservatism and illiberal authoritarianism of the far right.

By contrast, Orbán's Fidesz government has discursively framed anti-European sentiment in terms of a critique of Western European countries, blaming their history of colonialization for the refugee crisis, whilst expressing contempt for 'a perceived Western liberal cultural imperialism from the European Union' (Mark, Kalinosvky and Marung 2020: 24). From this point of view, Eastern Europe is presented as the 'real' centre of Christianity. Initially, discourses employed by the Hungarian government centred on the theme of 'welfare migration', based on claims similar to those made by far-right populist movements in Western Europe. These were new to the Hungarian public, 'given that prior to 2015, immigration rarely played a significant role on Hungarian political discourse' (Bocskor 2018: 554). From 2015 onwards, anti-immigration became a central topic of discourses employed by the Fidesz government, including the use of anti-Muslim stereotypes and an increasing focus on Christianity in government propaganda. This included the conflation of 'immigrants' and 'refugees' (diminishing their need for protection) and the association of 'immigration' with 'terrorism'. These discourses referred to acts of terrorism in Western Europe to present refugees as dangerous. The idea of a fundamental cultural difference between immigrant and native communities had already become apparent in Orbán's first interview in the aftermath of the *Charlie Hebdo* attacks in 2015. However, over time there was an increasing amount of references to religion in political discourses employed by the Fidesz government in the context of the refugee crisis. 'Otherness' of refugees and migrants became increasingly associated with Islam, while the idea of 'European culture', supposedly 'under siege', received also different interpretations tied partly to notions of Christianity.

As early as in January 2015, the Fidesz government called for an extraordinary 'debate day' in parliament. During a debate on the topic 'Hungary Does Not Need Welfare Immigration', government MPs used very harsh language about refugees, arguing, for example, that 'their clothes should be collected on the border to prevent Hungarians from touching them as those can bring diseases in the country' (*Országgyűlési Napló* 2015: 7418) and erasing the line between categories of 'economic migration', 'refugees' and 'asylum seekers'. A 'national consultation', a form of national survey introduced by the Orbán government in which the government asks the public leading questions, was announced on the topic of 'welfare immigration'. In April, a letter signed by Viktor Orbán and bearing his picture was posted to every Hungarian citizen explaining that the instances of terror in the news show that 'Brussels and the European Union is not capable of handling the question of immigration' and that 'welfare migrants posed as asylum seekers, but factually [were] coming for social benefits and jobs'. The questions included in this survey were very leading, asking, for example, 'Some say that welfare migrants put the jobs and welfare of Hungarians in jeopardy. Do you agree?' (*Nemzeti konzultáció* 2015: 1, trans. from the Hungarian original). In June, the government announced its billboard campaign against migration, costing more than a million Euros to the Hungarian taxpayers.

From the end of 2015, Viktor Orbán equated 'the European man' with 'the Western, Christian man' explaining what he meant by 'civilisation, the race [species] to which we belong'. Using these terms interchangeably, he opposed immigration in the context of an alleged 'invasion of Europe' (Orbán 2015, trans. from the Hungarian original). Orbán presented multiculturalism in terms of a coexistence of Christian Hungarians or Europeans with non-Christians, and claimed that this coexistence was not possible. These claims do not just bear serious consequences for Muslims. For instance, in the context of nineteenth-century Jewish immigration, these claims can also be regarded as strongly anti-Semitic.

## Conclusion

Our analysis of political discourses employed in Hungary, Germany, the UK and Spain in the context of the Syrian refugee crisis shows that they often mobilize national and transnational memories when presenting issues related to religious diversity and migration in contemporary society. References to collective memory have played an important role in discourses employed in these debates, for example, by creating links between national or European identities, to address or avert tensions between humanitarian principles, domestic pressures and expectations of the international community. Notions of race, ethnicity, culture and religion are often implicated, conflated and intertwined in these discourses, as are references to Judeo-Christian heritage and secular Enlightenment values.

Transnational memories employed within political discourses in these debates have often been embedded in national contexts and narratives, such as Spanish and British myths of tolerance, Germany's efforts to come to terms with its Nazi past or the notion of Hungary as the 'real' Christian centre of Europe. Notions of religious history and heritage, particularly Europe's Judeo-Christian heritage, have to different degrees been instrumentalized in these discourses in very different ways and for different, contrasting purposes: both to foster toleration and compassion, and to stoke fears of cultural, ethnic and religious difference, including the perceived threat of the 'Islamization of Europe'. Particularly in right-wing political discourses, there is little acknowledgement of the internal diversity of refugees (who are predominantly presented as young Muslim men) or of Islam as well as a tendency to conflate 'refugees' and 'migrants', but to distinguish between 'deserving' and 'undeserving' migrants (who allegedly have a hidden agenda, such as the Islamization of Europe).

The discursive framing of the arrival of large numbers of refugees as a 'crisis', and associations with security concerns in particular, highlight 'anxieties in Europe about diversity and change' (Holmes and Castañeda 2016: 13) and reflect insecurities and tensions around notions of European identity. While political discourses employed by the Fidesz government in Hungary stand out as particularly unwelcoming and hostile to Muslim refugees, there are clear parallels with discourses employed by right-wing populist movements in the UK, Germany and Spain that have been growing in popularity. Paradoxically, far-right populist parties have both utilized Eurosceptic sentiments in support of their anti-immigration stance, whilst also appealing to a sense of a common and shared European history, presenting Europe as both the centre of Christianity and of secularity.

The extent to which representations of history, and religious history in particular, have been weaponized and contested in political discourses in Europe about the refugee crisis highlights the important public role of academic research in offering nuanced, critical perspectives on the past. Given the specific interest of this volume in youth, this also highlights the need to promote and support the development of historical and religious literacy in education to equip young people to critically assess oversimplified representations of the past, and of religious history in particular, and raise awareness of the internal diversity and complexity of religious traditions.

# Commemorating the Good Friday Agreement (1998) and the Ohrid Framework Agreement (2001)

Lidija Georgieva, Naum Trajanovski and John Wolffe

## Introduction

Northern Ireland and North Macedonia, situated though they are at opposite ends of Europe, have many superficial similarities. They have comparably sized populations: at the most recent census in 2002, North Macedonia had 2.02 million inhabitants; at that in 2011 Northern Ireland had 1.81 million; projections for 2020 are 2.08 million and 1.91 million, respectively.[1] Both have substantial minorities for whom ethnic and national identity is closely bound up with religion. In Northern Ireland, in 2011, 48.7 per cent of the population had a Protestant upbringing and 48.4 per cent (including those with hybrid identities such as British and Northern Irish) identify as British; 45.1 per cent had a Catholic upbringing while 46.2 per cent identify solely as Irish or Northern Irish (Northern Ireland Statistics and Research Agency 2012). In North Macedonia, in 2002, 64.2 per cent of the population identified as Macedonian, 25.2 per cent as Albanian, 3.9 per cent as Turkish and 2.7 per cent as Roma, 1.8 per cent as Serbs, with the balance made up of smaller minorities (Georgieva, Memeti and Musliu 2011). Here too religious identifications closely align with ethnic ones: 64.7 per cent of the population are Orthodox Christians, and 33.3 per cent are Muslims. There is also a small Roman Catholic community: the Pope visited the country in 2019 for the first time.

There are also significant historical parallels. Both states emerged in the turbulent first quarter of the twentieth century as parts of larger entities, the UK, and in the Macedonian case the Ottoman Empire and, afterwards, the Kingdom of Yugoslavia. During that period both were shaped by the memory of experiences of heroic but failed rebellion, the Ilinden Uprising of August 1903 and the Easter Rising of April 1916, while Northern Ireland Protestants had a comparably emotive collective memory of the sacrifice of the two thousand men of the Ulster Division who died on the first day of the Battle of the Somme in July 1916. These years also saw the partition of both Macedonia and Ireland, by the Treaty of Bucharest of 1913 which separated what was to become the Republic of Macedonia and then North Macedonia from the southern part of Macedonia that became part of Greece and so-called Pirin Macedonia (Blagoevgrad Province), which became part of Bulgaria. The Anglo-Irish Treaty of 1921 separated the six counties of Northern Ireland from the twenty-six counties that formed the Irish Free State and subsequently the Republic of Ireland. Most recently, both countries have experienced escalation of internal violent conflict, the Northern Ireland Troubles of 1969–98 and the relatively short-lived confrontation between the Macedonian government and the Albanian National Liberation army in 2001. Such long and deep historical memories continue to shape the legacy of the respective settlements of these conflicts, the Belfast/Good Friday Agreement of 1998 (GFA) and the Ohrid Framework Agreement of 2001 (OFA), which are the primary focus of this chapter.

Current research on peace agreements aims to broaden the scope of investigation by discussing their contextual, social and legal aspects, as well as the complex phenomena of political violence, and the scope of the state- and non-state actors involved in violent conflicts (for an overview, see Bell 2008). From a conflict resolution studies perspective, two major approaches are traceable as paradigms within the most recent scholarship: one which places the agency of the international community as a prime concern (Richmond 2014), and the other one which highlights the need for recognizing the local context (Newman et al. 2009). In both scholarly streams, the role of religion in violent conflict and in its resolution emerges as a key issue, although caution should be exercised in labelling a conflict as 'religious'. It is thus a challenging task to identify and map the specific roles of religious actors in actual and discursive violence, and in complex wider conflicts, conflict resolutions, peacemaking and peacebuilding (Mayer et al. 2013).

This chapter draws upon these debates in exploring official and vernacular memories of the Good Friday and Ohrid Framework Agreements and post-conflict peacebuilding activities.[2] As part of the H2020 RETOPEA project, it draws on research on the various sociopolitical and commemorative features of the peace treaties within the project's scope. RETOPEA also provides an interdisciplinary platform for comparing various cross-country developments concerning the social memory of the conflicts under discussion. We argue that one should look at the various commemorations of the two agreements in order to better understand the sociopolitical dimensions and bottom-up reactions in the post-conflict situation and in peacebuilding. This chapter presumes an analytic dichotomy between official and informal memory, with the former being understood as a set of state-sponsored or elite memory practices and policies, while the latter is focused on mapping the informal, bottom-up practices of remembrance and commemorating.

## Memory, conflict, religion

Scholarly analysis of both Northern Ireland and North Macedonia has highlighted the importance of individual and collective memories in the state- and nation-building processes. Such theoretical approaches can be traced back to Maurice Halbwachs's concept of the 'social frameworks of memory' first enunciated in the 1920s, but only gaining widespread currency in the later twentieth century. Collective memory came to be seen as an important factor in the development of 'imagined communities' of an ethnic, national or transnational nature (e.g. Anderson 1983; Assmann 2010). While the literature has been largely dominated by social scientists and historians, a notable early contribution on Northern Ireland came from a primarily theological perspective (Falconer 1988). Since 1998, interest in both long-term collective historical memories (e.g. McBride 2001; Grayson and McGarry 2016) and the more personal recollection and commemoration of the Troubles by those who have lived through them (e.g. Conway 2010; Frawley 2014; Viggiani 2014; Smyth 2017) has gathered momentum. As for North Macedonia, Trajanovski (2020b) has recently examined post-2001 memory politics and memory regimes.

Most recently, contemporary debates in memory studies have shifted their focus from the initial Halbwachsian collective societal representations to the individual social actors' agency and their discursive practices (e.g. Gensburger 2016). There has been a wave of research on 'memory/mnemonic actors' (for an overview, see Kubik and Bernhard 2014a; 2014b), 'memory entrepreneurs' (e.g. Kaiser 2012) and 'memory agents' (e.g. Zelizer 2014). In Central and Eastern European scholarship, Jan Kubik and Michael Bernhard developed a theoretical model of 'memory regimes' as the interplay of the 'mnemonic actors' in a given national, political, societal and cultural synchronic constellation. According to the authors, the 'mnemonic actors' are defined as the 'political forces that are interested in a specific interpretation of the past' (2014a: 4).

Meanwhile the wider literature on memory and conflict resolution has generated insights relevant to both Northern Ireland and North Macedonia. The most active scholars propose novel methodological approaches and seek to determine the specific patterns and trajectories of social behaviour across different comparative contexts. In 2016, McGrattan and Hopkins explored the 'roles that memory may play in overcoming division'. This theme is also developed in a recent special issue of *East European Politics*, which builds upon earlier comparative research on the 'relationship between identity and war' while examining afresh 'the dynamics of grassroots peacebuilding, and the language of sexualized violence in war' (Harris and Baumann 2019: 404). Social memory, its politicization and securitization, its identity-building features, and its potential for social mobilization, becomes a basis for developing frameworks of interpretation for cross-national case studies. Harris and Baumann argue that 'history and the memory of it are not necessarily the same – the events and dates may be the same, but the interpretation of the context within which they happened is ... the matter of politics' (405). In similar vein, a 2019 special issue of *Innovation* journal addressed the subject through the concept of 'memory wars' (Pohoryles 2019). In his discussion of the 'politically constructed mnemonic tensions in the years preceding Yugoslavia's violent dissolution', Taylor McConnel (2019) coined the phrase 'memory abuse' with reference to the 'intentional manipulation of memory beyond an intangible threshold'. Recent scholarship has also explored memory activities in a variety of post-traumatic settings (e.g. Gray and Oliver 2004; Eyerman 2019).

Moreover, in both the case studies, religion has played a central role in the shaping of memory.[3] Although the immediate causes of the Northern Ireland Troubles were more political and social than religious, the confessionally polarized views of the past that have shaped Catholic and Protestant identities on the island of Ireland were a key precondition for the conflict (Elliott 2009). Conversely, since the publication in 1988 of *Reconciling Memories* (Falconer 1988), religious actors have been prominent in the endeavour to establish a narrative that highlights peacemaking rather than division (e.g. Falconer and Liechty 1998; Brewer, Higgins and Teeney 2011). As for North Macedonia, religion was an identity-marker during the late Ottoman Empire (see Clayer 2007 for an overview). The demise of the empire at the turn of the last century and the rise of local nationalisms further impacted the way religious boundaries were set in the post-imperial Balkans (for an overview, see Pandevska 2012; Pandevska and Mitrova 2019). After the Second World War the formation of the Macedonian state within socialist Yugoslavia was followed by institutionalization of the religious life of the two major communities in Macedonia: the Orthodox Christian one, which established the separate Macedonian Orthodox Church in the 1960s, and the Islamic community, which was organized by the Sarajevo-based Reis-ul-ulema during socialist Yugoslavia, and the Skopje-based Islamic Community of Macedonia after the state became independent in 1991.

# Ohrid Framework Agreement

## Introduction

Unlike the other constituent states of former socialist Yugoslavia, the Republic of Macedonia only experienced the escalation of violent conflict in 2001, almost ten years after its officially declared independence in 1991. The seven months of armed confrontations between the Macedonian state security forces and the ethnic Albanian rebels of the National Liberation Army (NLA) were mirrored by a heated public debate on the reasons for the escalating violence (Ackermann 2001: 117–35). Hitherto, interpretations of the *casus belli*, the military operations and the settlement are predominantly centred around two axes: the growth of interethnic hostilities in post-Yugoslav Macedonia and the impact of the regional violent contestations in Kosovo and southern Serbia on the Macedonian state and society. Both these approaches, however, recognize the different sets of identity-markers between the conflicting sides: the language, ethnicity and religious affiliation of the major ethnic group in today's North Macedonia, Macedonians, and the largest minority group, Albanians, as well as the means of political accommodation of the multiethnic population in the newly formed state.

Religious affiliation – with the Macedonians being predominantly Orthodox Christians and the Albanians Muslims – was identified as a lesser factor in the emergence of violent conflict in 2001 (for an overview, see Bellamy 2002). Rather, religious affiliation was part of the wider process of ethnonationalization in the 1990s. In this decade, there were several calls for an Albanian secession, while the Albanian political parties highlighted the 1991 constitution as a main generator of discontent – stressing its nation-centred configuration and favouring of Macedonian cultural, religious and ethnic symbols. On the other hand, the ethnic Macedonian political elites treated the non-voting of the Albanian MPs in the parliament and the organization of an Albanian plebiscite for independence in the early 1990s as proof of the Albanian citizens' disloyalty to the state *in toto*. These developments further challenged the ontological security of post-Yugoslav Macedonia and contributed to the hostilities in 2001 and the Ohrid Framework Agreement (OFA). The OFA was drafted in Villa Biljana, Ohrid, North Macedonia, in July and August 2001. It was concluded in Skopje on 13 August 2001 and signed by the president of the Republic of Macedonia, and the leaders of the state's major political parties, and brokered by representatives of the European Union (EU) and the United States.

From a present-day perspective, OFA is praised as an agreement that contributed to a ceasefire and stopped a full-scale civil war in the Republic of North Macedonia. According to historian Ulf Brunnbauer (2002), the violent conflict resulted in more than two hundred casualties and over a hundred thousand exiled and internally displaced persons. Hitherto, OFA – or the 'new chapter in the development of Macedonian democracy' (Aleksovska 2015: 55) – has been primarily discussed from peacebuilding, political power-sharing and conflict settlement perspectives. It is argued that OFA paved the way for a constitutional reform adopted in November 2001, which was instrumental for developing the so-called 'Macedonian model of soft power-sharing' (Bieber 2008; Ilievski and Wolff 2011; Georgieva, Memeti and Musliu 2011; Horowitz 2014).[4] The symbolic developments instigated by OFA were explored in recent scholarship, mostly relating to the 'Skopje 2014' project which was publicized in the late 2000s (see, inter alia, Frčkoski 2011; Bliznakovski 2013; Dimova 2013; Čupeska 2013; for an overview of the debate over 'Skopje 2014', see Trajanovski 2020a). The memory aftershocks of OFA and the 2001 conflict were discussed predominantly by foreign authors (see Ragaru 2008; Reef 2018), while several collections of oral histories of the conflict were published in the last decade (see the publications of Peace Actions and the Center for Human Rights and Conflict Resolution; also Stojanov et al. 2019). There has, however, been no systematic analysis of the memory regimes, bottom-up memory practices and state-sponsored activities relating to OFA and the 2001 conflict.

A close look at memory developments over OFA and the 2001 conflict is also critical for understanding the dynamics of religion in post-conflict North Macedonia. As observed by Alex J. Bellamy (2002: 120), 'religion has been something of a side issue in the Macedonian conflict, limited only to the demands that a reference to the Orthodox Church be removed from the constitution'. This was, in fact, accomplished in the OFA: the Agreement envisioned a Parliamentary Committee for Inter-Community Relations responsible for deliberation on issues concerning intercommunity relations, while freedom of religion and a recognition of other religious traditions alongside the Macedonian Orthodox Church (MOC) were introduced by amending Article 19 of the 1991 Constitution.[5] This resulted in MOC taking a critical stance towards OFA and a series of 'public exchanges' between MOC and the Islamic Community of Macedonia in 2001 (Latifi 2001). Religious affiliation, as an identity-marker in the post-conflict constellation, was instrumental for the engineering of what Ljubica Spaskovska (2012: 385) calls 'a specific *ethnizenship*' – or a citizenship regime where 'citizens realise their rights, duties and participation in the public and political sphere solely as members of ethno-national or religious communities'. This new citizenship regime also manifested as a particular 'ethnocracy' – in the words of Goran Janev (2011) – which delineates the 'binary logic' of the political representation of ethnonationalism and religion in the Macedonian public space in the aftermath of the conflict. The history of memory-related activities over OFA provides another critical standpoint from which to view these developments.

## The initial reception

The initial public discourses over OFA in Macedonia illuminate elite sociopolitical tensions over the 2001 conflict. In the early post-conflict years public narratives usually related the settlement to the memory of the war and there was a lack of any distinct memory discourse regarding OFA itself. To contextualize, just days before the signing of the OFA and under a general ceasefire, a massive ambush took place in the vicinity of Karpalak (8 August 2001), taking the lives of ten members of the Macedonian security forces (which in turn resulted in the demolition of the Bazaar Mosque in Prilep, the birthplace of the victims of the Karpalak ambush). A further attack took place near Ljuboten (10 August 2001), when the Albanian rebels killed eight members of the Macedonian security forces. These two events profoundly influenced the memory of OFA in the following years, shaping both the top-down and the bottom-up commemorative practices in ways that will be discussed in the next section. Moreover, initially, settlement of the conflict was by no means complete – sporadic shootings in Albanian-populated areas occurred until 2003 (Dnevnik 2003), the law on territorial organization projected in OFA was only enacted in 2004 (Markovikj and Damjanovski 2018), and Albanian was not inaugurated as a second official language in the city of Skopje until 2005.[6]

In this context, the Democratic Union for Integration (DUI), an Albanian political party formed in May 2002 and largely made up of former National Liberation Army fighters, promoted itself as the main custodian of the memory of OFA and organized the only commemorative events to take place on the anniversaries in 2002 and 2003. The 2003 commemoration, at the winter resort of Popova Šapka, is the best illustration of how it represented the memory: without endorsement from the state or representation from the ethno-Macedonian political camp, the reception was attended by representatives of NATO, the Organization for Security and Co-operation in Europe (OSCE) and members of the diplomatic corps who praised the agreement in their media statements (Vest 2003). The two subsequent OFA commemorations, organized by DUI, were in line with this partisan promotion of ethnonationalism and exclusivism, taking place in Albanian-populated Raduša (2004) and the ethnically mixed town of Struga (2005). The fifth anniversary of OFA in 2006 was also marked by a partisan commemoration organized by DUI in Ohrid, the place where the OFA was negotiated. Teuta Arifi, vice president of DUI in the early 2000s, commented that 'as every year', the diplomatic corps, state institutions and members of all the political parties are invited without exception to the celebration as the party (DUI) 'believes that the values of OFA are for all the citizens' of the state (A1 2006). It is important to note, however, that the then Macedonian president, Branko Crvenkovski, organized a reception in Ohrid on the fifth annual commemoration of OFA, just a few days after

DUI's ceremony – the first ever state-sponsored commemoration of OFA in the state. The event was attended by the US ambassador in Skopje, Gillian Milovanovic, whose absence from DUI's event was interpreted as shifting American support away from that political party (Opetčeska 2006).

However, the failure of the ethno-Macedonian political camp to commemorate OFA in a structured manner did not amount to a complete omission to produce memory discourses regarding the Agreement. In this period, the favourable reaction of the international community to OFA helped the ethnic Macedonian elites to articulate a positive view of integrating Macedonia into Euro-Atlantic alignments as its only viable sociopolitical future. Hence in 2002, Boris Trajkovski, then president of the republic and one of the OFA signatories, stated that the Agreement was a significant 'step forward' towards the consolidation of the Macedonian interethnic balance (A1 2002a). This position was restated at several post-2001 ceremonies commemorating the Ilinden uprising on Republic Day, the major Macedonian state holiday since the state's inception in the aftermath of the Second World War. Trajkovski, affiliated with the centre-right VMRO-DPMNE (Internal Macedonian Revolutionary Organization – Democratic Party for Macedonian National Unity), was the major proponent of this discourse at the Ilinden commemorations, aiming to establish the annual Kruševo-based event as a platform for celebrating the state's regional Euro-Atlantic aspirations (Trajanovski 2020b). A failed initiative for a cross-border, Macedonian-Albanian organization of the Struga Poetry Evenings in 2005, an annual festival with a tradition dating back to the early 1960s, can be seen in the same light.

However, this forward-looking position did not prevail in the political domain in the early post-conflict years. A newspaper article on 13 August 2002, the first anniversary of OFA, neatly summarized the dominant atmosphere in the Macedonian political camp: 'the anniversary of the Ohrid-Skopje agreement will be remembered as a successful period of NATO's and EU's political-peacebuilding mission. The day of the signing of OFA is a historical date only because of the ceasefire. It will not be celebrated as a date of the reshaping of Macedonia' (A1 2002d). This period was also formative in the articulation of a critical perspective on the OFA in the Macedonian political camp, as can be illustrated by examining the memory discourses of the relevant sociopolitical actors. Ljubčo Georgievski, former VMRO-DPMNE leader and one of the signatories of OFA, claimed that it questioned the 'history of good inter-ethnic relations', while the Socialist Party, in an official statement in 2002, stated that the signing of the Agreement is nothing else but a 'shameful treason' (A1 2002c).[7] Nikola Gruevski, minister of finance and prime minister in the second VMRO-DPMNE government (2006–16), which will be further discussed in the following section, also criticized the laws on territorial division and on self-government which OFA required. In his words, 'whether it will succeed or not, we will see, because there are still strong radical structures that see the Framework Agreement only as a means to reach another ultimate goal, which is called the realisation of some great dreams for another state (Albania), and that other state has territorial claims to the Republic of Macedonia' (A1 2002b). However, shortly after forming the second VMRO-DPMNE government, he changed his position and endorsed OFA as an important cornerstone for the future of Macedonia.

## Memory of the conflict and memory of the settlement

The year 2002 brought the second governmental change in the democratic history of North Macedonia. VMRO-DPMNE stepped down, and the centre-left Social Democratic Union of Macedonia (SDSM) formed a government in a coalition with DUI. However, although easing some of the immediate political tensions, the new coalition did not significantly change underlying stances towards the OFA. From an analytical standpoint there was a dichotomy between the memory of the conflict and the memory of the settlement. The memory of the conflict took a local turn, with local communities, actors and agencies stepping up as the major carriers of memory– often openly opposed to the activities of the establishment. The annual informal commemorations of the victims of the Karpalak ambush were a particularly significant example: initiated by families of the victims, the event consisted of an Orthodox Christian religious service in Prilep, the birthplace of the victims, and a small ceremony of laying flowers and erecting a memorial plaque at the scene of the assassination, approximately 130 kilometres from Prilep. The first commemoration in 2003 began a two-decade-long struggle over the memory site. The memorial plaque was violently removed after the commemorations in the early 2000s, thus becoming a media event both before and after the commemorations. Several commemorative plaques were also erected in Prilep and its vicinity and, in 2013, two memorials dedicated to the Karpalak victims were set up in Prilep. In August 2019, it was announced that the Karpalak memorial site would get a new plaque (see Figure 7.1) after the state acceded to NATO and the anticipated 'ease of the interethnic tensions' (Andonov 2019).

A brief overview of the first two years of the Karpalak ambush commemorations reveals the initial positioning of the major memory actors. The new SDSM Minister of Defence Vlado Bučovski appeared to be the focal point of the debate. At the 2003 commemoration, Bučovski depicted the ambush as the 'last attempt of the fools who thought that they could stop the peaceful settlement of the war-conflict in 2001.' This speech can be read as an attempt to shift the initial victim-centred commemorative discourse to a formal endorsement of OFA. However, the families of the victims, as reported in the media, boycotted his speech at the memorial site, arriving at the destination two hours afterwards (Dnevnik 2005). Bučovski also promised a new memorial plaque following its violent destruction in the mid-2000s, a statement which was criticized by the veteran fighters in the Macedonian media as Bučovski's government was perceived as sympathetic to the Albanian minority (e.g. Ristevska 2006). In the following years, the veteran organizations came to the forefront of the commemorations of the tragic events related to the 2001 conflict, often co-organizing them with the Macedonian army, the Ministry of Defence, and the Macedonian Orthodox Church. These ceremonies frequently served as a platform for expressing the demands of the organizations, criticizing selective justice, the improper treatment of the Macedonian war veterans and addressing various other sociopolitical concerns.

There was no state-sponsored commemoration of OFA until 2008, when one was organized by the secretariat for the implementation of the Agreement. This ceremony, however, was boycotted by both the VMRO-DPMNE former prime minister and the SDSM-backed president. In mid-August 2009, the secretariat again organized a

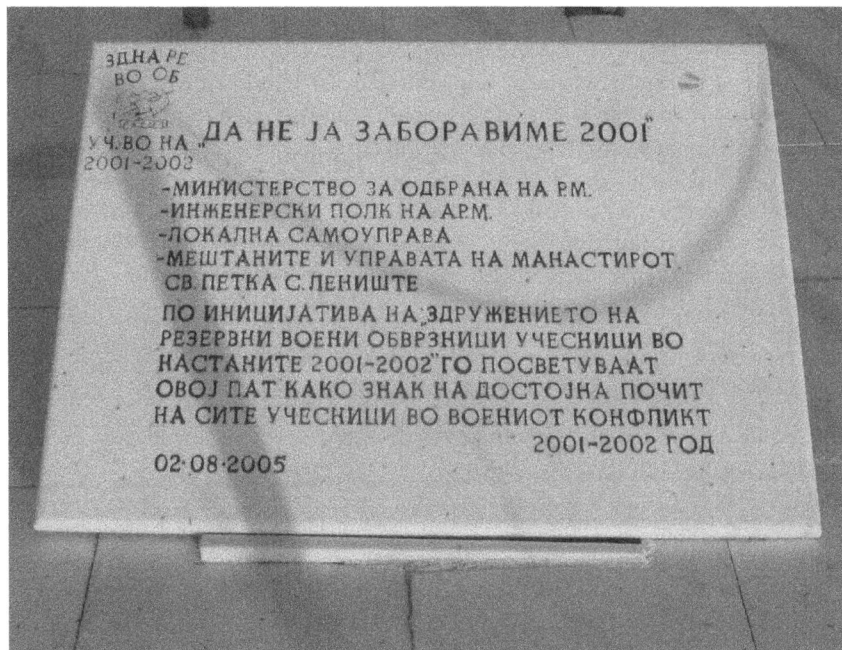

**Figure 7.1** A commemorative plaque in Leniše near Prilep

Note: The inscription in Macedonian states that it is 'dedicated to all the participants in the violent conflict in 2001–2002 as a sign of worthy respect'. *Source*: Courtesy Wikicommons.

ceremony in the Old Bazaar in Skopje, at which the new VMRO-DPMNE-backed President Ivanov praised the Agreement. In the course of his two presidential mandates, Ivanov argued that OFA was advancing a 'Macedonian model of multiculturalism' – a memory discourse that was promoted by several Macedonian artists in the late 1990s and was reimagined by the centre-right as a means of endorsing the OFA.[8] More specifically, Macedonia's Ottoman past was celebrated as a shared heritage and a model for multi-confessional tolerance.

On the eve of the OFA's tenth anniversary in 2011 high-profile politicians maintained an affirmative stance towards the Agreement, in line with the state's Euro-Atlantic aspirations. By contrast, less prominent politicians and experts still discussed the rationale, foundations and long-term impact of OFA. In the late 2000s the debate frequently revolved around the phrase 'spirit of the Agreement', regarded not merely as a ceasefire but as having as its main purpose the constitutional redesign of the republic of North Macedonia in the light of the 1991 republican constitution's inability to settle the growing interethnic tensions in the state.

In the 2010s Macedonian universities and research institutes also started to produce memory discourses about OFA (before this period, only foreign think-tanks and

NGOs based in North Macedonia had organized panel discussions and conferences on the OFA's anniversaries). For example, the tenth anniversary of the OFA in 2011 was marked by an academic conference held in the cities of Tetovo and Skopje by the State University of Tetovo, the South East European University and the University of Ss. Cyril and Methodius in Skopje. This event and the publications that followed in 2011 and 2012 had the ambitious goal of 'opening multidisciplinary research' on the OFA, despite the lack of a consensual discourse on the OFA within the academic community. In his introduction, the editor Blerim Reka, an international law expert, claimed that the OFA presented an opportunity for redefining the 'new political philosophy of the multi-ethnic state' (2011: 11).

### Recent developments: Ambiguous memory

The promotion of exclusively ethnocentric symbols within the public domain remains one of the prevailing trajectories of the memory of OFA and the 2001 conflict in contemporary North Macedonia. Even as from 2008 onwards, official OFA annual commemorations were organized by the governmental secretariat for the implementation of the OFA, the ruling VMRO-DPMNE-DUI coalition kept promoting divisive discourses over OFA and the preceding conflict.

After Greece vetoed Macedonia's membership of NATO in 2008, the second VMRO-DPMNE government set the promotion of ethnonational Macedonian identity high on their political agenda. The climax of this identity politics was the memory 'Skopje 2014' project, an umbrella term endorsing the 137 monuments and memorial objects erected in the cityscape. The project was described as a 'monumental and spectacular turning point in official narratives of Macedonian national identity' (Muhić and Takovski 2014: 138). As part of the project, a monument to the members of the Macedonian forces who lost their lives in the 2001 conflict was erected in 2011, while several other similar monuments were established in other Macedonian cities at the same period (see Figure 7.2).

The Albanian community in North Macedonia started promoting what Paul Reef calls 'a separate Albanian monument repertoire' (2018: 474) of the 2001 conflict. In November 2008, Albanian news agencies noted that, on the occasion of the Day of the Albanian Flag, DUI and the Municipality of Čair (part of Skopje) opened the Museum of Freedom, which exhibits materials on the history of the Albanians – from the period of the so-called 'League of Prizren (1878–81), to the events of 2001, the formation of the Kosovo Liberation Army (KLA) and the NLA' (Vreme 2008). In 2012, on the hundredth anniversary of Albanian independence, DUI opened a museum of the NLA and the 2001 conflict at Slupčane's cemetery complex. The museum, according to media reports, showcases wartime memorabilia and publications on the conflict (Makfaks 2012).

Several other monuments dedicated to the 2001 conflict, the Kosovo crisis and KLA were erected in Albanian settlements.[9] In 2013, Ali Ahmeti, DUI's leader, opened a memorial complex dedicated to 'Mother Albania' in Zajas, while several years after the promotion of 'Skopje 2014', a parallel project was launched at the nearby Skenderbeg Square in Skopje. This square, located in the predominantly Albanian part

**Figure 7.2** Monument 'Macedonian Defenders' in Skopje

*Source*: Courtesy Wikicommons.

of the city, now hosts a large mural depicting both ethnic Albanian historical figures and the radicals fighting for the minority cause in 2001 (see Figure 7.3). In 2017, the Kumanovo chapter of DUI announced that it would erect a monument dedicated to the NLA as a response to the city's mayor, who was proposing to set up a monument dedicated to the Macedonian forces active in the 2001 conflict.

However, these exclusive approaches to memorialization were rarely translated into the political arena.[10] Indeed during the 2010s political elites promoted reconciliatory discourses. For instance, the fifteenth anniversary of the signing of OFA in 2016 was marked by a conference on the subject of 'OFA – a Challenge and a Guarantee for Integration'. It was attended by Ali Ahmeti, leader of the DUI, and other high-profile politicians and members of the diplomatic core. 'There was no way to avoid what happened,' Ahmeti said in a statement, speaking of Albanian dissatisfaction since the time of the former Yugoslavia and the protests in Priština before the 2001 conflict. He

**Figure 7.3** 'Skenderbeg Square' in Skopje

*Source*: Courtesy Wikicommons.

thanked NATO and all mediators and statesmen for their efforts to address what he called 'the unresolved problems of the time'.

On 14 December 2018, seventeen years after the 2001 armed conflict, the first joint commemoration of the civil victims took place in the village of Lipkovo. The leading figures in the commemoration were Stojanče Angelov, former general major of the Special Macedonian Forces, and Abedin Zimberi, former commander of the NLA Military Police. Both Angelov and Zimberi laid flowers on the graves of the civil victims and made public statements in favour of interethnic reconciliation. In Angelov's words, 'Even though we may have completely different views of past events, we should be ready to fight together for the future.' This initiative well illustrates the present situation of the memory of the OFA and the 2001 conflict: a varied set of reconciliatory discourses are being promoted to the general public, while other, exclusive and ethnocentred narratives are maintained within the ethnic communities. Nevertheless, the Angelov-Zimberi initiative shows there is room for a different approach to the OFA and the conflict through a bottom-up dynamic, focused on the state's multi-ethnic prospects.

The gap between ethnocentred memory discourses and reconciliatory initiatives is also observable when speaking with Macedonian youth. The focus groups with young people organized by the Macedonian RETOPEA team showed that the generation born in the midst or immediately after the conflict perceive Macedonian society as polarized along ethnic and religious lines, and they believe that this polarization has not changed in recent years. According to the young people interviewed, who are enrolled in separate educational institutions, there is also a lack of interreligious dialogue; moreover they see this issue as a consequence of educational policy. A positive sign, however, was the ability of most of the young people to recognize the nationalistic content of syllabi – primarily in relation to history, religious history and ethics.

## The Good Friday Agreement

### Background

Unlike the OFA, which was rapidly drafted to bring an end to a short period of violent conflict, the GFA (also known as the Belfast Agreement after the city in which it was concluded on Good Friday, 10 April 1998) was the culmination of repeated and prolonged attempts to end the Northern Ireland 'Troubles', which had continued since 1969. The origins of the conflict lay in the historic polarization between the Protestant majority and the substantial Catholic/nationalist minority. The Protestants, politically known as Unionists or in more extreme form as Loyalists, saw the province as an integral part of the UK, whereas most Catholics, politically known as nationalists or republicans, hoped for the eventual unification of Northern Ireland with the independent Republic of Ireland. This underlying religious and political division was exacerbated by the particular terms on which the semi-autonomous Northern Ireland state was established in the early 1920s, with Protestants entrenching their political dominance at both regional and local level through manipulation of electoral boundaries and consigning representatives of the Catholic community to perpetual largely impotent opposition. Catholics were also under-represented in government service, especially at senior levels, and the police force was similarly dominated by Protestants. Although the consequent resentments and tensions were suppressed for decades, they exploded in the late 1960s in the context of the wider international civil rights movement. Initially peaceful Catholic protests provoked a backlash from Protestants. The situation rapidly deteriorated into violence, leading to the British army being sent on to the streets to restore order.

Although the army's presence was initially welcomed, it was soon perceived by Catholics as an occupying force, an impression reinforced by heavy-handed tactics, above all the fatal shooting of fourteen unarmed civil rights demonstrators in Derry/Londonderry on 'Bloody Sunday', 30 January 1972. By this time violence had become endemic and was pursued by both Catholic and Protestant paramilitary groups, notably the Irish Republican Army (IRA) and the Ulster Volunteer Force. There was a seemingly endless cycle of bombings, assassinations, random sectarian killings and assaults, which by 1998 had left over 3,600 people dead and tens of thousands injured or bereaved. The violence sometimes spilled over to other parts of the UK with IRA attacks on targets in England, notably the attempted assassination of the prime minister, Margaret Thatcher, and other members of her government in the Brighton bombing of 1984. The first serious attempt at a settlement, the Sunningdale Agreement of December 1973, rapidly broke down in the face of Protestant/Unionist intransigence. The Anglo-Irish Agreement of November 1985 suffered a similar fate, as a compromise that proved unacceptable to hardliners on both sides.

By the early 1990s, however, the mood was changing. There was growing revulsion against violence that seemed to perpetuate a futile stalemate, while the increasing electoral success of the IRA's political counterpart Sinn Féin encouraged Irish republicans to feel that they might eventually achieve more through the ballot box than through guns and bombs. The Downing Street Declaration of December 1993 committed the British and Irish governments jointly to search for peace based on the consent of the people of Northern Ireland. During 1994 the paramilitary groups declared ceasefires and, despite some continuing violence, momentum began to build towards a negotiated settlement. It received increased impetus following general elections in mid-1997 in both the UK and the Republic of Ireland, with the newly appointed prime ministers, Tony Blair and Bertie Ahern, both firmly committed to securing a deal. The final rounds of talks in the spring of 1998 were nevertheless prolonged and tortuous. They were chaired by a leading former American senator, George Mitchell, and the US president, Bill Clinton, was also actively involved in efforts to persuade the Northern Ireland parties to reach a compromise.

The resulting GFA consists of two documents, an agreement between the Northern Ireland political parties and an international treaty between the UK and Irish governments as joint guarantors of that settlement. The central compromise was a commitment that Northern Ireland would remain a part of the UK unless and until the people of both Northern Ireland and the Republic of Ireland voted in referenda for a united Ireland. A devolved Northern Ireland assembly and government would be reinstated – having been in abeyance since the early 1970s – but rather than restoring control by the Protestant majority, there would be a power-sharing executive with the Protestant/Unionist first minister having a Catholic/nationalist deputy. Other provisions included commitments to secure the decommissioning of the arsenals of weapons held by the paramilitary groups, to review and reform the police service to address its perceived sectarian bias, and to establish structures to advance equality and human rights (for a fuller albeit summary account of the Troubles and the events leading up to the GFA, see Fenton 2018: 15–80).

## Implementation and commemoration

The GFA faced the immediate obstacle of ratification by referendums on 22 May in both Northern Ireland and the Republic of Ireland. While positive outcomes were never seriously in doubt, the campaign preceding the votes exposed the degree of continuing opposition to the settlement, notably from the Democratic Unionist Party (DUP) led by Revd Ian Paisley, who had since the 1960s combined religious conviction and political rhetoric in diehard opposition to any concession to either Catholicism or Irish nationalism. Then on 15 August 1998, dissident republican paramilitaries opposed to the GFA planted a car bomb in the town of Omagh killing twenty-nine people, the highest death toll in any single incident in the Troubles. The dual challenges of political intransigence, primarily on the Protestant/Unionist side and continuing rogue paramilitary activity, primarily on the Catholic/nationalist/republican side, continued to delay full and successful implementation of the GFA (for a survey of political developments between 1998 and 2018, see O'Kane and Dixon 2018). The early years after 1998 saw a cycle of short-lived attempts to sustain the power-sharing arrangement, which then collapsed amid mutual distrust and recrimination. Unionists feared that a renewal of paramilitary violence would be used to exert political leverage, and so insisted that the commitment to decommission IRA weapons must be honoured before they would co-operate further. The process, overseen by a Catholic priest, Alec Reid, and a Methodist minister, Harold Good, eventually began in late 2001, but distrust of the IRA's intentions persisted until it was reported complete in 2005.

Hence at the time of the fifth anniversary of the Agreement in April 2003, both the power-sharing executive and the assembly were suspended. The occasion was therefore a cause not for celebration but rather for exhortations to complete unfinished business. Ahern, Blair and the US President George W. Bush issued a joint statement to that effect (*Irish Times* 9 April 2003). Unionists were noticeably silent, but Irish nationalists such as the Sinn Féin leader in the Irish parliament and participants in a conference of the Connolly Association in London also urged the need for further progress (Sinn Féin 2003). A rather different note, however, was struck by Nicholas Frayling, a senior Church of England clergyman who spoke of the need for repentance, crucially by the British for their actions in Ireland over the centuries. Frayling advocated a truth and reconciliation process on the lines of the one recently conducted in post-apartheid South Africa. In his opinion there was a need for 'working through history together' if there was to be meaningful reconciliation in the future (*Irish Democrat* 2003).

By the time of the tenth anniversary, however, prospects had improved. The St Andrews Agreement of October 2006 (named after the Scottish town where the talks were conducted) paved the way for a restoration of the assembly and the executive in May 2007. Remarkably, Ian Paisley of the DUP and Martin McGuinness of Sinn Féin developed a successful working relationship as first and deputy first ministers. In June 2007 the need to address the painful legacy of the Troubles was recognized by the setting up of the Consultative Group on the Past, co-chaired by Robin Eames, the former Anglican archbishop of Armagh, and Denis Bradley, a former Catholic priest. The commemorations in April 2008 reflected this more positive mood: the *Irish Times* editorial (10 April 2008) hailed the GFA's achievement of embedding an 'ethos of mutual recognition, respect and toleration in inter-community and inter-state relations' while Prime Minister Ahern affirmed that 'we have closed the bloody chapters and opened a new chapter of reconciliation and renewal' (Ahern 2008). There were, however, discordant notes: Paisley and his fellow DUP ministers were notable for their absence from a commemorative symposium in Belfast, and the *Irish Times* felt that the Agreement's promise of 'community reconciliation, solidarity and inclusiveness' was yet to be fulfilled. The continuing obstacles to full reconciliation were painfully exposed in early 2009 when the Eames-Bradley group reported. They made a number of thoughtful recommendations regarding processes for addressing the hurts and divisions of the past, but these were drowned out by the furore caused by their proposal that the nearest relative of *all* those killed in the conflict should receive a payment of £12,000. For Unionists, the implied moral equivalence between republican paramilitaries, British soldiers and Protestant civilians was wholly unacceptable. This reaction ensured that the attempt to establish a truth and reconciliation process in Northern Ireland on South African lines failed to gain momentum.

Paisley stepped down as first minister in June 2008, and his successors failed to establish the kind of warm relations with McGuinness that had led to the duo being known as the 'chuckle brothers'. Nevertheless, the power-sharing executive now survived for a decade until it collapsed in early 2017 due to McGuinness's own resignation over a failed energy scheme for which he held the DUP responsible. Meanwhile the fifteenth anniversary of the GFA in April 2013 took place in a climate of relative political stability. While acknowledging that much remained to be done, the UK prime minister, David Cameron, issued a statement hailing it as the platform for building a 'new confident and inclusive Northern Ireland' (Prime Minister's Office 2013). In Belfast, at an event for young people, the UK secretary of state for Northern Ireland Theresa Villiers shared a platform with the Irish Foreign Minister Eamon Gilmore (Irish Foreign Ministry 2013). Villiers initially sounded complacent, highlighting the UK government's achievements in Northern Ireland since 1998, but she went on to express concern at the continuing legacy of sectarianism that was transmitting itself to young people who had grown up since the Agreement. Gilmore was more challenging, highlighting the need for mutual respect between different traditions and calling on his youthful audience to consign the politics of the past to the past. Alluding to the so-called peace walls that continued to separate polarized communities in Belfast, he acknowledged that deep divisions continued and urged his hearer to break down the walls in their hearts.

The most recent significant anniversary, the twentieth in April 2018, occurred against a much-changed and substantially bleaker political landscape. Not only had the assembly and the executive now been suspended for over a year, but the UK's vote to leave the EU in the referendum of June 2016 was straining relations with the Republic of Ireland, and raising serious practical questions about how to maintain the open border between the two jurisdictions that was an essential precondition for the settlement. A further complication, following the UK general election in June 2017, was the British Conservative government's dependence on the DUP to maintain its fragile majority in the Westminster parliament, which undermined its ability to act as an honest broker in Northern Ireland.

April 2018 saw a variety of public statements, newspaper articles and interviews by both present-day leaders and surviving participants in the 1998 negotiations. The most high-profile event brought many of these together for a conference at Queen's University Belfast (2018) on the actual anniversary of the GFA. The speeches were preceded by a moving film that combined footage of 1998 with reflections from present-day young people, from university students to small children, on their appreciation of growing up in a peaceful Northern Ireland and on their hopes for the future. The forward-looking theme was pursued by the Irish foreign minister, Simon Coveney, who stressed the importance of remembering how things had been before 1998 and the continuing need to make progress on the legacy of the past. He called for a fresh spirit of renewal and reconciliation. Former prime ministers Ahern and Blair shared a platform with former president Clinton and senator Mitchell. Their emphatic joint message was that the Agreement had been a hard-won triumph of the democratic process. It was not perfect and could not on its own solve all of Northern Ireland's problems, but it had brought vast improvements and remained an essential foundation for further progress.

Successive speakers urged unremitting efforts to restore functioning of the devolved government and emphasized the vital importance of avoiding a hard border if the achievements of the last twenty years were to be sustained. The conference's sense of a vital unfinished task was also echoed in a joint statement by the Anglican and Catholic archbishops:

> The peace we have today took a great effort to achieve; it will equally take risk, and leadership at all levels, to maintain. It is therefore our sincere shared prayer that this anniversary will help to rekindle a spirit of opportunity, healing and hope for lasting peace which is now needed more than ever. (Church of Ireland 2018)

## Commemorating and perpetuating conflict

The above events and pronouncements commemorating the GFA were elite activities, bringing together protagonists from 1998 with current political leaders and a supporting cast of academics, journalists and religious leaders. The importance of influencing the young was emphasized, but direct interaction with them was limited.

At a more popular level, in Northern Ireland as in Macedonia, commemoration of the past took very different forms. These related not only to the Troubles of the later twentieth century but also to much more distant history. In particular, Protestant Orangemen continued to assert their right to march and celebrate on 12 July to mark the anniversary of the Battle of the Boyne in 1690, the decisive victory of the forces of the Protestant King William of Orange over his Catholic rival James II. The sacrifice of the Ulster Division at the Battle of the Somme in 1916 is also commemorated on the 'Twelfth', as this too occurred in early July. At the time of the GFA in 1998 there were acute tensions associated with the Orange parade to the church at Drumcree near Portadown, because the Orangemen had recently been banned from returning along their traditional route in order to avoid provoking Catholic residents. In July 1998 up to twenty thousand people gathered near Drumcree church, and although most were peaceful some violence ensued. Similar events followed in the next few years (Pickering 2009). Although the Drumcree protests gradually subsided in the early 2000s, Orange marches in Belfast and elsewhere have continued to be a source of ongoing tension.

Since 1998 the desire to commemorate the more recent Troubles, especially those who died in them, has led to the erection of numerous memorials. For example, on the Catholic/republican side there is the Clonard Martyrs Garden in Bombay Street, Belfast, unveiled in August 2000, off the Falls Road in West Belfast, in an area burned by Protestants at the outset of the Troubles in 1969 (see Figure 7.4).

There is a cluster of memorials at Free Derry Corner (Londonderry) including the original memorial to the victims of Bloody Sunday, which was renovated around the time of the twenty-fifth anniversary in 2007, a memorial to ten republicans who died on hunger strike in 1981 at the height of the Troubles and the Museum of Free Derry, opened in 2005 (Conway 2010). Protestant counterparts include memorial gardens built by the Ulster Defence Association in Sandy Row and Roden Street,

**Figure 7.4** Clonard Martyrs Memorial Garden

*Source*: Photo by John Wolffe, 25 April 2018.

Belfast, both opened in 2006. These memorials associate the deaths of Loyalist paramilitaries in the Troubles with the historic sacrifice of the Ulster Division on the Somme (Viggiani 2014). An impressive new memorial to the First World War dead, erected on the Protestant Shankill Road in West Belfast in 2009, implies a similar continuity. Both communities also adorned walls in their respective territories with murals reflecting their distinct interpretations of history and the Troubles. The example in Figure 7.5, also on the Shankill Road, commemorates the centenary in 2012 of the Ulster Covenant, in which most of the Protestant population had pledged themselves to diehard resistance to a proposed devolved parliament in Dublin beginning the chain of events that led to the division of the island of Ireland in the 1920s.

Contemporary events also stirred divisive popular reactions, notably the decision of Belfast City Council on 3 December 2012 to cease to fly the Union Flag throughout the year, and instead only to fly it on eighteen officially designated dates. This merely brought Belfast into line with usual practice in other parts of the UK, but in the eyes of Protestant Loyalists it was an unacceptable concession to Irish nationalism. There were prolonged street protests, which although non-violent, were disruptive of normal life and indicative of ongoing Protestant resistance to even limited compromise, particularly in working-class communities that were still suffering high levels of deprivation and unemployment and felt left behind by the growing prosperity of other parts of Northern Ireland (Jarman 2019).

It was understandable that those who had lived through the conflict, especially former paramilitaries and those close to them, were reluctant to let go of past attitudes. Hence more than twenty years on from the GFA Northern Ireland remains a deeply divided albeit largely peaceful society. Attention has therefore focused on the prospects for change through a younger generation who have grown up since 1998. However, although some young people, such as those featured in the film shown at the 2018 anniversary event, take a very positive view of the future, wider attitudes are mixed. Despite some slow progress in developing integrated schools, over 90 per cent of Northern Ireland children continue to be educated in institutions with student bodies that are almost exclusively either Catholic or Protestant (Morrow 2019: 25). Although there are projects to foster collaboration between schools of different traditions, unless and until they enter university or the workplace most young people are unlikely to have much social or other contact with 'the other side'. In a 2018 survey, 66 per cent of Northern Ireland young people (between eighteen and thirty) thought discrimination and prejudice were still a problem to a 'great' or to 'some' extent. They were alienated from the political process, with only 10 per

**Figure 7.5** Mural on the Shankill Road

*Source*: Photo by John Wolffe, 28 May 2019.

cent giving a positive trust rating to the Northern Ireland assembly and only 11 per cent to the Westminster parliament. There was also nervousness about future economic prospects, with 90 per cent concerned about a lack of jobs for young people (Connolly et al. 2018: 21, 27, 32). There is a risk that the alienation and boredom consequent on youth unemployment could become a breeding ground for renewed sectarian conflict. Hence a recent report on addressing sectarianism in Northern Ireland placed a particular emphasis on the young, including mentoring and intergenerational engagement, fostering youth leadership and participation, and ensuring schools have shared programmes with other communities. It also stressed the importance of investing in youth work (Morrow 2019: 42–5). While the passage of time indeed offers hope that the politics and conflicts of the past will eventually be consigned to the past there is no room for complacency.

## Conclusion

Both Northern Ireland and North Macedonia retain high levels of religiosity. In Northern Ireland in 2011, 83 per cent of the population identified with a religion, a lower proportion than the 94 per cent who had had a religious upbringing, but still an overwhelming majority (Northern Ireland Statistics and Research Agency 2012: 3). In North Macedonia in 2012, 90 per cent of the population identified as 'religious persons' (Zdravkovski and Morrison 2014: 241). In both countries, populist right of centre political parties – the DUP in Northern Ireland and the DPMNE in North Macedonia – have sought legitimacy through alignment with dominant religious groups – Ulster Presbyterians and Macedonian Orthodox Christians. Hence the continuing polarizing effect of rival religious identities at a popular level has inhibited any aspirations they might have to bridge divides and facilitate inclusive collective memorialization of the peace settlements. Although religious actors have been involved in some significant peacebuilding initiatives in Northern Ireland, in general religion has been subordinated to political agendas much more than it has shaped them.

Against this background, organized commemorations of the settlements have tended either to be elitist and academic – such as the conferences held by Macedonian universities in 2011 or that by Queens University Belfast in 2018 – or obviously partisan – such as the Connolly Association conference in London in 2003, or the DUI event in Ohrid in 2006. Official attempts to hold more inclusive commemorations, notably those by the secretariat for the implementation of the OFA, have largely founded on the rocks of political partisanship and popular apathy. On the other hand, physical memorials and museums recalling the conflicts themselves have had more popular resonance. Such material commemoration of past violence is disturbing for those who want rather to celebrate peace, but it may well have a cathartic function for those who might otherwise be tempted to resume hostilities. It offers them a sense that justice has been done to the past, and that they can now look to the future as in the joint commemoration at Lipkovo in December 2018.

It is evident therefore that in both societies the building of peace and acceptance of diversity based on the respective peace settlements of 1998 and 2001 is a long-term process. It is accordingly crucial to look to the formative influences on young people and to foster education systems that promote mutual understanding and tolerance even when they still unavoidably separate children on religious lines. The cultivation of a balanced understanding of recent history that questions divisive collective memories and affirms consensual ones can make an important contribution to this process.

# Religious pluralism in the Islamic tradition in late al-Andalus and in contemporary Islamic transnationalism: A conceptual approach

Nadia Hindi Mediavilla, Antonio Peláez Rovira
and María Dolores Rodríguez Gómez[1]

'Islam has a proud tradition of tolerance. We see it in the history of Andalusia and Cordoba' (The White House 2009). This excerpt from a speech by Barack Obama at Cairo University in 2009 encapsulates the powerful metaphor of al-Andalus as a historical example of Islamic tolerance. The eight centuries of Muslim presence in the Iberian Peninsula are often evoked as a period of peaceful coexistence. However, this representation is not only a matter of historiographical controversy as regards its interpretation and the uses of the past, but it also mobilizes different imaginaries of self-identification and otherness that have little to do with that stage in history and instead reflect the paradigms of the present and the way it is projected onto the past.

Studies of religious pluralism in Islamic tradition and its historical transformations could contribute to a more in-depth understanding of how Muslims deal with religious diversity in the past and in the present, and would certainly offer a more balanced picture of Islam. Thus, looking back into history and comparing it to the current world situation could help build a more critical understanding of our present-day reality. As Chapter 2 makes clear 'relating past and present is a valuable approach to enable young people to "think outside the box" and construct their ideas', and this is what this chapter sets out to do: establish a complex relation between past and present focused on the very concepts that describe the social and political dynamics of religious pluralism in Islam.

This chapter explores Islamic tradition to see how religious diversity was experienced in the past and is evoked in the present. The main object of this study are some key concepts that are used in relation to religious pluralism in legal and political documents such as fatwas, court testimonies, pacts, treaties, capitulations and Islamic initiatives in favour of peace and tolerance. A diachronic analysis of these documentary sources shows us that the concept of religious tolerance had a different meaning within Islamic tradition than it has today. The documents we will be analyzing date from two different periods in history. The first period covers the final era of al-Andalus, with the decline of the Nasrid Kingdom of Granada and its surrender to the Catholic monarchs, while the second refers to the post–9/11 era, which was characterized by Islamophobia and a global war on terrorism. Both crises, the collapse of al-Andalus in the fifteenth century and the securitization of Islam in the twenty-first century, triggered significant reconceptualizations of religious pluralism.

The first section of this chapter provides a historical account of these two historical crises. The second section explores the issues that dominated interreligious relations before the Conquest of Granada, underlining the importance of pacts and treaties as sources of stability between Christian and Muslim territories. It also assesses different approaches to *dār al-islām* (the domain of Islam) and *dār al-ḥarb* (the domain of war) and the juridical attempts to overcome this binary in both historical contexts, within which there is a degree of continuity rather than a sharp division. To this end, we will be analyzing the results of an important transnational Islamic initiative – the Conference of Mardin – which problematizes this dichotomy and (re)evokes the notion of pact (*'ahd*) as the framework through which justice (*'adl*), and common good (*maṣlaḥa*) – or public interest (*istiṣlāḥ*) – between individuals and communities should be articulated in interreligious and 'glocal' societies. The third section of the chapter takes a more detailed look at peace treaties between Muslims and Christians in al-Andalus and at the way they articulate peace (*ṣulḥ*), reconciliation (*iṣlāḥ*), equality (*siwā*) and freedom (*sariḥa*). Finally, it moves onto two other contemporary transnational initiatives – the Amman Message and the Declaration of Marrakesh – that evoke an ethical dimension of Islam linked to the idea of tolerance (*tasāmuḥ*) and broaden the understanding of concepts such as pacts (*'ahd*) in order to support the idea that plural societies are inherent to the Islamic world view.

As a starting point, we should perhaps begin by exploring the concept of 'tolerance' (*tasāmuḥ*), which is probably the first term that springs to mind when talking about religious pluralism, especially with regards to al-Andalus, together with the Spanish concept *convivencia* (coexistence or living together). The first questions that should be addressed are: How was the concept of tolerance used in Islamic tradition and to whom did it apply? Or in other words who did it extend to and who were excluded from the equation or ignored? An exhaustive answer to such a broad question would be impossible and instead must be limited to the scope of this study. *Tasāmuḥ* derives from the VI form (*tafā'ul*) of the trilateral Arabic verb *samaḥa* (to permit, admit, allow), which also conveys a sense of reciprocity and mutuality. *Tasāmuḥ* therefore means, and is often translated as, 'mutual tolerance' or 'mutual forgiveness'. This word is not mentioned in the Quran, although the implicit idea can be found in other Arabic words such as *'afā* (pardon/forgive): 'The recompense for an evil is an evil equal thereto, but who forgives (*'afā*) and reconciles (*aṣlaḥa*), his recompense is from God' (Quran 42:40, Amman's Message translation). There is no evidence of the use of the word *tasāmuḥ* during Medieval Islam, although it is commonly used by Islamic scholars today. As regards the second question as to who are included/excluded from the bidirectional meaning of 'mutual tolerance', in al-Andalus, as in other parts of the Islamic world, tolerance did not imply equality as we understand it today. The relationships between religions and their implicit ethno-religious hierarchies were based much more on convenience and the need to ensure social stability by reaching agreements between the parties, Muslims and Christians. Today, toleration is closely related to equality and religious freedom. The non-Muslims included in the recent transnational initiatives examined here are mainly Christian and Jews, and include indigenous Christian and Jewish communities and other non-Muslim religious groups such as the Yazidists of Iraq, along with non-Muslim foreigners who are resident in countries with Muslim majorities. Some groups, however, are ignored. These include, for example, Muslims who converted to Christianity and minority Islamic communities in certain countries such as Morocco and Saudi Arabia, not to mention atheists or agnostics. The very limits of contemporary Islamic inclusiveness point to a new range of upcoming challenges, which appear to be accumulating in number rather than easing.

## Concepts of religious pluralism: A historic contextual analysis

### In classical Islam

Religious pluralism in al-Andalus was part of a longstanding tradition that was rooted in the very origins of Islam, as set out in the first Islamic treatise known as the 'Constitution [or Charter] of Medina' (622), which established the principles governing the community of believers (*umma*), including Jews. This was followed by the 'Pact of 'Umar' (traditionally dated 637), which adopted the term *dhimma* ('protection') to describe the status of the followers of the revealed religions in *dār al-islām*. Those who assigned this status were allowed to preserve their religious practices, property, legal systems, and so on, in exchange for the payment of certain taxes. This arrangement appeared within the context of the dynamic expansion of Islam driven by the imperative to spread the faith, by force if necessary (the 'lesser' *jihād*),[2] as seen, for example, in the arrival of the Umayyad armies in the Iberian Peninsula in 711. In order to continue their expansion, they adopted a pragmatic policy of pacts (*'aqd/'ahd*) with Iberian noblemen, which enabled them to extend their territorial dominance with only minimal losses (Chalmeta Gendrón 2004). Indeed, the favourable conditions of *dhimmī* status contributed to the success of these pacts and allowed Muslim troops to reach southern France just a few years later.

The rise of reactionary and hardcore militant movements within Western Islam such as the Almoravids (1056–1147) and Almohads (1130–1269), together with the Muslim loss of Sicily in 1061, the fall of Jerusalem to the Crusaders in 1099 and the seizure of Baghdad by the Mongols in 1258, all contributed to the emergence of theories about the struggle between two 'houses': *dār al-islām*, the 'domain (house) of Islam' (also known as *dār al-salām*, the 'domain of peace'), and the land ruled by the infidel, *dār al-ḥarb*, the 'domain (house) of war' (also called *dār al-kufr*, the 'domain of unbelief'). The seizures of Jerusalem and Baghdad left the strongest mark on Islamic political and religious thought by giving the term *hijra* an additional connotation of 'emigration by Muslims to *dār al-islām*' (Fierro 1991). Indeed, the very first Islamic community was established after the flight (referred to in Islam as *hijra*) of the Muslims from Mecca to Medina in times of the Prophet. In this latter context *hijra* also became a juridical term to refer to the situation in which Muslims were forced to flee to Islamic-ruled lands in order to safeguard their religious practices and mores. Therefore, the evolution of these concepts regarding the relations between Muslims and non-Muslims in the Middle Ages was closely linked to the notion of territorial control, which fluctuated widely from Islam's initial expansionist phase up to its gradual loss of territory and the collapse of central power, succumbing to the advance of other religions or foreign dynasties, or to tendencies within Islam that were opposed to the dominant ideology.

Our decision to focus on the Nasrid Kingdom of Granada (1232–1492), the last Muslim state in the Peninsula, in the fifteenth century and its later Mudejar period (1492–1501) is not an arbitrary one. The great crisis in this region that led to the end of al-Andalus and the transition from being the dominant community in a part of *dār al-islām* to a subordinate one in a Christian kingdom led to a rethinking of the criteria about religious pluralism that can be compared to that taking place today. In fact, the fall of al-Andalus is often cited in jihadist propaganda, in which parallels are drawn with the current situation.

In the history of Islamic Granada there are two clearly distinct stages before and after the fall of the city:

1.  Islamic rule (1091–up to 2 January 1492): during this period, in contrast to the pre-Almoravid era (756–1091), the population of Granada was almost entirely Muslim and there was little religious diversity. Christians and Jews had for the most part decamped to 'the other side of the border' while those who lived in Islamic territory on a temporary basis received the traditional *amān* or safe-conduct. There were very few native Jewish communities and Christians are hardly mentioned. As for external relations with the other kingdoms in the Peninsula, there were peace agreements in place during most of the fifteenth century, which were necessary for regulating trade and protecting captive prisoners. On the frontier between Christian and Muslim domains, there were frequent examples of collaboration and understanding, thereby enabling a degree of coexistence even within the prevailing atmosphere of hostility. This stage culminated with Castile's war on Granada (1482–92), which ended with the signing of the Capitulations or surrender agreement and the handover of the city to its new Christian rulers (Garrido Atienza 1910: 269–95, doc. LX). The whole of the Iberian Peninsula was now under Christian rule, and the Muslim inhabitants of Granada acquired the same status as their coreligionists in the rest of the country. They were now classified as Mudejars (*mudajjan*), that is, Muslims who lived in areas under Christian rule, and had a similar status to the *dhimmī* status that had previously been afforded to Christians in areas under Muslim control (see Figure 8.1).

2.  The stage of Christian dominance (from 2 January 1492): The fall of Granada in 1492 ushered in drastic changes for its Muslim population. From 1492 to 1500 the Christians ruled over the Muslim majority in Granada according to the clauses and regulations set out in the Capitulations. These Muslims faced a

**Figure 8.1** Capitulations of Granada, Archivo de los Duques de Frías (Sección Nobleza, Archivo Histórico Nacional)

*Source*: Courtesy Wikicommons.

difficult dilemma between *hijra* (emigration to *dār al-islām*) and *taqiya* (staying in *dār al-ḥarb* while hiding their beliefs). The ensuing debate generated various religious statements (*fatāwā*, sg. *fatwā*) both for and against. Although most of the muftis insisted on the obligation to emigrate, just as Muḥammad had done from Mecca to Medina, others defended the right to remain in the land of their forebears. Many Muslims decided to stay. Since coexistence proved difficult mainly due to the tremendous pressure exerted by the Christians; in 1501 the Catholic monarchs decreed that the Muslims of Granada must choose between conversion and expulsion, a measure they had previously imposed on the Jews in 1492. The decree was eventually extended to all the Muslims in the Peninsula. Newly converted Muslims were assimilated and became Moriscos or *cristianos nuevos de moros* ('New Christians descended from Moors'). But this was not enough for the Christian rulers and thousands of Moriscos were finally expelled from the Peninsula in 1609. These events and the articulation of otherness were of great significance as they formed part of a major geopolitical shift: the internationalization of power in the sixteenth century, the expansion of the Spanish Empire, the conquest of America, further European colonization and the establishment of international markets. From then on, the contacts between Europe and the Islamic world would be driven mainly by colonial interests.

**In contemporary Islam**

After analyzing the situation at the end of al-Andalus we will now move on to examine religious pluralism in other parts of *dār al-islām*. Arguably the greatest Islamic power at that time was the Ottoman Empire, which held sway over large swathes of Europe and North Africa over a long period stretching from the late Middle Ages until the early twentieth century (1299–1923). The political dynamics behind religious pluralism vary greatly from one context to another, as we have already seen. The territories that remained under the control of the Almoravid and Almohad dynasties in western Islamdom enjoyed less and less religious freedom, whereas the Ottoman Empire became ever more multi-confessional as it expanded into traditionally Christian areas of Europe and welcomed Sephardic Jews and Moriscos from the Iberian Peninsula. During the nineteenth century, however, the Ottoman Empire went into decline, losing territory to rival European powers. Nationalist movements began to appear all over the region often based in non-Muslim communities. In order to overcome these internal and external challenges the judicial system was completely overhauled. *Dhimma* status was replaced by that of citizenship and a constitutional system was established, although not without great difficulty (Kern 2011). Throughout this period reformers from both inside and outside the declining Ottoman Empire sought to transform society by establishing a legal foundation for the changes that were taking place and imagining what their ideal *waṭan* (nation/homeland) or *umma* (nation generally understood as a broader spiritual Islamic community) might look like. They offered vague, competing notions as to where future borderlines should lie, in the face of an increasing need to combat both foreign powers and internal division derived from the old socio-religious hierarchies and the political use of religious identities (*ṭā'ifiyya*) (sectarianism) in parts of the empire such as today's Egypt and Syria (Makdisi 2000; Kutelia 2011).

The First World War (1914–18) gave rise to a new international order, the collapse of the last Islamic caliphate and the founding of nation states, mainly under the influence of the European colonial powers. From that point onwards and throughout the entire twentieth century, the regions known today as the Middle East and North Africa underwent a series of upheavals: anticolonial nationalisms; implementation of the principles of *waṭan* (nation/homeland) and *muwāṭana* (citizenship); transformation of communal loyalties; struggles for independence and the founding of secular authoritarian regimes; the formation of a Jewish state at the expense of the local Palestinian population; re-Islamization and the strengthening of Islamist currents, mass migration and so on. The above was also affected by the establishment of global capitalism and the globalization of power since the Second World War (new technologies, financial capitalism, supranational institutions and information societies).

The accumulative effects of the colonial and postcolonial experience in these regions were distorted even further at the dawn of the twenty-first century. After the attack on New York's Twin Towers in 2001 and the resulting 'War on Terror' (Managhan 2020), Islam, and hence Muslims, came under attack from a range of different interconnected geopolitical forces and phenomena, thereby becoming a target for terrorism, sectarianism, Islamophobia and war. In this atmosphere of crisis, during the first two decades of the twenty-first century prominent Islamic *'ulamā'* and organizations, on their own initiatives or spurred on by governments, have turned to Islamic legal tradition in an attempt to promote principles of 'tolerance' (*tasāmuḥ*), reopen the debate on citizenship and religious pluralism, and revise the territorial concepts of *dār al-islām* and *dār al-ḥarb*. In so doing, their aim has been to defend and revive a 'true', 'moderate' and/or 'normative' Islam that has nothing to do with Islamist or jihadist terrorism, as a means of reducing Islamophobia within a global context that Yahya Michot described as 'a power struggle to represent Islamic authority after 9/11' (2011: 133). The concepts of religious pluralism that arose at different points in this long and complex process show how their meanings could evolve without altering the fundamental religious principles on which they are based.

## Juridical documents: Beyond *dār al-Islām* and *dār al-ḥarb*

### The frontier: A pragmatic coexistence

One might imagine that the relations between Muslims and Christians on the frontier between their respective domains in the Iberian Peninsula would have been fraught with tension and in a state of permanent conflict, but this was far from true. In fact the norm was for agreements to be reached in cases of potential confrontation between the two communities.[3] Continuous contacts were shaped by peace treaties and truces with clauses that permitted cross-border activities between the two communities, such as trading and supplying basic needs, herding, tracking and exchanging captives and their possessions, as well as religious freedom and mobility for converts, among others. They also forbade raiding and seizing hostages, imposing punishments on those who disobeyed. Some scholars claim that in frontier areas war and peace took on special form (Carriazo y Arroquia 2002: 215–16). Instead of being black and white, these concepts were full of shades of grey (Argente del Castillo 1988: 222–3); and fluctuating, ambiguous situations were common on either side (Rodríguez Molina 1997: 258). 'Truces were clearly an effective formula, especially during the fifteenth century, for fulfilling the peaceful aspirations of both camps,' and became 'a significant feature in the development of the Sultanate of Granada' (Melo Carrasco 2012: 271).

In general, the regulations on the Muslim side were drawn up in line with Islamic law (*fiqh*) and the Mālikī School of jurisprudence, the dominant school in al-Andalus, and were therefore able to adapt to the particular requirements at any given time. According to María Arcas Campoy (2003), at the borders, this School took account of necessity (*ḍarūra*) and justice (*'adl*), to which we might add another element of Mālikī jurisprudence, the public interest (*istiṣlāḥ*).

### What shall we do now that al-Andalus is gone? The choice between staying and leaving

The Capitulations of 1491 by which the Sultan of Granada surrendered the city followed a model that had already been widely applied in other towns conquered by the Christians. Among the clauses that benefited the Muslim population, now called Mudejars, were those that enabled them to preserve their possessions, their religious and legal practices, customs, language and so on, in exchange for the payment of certain taxes. They were also given the opportunity to emigrate to *dār al-islām* and even to return from it if they wished.

The dilemma about whether Muslims should emigrate (in a *hijra*) from their ancestral lands was presented first to the Mudejars and later to the Moriscos (Muslims who had converted to Christianity), not only as an ethical/moral question or a religious imperative but also as part of a sustained campaign against them by their conquerors, involving increased taxes, forced conversions, extortions and other outrages. Faced with this difficult choice, Muslims turned as usual to their legal authorities (*fuqahā'*, sg. *faqīh*) asking for fatwas to guide them. There was never a consensus, however, in favour of one position or the other (García Sanjuán 2015: 15).

One of those consulted was al-Wansharīsī (d. 1508), the mufti of Fez, who had already witnessed the emigration of Mudejars to his native Tlemcen. When a group of Muslims who wanted to return to the Peninsula turned to him for advice, he took one of the most inflexible positions followed by the majority of *fuqahā'* in his famous fatwa *Asnā al-matājir*, which declared it obligatory for Muslims to reside in *dār al-islām*. He issued this same juridical opinion in a shorter fatwa called the 'Fatwa of Marbella' (among others Verskin 2015: 11–7 and appendices).

Other muftis, however, such as al-'Abdūsī of Fez (d. 1445), judged the matter differently, arguing in favour of remaining in one's native land, applying the principle of *istiṣlāḥ* or preference for reasons of general interest. We have evidence that many Andalusis chose the latter path, including – and this is very revealing – members of the legal and religious authorities: *fuqahā'*, *'ulamā'*, notaries, and so on (Galán Sánchez 2008; Zomeño 2015). In the latter case some *fuqahā'* preferred the expressions *dār al-ṣulḥ* or *dār al-'ahd*, 'domain of the pact' (García Sanjuán 2015: 18). Maribel Fierro (1991: 19) noted that the conditions under which Muslims were allowed to stay brought about a change in the Sunni definition of *dār al-islām*, which became 'both a land governed by a Muslim and a land where, although its ruler is not Muslim, Muslims are allowed to practice their religion'.

## The Mardin Declaration: A new proposal for deconstructing the territorial binomial

The Mardin Conference, held in 2010, was convened by Muslim non-governmental organizations based in the UK that were linked to prominent personalities, chief among them the Mauritanian sheikh Abd Allah bin Bayyah (b. 1935), president of the Forum for Promoting Peace in Muslim Societies based in Abu Dhabi and a prominent Sufi scholar in transnational Islamic organizations. The conference, attended by a diverse group of Islamic scholars, took place at Mardin Artuklu University in Turkey. The participating theologians examined various concepts of classical jurisprudence related to religious pluralism in the light of Sharia and the new realities of the twenty-first century, with particular attention to the division of territory into two basic spaces, the domain of peace (*dār al-islām*) and the domain of war (*dār al-ḥarb*). The meeting's chief aim, according to its final Declaration, was 'the grounding of peaceful and harmonious coexistence and cooperation for good and justice between Muslims and non-Muslims, provided that it is understood in consonance with normative religious texts, and maxims, and in light of higher objectives of Islamic Law' (The Mardin Declaration 2010, organisers' translation). The central topic of the conference was the 'Mardin Fatwa' a judicial opinion by the famous Syrian theologian Ibn Taymiyya (1263–1328), in which instead of being assigned to *dār al-islām* or *dār al-ḥarb*, Mardin was assigned to a new third category required by the particular context of its time.

The controversial thirteenth-century theologian has been repeatedly invoked by modern Muslim thinkers of varying backgrounds. He has inspired and legitimized positions as contradictory as 'middle-ground' Islam (*wasaṭiyya*) on the one hand and jihad against both non-Muslim and Muslim infidels on the other (Hoover 2016; Baylocq 2018; Gómez García 2018). This is why Ibn Taymiyya became the main focus of the Mardin Conference. But what is his fatwa about, and how significant is it today? At the time the fatwa was issued, Mardin was a multi-confessional city that was part of the Ilkhanate (1291–1335), a state first established by the Mongol expansion, whose ruling dynasty converted to Islam in 1295. However, its Muslim community, and Ibn Taymiyya himself, believed that Islamic law was not being properly applied there. The famous scholar was asked whether Mardin was living under the legal status of *dār al-islām* or *dār al-ḥarb*, and whether Muslims were obliged to emigrate to areas under Islamic rule. In response, Ibn Taymiyya issued his fatwa affirming that there was no inevitable obligation for a Muslim to emigrate so long as he could perform his religious duties. He designated the city of Mardin as a third category, a 'composite' (*murakkab*): while the domain of peace is a territory whose 'army is Muslim' and thus 'the institutions (*aḥkām*) of Islam are implemented' (Michot 2006: 65), the domain of war is inhabited by infidels. According to Ibn Taymiyya, Mardin did not wholly fulfil either of those conditions. He concluded, therefore, that it was a space in which 'the Muslim shall be treated as he merits and in which the one who departs from the Way/ Law of Islam should be treated as he merits'[4] (Michot 2011: 146, author's translation).

The Mardin Fatwa proposed that this binary view of space was no longer valid, opening up the possibility of a stable life for Muslims and non-Muslims in plural societies. The fact is, however, that similar situations had existed almost since the early period of rapid expansion of Islam in which *dār al-islām* and *dār al-ḥarb* had continually shifting boundaries and it was common to find non-Muslim subjects under Islamic rule and vice versa. This political and military domination by one side or the other did not necessary entail an attack on religious and cultural identity. Indeed, some scholars, such as Ḥusayn Mu'nis (1996: 11–12), argue that the fatwa issued by al-Wansharīsī was in many ways a reaction to the persecution of the Moriscos by the Christian rulers of Spain. It did not resonate much with Eastern Islam and had little impact on its relations with foreign political and religious powers like the Byzantines.

If we move forward again to modern times, the Mardin Declaration encouraged modern Muslim jurists to take another look at this classical legal distinction between *dār al-islām* and *dār al-ḥarb*, which was a reflection of particular conditions in the history of Muslim expansion, adapting it to the reality (*wāqi'*) of the modern day. The Declaration affirms that nowadays Muslims mix with non-Muslims at every level – social, economic and political – and are subject to international treaties and conventions, while enjoying the rights and freedoms that states grant their citizens. It also sets up a parallel between modern times and foundational Islam in terms of the Sharia. It therefore postulates that the principles of coexistence (*ta'āyush*), justice (*'adl*) and the common good (*maṣlaḥa*) contained in international treaties (*mu'āhadāt*) are the same principles that the Sharia has proclaimed to humanity ever since Mohammed emigrated to Medina and established the Constitution of Medina with the city's non-Muslim inhabitants – a *mu'āhada*, the same term now used for an international treaty – in order to establish principles of justice and the common good.

*Mu'āhada* is derived from *'ahd* (pact), a word of considerable religious significance not only in Islamic political history, as we have seen, but also in the Quranic prescription about adherence to pacts (Quran 16:91). Further, the aforementioned concept of *dār al-'ahd* (domain of the pact) had already been introduced by the Shāfi'ī legal School to refer to either 'the absence of war' (Ramadan 2002: 181) or 'a truce' (The Mardin Declaration 2010), thereby adapting itself to the classical construction, without denying the existence of domains of peace and of war (Gómez García 2019: 100). The domain of the pact was proposed by a group of well-known *'ulamā'* at a seminar organized in France in 1992 by the Federation of Islamic Organizations in Europe, as a legal basis for the residency and citizenship of Muslims in Europe (Caeiro 2011: 121–41). Nonetheless, according to the influential scholar Tariq Ramadan (2002: 181–3), *dār al-'ahd* does not entirely supersede the dichotomy inherent in the classical concept. The Mardin Declaration, meanwhile, includes the domain of the pact within the classical tradition, seemingly without questioning its contemporary relevance. The theologians who signed the Declaration did not issue a fatwa on the subject; instead, as indicated above, they presented the fatwa of Ibn Taymiyya as a legal precedent for condemning violence and rethinking the notion of space in the light of Sharia, attributing a crucial role to treaties and pacts (*mu'āhadāt*) in Muslims' relations with the rest of the world.

## Political documents: Normative frameworks for coexistence

### The classical political treatise: An agreement about territory with an egalitarian approach

The Nasrid Kingdom of Granada applied several political strategies in an attempt to regulate its relations with Castile, its main rival for centuries until it was finally absorbed by it in 1492. Diplomacy was essential to Granada's existence, through treaties that governed peaceful relations and permitted dialogue between rival states (Melo Carrasco 2012). These followed the pattern of the Treaty of Jaén (1246), the first of its kind (Vidal Castro 2000: 52), with adaptations to suit the prevailing circumstances. The document we have chosen to study here is the three-year Peace Treaty between Abū l-Ḥasan 'Alī of Granada and Henry IV of Castile, as it contains various aspects common to all other treaties of the time. This Peace Treaty was signed in 1472 (García

Luján 1998: 92–105; Monferrer Sala and Pinilla Melguizo 1998: 251–9) when an agreement was reached after several conflicts between Castile and Granada. Notable facts about Abū l-Ḥasan (1464–1482) include his leadership, his close relationship with Castile (Melo Carrasco 2015: 204–13) and his capacity to unite scattered elements (Vidal Castro 2000: 191–8).

Every peace treaty is an *'aqd* (agreement or pact). This treaty employs the verb *'aqada* twice, on both occasions when the Nasrid Emir addresses the king of Castile on equal terms: 'We pact with You – King of Castile – by land and sea, for a period of three consecutive Christian years'[5] and 'we pact with You and you have agreed with Us in this aforesaid treaty of peace.' The text makes clear that the two heads of state shall be equal for the duration of the agreement: 'We and You during the time of this peace treaty shall be equal (*siw*^(*an*)) and like to each other.' This equivalence between the monarchs extended to their subjects, who shared the same rights and duties. The document's normative framework reveals its egalitarian spirit: 'Everything obligatory for Christians is obligatory for Muslims, and everything obligatory for Muslims is obligatory for Christians, in the same measure (*siwā*) and alike.' The clauses and conditions (*shurūṭ*) of the treaty define these obligations as usual in these kinds of documents (Melo Carrasco 2015).

Coexistence within both the Nasrid and the Castilian domains was guaranteed. The treaty grants an *amān* (safe-conduct) to non-Muslim subjects in Islamic territory (named *mulk*/kingdom or *waṭan*/homeland) to protect their life and property, and religious communities – 'Muslims, Christians, and Jews on both sides' – are likewise given safe-conducts. This provision implies freedom of action (or *sariḥa*/walking in freedom) enabling subjects to buy and sell in both territories regardless of their religion; even if this is not the same as individual freedom (*ḥurriya*), it falls within the same semantic field of freedom of action. When conflicts arise between members of different religious communities, the treaty activates mechanisms for obtaining *iṣlāḥ* (reparation, reconciliation) between the parties and a return to peaceful coexistence. The term for 'peace treaty' is *ṣulḥ* (agreement, peace), which means that peace is the dominant semantic thread of the clauses of the treaty: peace and war become two necessary elements in the order of life (Viguera Molíns 1997), but peaceful relations agreed in official documents were clearly more common (Rodríguez Molina 1997).

### The Capitulations of Granada: Regulated ethical coexistence with the vanquished

In the final years of the war, several conquered towns signed surrender agreements with Castile that were meant to protect Muslim lives and property. The Capitulations, an agreement for the surrender of Granada signed between the Catholic monarchs (Queen Isabella and King Ferdinand) and Boabdil, the sultan of Granada, on 25 November 1491, decreed the right of the Muslim community to remain in Granada while retaining their possessions, religion, customs and fiscal arrangements. It also facilitated their emigration to the Maghreb (Vidal Castro 2000: 206). In addition to the Spanish text of the document (Garrido Atienza 1910: 269–95, doc. LX) there is also an extract of nineteen clauses from it in Arabic in the *Nafḥ al-ṭīb*, an encyclopaedia about al-Andalus by al-Maqqarī (d. 1632) (1968: IV, 525–6). These Arabic clauses are of great historic and legal significance (Velázquez 2002: 481–4).

The Capitulations consist of *shurūṭ* (clauses, conditions) that regulate coexistence under Castilian rule; that is, they allow for peaceful relations and establish ways of dealing with conflict. Although they are not defined as 'rights' (*ḥuqūq* in the contemporary terminology), the clauses do provide a clear series of guarantees in relation to the ethical treatment of the conquered. This can be seen as early as Clause 1, which deals with *ta'mīn* (from the same root as the term *amān* – safe-conduct or surety – which is widely used in political texts), which assures the right to remain and the security of persons, families, goods and real estate (al-Maqqarī 1968: IV, 525–6; trans. Velázquez 2002: 535–6). Freedom of worship is also guaranteed to Muslims. Ethical treatment extends so far that 'anyone who mocks [a conquered subject] shall be punished'. Conversion to Christianity is made conditional on exploring the potential convert's true intentions, but is not forbidden outright, as one might expect from the Islamic point of view. This should not be viewed as religious freedom, but more as a regulation of a practice that might become a form of coexistence with the Christian conquerors. The text is clear: 'A Muslim who has embraced Christianity should be given a few days to be certain of his wish and to renounce any return to Islam.' Finally, members of the Granada community will be accommodated if they decide to move to Christian territory, 'with protection of their persons and goods', and they will be placed on an equal footing with subjects of Castile in that they will not be forced to wear 'any distinctive sign like the Jews and Mudejars' who lived in Castilian territory.

### Religious pluralism at the turn of the twenty-first century

In addition to the Mardin Declaration, various other initiatives in different Arab countries have sought to promote peace and tolerance within the international framework described above. Jordan and Morocco, for example, have both raised the banner of *wasaṭiyya* ('middle-ground' Islam). The pioneer was King Abdallah II of Jordan, with the Amman Message of 2004, which recognized the diversity within Islam, including all the legal schools and the other recognized currents and traditions, as part of an intrinsically moderate, orthodox Islam.[6] This effort enjoyed considerable success at the time, encompassing twenty-four fatwas by the best-known authorities from the various legal schools, thus achieving a broad transnational Islamic consensus (*ijmāʿ*). This general agreement was developed in the years that followed through a series of meetings and conferences that focused on different issues of contemporary concern (Shalabi and Khalayleh 2007), including interreligious relations. These led to new versions of the Amman Message in the form of the Amman Interfaith Message (2005) and A Common Word between Us and You (2009). Morocco, for its part, has launched several initiatives for interreligious dialogue (Peyret 2019), most importantly the Marrakesh Declaration on the Rights of Religious Minorities in Predominantly Muslim Majority Communities, which was issued by a conference of the same name held in Marrakesh in early 2016. Although the Declaration was issued under the auspices of King Mohammad VI, the initiative itself was organized by the Forum for the Promotion of Peace in Muslim Societies, with headquarters in the United Arab Emirates and whose president is the aforementioned sheikh Abd Allah b. Bayyah. In both initiatives, concepts related with Islamic ethics and human relations occupy a central position. The celebrated word 'tolerance' (*tasāmuḥ*), as applied to interreligious relations in the modern age (Seeberg 2017; Ramadan 2012: 40–50), appears frequently, together with other terms such as peace (*salām/ṣulḥ*), religious freedom (*ḥurriyyat al-dīn/ḥurriyat al-ʿibāda*), fraternity (*ukhuwwa*) and so on. Some of these, such as coexistence (*taʿāyush*), pluralism (*taʿadudiyya*) and religious freedom, are part of a common global terminology that may or may not have been employed in the past. But others such as *raḥma* (compassion), *maṣlaḥa* (the common good), *ʿadl* (justice) and *ḥikma* (wisdom) fall firmly within the Islamic tradition. Hence, there is an overlapping of two different frames of reference: the language of Islam and that of human rights. As mentioned earlier, the word *tasāmuḥ* (tolerance) was not used in Medieval al-Andalus, although this does not mean that peaceful coexistence and reconciliation were not pursued through peace agreements during periods of conflict. Today, however, this concept is widely used in religious discourse along with other similar concepts (Fahy 2018; Kayaoglu 2015; Browers 2011).

We finally turn to the Declaration of Marrakesh on the Rights of Religious Minorities in Predominantly Muslim Majority Communities, which was issued during a convulsive period in which religious minorities, from mainly Christian, Yazidi and some Shia communities, and the population at large felt threatened by the war and the conflicts in Syria and Iraq. Against this backdrop the Declaration took the Constitution of Medina as a legal basis for constitutional principles of 'contractual citizenship' (*muwāṭana taʿaqūdiyya*), such as justice (*ʿadl*) and equality (*musāwā*) before the law, so introducing a renewed approach to the concept of citizenship (*muwāṭana*), which in Arabic derives from the word *waṭan* (homeland/country of birth and/or residence).

As regards the ethical dimension of many of these concepts, in the Constitution of Medina they are proposed as the fundamental values that inspire the citizens of plural societies: 'kindness, honor, cooperation and solidarity, reconciliation, human fraternity and interaction, wisdom, commonweal, being just with others, mercy and peace' (Bayyah 2016a: 8–9, organizers' translation). Likewise Abd Allah b. Bayyah's keynote address, which lays out the theoretical framework behind the Declaration, seeks to examine the concepts of identity and legal status. First, he revises certain classical concepts like *dhimma* and jihad, emphasizing the acceptance of diversity and religious freedom based on the common good, justice and obedience to pacts (Bayyah 2016b: 18–22, 28), and second, he adapts the notion of *umma wāḥida* (a single community)[7] to the contemporary relationship of citizens with their states, tied internally to a constitution and externally to international agreements (*muʿāhadat*) and law (Bayyah 2016b: 28). *Muwāṭana* is therefore based on an accord or contract (*ʿahd/ʿaqd*), equality (*musāwā*) before the law and the notion of collaboration and solidarity among the components of a single community, in which religious and cultural pluralism is 'a virtue in itself, since it establishes opportunities for peace, which is the natural state of mankind' (Bayyah 2016b: 15, our translation). Hence the 'intrinsic' (Bayyah 2016a: 11) plurality of the Islamic *umma* is endowed with a broader meaning in order to define plurality in contemporary societies.

# Conclusions

Al-Andalus offers a magnificent example for assessing the adaptability of Islam to changes in interreligious relations. This is especially true in fifteenth-century Granada under the Nasrids, who were striving to maintain the final frontiers of Islam in Western Europe.

The general normative frameworks in the Islamic world were designed for an expanding empire and were complemented as time went by with adjustments that permitted a relaxation of those initial positions. During this final phase of al-Andalus, which was one of territorial retreat, peace treaties and truces created frequent 'exceptions' to the original norm, especially in frontier regions.

The concept of *dār al-ḥarb* grew less rigid and new solutions were found, such as *dār al-ṣulḥ* and *dār al-ʿahd* (domain of the pact). These treaties and the opinions of some of the muftis revealed an inclination towards ensuring governability, based on resources found within Islamic law itself such as *istiṣlāḥ* or preference for the general interest.

Moreover, the authors of these documents show a clear inclination to peaceful agreements between states when they establish the egalitarian treatment of all their subjects, who should, at least in theory, enjoy the same rights in terms of the preservation of their lives and property, even when standing on the other party's territory. The clauses of the Capitulations insist that the rights of the members of the Muslim community must be preserved and, by signing the agreement, the Christian conquerors of Granada were ethically obliged to honour the commitments they had made therein. However, this peaceful *convivencia* proved short-lived, thwarted by political and ecclesiastical pressures to the contrary.

In summary, the agreements analysed in our two case studies have the following in common:

1. A tendency to safeguard human security and integrity irrespective of who is governing the territory, while guaranteeing economic and sociocultural relations and activities.
2. The pragmatism of the main actors, who established normative frameworks that satisfied the needs of their time. One clear example was the fatwas that broadened the definitions of territorial domains in order to adjust to new situations in both the past and the present.
3. The flexibility of these concepts was determined above all by the real situation on the ground (*wāqiʿ*). Nevertheless, the diversity and adaptability of Islam in these situations did not alter its basic principles.

The present-day initiatives reveal that it is still necessary to trace an Islamic genealogy for concepts that link the past to the present and the future, and offer ways of imagining societies that go beyond a presumed hegemonic universality. Arguably, the limited impact of these projects is due to the fact that they are top-down initiatives that emanate from an elite group of religious scholars, and are sponsored by countries and agendas that eventually hijack the concepts that could potentially be used to shape a more positive future.

We have identified two main groups of semantic fields that are closely related and could lead to further studies. The first concerns the individual and his/her relation to territory and belonging: *dhimma* (the legal status of non-Muslims under Islam), *mudajjan* (the legal status of Muslims under Christianity), *dār al-islām* (the domain of Islam) and so on. The second field concerns the individual in relation to ethics and human relations: *ʿadl* (justice), *istiḥsān* (the public good), *tasāmuḥ* (mutual tolerance) and so on. The latter field has proved to be more contextual, contingent and pragmatic, and is therefore better able to model, to a certain degree, how subjects relate to each other and to the territory and, something even more crucial, how these relations impact political and legal frameworks.

Thus, violence and war were not inevitable outcomes of interreligious contacts. Past and present are contingent and subjects had room for agency by opening up conceptual and societal boundaries without endangering their identities. Understanding this could contribute to a deeper learning that goes beyond facts and figures, and might offset the presentism to which many young people are prone. Approaches of this kind could also inform history educators in their efforts to create more critical-thinking, open-minded young citizens who resist stereotyping and homogenizing discourses.

# From dialogue to peace: Organizations for interreligious and interconvictional dialogue in Europe

Elina Kuokkanen and Patrick Pasture[1]

Although contemporary Europe, and in particular north-western Europe, is perceived as profoundly secular, religion has acquired a new salience in the public debate, partly as a result of immigration and violent terrorist actions. In an increasingly diverse world, in which people are searching for stability and identity but are torn between conflicting messages, conflicts are sometimes associated with religious belonging. One way to counter such conflicts is by promoting intercultural and interreligious dialogue and stressing the importance of 'encouraging cultural pluralism', 'discouraging expressions of extremism and fanaticism' and 'highlighting values and principles that bring people together' (UNESCO n.d.). Although some consider religions as intrinsically violent, religious actors are also being called upon to act as promoters of peace and understanding (Mandaville and Noze 2017) and as a result interreligious and interfaith movements have been attracting a lot of attention recently.[2] In this chapter we explore the efforts these movements are making to foster cultural dialogue as a means of countering violent religious extremism, while broadening their perspective to include various kinds of organizations that promote interreligious and interconvictional dialogue (OIID). These include both faith-based and pluralistic organizations, which make an important yet undervalued contribution to this objective, particularly at local level.

There can be little doubt that exact definitions of both religion and extremism are unattainable, and this begs the question as to whether a specifically 'religious' form of violence actually exists, and how this differs from other kinds of violence inspired by non-religious ideologies such as nationalism. Once we have established whether there is anything special or unique about 'religious violence' that would justify analysing it separately, the next important question would be to assess if and how religions can contribute to combatting this 'religious violence': both the European Union (EU) and the United States Institute of Peace, for example, have expressed scepticism about suggestions that religions could be part of the solution to violent extremism (Mandaville and Noze 2017: 5). Both questions, however, largely exceed the scope of this chapter (see Cavanaugh 2009, who also reflects on the definition of religion;

Hellyer and Grossman 2019). Here we will be assessing above all to what extent and in what ways OIID activities seek to combat what is often referred to as 'violent religious extremism'.

The research for this chapter is based on interviews, an analysis of (mainly online) documents, and participant observation of some OIID activities in Brussels. We focus on a selection of OIID from large international organizations to local groups, some well-established and others more recent. We do not aspire to produce a comprehensive or representative analysis of this issue, although we do hope to provide some insight into existing dynamics in Europe. The organizations covered are Religions for Peace (RfP), United Religions Initiative (URI) – Europe, Coexister, Axcent, Orbit and Expertisepunt IDB. Occasionally we refer to other OIID, such as KAICIID, which is also active in Europe, and the Quilliam Foundation, an organization with roots in the UK that (until its dissolution in 2021) profiled itself as 'the world's first counter-extremism organization' (n.d.).[3]

## Interfaith and interconvictional dialogue in Europe

Although there are historical antecedents – most notably the 1893 World Congress of Religions in Chicago – OIID are largely a post–Second World War phenomenon, which became increasingly significant after the Rushdie Affair in 1989. They are actively promoted by international organizations such as the UN, the Council of Europe, the EU (within the framework of art. 17 of the EU Treaty), and engage people of all ages and classes (see e.g. Halafoff 2013; Yukich and Braunstein 2014; Kollar 2016; Fahy and Bock 2020a; Fahy and Haynes 2018; Patel and Brodeur 2006; Lehmann, ed.,. 2020), even if their leadership, especially as regards the larger umbrella organizations, is often dominated by men (Furseth et al. 2018).

There are important differences between the different OIID as regards inclusiveness and organization: some of the best-known OIID are international and focus on international organizations such as the UN. One particularly noteworthy example is Religions for Peace (RfP), which was established in 1970 as a global association of faith communities. Other interesting initiatives include those sponsored by Muslims in the United States, which arose in response to the 9/11 attacks and the emerging Islamophobia in the West. Similar initiatives also appeared in Islamic states around the world. Their aim was to promote, at least in their international relations, an image of a modern, moderate Islam. These include, for example, the Doha International Centre for Interfaith Dialogue (DICID) and the King Abdullah bin Abdulaziz International Centre for Interreligious and Intercultural Dialogue (KAICIID). The latter has become one of the best-known of such organizations. It was established in Vienna in 2012 by the Kingdom of Saudi Arabia, the Republic of Austria and the Kingdom of Spain, on the initiative of Saudi King Abdullah. However, notwithstanding its support by the UN and even the Holy See as a 'founding observer', it is also quite controversial because of Saudi Arabia's poor human rights record, including with regards to religious freedom (for a discussion of the particular situation in the Middle East, see Fahy 2018a; Kayaoglu 2015; see also Browers 2011; Fahy 2018b).

OIID can be created by a single confession or faith community, or by several, as well as by non-religious pluralist associations and public authorities. They promote dialogue not only between religions but with all world views, including atheists and secularists; often then representing themselves as multicultural, interreligious and interconvictional (Sclafani 2019; Becker 2016; contrasting views in Mandaville and Noze 2017; Griera and Nagel 2018; Nagel and Kalender 2014; Neumaier and Klinkhammer 2020). While Muslims took the lead in the Middle East and also in the United States, in Europe Christian churches were often the source of initiatives for interreligious dialogue. Some of these originated in the ecumenical movement or, particularly in Germany, in the attempts at reconciliation between Christians and Jews. Public authorities sometimes appeal to majority churches to encourage interfaith activities not only as an instrument to prevent potential conflicts and the emergence of extremism, but also to promote moderate forms of religion and civic education (Galal, Liebmann and Nordin 2018; Griera and Forteza 2011). Some Muslim communities in Europe are also striving to foster interfaith dialogue, especially those affiliated with Ahmadiyya and the Gülen-informed groups (such as the Dialogforum in Norway and Sweden). Secular, non-religious, lay movements also play a major (albeit often overlooked) role, though they are not important everywhere (Galal, Liebmann and Nordin 2018: 334–5). Our sample in this research includes several pluralistic organizations such as the French youth movement Coexister and the Belgian associations Orbit and Axsent.

Most European OIID are NGOs that operate at grassroots level (Klinkhammer et al. 2011: 48; Klinkhammer 2020). Some of these local OIID collaborate or are associated with larger OIID 'conglomerates' such as RfP and URI, and others work completely independently. Together they constitute a recognizable 'nebula' of like-minded associations whose real impact is hard to measure.[4] They are far from marginal however: in a survey conducted in 2011, Klinkhammer et al. counted more than 230 independent interreligious dialogue groups throughout Germany, not including regular contacts and dialogues between local parishes and mosques.

One of the most complex issues when assessing OIID is to define dialogue, which the Leuven theologian Terrence Merrigan dubbed 'the most ambiguous term in the vocabulary that has developed around the challenge to religions posed by globalization and pluralization' (Merrigan 2017: 2; Melnik 2020; see also Moyaert 2013). In principle, OIID do not aim to find unity or even common ground and instead accept that fundamental differences exist, with some claiming that diversity is a value in itself. This distinguishes them from ecumenical movements. The OIID's objective of dialogue is to prevent mutual misunderstandings and to engage participants to act for peace and global justice. In that sense, the participants in the dialogue should share a basic acceptance of the values of pluralism, although this may not be true for all interlocutors (see below).[5] It seems, however, that for religious OIID (interfaith organizations in a strict sense) – particularly Christian ones? – the minimum requirement to participate in a dialogue nevertheless includes common acceptance of the value of faith. The renowned German advocate for interreligious dialogue, the Protestant theologian Theo Sundermeier, for example, in his particular interpretation of *Konvivenz* (referring to the *convivencia* in al-Andalus) claims that dialogue should revolve around issues of religious truth or salvation (Klinkhammer et al. 2011). As a result some OIID differ as to whom they want to dialogue with. The Expertisepunt IDB, a local project run by the Catholic Church in Brussels which facilitates multicultural coexistence and interreligious dialogue, excludes atheists on the grounds that the goals of dialogue with atheists would be different from those of 'interreligious' dialogue (interview Van Eycken 2018). Dialogue partners are carefully selected, and controversial topics are avoided. Selecting participants necessarily involves selecting certain religions, and also certain individuals within those religions – namely people who 'express themselves calmly' and 'do not get involved in disputes' or try to convert others. IDB believes that an essential ingredient of a successful dialogue is mutual trust, and therefore that excessive diversity could have negative results. IDB, however, constitutes an exception: the other OIID in our sample do not select their interlocutors in this way.

In practice, OIID have a broad range of objectives, and this means that the projects, platforms, groups and initiatives that they implement are inevitably very diverse. The following goals can be identified: (1) Fostering dialogue between local faith communities and local governments; (2) Promoting knowledge dissemination about religious diversity; (3) Mediating and solving controversies; (4) Advising; (5) Lobbying for the rights and values of religious organizations and (6) Symbolic representation. OIID may also act as interlocutors between religious groups and government, so as to help establish which groups are legitimate religious organizations, although in general they do not involve the public authorities in their activities (Griera and Forteza 2011; see also Griera and Nagel 2018). An issue could arise as to whether those speaking in the name of a certain community might legitimately represent the views of all of their 'co-believers' (Furseth et al. 2018). OIID, however, mainly engage individuals who are acting in their own personal capacity and not as representatives of institutions, and therefore cannot enter into binding agreements on their behalf.

John Fahy and Jan-Jonathan Bock propose that OIID should be considered as social movements, given that, in their view, they promote a normative programme of societal change. On similar lines to Fred Kniss and Paul Numrich (2007: 227), they describe them as a 'decentralised social movement of individuals, groups and organisations seeking to foster mutual respect and understanding across religions in order to achieve positive individual, social, cultural and civic change' (Fahy and Bock 2020b: 1–17, 14). This definition seems to tick a lot of boxes in terms of the roughly similar goals, repertoires of action and focus on 'identity spaces' that all OIID share. However, they focus exclusively on interfaith associations and perceive them as an essentially 'reactionary movement that seeks both to re-inscribe religious values and to provide a platform for religious voices in a modernizing, globalizing and, most of all, secularizing world' (18). This appreciation is questionable though. First, not all interfaith organizations and OIID support 'reinscribing' religious values in society as Fahy and Bock suggest, even if they often support the recognition of religious institutions as genuine actors in society and defend their interests, including requesting public funding for their activities. As a recent study on Nordic OIID shows, they also speak out on public issues; they actually behave in the public as many civil societies (Furseth et al. 2018). Nevertheless, stimulating dialogue, understood as an exchange of views to promote mutual understanding and respect, is a goal substantially different from the more concrete political and societal objectives pursued by social movements; it does not imply anything close to a conversion nor even increased impact of religion in society (although recognition and respect for religious concerns are an issue). It is also important to highlight that many OIID include secular and pluralist actors, who, especially at grassroots level, constitute an important part of the OIID 'nebula'. OIID then highlight a more complex (less tense?) relationship between the religious and the secular. In this respect one may observe that boundaries between the secular and the sacred have evaporated or at least weakened (thereby forming an interpretation of post-secularity that is quite different fromHabermas's concept).[6] As Nathan Kollar argued, in reference to Victor Turner's understanding of liminality, this goes beyond divisions between modern and pre-/postmodern (and secular/post-secular), and instead considers change and fluidity as essential parts of contemporary culture. Following Kollar, one could contend that although OIID do not necessarily strive towards social change, they do (1) break with traditional divisions (associating religious and secular instances in new ways) and (2) engage in activities that transform all those involved individually – and perhaps in the long run society as well. This transformation, however, is far from being a 'conversion' or establishing a common truth, but offers 'a view of the world and religion that has not heretofore existed', in which participants become 'healers of division within their own religion and among religions' (Kollar 2016: 15; Tracy 1987: 65–71; see also Bauman 2000). This ambition still distinguishes OIID from traditional (or modern) social movements.

## Encountering the religious 'other' in OIID

Timothy Garton Ash (2016: location no. 8307–8) argues in favour of dialogue even in situations where the positions of the participants are irreconcilable. But how can dialogue be possible if all the participants observe each other through their own theological lenses and firmly believe that they are the only ones in possession of the ultimate truth? Peter Phan argues that the idea that one's own religion (or world view) contains the ultimate truth (exclusivism), the idea that all religions and world views are equally valid (pluralism), and the idea that other religions draw from one's own (inclusivism) have all failed to appreciate the 'otherness' of various religions, because they continue to view the other through a particular filter. He suggests that the best way to overcome the problem of conflicting claims to truth would be 'deep intellectual and spiritual humility' in order to recognize that 'one's religion offers a true but ever partial insight into reality' (Phan 2012).[7]

In a speech for the UN Department of Public Information in December 2016 United Religions International Secretary General Victor Kazanjian presented interreligious dialogue as a positive, non-military approach to dealing with violence caused by religious extremism, in a context in which military approaches have failed to bring about sustainable solutions. In terms of countering extremism, interconvictional dialogue seems to have a dual goal: first, to reach out to extremists, who are seen as people who were attracted to extremism because of the particular environments in which they were raised; and second, to strengthen the middle ground, limiting the influence of extremists and developing young people's critical-thinking skills and knowledge in order to make them less receptive to extremist narratives, that is, a preventive approach. KAICIID is an example of the first approach. They argue that dialogue should be encouraged as a means of dealing with ongoing conflicts. URI and RfP also aim to include those on the extremes and bring them closer together. The second approach is clear in the work of Coexister, while Orbit has two main goals in its counter-extremism strategy: first, to counter and expose extremist arguments for what they are, which would be targeting the poles, and second, to send a signal to those who read the posts and to the people these posts insult, which would be strengthening the middle ground (interview Maiky 2018). But as the exclusive premises of Expertisepunt IDB illustrate, not all OIID engaged in these kinds of activities.

How do OIID discuss sensitive topics and how do they counter extreme ideas? KAICIID's approach to dealing with polarization is to learn how to regulate the conversation so that diverse opinions can be expressed in a way that is bearable for those involved. This leads automatically to bringing opposing groups and individuals together to discuss and debate the issues that most concern them, instead of resorting to violence. To this end, they also train participants regarding the best ways to handle controversial topics. Cosette Maiky, KAICIID's Iraq and Syria Field Expert, emphasizes the need for a holistic approach. She sees extremism as a symptom of wider problems in society and, given that extremism has many root causes, so the solution must also take place on multiple levels. Interreligious dialogue and social media approaches are part of a wider range of actions that have to be taken. This does not mean justifying the extremists' actions in any way, but it does require a realistic assessment of the environment within which extremism can take hold. The root causes such as poverty, ignorance, social exclusion and unemployment need to be addressed (interview Maiky 2018).

The fact that OIID are united in their condemnation of violent extremism means that they must share some common values, such as respect for human life and dignity, which are clearly being violated in cases of violent extremism. It is therefore necessary to emphasize that some values are universal, thereby contradicting the assumption that there is no common ground between religions. As the premise underlying interreligious dialogue, as opposed to ecumenical dialogue, is not so much to find common ground as to accept differences, total acceptance would mean there was no need to bring up issues in which opinions differ or to criticize or discuss them.

Not all OIID, however, have an explicit strategy for countering extremism, and those that do tend to focus on 'strengthening the middle' instead of reaching out to extremists. In fact, one might ask to what extent, if at all, they actually involve extremists. After all, participation in OIID activities is voluntary. In extensive research on OIID in Germany, Gritt Klinkhammer observed that many participants in OIID activities had never actually met anyone from another faith before getting involved in OIID, other than indirectly via the media. She also noted that one of the reasons for engaging in OIID, in particular for Muslims, is to counter prejudice spread by the media, though their motives, as those of others, are more complex and include more practical reasons such as a desire to improve their own personal image. Engaging with popular images and the media is therefore a powerful reason for joining in OIID activities and can help deal with negative stereotypes (Klinkhammer 2020).

Some interfaith organizations tend to view extremists as people who abuse religion for their own purposes (interview Hasandedić 2018). On the other hand, they consider those who join extremist organizations as normal, if misguided people, who are attracted by the extremist narrative for various reasons (interview Maiky 2018). This contrasts with the idea of extremists 'weaponizing' religion, which is based on the assumption that extremists deliberately 'abuse' religion, consciously exploiting it to achieve their own goals. OIID, on the other hand, regard extremists as both 'abusers' and 'abused', acknowledging that they might not be consciously weaponizing religion. But what is 'the right interpretation' of religion or the scriptures? Certain Islamist extremist groups, for instance, insist that 'only they speak in God's name, and only they are agents of His will' (Harris and Nawaz 2015: 96). By claiming that the extremist groups are misguided and that they interpret religion and the scriptures wrongly, those who seek to combat extremism are in fact using the very same arguments as the extremists, presenting themselves as the holders of ultimate truth. Religions for Peace (RfP) in this respect did not identify any specific problematic groups besides ISIS. RfP Secretary General Azza Karam has criticized PVE (preventing violent extremism) and CVE (countering violent extremism) for focusing too much on Islamist extremism and largely ignoring other ideologies behind violent acts, such as anti-Semitism, and by doing so enforcing the division between 'us' and 'them'. Karam (2021) suggests that replacing a narrative with another could end up affirming the us-versus-them world view: 'our narrative was, would be, better than theirs'. Instead of countering one narrative with another, she recognizes the power inherent in our diversity as an antidote against othering and hatred. 'All faiths teach that diversity is manifestations of the Divine, and/or that the Divine resides in diversity – sometimes polar opposites (e.g. Destructor – Creator)' (Karam 2021).

RfP considers countering 'religious violent extremism' as one of their action areas. The organization defines this as 'violence justified by an extremist religious ideology that does not acknowledge and honour human dignity and the rights that flow from it' (Religions for Peace 2018). As mentioned earlier, they distinguish between religious extremism and violent political and ethnic ideologies, while they also condemn them. As religious leaders they believe they have 'a special responsibility to reject, condemn and take action against violent religious extremism'. They go on to define violent religious extremism as 'false religious ideologies of hatred, not peace'. RfP distinguishes between the religious-ideological, socio-economic and psychological/spiritual drivers behind extremism, calling for further analyses of these drivers and a multi-stakeholder approach to address them (Religions for Peace 2014). Interreligious dialogue, or a 'multireligious approach' as they prefer to call it, is itself a demonstration that peaceful coexistence is possible. The movement, however, mainly operates at the level of global politics and conferences, while offering support and enhanced legitimacy to local interfaith initiatives all over the world and to religious leaders as promoters of peace. How important or effective this kind of action is remains open to discussion: it has had little effect, for example, on the global debate at the UN, though much of the criticism regarding the inefficacy of global action could equally be directed at the UN itself (for a recent critical assessment of the global interfaith dialogue, with special attention to the RfP as well as URI, see Haynes 2018).

The different OIID organizations have different approaches, some are top-down while others prefer to operate from the bottom-up. Both RfP and KAICIID opt for a top-down approach, but with strong links to the real situation on the ground. They empower local actors to maintain and facilitate dialogue. The idea is for their top-down activities to have lasting effects through transformative relationships, as those who attend the dialogue become influential role models in their local communities (interview Maiky 2018).

URI (United Religions International),[8] created in San Francisco in 2000, in contrast focuses on the local level and describes itself as 'a global grassroots interfaith network that cultivates peace and justice by engaging people to bridge religious and cultural differences'. URI is geographically the most far-reaching OIID, acting globally, regionally and locally. At its core, it is made up of Cooperation Circles, small self-organizing groups encompassing members from 'at least three religions, spiritual expressions, or indigenous traditions, including atheists and agnostics'. There are more than one thousand such Circles around the world, sixty-one of which are in Europe. They give people from different backgrounds the chance to work together and to tackle local community issues. Their strategy for reducing violence consists of interreligious bridge-building and local community-based actions that address the causes of conflict. For URI, the strength of interreligious dialogue lies in the wide reach of religious communities as they cross geographical, political and class borders, and in the ways that they 'touch hearts' (United Religions Initiative n.d.). The benefits of grassroots activities are illustrated by a deeply symbolic event in Mostar (Bosnia and Herzegovina), as recalled by Lejla Hasandedić, URI Europe Corporation Circles liaison officer and coordinator of URI Europe. The organization started forging links between the communities on either side of the river, with Catholics on one side and Muslims on the other. After a year of preparations, their efforts culminated in the symbolical event of crossing the Old Bridge together. For those involved, however, it was also a question of breaking down deeply ingrained, mental boundaries. The city had been divided by a conflict, and since then the paths of those from the warring factions had very rarely crossed (interview Hasandedić 2018). According to OIID activists, it is the most local events that lead to the most lasting change.

The interconvictional youth movement Coexister, which is originally from France, is associated with the URI and also participates in the activities of the RfP. It focuses on young people between fifteen and thirty-five years old and is active today in France, Germany, the UK, Belgium and Switzerland. It started as a grassroots movement of Muslims, Christians, Jews and atheists that sought to combat the hatred and violence between Palestinians and Israel, but since then it has broadened its perspective and built up networks with other similar interconvictional organizations promoting peaceful coexistence, such as URI. It is an NGO, but also receives support from the French state for its educational and philanthropic activities. Coexister identifies dialogue, solidarity and raising awareness as three methods through which the organization aims to encourage 'Active Coexistence' and to teach young people to embrace differences instead of considering them a source of problems (Coexister n.d.). Although terms such as 'violent extremism' do not feature in the content displayed on their website, in the specific activities they organize, the idea of countering extremism is vividly present, especially as a means of preventing radicalization (see e.g. Alouti 2018).

Coexister has forcefully pleaded for solidarity and peace in reaction to the Islamist attacks in France in 2015 and 2020. Nevertheless their actions provoked fierce criticism from radical secularists, who accused them of 'naivety' and 'ambiguous relations' with Islamist movements, in particular the Muslim Brotherhood (Pérou and Pétreault 2020; see the French Wikipedia page on Coexister for updated references to media coverage). While reacting against these criticisms, the movement's leaders have actually strongly subscribed to the French principles of *laïcité*, not only with regards to the 'neutrality' of the French state but also in terms of respect for the secular nature of the 'social spheres'. They explicitly reject the suggestion that they are seeking to 'replace the *laïcité* regime (the separation of church and state) of 1905 with a system of toleration or multiculturalism' (Bakkouch 2016).[9] Respect for republican values also figures prominently in the movement's activities and social media output, in which *laïcité* is presented as a context that facilitates debate and coming together, emphasizing the neutrality of the state.

Though more local than Coexister, the Belgian associations Axcent and Orbit defend similar goals. Neither could be considered an interfaith movement. Axcent describes itself as a pluralistic organization – which in the Belgian context means lay and non-religious – that seeks to promote intercultural and interconvictional dialogue in Brussels, one of the most diverse cities in Europe, and to this end develops pedagogical tools for young people, including games (Axcent n.d.a). Orbit, on the other hand, focuses on promoting equality and justice for migrants, whatever their legal status, and on combatting racism, but similarly promotes democratic and intercultural, interreligious and interconvictional dialogue and collaboration, while respecting each other's diversity, which it regards as a value and an asset. Recently, the fight against Islamophobia and anti-Semitism seems to have subsided to some extent, and 'racism' is now being prioritized, although they continue to target individuals who express extremist religious opinions, and try to counter their ideas in a polite, respectful manner (Orbit 2017a). Their strategy is to provide information and tools that can be used in everyday life. As regards structural racism or racially motivated violence, they recognize that there is a need for a more judicial approach and, in such cases, they cooperate with other organizations, while recognizing that even in these cases for the judicial approach to be effective, it must have an educational component (Orbit 2017b). While neither specifically talk about religious extremism supporting violence, they do focus on people who hold beliefs that undermine the rights of others, such as racism, and they identify interreligious dialogue as a way to build a future together. Their point of departure for dialogue is that cultural and religious diversity is a reality and that dialogue is a way to form a climate within which we can coexist.

In contrast to Axcent and Orbit, Expertisepunt IDB seems to aim more at finding common understanding through knowledge-exchange and building contacts between different local religious communities. Expertisepunt IDB wants to make religions more easily approachable and create possibilities for dialogue and encounters (Expertisepunt IDB n.d.). The goal here seems to be the dialogue itself, or maybe even defending the religions' right to exist.

## Challenges to the dialogue

Conducting a dialogue may not be easy. Bart Brandsma (2016: 80), a Dutch philosopher and expert in combatting polarization, is cautious when talking about dialogue and states that many things can go wrong, and that dialogue can actually end up worsening the conflict. He points out that interreligious dialogue often focuses on the identity of the participants, which can heighten polarization. Instead of identity, Brandsma suggests that dialogue should focus on concrete problems. Finding solutions to these problems requires self-reflection and conflict-management skills (where religion can play a positive role). A successful dialogue might require recruiting participants, instead of only choosing those who are already interested in taking part. According to Brandsma, the type of dialogue that is chosen is not always suitable for the type of polarization or conflict. Preventive dialogue is not suitable after terrorist attacks, for instance. It is important to identify the phase of the conflict and choose the type of dialogue accordingly, and this does not always result in harmony. In fact, to be able to discuss peace, it is necessary to have lived through conflicts. The pain and grief have to come to the surface and be discussed in order to create space for questions about how to solve the issues.

The OIID investigated in this research cited a diverse set of challenges that they identify as problematic for dialogue. In some cases, fear of extremist groups limits how freely people can express their personal views. In addition, not all content can be posted online, and photos and films cannot be spread freely (interview Maiky 2018). Lejla Hasandedić from URI also pointed out that some might be restricted from attending interreligious dialogue, especially young people who need permission from their parents. Another challenge is the intergenerational gap they often see between religious representatives and the younger generation – the former do not know how to communicate with the latter, and the latter are not interested in interreligious dialogue or religions. In post-conflict situations, however, attitudes and knowledge are passed on through an intergenerational learning process, and young people who grow up in post-conflict environments learn to consider the 'other side' as violent and dangerous and absorb the idea that they are not supposed to communicate with them. Another challenge is the reluctance in wider society to create space for interreligious dialogue: dialogue is not considered to be of great importance (interview Hasandedić 2018). While there is international recognition of the benefits of interreligious dialogue, local communities are sometimes more sceptical, and it is difficult or impossible to measure its impact. If the causal link between hateful speech and violence is hard to establish, it is even more difficult to establish a connection between bridge-building speech and the absence of violence (Ash 2016: location no. 3235).

The fact that more than one OIID emphasizes the essential nature of dialogue shows that it is not self-evident, even for those who participate in it. Lejla Hasandedić mentioned the difficulties they had with people who instead of entering into dialogue try to convert the other participants, and aggressively share their own, quite extreme views, apparently guided by outside influences opposed to dialogue (interview 2018). KAICIID provides training on dialogue, interreligious dialogue and social media – the very fact that training is needed suggests that dialogue is not automatically successful. Expertisepunt IDB also had negative experiences when those attending seemed more interested in converting others than engaging in dialogue (interview Van Eycken 2018).

Amine El Asli, a member of the youth committee of RfP Europe, mentioned the additional problem of putting the highbrow theories about dialogue put forward in meeting rooms into practical effect in the classroom. When working with schools in Brussels on radicalization, he found it especially problematic that schools – the institutions that should teach young people the skills they need to live together and engage in dialogue – lack the necessary support to maintain continuous dialogue. When asked about the situation in Brussels, El Asli argued that schools should have more information on radicalization, and that there are people within OIID with the expertise and willingness to share that knowledge. The problem is that there is no systematic way to provide schools with the information they require. There is no institution to contact in the event of concerns about radicalization and, if help was requested, this could stigmatize the school as a hotbed of radicalism (interview El Asli 2018). Another problem is that even when information and training are provided, implementing these newly acquired skills in practice has proven very complicated.

These issues were also addressed by the Facebook Digital Challenge team in 2018. During the project, the team introduced these themes as a game that could be used in the classroom. The children were asked to do tasks aimed at increasing their factual knowledge about religions and cultures, and were also encouraged to reflect and express their own ideas. Both of these skills are basic elements of interreligious dialogue. It was reasonably easy to find schools that wanted to participate, and there was also initial interest from the local media and the Flemish Ministry of Education. This implies that while there was a need and a demand for dialogue in schools, it was not viewed as a high priority, and the right tools were not available to sustain it. It does seem, nevertheless, that this issue has been recognized both on the ground and by decision makers (Bonding Beyond Borders 2018).[10]

In the interview mentioned earlier, Amine El Asli observed that there is a lack of connection between immigrants and the religious traditions in their respective home countries (e.g. Morocco, Algeria). As Islam in Brussels cannot be taught at public schools, the parents send their children to Quran schools which are privately run and often transmit a Gulf State view of Islam. This disconnects children from their own national religious traditions and prevents the development of local or European versions of Islam (interview El Asli 2018; see also Pasture 2009: 336). This specific issue cannot be directly solved by interreligious dialogue initiatives, although they might help by portraying religion in a less threatening light, making it more approachable. Eventually, they could help to depolarize the discussion around immigrants and religious minorities.

## OIID and the young

All OIID consider young people to be extremely important. Several of the URI Cooperation Circles involve youth work or are youth led, including Eastern European

Forum for Dialogue – BRIDGES (Bulgaria); Coexister (France); Youth for Peace (Bosnia and Herzegovina); Student Aid Drop (Bulgaria), and Udhetim I Lire (Albania). Sometimes there are signs of a generation gap, between the older generation, who are closer to ecumenical ideas, and young people whose faith gives them a sense of identity but not necessarily to the point of viewing it as exclusive (interview Hasandedić 2018). The main activity of these groups is to organize interconvictional encounters and provide information about different faiths and world views, thus improving religious literacy. In the case of Coexister, for example, this includes (quite prominently) information about the separation of church and state, French 'republican values' and *laïcité*, as well as about non-belief, agnosticism and atheism. Visits to places of worship and particular sites of memory – masonic temples and concentration camps included – rank high. They even organize foreign trips (e.g. to Auschwitz), and visits by faith representatives and testimonies, especially of young people, for example, in schools and local community centres (Axcent n.d.b). Videos and clips on social media are also increasingly popular as a means of presenting information about different faiths and world views. Coexister has made videos '(about) three minutes-long' to introduce different religions (Christianity, Islam, Judaism) as well as atheism and *laïcité*, which stresses the neutrality of the state and the freedom of religion in a system of state-church separation. Remarkably, also the videos on religions conclude by praising the French model of *laïcité*, 'which allows all citizens, of whatever religious, ideological or spiritual worldview to live well together' (Coexister n.d.; also see Coexister 2016). These videos offer an overview of history, inevitably – given their short duration – focusing on key moments rather than on interactions with others, and offer quite a positive outlook. Coexister organizes regular meeting points called *Kawaa* ('a café-debate on living together and secularism. Its goal is to create a space for friendly exchange on the levers of interconvictionality to live better together'). They organized 94 *Kawaa* in France in 2019–20. The association particularly emphasizes 'awareness-raising actions' to teach young people to express their views while respecting those of others. They also highlight the importance of France's secular 'republican values', which in their view underpin coexistence and living together, a statement that is hard not to interpret as a response to strong pressure from secularist lobbies. Coexister (2020) has also developed extensive pedagogical information kits for educators and educational facilitators (*animateurs*).

Other OIID use similar techniques. Axcent produced a DVD called *I Worldview You* (*Ik levensbeschouw jou*) in which young people express their ideas about the history of diversity as a starting point for exploring contemporary experiences of pluralism. It also includes testimonies to encourage reflection about the value and the risks of having strong convictions, be they religious or non-religious. Orbit has created postcards about religious feasts to be distributed among young people, and flashcards with subjects that arouse reflection and debate have been created as a means of informally introducing interconvictional themes into classroom discussions. During the Facebook Global Digital Challenge in 2018 a team created a game that could be used by teachers to help them initiate dialogues on sensitive topics in the classroom. The team did initial research to identify local issues that could be tackled in class. After producing the game, they then visited schools to test it out and measure its impact in terms of changes in attitudes. The game was designed to increase factual knowledge of religions and cultures, as well as to develop reflective skills and to encourage young people to express their own ideas (Bonding Beyond Borders 2018). The concept has recently been commercialized by a young start-up called Bonding Beyond Borders in Flanders, which sells its educational card game to schools and teachers.[11]

Western European OIID groups try to create dialogue and openness with young people from migrant backgrounds (including second or third generation) and refugees, while also addressing recurrent issues in European history, most notably anti-Semitism or anti-Judaism – hence the excursions to Auschwitz. In the Southern Balkans, however, and in particular in the former Yugoslavia, emphasis is also placed on building bridges between local communities who not long ago were at each other's throats, as well as on relations with minorities, in particular Romani. Typical activities organized in these areas include youth camps, workshops, exchanges and interfaith café encounters (see Youth for Peace n.d.). In many cases they are 'preaching to the converted', in the sense of reaching out to young people who are already convinced of the need for peace and understanding. Nonetheless, they could help to change the climate, as similar bridge-building experiences after the Second World War, particularly between Germany and France, show (compare also Chapter 7). They also organize gatherings in which young people from different religious backgrounds and different parts of the world gather together to get to know each other and reflect about their differences and similarities, and about ways to promote peace through non-violent means.

## Conclusion

Since the 1960s, religious diversity in Europe has increased considerably, with the main European capitals and other big cities becoming hyper-diverse. This creates multiple challenges, especially as European culture is characterized by a deep longing for homogeneity with which cultural and religious diversity tend to clash (Chapter 1). Religion has been a particularly contentious issue, with the influx of migrants from different religious backgrounds, many of them Muslim. Although cultural and religious diversity was never even a minor concern until the 1980s, coexistence has come under stress with the rise of political Islam in the Middle East and the terrorist attacks inspired by extreme Islamist organizations such as Al Qaida and ISIS. The radicalization of Islam has also affected local and immigrant Muslim communities in Europe, although only a miniscule minority become violent. However, these developments have provoked reactions from autochthonous populations and politicians, who either emphasize Europe's Christian origins, or liberal, secularist 'republican' values or, sometimes, both.

The polarization around religion and world view, and the increased public visibility of religion, challenges established narratives about the 'secularization' of Europe, although in fact what they really highlight is that the very meaning of religion has profoundly changed. This new situation is usually referred to as 'post-secularism', although there is no consensus on what this actually means in practice. OIID offer some answers though. They first of all recognize that for many people religion remains an important source of identity and therefore must be taken seriously. They moreover testify that faith – religious or secular – is not just a source of conflict but can also offer solutions, showing at the very least that a peaceful dialogue is possible, although the contribution it makes to the resolution of conflicts remains hard to quantify. They also illustrate that 'secular' and 'religious' are not necessarily opposites – a possible definition of 'post-secular' could be the blurring of such boundaries and oppositions, perhaps, because 'belief' has largely replaced 'faith', and people can more easily accept different beliefs in the modern sense (i.e. 'liberated' above all from their Christian – but arguably also secularist – straitjacket) (Shagan 2019: 293). The above assessment, however, also shows that 'vestiges' of the old antagonisms still remain, for example, in the exclusion of non-religious people by some faith-based OIID, as well as in the secularist assault against associations that combat Islamophobia and promote dialogue. Insofar as they are grassroots movements – not all are – OIID can shift their focus away from established boundaries and theologies and focus instead on the many hybrid varieties of contemporary 'world views', where convictions are multiple and often overlap. This is particularly true for young people, whose hybrid experiences seem hard to fit into established traditions, be they religious or not (see e.g. Lee 2015; Bock, Fahy and Everett 2019; Boubekeur and Roy 2012; Lamine 2013). From that perspective, OIID also appear to offer a real answer to the demands of European youth, as came to light in the pilot studies discussed in Chapter 2 of this book. How effective they are in preventing radicalization and the emergence of violent extremism still remains an open question though.

Interreligious and interconvictional dialogue has been criticized because it focuses on identity and in so doing may fuel polarization, as identities often emphasize differences. It is argued that to ensure effective depolarization, these dialogues should focus on concrete issues and forget these differences for a while. We did not find evidence to support this claim, however. In practice, the opposite seems to occur, in that OIID tend to generate new hybrid 'transconvictional' identities. A preselection of participants might lead more easily to the formation of such an 'transconvictional' group identity – one way of encouraging this would be to cast the net wider to bring people into dialogue from outside the 'already interested' circle. In cases in which the dialogue centres on a concrete problem or topic, the group identity is less obvious. For instance, Coexister organizes events which aim to make practical improvements to local communities, such as giving food to the homeless, and Orbit tries to uncover concrete reasons behind racism, thereby making the discussion more problem-focused rather than circling round identities. The main thing these associations achieve is arguably the meeting place, the dialogue itself, creating an environment of trust and respect.

There is little indication that these OIID offer an immediate cure for violence; we did not encounter examples where OIID or religious leaders were able, or even directly tried, to effectively engage with radicalized persons – arguably our research was too small and too limited for that. The fact that the OIID could not use social media effectively in this respect (other than as instruments of self-promotion) is also very significant. There are, however, signs that they contribute to creating a less polarized environment, and hence act as preventers of violence. That OIID are not necessarily just 'interfaith' organizations may be important here, as this implies that they also overcome the secularist–religious divide that has also been at the heart of much conflict in European history (albeit less violent than the religious wars of the sixteenth century or contemporary Islamist terrorism). This blurring of the lines between secular and religious has, however, opened them up to attack from secularist milieus, as experienced by the French OIID Coexister.

Anna Halafoff (2013: 169) argues that OIID contribute to what she calls 'netpeace' by emphasizing the interconnectedness of global problems and solutions, and particularly by creating 'critical and collaborative networks, including state, non-state and religious actors co-committed towards common good, to solve the world's most pressing problems'. Although she may be slightly overstating the role they play, this explains quite succinctly why OIID must be taken seriously.

## Interviews

- Amine El Asli (member of the Youth Committee of RfP Europe), interview by EK, 15 May 2018.
- Lejla Hasandedić (URI Europe Corporation Circles Liaison Officer and coordinator, URI Europe), interview by EK, 6 April 2018.
- Cosette Maiky (Iraq and Syria Field Expert, KAICIID), interview by EK, 20 March 2018.
- Jan Van Eycken (coordinator, Expertisepunt IDB), interview by EK, 2 May 2018.

# Religious toleration in the new spirituality subculture: The Estonian case

Lea Altnurme

## Introduction: History of new spirituality

Tolerance is one of the central principles in today's liberal, multicultural, pluralist society. It has become a cornerstone for diversity, coexistence and the integration of social differences. The principle of tolerance underpins the fulfilment of civil liberties and human rights and protects the right of individuals to act according to their fundamental convictions (Murphy 2020). In general, 'tolerance' is understood as voluntary, conditional acceptance of any beliefs, acts or customs that are seen as flawed, incorrect or different, but still bearable. Tolerance, and in particular religious tolerance, can be interpreted in several different ways (Forst 2017). In this chapter, 'tolerance' is used in the sense of acceptance of difference.

New spirituality, previously also known as New Age, originated in the hippie movement that was part of the counterculture of the 1960s. The basic attitudes of new spirituality towards religion stem from the same source, justifying a closer look at the history of this phenomenon. The hippie movement, in general, was not religious in nature, despite being clearly influenced by Eastern religions, particularly Buddhism. It also incorporated aspects of shamanism and neo-shamanism, especially in the context of using psychedelic substances to facilitate spiritual experiences.

Buddhism had a notable impact on political agendas. Specifically, the two slogans, 'Make Love, Not War' and 'Flower Power', adopted by the hippie movement in the United States as they protested against the Vietnam War in the mid-1960s, were aimed at ending war and violence, not through frontal confrontation but through peaceful campaigns that promoted love. The latter slogan and the associated programme for action were formulated by the Beat poet Allen Ginsberg (1926–97), who had discovered Buddhism as early as 1953 (Kent 2001: 9). War and violence can be seen as extreme manifestations of intolerance. Having rejected violence, hippies promoted the ideas of love and tolerance as the alternative.

The principle of non-violence or Ahimsa argues that one should not cause harm to any life form and is a key concept in Indian religions, particularly Buddhism and Jainism. In Buddhism, it is associated with compassion. The great Indian activist

Mahatma Gandhi (1869–1948) was the first to incorporate the idea and practice of non-violence into the struggle against British rule. He believed it was the ultimate human value (Mäll. Läänemets and Toome 2006: 246) and was an inspiration for many civil rights and liberation movements throughout the world.

In the hippie counterculture, the ideas of non-violent resistance, insubordination and refusal to be part of the 'system' were linked to protest not only against war but also against capitalist society with its institutions and authorities. The state, the police, the military industrial complex, the civil order – all these structures had, according to hippies, been established through violence and brutality (Hall 2007: 155). 'Flower Power' represented spiritual politics by 'other means', aimed at undermining the system from within (Hall 2007: 163). Previous moral norms and social conventions were rejected. This also applied to the established Christian church, which was regarded as an institution of power that aroused strong opposition.

In general, hippies placed great value on feelings and despised 'robotic' rationalism. They believed that the world, other people and one's own self had to be experienced directly, without the ambition of gaining control. They opposed technological activity that views life as just a series of problems that need to be solved, and concluded that this manner of constantly reworking and reassembling the world was pointless because the world was already a whole. They pointed out that people in Western society had been reduced to performing the functions for which they had been trained and employed, to the detriment of the integrity and dignity of the individual. Hippies also tended to reject the ethics of achievement that focused on status, wealth, power and career (Tipton 1982: 21–3). They blamed institutions for violent, destructive levelling and standardization of individuals, resulting in the elimination of everything that was different and original, that is, intolerance towards difference. It is therefore not surprising that integrity, uniqueness, authenticity and diversity were highly valued in the hippie counterculture.

However, the political 'Flower Power' protest did not produce the expected results. A new, better society was not born and violence persisted. Although great efforts had been made, they had apparently come to nothing. This led to frustration and a mental shift. If social revolution could not be achieved through political means, then alternative religious movements and associations, some of them of Eastern origin, could perhaps be the source of new hope. As previously noted, the influence of such movements was noticeable in the hippie counterculture from the beginning. The apparent leap from protesting on the streets to learning to meditate in ashrams was in fact surprisingly easy. These attempts to find shelter in new religious groupings became increasingly popular and started to attract wider attention. This search for religion was guided by the principle that if we cannot change the world, we can at least change ourselves (Kent 2001: 27–40). It was within this context that the idea of a 'New Age' came to the fore. If a New Age could not be achieved through political protest, it would have to come about through a cosmic event based on astrological predictions.

The New Age did not suddenly appear out of nowhere. It was based on an existing network of esoteric groups and communities, within which the old idea of a new age was already circulating through the works of Alice Bailey, who proclaimed that humanity had reached a turning point after the Second World War and was now moving into a different spiritual reality. There was talk of the end of the Age of Pisces and the beginning of a New Age, the Age of Aquarius, which would begin when the Sun left the constellation of Pisces and entered the constellation of Aquarius at the Spring equinox (Clarke 2006: 26). Wouter Hanegraaff (1996: 97) has described this stage of development as a New Age *sensu stricto* (in a strict and limited sense).

The emerging New Age subculture adopted the idea, popularized in the 1960s, that it was important to find oneself, to discover one's true nature and live by it, instead of surrendering to external conformity created by society, previous generations or religious and political authorities. Freedom of choice, personal experience and authenticity became important ideals (Taylor 2002: 83). The integrity of the individual and of nature had been destroyed by the capitalist system and had to be rebuilt through psychotherapeutic self-integration, a mystical fusion of self and others, and heightened environmental awareness and protection (Tipton 1982: 22). It was hoped that the growing number of people who chose the path of personal transformation would eventually make the world a better place.

The New Age subculture, or new spirituality, inherited a great deal from the hippies, but its role as a counterculture in opposition to established society gradually weakened over time and it lost its millennial edge (Sutcliffe and Gilhus 2014: 3–4). This New Age *sensu lato* (in a much broader sense) developed on the basis of a wide variety of 'alternative' ideas and pursuits, to use Colin Campbell's terminology, and could be regarded as 'the cultic milieu having become conscious of itself ... as constituting a more or less unified "movement"' (Hanegraaff 1996: 97).

New spirituality has also inherited an ambivalent attitude towards religion. On the one hand, it is tolerant, providing that the debate is about the voluntary religious choices made by the individual, while on the other, it is confrontational and critical when it comes to an institutional religion that has power over its members, like the church. This attitude towards institutional religion in the New Age arose not only out of the hippie movement but also from esoterics, where it has a long history (Hanegraaff 2006: x).

The participants in the new spirituality subculture do not usually describe themselves as 'religious' because, in their minds, this term is associated primarily with institutional forms of religion, which they see as violent and restrictive of spiritual development. If they use such descriptions at all, they prefer to define themselves as 'spiritual'. In the nineteenth and twentieth centuries, the word 'spiritual' was used to emphasize inner life and, from the 1950s onwards, it was also used to denote religious traditions that had separated from the standard institutional form. In the 1960s, Abraham Maslow created a new theory of transpersonal psychology in which spirituality acted as a means towards 'self-actualization'. In the 1990s, it also became a label or brand under which both products and dreams could be bought and sold (Pasture 2011: 67–8).

One of the most spectacular, profound and yet undervalued phenomena of the post-war transformations of religion was what was once described as 'the end of the missionary ideal'. This was clearly related to decolonization, but was arguably also part of a broader phenomenon of respect for other faiths and individual religious freedom

(Pasture 2011: 95). In Estonia, too, there is a widely held belief that 'you should not impose your faith on others'.

However, as a syncretic, perennial phenomenon, new spirituality has assimilated many ideas and practices from other, particularly Eastern, religions, such as Buddhism and Hinduism. It has also borrowed from indigenous religions, usually in the form of neo-shamanism (Altnurme 2013: 24–8). Unsurprisingly, its followers have a respectful, amicable attitude towards these religions, which contrasts with their normally critical stance towards monotheistic religions from which they have borrowed very little.

Today, new spirituality represents an environment, a religious culture with a global reach that produces its own specific resources in the intellectual (books, magazines, online portals, forums, videos), creative (music, dance, visual arts) and practical (self-development groups, training groups, lectures, workshops, camps, festivals, etc.) domains. This environment includes different spiritual leaders, teachers, group and practice instructors, and event organizers, who together form a large number of activists. These are joined by regular or occasional participants and lifestyle practitioners who come together to form communes, communities and communication networks of varying sizes that have a perceptible influence beyond their own subculture. The basic discourse of new spirituality talks about striving towards spiritual development and well-being. The resulting doctrines and practices focus primarily on meeting the needs of the individual, even if activities are conducted in a group setting. For instance, those taking part in a yoga group are focused on developing themselves, rather than on advancing as a group. This individualistic discourse of spiritual development has been described in research literature as *self-spirituality* (Heelas 1996: 18), *me-spirituality* (Stoltz and Engelberger 2016: 102) or *me-centredness* (Stolz and Engelberger 2016: 101).

Religious individualization was the result of the individualization of society. The decline of the social order and hierarchies ushered in the wholesale abandonment of established traditions and practices, allowing individuals to become masters of their own destinies. At the same time, social boundaries evaporated, leading to a reduction in social cohesion and increased interaction and hybridization (Pasture 2011: 70).

The aim of this chapter is to describe the attitude towards religion among the members of new spirituality groups in the Estonian historical and sociocultural context, focusing particularly on the issues of diversity, pluralism and tolerance.

## The Estonian case: Religious diversity

The emergence of religious diversity is contingent on several legal, social and cultural prerequisites. For a start, the general sociocultural situation should regard diversity as something that is permissible and tolerable from ideological and religious perspectives. Religious diversity should not be confused with religious plurality, which refers to a prevalent social situation in terms of pluralism, that is, the attitude towards diversity. Different societies with a greater or lesser degree of religious plurality may or may not be pluralist, that is, tolerant of diversity (Bouma and Ling 2009: 508).

Religious diversity in what is today Estonia first began to emerge after the Great Northern War in the early eighteenth century when this area was incorporated into the religiously varied Russian Empire. By the time the Republic of Estonia was proclaimed in 1918, religious diversity had become a factual reality. The Estonian population was predominantly Lutheran but there was a significant number of Orthodox Christians and a growing share of free churches influenced by the Brethren Movement. There were also Jewish and Tatar Muslim communities (Au and Ringvee 2007: 117–23). Some groups in Estonia practised spiritism, occultism or parapsychology, and there was also a Freemasonry lodge. The ideas of theosophy and anthroposophy, which are sometimes regarded as predecessors of new spirituality, had been circulating even before Estonia became an independent state. Eventually, the respective associations were officially registered: the Estonian Anthroposophical Society in 1924 and the Estonian Society of Theosophy in 1927 (Abiline 2013: 37–63). Freedom of religion had been guaranteed by the Constitution of the Republic of Estonia, and the Religious Associations Act of 1925 stipulated that 'everyone is free to decide on their membership or secession of membership in religious associations'. This meant that by law everyone was permitted to choose their religion or to not follow any religion at all. In legal terms, religion had become a matter of individual choice. All religions without distinction were tolerated by the state institutions (Altnurme 2018: 300).

This situation was radically reversed under the anti-religious Marxist ideology of the Soviet period (1945–91). Even though freedom of religion in the sense of celebrating rituals was notionally guaranteed, in fact the work of religious associations was hindered – they were kept under surveillance and the government promoted anti-religious propaganda. Dissemination of religious ideas was prohibited. Believers who confessed their faith in public encountered obstacles in education, employment choices and career advancement. They were also considered ineligible for any benefits (e.g. apartment tenure rights, car purchase permits, foreign travel clearances). While the official Marxist ideology never gained widespread popularity, its negative attitude towards religion, including Christianity, did take root. Estonia underwent significant secularization in the Soviet period. The majority of the population became detached from the church and the custom of passing on religious traditions at home was interrupted.

Even though the Soviet period was a difficult time for religions due to the ban on the promotion of religious beliefs, several new players were, nevertheless, able to enter the religious playing field. Eastern religions became more influential and from being the norm, Christianity now had to compete with a range of religious options (Altnurme 2006: 153–217). Lectures on Asian culture became increasingly popular in the 1970s. These were held in the University of Tartu and elsewhere on the initiative of Linnart Mäll, an Estonian Orientalist who translated a range of Buddhist, Taoist and Confucianist texts into Estonian. These lectures attracted significant interest among students and intellectuals. The first Buddhist association, the Estonian Buddhist Brotherhood, was formed in Tallinn in 1984 (Põlenik 2004: 67–95). Another noteworthy addition was the arrival of the Hinduist Hare Krishna cult in Estonia in 1977, interest in which was spread by word of mouth within a mixed Russian-Estonian circle of friends. Krishna devotees from Estonia travelled to other republics of the USSR, promoting their beliefs mainly through lectures on Vedic philosophy, but also through chanting, recitation of mantras and sacred food (Ellermäe-Reimets 2004: 96–116). In 1983, Eastern religions became the target of government persecution (Altnurme 2006: 77).

Another interesting development was the spread of new spirituality literature and practices in Estonia, which occurred at the same time as in the West, initially also in the wake of the hippie counterculture. Religious literature that was smuggled in from the West was translated, copied and distributed in secret, mostly among tight circles of intellectuals and artists, without gaining much traction beyond them. The subjects discussed in this underground literature included esotericism, parapsychology, alternative medicine, yoga, meditation, natural mysticism, Buddhism, Hinduism and Taoism. The first yoga groups were formed. Alternative healers and psychics garnered unprecedented popularity in the late 1970s and early 1980s, often being invited to give semi-legal public presentations and it was difficult to get an individual appointment with them due to the high level of interest. In addition to healing, they were also seen as sources of alternative philosophies and ways of life, with many people expecting them to confirm the ideas, theories and parapsychological phenomena they had read about in underground literature. People turned to them in search of spiritual guidance (Altnurme 2006: 78–9).

Something unexpected happened in the field of religion at the end of the Soviet period, during the Singing Revolution (1987–91), in which there was a religious upsurge because everything that had been prohibited was now suddenly legal. People were baptized in large numbers. There was an outburst of enthusiasm for religion and esotericism. Several new religions started to arrive from the West. Former underground religious groups, such as the Jehovah's Witnesses, the Hare Krishna movement and others, were now able to operate openly in public (Altnurme 2006: 80–3). This was a period of unprecedented tolerance at both official and individual level, if by tolerance we mean acceptance of difference.

The religious surge started to abate at the start of the second period of independence, from 1991 onwards. As Estonians were not accustomed to seeing missionaries at work on the streets – primarily from the Christian Word of Life Church, Jehovah's Witnesses, Mormons and the Hare Krishna movement – they began to regard the new religious groups as a problem. The Estonian media raised the issue of possible brainwashing, asking whether the members of such movements could be regarded as completely sane. The initial enthusiasm for religion witnessed during the transformation period gave way to a degree of scepticism (Altnurme 2018: 306).

The Singing Revolution (1987–91) was also a time of mass popularity and local reshaping of the global New Age culture, with the result that the Estonian new spirituality subculture started to distance itself from the 'New Age' tag at the end of 1990. This was not replaced by any other common self-description, resulting in an ambiguous situation as regards an appropriate label. The academic description 'new spirituality' is generally accepted by those involved in New Age practices, despite some perceptible mistrust of any designations, labels or frames (Uibu 2015: 109–10). The study by Marko Uibu (2015: 114) confirmed that three-quarters of partakers were opposed to labelling new spirituality as a 'religion' and preferred to describe themselves as 'spiritual but not religious'. The analysis of responses to the survey of 'Religious Trends in Estonia

2014' supported the conclusion that those who described themselves as 'spiritual but not religious' were influenced less by Christianity, that is, religion, and more by the new spirituality subculture, as compared to the average for the Estonian population as a whole (RTE 2014). In the light of the results of several surveys, it would seem that an estimated one-third of Estonians have been influenced by new spirituality, and a roughly similar share of the population would describe themselves as 'spiritual but not religious' (RTE 2014, 34 per cent; LFRL 2015, 28 per cent; Religio 2 2017, 28 per cent).

Having started out as an alternative spiritual movement, it did not take long for new spirituality to become part of the mainstream (Uibu 2016: 262). Society is generally tolerant of the New Age subculture, which is usually not seen as a religious phenomenon. However, there are some signs of growing scepticism about it (Uibu 2012: 337–57).

At present, there are two major religious paradigms in Estonia – Christianity and new spirituality. Based on different surveys, one-fifth to a quarter of ethnic Estonians support Christianity while, as mentioned earlier, one-third have been influenced by new spirituality. The new spirituality subculture has a critical disposition towards Christianity as an institutional religion. Similarly, many of the statements made by spokespersons of Christian institutions labelling new spirituality as a false belief or fallacy have not been particularly friendly, either. However, neither party is interested in inciting a conflict. There is mutual tolerance in the sense of putting up with each other's presence. There has also been at least one known instance of attempted co-operation. In 2011, a rebirthing breathwork group, belonging to the new spirituality subculture, held some sessions in St John's Lutheran Church in Tartu. Having identified St John's as a focal point of spiritual energy in Tartu, members of the group asked for permission to hold one of their sessions in the church. As the management board of the congregation did not find the world view of the group inappropriate, they decided to grant them permission, based on the principle of openness as stated in their development plan, that is, that the church is open to new people, ideas and spiritual diversity, while carrying on and upholding traditions (Pekko and Koppel 2013: 154–5).

It is also worth noting that there have been no conflicts between different religions in Estonia at societal level since the gradual emergence of religious diversity from the eighteenth century onwards. According to the latest Census of 2011, there are ninety religions in Estonia (Census 2011). It may seem a lot, but apart from Christianity (28 per cent of the population said they were Christians), the members of all the other religious associations total less than 1 per cent of the population. The Census, however, did not provide a complete picture of religious diversity in Estonia in that new spirituality was not included in the results, because of the way the questions were framed. Other surveys which include new spirituality attest to its widespread influence, as mentioned earlier.

The existence of religious tolerance at a public, institutional level does not necessarily mean that it exists at the individual level. A study of religious biographies of three generations (a total of seventy-seven biographies, collected in 1999 and 2000) indicated that tolerance towards people with different religious affiliations takes time to develop. The biographies of the generation that became religious in the first half of the twentieth century reflected disputes about the right or wrong religion. In general, Lutheranism – and with some reservations, Orthodoxy – were seen as the correct and appropriate faiths, while all other religions were regarded as foreign and untrustworthy. There were horror stories about free churches along the lines of 'I was forced to become a follower' or 'their teaching will drive you crazy', which resemble the stories told today about new religions (Altnurme 2006: 121–3). Buddhism seemed suspicious (Altnurme 2006: 184), and the neopagan Taara faith was accused of being artificial and lacking authenticity. This indicated a continued mistrust of other ways of believing, even though there was already quite a range of different options available.

The situation changed at the end of the Second World War with the arrival of the Soviet regime, under which religion was officially persecuted and became the subject of negative stereotypes. As a result, the majority of the population distanced themselves from the church and established religion. This had an unexpected effect in that it led to increased communication across denominational boundaries among Christians in the 1970s and 1980s, especially young people who became religious during that period (Altnurme 2009: 197). They started to assemble in various groups, ensembles, discussion panels and camps, establishing a pattern of ecumenical communication at a grassroots level. Compared to the preceding generation, they were more tolerant of other religions, such as Buddhism and Hinduism, and of esotericism. The same could be said about the attitude of Buddhists and Hare Krishna devotees towards Christianity (Altnurme 2006: 184–6).

As to the people who became religious after the restoration of Estonia's independence in 1991, their biographies generally indicate that they were tolerant of other religions and believed that different religions should foster friendly coexistence for the sake of a future without wars. The intolerant minority was, for the most part, made up of members of extreme religious groups (Word of Life, Jehovah's Witnesses). The spread of the idea of perennialism and syncretism was also noticeable (Altnurme 2006: 238–43; Pekko and Koppel 2013: 146–52). The acceptance of difference was increasingly seen as a value in itself. However, it is probably not surprising that Christians tended to be more lenient towards other Christian denominations and more reserved about Eastern religions and New Age, and vice versa (Altnurme 2006: 238–43).

In conclusion, even though one-third of Estonians have a critical attitude towards the church (RSE 2014) and there is a prevalence of negative stereotypes about religion (e.g. religion makes you stupid, passive and weak or, conversely, violent), the current overall atmosphere is characterized by tolerance at both societal and individual levels.

## Qualitative study: Religious toleration in the new spirituality subculture

### Method

Within the framework of the RETOPEA project, I interviewed ten respondents from three different new spirituality groups: Lilleoru Community (3), Spiritual Lecture Hall (4) and Gaia Academy (3). It is important to note that new spirituality groups are not exclusive – people are free to move between them and to be members of several groups at the same time. I chose these groups because they have a more permanent, enduring mode of operation than most new spirituality groups, which tend to emerge and disappear quite quickly.

The oldest of them is the Lilleoru Community (www.lilleoru.ee), which is located in a rural area close to Tallinn, the capital of Estonia. It was established in 1993 and its central figure is the spiritual teacher Ingvar Villido. The group has undergone several transformations, in keeping with the shifting relevance of different topics and practices (e.g. yoga, neo-shamanism according to Carlos Castaneda, Native American teaching in the spirit of Toltecs and Arizona tribes, the Hinduist doctrine of Haidakan Babaji, Buddhism, Dzog-Chen, etc.) within the wider new spirituality subculture (Tamm 2012: 85–6).

The Spiritual Lecture Hall (www.lektoorium.ee) was launched in 2007 with the aim of establishing a network of groups throughout Estonia, in order to enable people to think and grow together so that they could generate original ideas and suggestions that would, it was hoped, lead to a spiritual awakening of the entire country. This ambitious plan did not succeed. Nevertheless, one group still remains active in the city of Tartu. It is guided by Peeter Lepisk and provides those interested in new spirituality with an opportunity to come together in a club format.

The Estonian Gaia Academy was established in 2015 by Toomas Trapido, although Estonia joined the Global Ecovillage Network much earlier in 2006. Gaia Academy is an educational school that specializes in adult education. Its website (www. gaiaakadeemia.ee) presents the school as follows:

> Gaia Academy is a comprehensive lifestyle institution that operates within the framework of the Estonian Eco-Communities and contributes to promoting sustainable development education. Gaia Academy is guided by the international Gaia curriculum, whose keywords are a holistic approach to life and experientiality. Gaia Academy is an education institution for holistic lifestyle studies. Gaia Academy is part of the Estonian Ecovillage Association and both are working together to contribute to sustainable development education. We offer different Gaia Education based courses for adults and host other different holistic courses.

Five of the respondents were female and five were male, with ages ranging from thirty to seventy years old. I found the respondents through personal contacts. The goal of the interviews was to examine the respondents' attitude towards religion. I started each interview by talking about specific religious personalities, either from a film where religion is depicted in a neutral or positive light or from the person's own group of acquaintances, and I tried to guide the respondents to express their attitude. I followed this up with the general question 'What do you think about religion?' I adopted this approach because attitudes expressed with regards to specific, personal relations or emotional experiences (films) can be quite different from those offered as general statements. The remaining questions were different for each respondent, depending on their previous answers. Saturation of the sample occurred quickly, as the respondents repeated previously known attitudes and explanations that were presented above.

In analysing the text of the interviews, I combined deductive and inductive content analysis as described by Philipp Mayring (Mayring 2014: 104). The inductive analysis was performed in seven steps according to Mayring's step-by-step model for summarizing content analysis (Mayring 2014: 66). I compared the interviews based on the derived categories, using the principle of cross-case analysis.

## Results

The results of the interviews coincided quite well with the general beliefs that are prevalent in the new spirituality subculture. I divided the answers into three thematic groups.

### *1. Recognition of individual free choices*

As is common in the new spirituality subculture, the interviewees recognized the right of individuals to make free choices, including the choice of a world view or religion. For example:

> It is my own internal feeling, what I believe, what I perceive and what I think. Every person has their own path; if someone interprets that there is only matter and nothing else, that we somehow appeared on this earth completely by accident, that we simply live and then die and after that there is nothing and never will be again, then this is equally their belief. It is not up to me to argue for something else. I am amenable and I don't feel that it is my duty to guide someone to believe something different to what they currently believe. (female)

Individual choices were recognized even when they entailed the decision to be a member of an institutional religion. The respondents reckoned that religion could have several benefits for such individuals: helping to solve problems, counterbalancing excessive materialism, providing a source of truth, integrating life into a whole, providing support in difficult situations, and so on. Some examples are given below:

> Very often, people turn to religion if they have problems. If the solutions they learned at home do not work, they start looking for other possibilities. A religious path is one option. It is important for people to find some kind of spirituality in their lives, to achieve a balance within their highly practical, highly material lives. If a person comes to spirituality or religion during a crisis, then there is the risk that this may happen in a very extreme manner. Especially at the beginning. A person who is drawn to the extremes is no longer tolerant and open, and they see in religion only a very narrow truth. (female)
>
> Religion has a place in human lives. It is justified. The specific direction is a matter of individual choice. I accept them. Religion helps people to find a direction, a balance, their own truth. (female)

If someone has religion in their heart, it is better than nothing. Then they have the ability to turn towards God. A person that does not even aspire to find God flutters in all the winds of the world, no matter where they come from. If you pray to God in a difficult situation, you will have support. (female)

Religion, Christianity, is for those who want an escape from life. It is necessary and good for them. I will not say that it is bad to be religious. They are doing what is right for them. But it cannot be recommended to anybody else. (male)

While the respondents acknowledged that the choices people make deserve respect, they also highlighted potential problems, as can be seen from the above examples: religion as escapism, the risk of fanatism. This option was also seen as less valuable than their own decision to engage freely in spiritual practices. The respondents did not see their membership of the Lecture Hall, Gaia Academy or the Lilleoru Community as restricting their spiritual journey because, as noted above, membership of new spirituality groups is not exclusive and not even constitutive of identity, as people are freely moving between groups and associations. These groups do not impose restrictions or demands on their members. This facilitates the feeling of spiritual freedom among participants.

2. Criticism of institutional religion

As expected, the respondents were critical of institutional religion. The examples below indicate the aspects that the respondents found objectionable: the church and spiritual leaders are authoritarian; they impose external rules, restrictions and obligations; they demand obedience and deprive individuals of responsibility; the church represents a narrow, limited way of thinking; it is artificial, inauthentic, striving for money and power, and degenerate:

The word 'religion' creates associations with the word 'church' or with a sect. A leader or guru of a sect, however you like to call them. I have never had, and hopefully will never have, an external authority who tells me how I should think, what my opinion should be or what I should believe. It is a matter of definition. (female)

The Church is an escape. Perhaps I will no longer think this way in a year. For me, the Game (i.e., life) offers much more opportunities than the Church. The Church provides a safe environment to escape from the opportunities of the Game. The people who are in the Church want someone to save them. There is nothing that people need saving from. Human beings need to maintain their humanity and love in difficult situations. If they leave a difficult situation and someone saves them, they will have much less opportunity to maintain their humanity and love. (male)

Religion is something that has a doctrine, a scripture, rituals, priests. Religions are large, organised systems. Even though I am baptised, I do not consider myself a Christian. Religion is too restrictive for me. Why do clergy think that they have the right to speak on behalf of God, while relying on words written by humans?

God is everywhere; you don't have to go to a stone building to meet God. If your feet do not take you there, it means you are not interested. (male)

Religion is a bad word. Why would you be religious? Rely on your experience and test what you are told. If you sense that someone has a connection to the spiritual aspect, to their deeper self, then their words are based on actual experience and are worth listening to, but if all they do is quote the Bible, albeit convincingly, then ... let them keep talking. But if they start prescribing rules and demand that people follow them, even though the rules are unnatural and harmful, then this is something I do not support. (male)

For me, religion is an institutional phenomenon. Religious-institutional is associated with certain formalities. The institution retains the form, but its content is no longer understood. People start to practice the form. They perform a ritual, without necessarily comprehending the content; it is done purely on the basis of faith. The form, such as a church, was used to record information, experiential knowledge, that has been lost over time. It has become something to be taught and blindly followed, thinking is not allowed, you only have to believe. (female)

For me, religions have lost their value, even though I consider myself religious. I definitely do believe, but I don't know what to call it, whether universal energy or something solemn. Religions should be focused on the spiritual, but they are more interested in material gain, and this is what debases them. The present-day religions depend on money. They are involved in extensive cooperation with the material. They cannot reach the human soul. But they should be bearers of faith, hope and comfort. (male)

Religion is blinding if you don't have freedom of thought. (male)

It closes certain doors. If your mind is turned in one direction, you no longer notice anything else. Your thoughts have been firmly fixed by the system. (female)

Obviously, these examples cannot cover the entire spectrum of criticism. The list could be continued, but the principal, most common positions of new spirituality seem to be as follows: institutional religion represents a threat to spiritual development (in whatever sense); its rigid dogmas, outdated moral norms and the requirement of subordination to external authorities tend to hinder, rather than facilitate, development.

3.   Self-positioning in relation to religion

While the respondents were, unsurprisingly, tolerant of individual religious choices and critical of institutional religion, seeing themselves as free spiritual travellers, they were quite amenable to the word 'religious' and some even used it to refer to themselves. Previous studies have indicated that participants in the new spirituality subculture tend not to define themselves as religious (Uibu 2015: 114; RTE 2014). Some examples are as follows:

For me, there has never been any conflict between religions since I was a child. I think all religions are like languages that talk about the same thing. The object they describe is the same, only the languages are different. Religion is like a pointing finger. What is it that religions point to? It is what human beings are seeking. They seek a deeper meaning in their daily lives. They seek transcendence. (female)

I could also define myself as religious if it means that I believe there is something invisible in addition to the material. I would not want to bind myself to any external authority, be it an institution or an individual or whoever, who starts to tell me what is right or how I should act. (female)

The two examples below illustrate the typical attitude of respondents by which they distance themselves from religion:

But I am now a self-made philosopher, I have no fundamental religious beliefs. I would not even consider this right. I believe that the original teaching was communicated verbally, without any church or scripture. The prominent yoga teachers even ruled out the written word as such, because it loses the sentiment that comes with verbal teaching. As soon as you write a teaching down and someone else reads it, it has already changed. (male)

I find that no religion is right for me. My current life is a time of faith in myself and of exploring who I am. I feel uncomfortable when I have to fit in. Religion is not my way. In that regard, you need to be a psychic to sense your inner core. You need to engage it or provide it with a chance to exist. This is something to keep in mind above all. Then you will live your life without having to do too much. Your life will be difficult if you try to hide or suppress that core. My core is completely separate from the Church. I see God in another human being. (male)

It is important to add that, even though generally disliked, the church had certain valuable aspects for some respondents. In particular, they appreciated old church buildings as powerful or mystical places that elicit a specific state of mind. This phenomenon has been observed before (Altnurme 2010: 202–3). In the context of this study, there is one relevant example:

I am not bound to any specific religion; I go to church because it has good energy, it is a good place to find harmony in yourself. Liturgies are also good; they provide a good meaning. I fully support the work of this church; it is part of the culture of the region. It has, after all, a good message. For instance, the Book of Wisdom from the Bible. (male)

The man who had previously criticized the church as being debased by its lust for power and money also saw something good in it: the space, the liturgy and the Word, which he claimed helped him find harmony in himself. In addition, he saw the church as part of local ethnic culture, an opinion that is quite unusual in Estonia. A more common belief is that the church signifies being part of European civilization.

## Conclusions and discussion

It would seem then that the members of new spirituality groups have a generally tolerant attitude towards religion in several respects. If tolerance is understood as tolerating or putting up with something in return for some benefit, then they are ultimately prepared to tolerate even institutional religion, because there are people who choose to belong to a church as something important and necessary for them. The free choices of individuals are respected. If tolerance is understood as acceptance of difference, then the new spirituality subculture is open to borrowing from a wide spectrum of religions. Its members are also characterized by openness and amenability. Many of them believe that all religions have the same core and, that ultimately, they all express the same thing.

While members of new spirituality groups are generally tolerant of religion, and particularly of religious individuals, they also look down on them to some extent. They contrast free spiritual development presented as a personal choice with opting for dogmatic, restricted faith like members of institutional religion. When they compare the two, it is obvious that they do not regard them as equally worthy choices. The first option is high up in their hierarchy of values, while the second has a relatively lowly position.

If we place the results of this small study within the context of the history of religion and society in Estonia, it would seem that the members of the new spirituality subculture are not much different from anyone else. The dominant attitude towards religion in Estonia today is one of calm, tolerance and even indifference. All the ideas expressed by those participating in the interviews can also be encountered in Estonian society outside the new spirituality subculture. As a result, the people interested in new spirituality find external confirmation of their opinions and beliefs, while they in turn contribute to maintaining a tolerant atmosphere within society.

## Surveys

Census 2011: Statistical Database: 'Religious Affiliation', 22 March 2019. Available online: http://andmebaas.stat.ee/Index.aspx?lang=et&DataSetCode=RL0451 (accessed 21 September 2021).

LFRL 2015: Poll 'On Life, Faith, and Religious Life 2015' (EUU 2015). The poll was carried out by Saar Poll Ltd. A total of 1,002 people, 683 of them Estonians, were questioned in live interviews. Responses were recorded on paper. The sample was selected using the proportional model of the population set.

RTE 2014: Poll 'Religious Trends in Estonia 2014' (RSE 2014). The poll was carried out by TNS Emor by means of telephone interviews in February 2014 (50 per cent by mobile phone and 50 per cent by desk phone) as a CATIbuss study. A total of 1,100 residents of Estonia over the age of fifteen were questioned; there were 756 Estonians in the sample. The sample was selected using the proportional model of the population set.

Religio 2 2017: Poll 'Religio 2' (Religio 2 2017). The poll was carried out by Kantar
    Emor by means of telephone interviews in spring 2017 as a CATIbuss study.
    A total of 1,100 residents of Estonia over the age of fifteen were questioned; there
    were 664 Estonians in the sample. The sample was selected using the proportional
    model of the population set.

# Notes

## Introduction

1. I would like to thank Elena Arigita, Riho Altnurme, Stefanie Sinclair, Karel Van Nieuwenhuyse, Nigel Walkington and John Wolffe for their constructive comments on earlier versions of this text, for which nevertheless I alone bear responsibility.
2. This book is based on the findings of the European H2020 research project RETOPEA (Religious Toleration and Peace). This project's main aim was (and is) to explore how the experiences of historical peacemaking processes can be 'used' to help young people obtain a more nuanced understanding of religious diversity, on which they can reflect, and to develop an appropriate instrument to bring this about. For more information see http://retopea.eu. The project has received funding from the EU under the European Union's Horizon 2020 research and innovation programme (GA no. 770309).
3. Secularism is more often used to refer to 'the governance of religion' than secularities (Taylor 2007, 2014; Bigrami 2014; Modood 2017; Modood and Sealey 2019; Triandafyllidou and Magazzini 2021), but has the disadvantage of the ideological load, which also explains why spirituality is usually ignored. Compare Fox (2015); Kleine and Wohlrab-Sahr (2020); Schnabel, Behrens and Grötsch (2017).
4. As Ronald Inglehart (2021) and others argue, the politicization of religion may have led to a decline in churching in the United States. But religion remains, perhaps even more than ever, an important (yet divisive) factor in US politics.
5. As David Nirenberg (2013) observes, however, (anti-)Judaism is much more than about a certain people or faith, and is rather used as 'a category, a set of beliefs and attributes with which non-Jews can make sense of and criticize their world' (3)). Here the emphasis is on the religious dimension, though I am aware that it is not that simple.
6. Compare Furseth (2018a). It should be clear that this approach is different from the mediatization of religion.
7. The difference between religious and history textbooks is not discussed in Chapter 3 of this book, but is one of the conclusions of research conducted by Madis Maasing and Karel Van Nieuwenhuyse within the framework of the RETOPEA project.
8. This assessment also came to the fore in some two hundred review papers of the House of European History conducted within the framework of the international Master's Programme in European Studies: Transnational and Global Perspectives at KU Leuven in 2018 and 2019 (which offered quite divergent interpretations and appreciations of the museum). See also Chapter 4.

# Chapter 1

1. Thanks to Riho Altnurme, Elena Arigita, Irene Dingel, Lydija Georgieva, Henning Jürgens, Brigitte Meijns, Violet Soen and John Wolffe for comments on an earlier draft. As always, the authors bear sole responsibility for errors and interpretations expressed in this chapter.
2. Rainer Forst (2011) distinguishes between horizontal toleration – how people accept differences among each other – and vertical toleration by the state. This is similar to the distinction between institutional and legal *toleration*, and tolerance referring to attitudes and/or daily practices (e.g. Murphy 1997). Classen (2018) views toleration as the acceptance of a minority by a majority and tolerance referring to a wider range of differences.
3. The literature is extensive. Forst (2011) offers a historical-philosophical assessment (albeit in a teleological frame of progress). For the Christian contribution see Shah (2016) and Wilken (2019).
4. The literature on the development of religious diversity in North America is vast. Haefeli (2021) offers a brilliant starting point for discussing this evolution in a global transatlantic perspective.

# Chapter 3

1. In collaboration with the Spanish research project Representations of Islam in the Glocal Mediterranean: Conceptual Cartography and History (FEDER-MICINN: RTI2018-098892-B-100).
2. In the case of Estonia and Germany, we also had to include sixth grade textbooks, as Ancient History is studied in this grade. In the case of Finland, we analysed both fifth and sixth grade textbooks, as history from the Ancient to the Early Modern Period is studied in these grades.
3. As Germany is a federal state, it has a federal school system in which each state uses its own textbooks, with their own specific (and different) contents, approaches and mentalities. The textbooks in predominantly Catholic Bavaria are quite different from those used in mostly Protestant and more secular Brandenburg.

# Chapter 4

1. See http://www.culturaydeporte.gob.es/msefardi/home.htmluseum (accessed 16 September 2020).
2. The Macedonian case study is surprisingly under-researched and there is little new literature on museums and the various nation- and identity-building processes. See, for instance, Aronsson and Elgenius (2011); Whitehead, Eckersley and Mason (2012); Peressut and Pozzi (2012); Whitehead et al. (2013); Perresut, Lanz and Postiglione (2013a), (2013b) and (2013c).
3. One of the first museological texts published in North Macedonia, 'Art and Museum Aesthetics', by PavaoVuk-Pavlović, professor at the Faculty of Philosophy in Skopje, can be read from this perspective. Published in 1963 the author argued that the epistemological function of the museum is 'intellectual, and not emotional', while

claiming that the museum as an institution should be in constant need of 'refreshing' (1963: 11–3).
4. Similar continuity was observed throughout the former Yugoslavia as museum exhibitions remained virtually unchanged for some time after the country disintegrated. Some authors described the museums in the former Yugoslav states as 'time-capsules' filled with content from a different political 'era' (Puttkamer 2015; Jagdhuhn 2016).
5. Berenbaum played a leading role in the creation of the US Holocaust Memorial Museum in the 1990s, while Jacobs is his close associate and co-founder of Berenbaum Jacobs Associates – an educational experience design firm.

## Chapter 6

1. This referendum asked the question: 'Do you want the European Union to be entitled to prescribe the mandatory settlement of non-Hungarian citizens in Hungary without the consent of the National Assembly?' (see the official election pages: https://static.valasztas.hu/dyn/onepsz201610/szavossz/en/eredind_e.html).
2. PEGIDA stands for *Patriotische Europäer gegen die Islamisierung des Abendlandes* (Patriotic Europeans against the Islamization of the Occident).

## Chapter 7

1. On the failure of the 2011 census in Macedonia, which is itself indicative of the difficult post-2001 interethnic relations in the state, see Visoka and Gjevori (2013).
2. The two agreements have a history of mutual reference and cross-national transfer of knowledge. As an example, in March 2010, six experience-exchange visits took place in Skopje as part of the EU-funded MOST project – International Dialogue for Civic Leadership, organized by the Macedonian Center for International Cooperation and Mediation Northern Ireland. The workshops were focused on sharing experiences from the implementation of the GFA and the OFA (more in MCIC 2010).
3. Kubik and Bernhard also recognize the 'churches' among the 'governments, political parties, schools, families, museums and so on', as agencies which 'work hard to reproduce both the themes (cultural heroes, myths of origin, narratives of greatness, etc.), that are defined as constitutive units of one or more specific visions of "national heritage", and scripts or scenarios of action that together amount to what is often defined as (a version of) the "national character"' (Kubik and Bernhard 2014b: 286).
4. The OFA stated: 'This Framework agreement will promote peaceful and harmonic development of the civic society and it will simultaneously respect the ethnic identity and the interests of all Macedonian citizens'.
5. Until 2001, the 1991 Constitution mentioned only MOC and 'the other religious communities and groups' as 'separate from the state and equal before the law' (Macedonian Constitution 1991, art. 19). The full 2001 Amendment VII to the Macedonian Constitution reads as follows:

'(1) The Macedonian Orthodox Church, as well as the Islamic Religious Community in Macedonia, the Catholic Church, Evangelical Methodist Church, the Jewish Community and other Religious communities and groups are separate from the state and equal before the law. (2) The Macedonian Orthodox Church and the Islamic Religious Community in Macedonia, the Catholic Church, Evangelical Methodist Church, the Jewish Community, and other Religious communities and groups are free to establish schools and other social and charitable institutions, by way of a procedure regulated by law. (3) Item 1 of this amendment replaces paragraph 3 of Article 19 and Item 2 replaces paragraph 4 of Article 19 of the Constitution of the Republic of Macedonia. (Macedonian Constitution 1991, amend. VII)

6. More than 130 laws, legal changes and amendments have been adopted by 2019 – the eighteenth anniversary of OFA – most of which are laws on non-discrimination and equitable representation (59), while 40 of them are legal interventions in the fields of culture, education and decentralization.
7. Nadège Ragaru (2008: 9–10) notes that DPMNE understood OFA as a 'reward to terrorism forcibly imposed by the international community' during the first post-conflict year, which in turn resulted in a political blockade of 'the reforms included in the Ohrid package'.
8. One of the most prominent artistic projects was 'Komsi Kapicik' – a Turkish phrase depicting a small garden door that connects two neighbouring estates. The door was present in most households, whatever the families' religious denomination or ethnic origins. The door, thus, was artistically reimagined as a metonymy to the history of multi-ethnic and multi-confessional tolerance in Macedonia.
9. An early unsuccessful, initiative to memorialize the 2001 conflict by an ethnic Albanian political actor occurred in Struga in the mid-2000s, when the newly appointed head of the municipality launched a project to erect 'a memorial to the killed municipal councillor, Nura Mazar, aka Commander Struga, an alleged former NLA member' (Ragaru 2008: 26).
10. One of the rare exceptions was the Ahmeti initiative for a meeting of Albanian party leaders on 13 August 2020 following parliamentary elections, which was rejected by the partisan leaders.

# Chapter 8

1. We are very grateful to the editors and to Luz Gómez for their careful reading of this chapter and their useful and thoughtful comments.
2. Nieves Paradela Alonso provides a revealing definition of *jihād* based on the classical theories of Muslim theologians: it is 'any effort performed by a Muslim to gain spiritual betterment for himself or a collective benefit for Islam'. The 'greater' *jihād* is spiritual and peaceful, while the 'lesser' *jihād* requires fighting against the infidel (Paradela Alonso 2001: 655).
3. The area under Nasrid control in the fifteenth century stretched from Vera in the East (until 1488) to Gibraltar (until 1462) and then Marbella (until 1485) in the West, on both land and sea.
4. In an edition dated 1327 that later circulated widely, the expression 'shall be treated' (*yuʿamal*) at the end of the text was replaced by 'shall be fought' (*yuqatal*), so producing a drastic change in meaning. Abd Allah b. Bayyah, principal promoter of

the Mardin Conference, drew attention to this emendation after consulting the original manuscript, no. 2757 in the Ẓāhiriyya Library in Damascus (Michot 2011: 145–6).

5. The use of Christian years in Nasrid documents should not be understood as a sign that the Christians were the dominant partner, nor that it was an act of courtesy towards them. 'Christian years' were used to have a common calendar that reflected the difference between solar years and lunar years so that the two sides could reach an agreement more easily.

6. This recognition includes the eight schools of Islamic jurisprudence; the Ashʿarī creed; the 'real' *Taṣawwuf* (Sufism); and 'true' Salafi thought (Bin Talal 2006: xix–xx).

7. *Umma* has the general sense of 'community', which in religious terms usually means the community of Muslims. In the Constitution of Medina, however, the term is not used in a religious sense and refers more to a sociopolitical entity dependent on a legal framework that governs the relations between parties (Gómez García 2019: 388–90).

# Chapter 9

1. This chapter is based on a master thesis by Elina Kuokkanen (Master in European Studies: Transnational and Global Perspectives, KU Leuven) (referred to as EK below) and has been edited and updated by Patrick Pasture and Elina Kuokkanen, and includes material collected by Priit Rohtmets (University of Tartu). Special thanks to Angelina Vladikova (URI Europe CC Liaison Officer, Chair of Bridges), the interviewees, and co-editors.

2. We use interreligious and interfaith interchangeably, referring to the dialogue between religions/faiths and between (Christian) denominations.

3. Elina Kuokkanen (EK) attended four events organized by three of these organizations: a visit to a Protestant church in Brussels organized by Coexister, a yearly meeting of Religions for Peace, a meeting of religion teachers and a meeting to plan an event for young people, both organized by Expertiesepunt IDB. She also joined the Quilliam Circle to gain access to their publications and followed two activities by the Quilliam Foundation on the development of Islamist ideology. She also took part in a Facebook Global Digital Challenge in 2018. The Global Challenges are part of Facebook's Counter Speech initiative, and engage students worldwide to challenge extremist narratives by creating content on social media and organizing offline events. The Quilliam Foundation was dissolved in April 2021.

4. The metaphor of the nebula is borrowed from the French sociologist of religion, Françoise Champion, who uses the concept of *nébuleuse* to refer to an undefined whole of groups, associations and networks which are like-minded, not necessarily connected but still recognizable.

5. Here we disagree with Moyaert (2013) and are closer to what Lehmann (2020a) describes as a 'cultural context approach'.

6. Fahy and Bock (2020a) refer to Habermas's concept of the post-secular as a secular society in which religious actors again play an active role in the public sphere. On different (critical) views on the concept see Beckford (2012) and Hjelm (2015). For a creative attempt to interpret interfaith organization as secularization, see Lehmann (2020b).

7. It is important to observe that the claim to hold the absolute truth is common to the main monotheistic religions, but is not necessarily universal. Neither Buddhism

     nor Hinduism, at least in their manifestations prior to their 'modernization' under Western Christian influence, claim to possess the truth in this sense, nor does contemporary New Spirituality (see Chapter 10). OIID do not claim absolute truth either, although some individual interlocutors may.

8. Not to be confused with United Religions, which is an intergovernmental organization created in Geneva in 2018. See https://unitedreligions.org/ (accessed 21 September 2021).

9. It should be noted that this is quite a radical secularist interpretation of the principle of *laïcité*. In its daily activities and information Coexister adopts a more moderate interpretation which emphasizes the liberating nature of *laïcité*, which allows everyone to express their own world view. The most radical interpretation advocated today by the French authorities argues for the ideals of secularism to impregnate all levels of society, completely marginalizing religions, which only have the right to practise their rituals. On the complexities of the concept (though largely ignoring the fact that there are multiple interpretations), see Balibar (2018), esp. chapters 8, 12 and 15.

10. The new end terms that the Flemish Parliament adopted in January 2021 explicitly focus on dialogue and active participation in society: https://www.kwalificatiesencur riculum.be/sites/default/files/atoms/files/Sleutelcompetentie%20Burgerschap.pdf (accessed 21 September 2021).

11. EK is one of the founders of Bonding Beyond Borders. See Bonding Beyond Borders (2018).

# References

## Introduction

Angvik, Magne, and Bodo von Borries (1997), *Youth and History: A Comparative European Survey on Historical Consciousness and Political Attitudes among Adolescents*, Hamburg: Körber-Stiftung.

Asad, Talal (2003), *Formations of the Secular: Christianity, Islam, Modernity*, Stanford: Stanford University Press.

Asad, Talal (2013), 'Trying to Understand French Secularism', in Hent de Vries and Lawrence E. Sullivan (eds), *Political Theologies: Public Religions in a Post-secular World*, 494–526, New York: Fordham University Press.

Aupers, Stef, and Dick Houtman (2006), 'Beyond the Spiritual Supermarket: The Social and Public Significance of New Age Spirituality', *Journal of Contemporary Religion*, 21 (2): 201–22.

Balibar, Étienne (2018), *Secularism and Cosmopolitanism: Critical Hypotheses on Religion and Politics*, New York: Columbia University Press.

Bardon, Aurélia, Maria Birnbaum, Lois Lee and Kristina Stoeckl (2015), 'Introduction: Pluralism and Plurality', in Aurélia Bardon, Maria Birnbaum, Lois Lee and Kristina Stoeckl (eds), *Religious Pluralism: A Resource Book*, 1–10, Florence: European University Institute – ReligioWest.

Beckford, James A. (2003), *Social Theory and Religion*, Cambridge: Cambridge University Press.

Beckford, James A. (2010), 'The Return of Public Religion? A Critical Assessment of a Popular Claim', *Nordic Journal of Religion and Society*, 23 (2): 121–36.

Beckford, James A. (2012), 'ASSSR Presidential Address Public Religions and the Postsecular: Critical Reflections', *Journal for the Scientific Study of Religion*, 51 (1): 1–19.

Bejan, Teresa M. (2017), *Mere Civility: Disagreement and the Limits of Toleration*, Cambridge, MA: Harvard University Press.

Bilgrami, Akeel (2014), 'Secularism: Its Content and Context', in Alfred Stepan and Charles Taylor (eds), *Boundaries of Toleration*, 79–129, New York: Columbia University Press.

Bock, Jan-Jonathan, and John Fahy (2019), 'Emergent Religious Pluralisms: Ideals and Realities in a Changing World', in Jan-Jonathan Bock, John Fahy and Samuel Everett (eds), *Emergent Religious Pluralisms*, 1–21, Basingstoke: Palgrave-Macmillan.

Borries, Bodo von (1994), '(Re-)Constructing History and Moral Judgment: On Relationships between Interpretations of the Past and Perceptions of the Present', in Mario Carretero and James F. Voss (eds), *Cognitive and Instructional Processes in History and Social Sciences*, 339–55, Hillsdale, NJ: Lawrence Erlbaum Associates.

Bruce, Steve (2002), *God Is Dead: Secularization in the West*, Oxford: Blackwell.

Calhoun, Craig, Mark Juergensmeyer and Jonathan Van Antwerpen (eds) (2011), *Rethinking Secularism*, Oxford: Oxford University Press.

Casanova, José (1994), *Public Religions in the Modern World*, Chicago: Chicago University Press.

Christensen, Henrik Reintoft (2018), 'Religious Diversity and the News: Critical Issues in the Study of Religion and Media', in Lene Kühle, Jørn Borup and William Hoverd (eds), *The Critical Analysis of Religious Diversity*, 252–71, Leiden: Brill.

Christie, Nancy, and Michael Gauvreau (eds) (2013), *The Sixties and Beyond: Dechristianization in North America and Western Europe, 1945–2000*, Toronto: University of Toronto Press.

Cooper, Laurence D. (2016), 'The New Spirituality, or The Democratization of Divinity and Vice Versa (Has the New Age Come of Age?)', *Perspectives on Political Science*, 45 (4): 1–13.

Corm, Georges (2005), *Orient-Occident, la fracture imaginaire*, Paris: La Découverte.

Corm, Georges (2009), *L'Europe et le Mythe de l'Occident: La Construction d'une Histoire*, Paris: La Découverte.

Costa, Paolo (2019), *La città post-secolare: Il nuovo dibattito sulla secolarizzazione*, Brescia: Queriniana.

Delanty, Gerard (2013), *Formations of European Modernity: A Historical and Political Sociology of Europe*, Basingstoke: Palgrave-Macmillan.

Dobbelaere, Karel (2002), *Secularization: An Analysis at Three Levels*, Brussels: P. I. E.-Peter Lang.

Eck, Dianne (2016), 'What Is Pluralism? The Pluralism Project'. Available online: http://pluralism. org/what-is-pluralism/ (accessed 21 September 2021).

Ferrari, Silvio (2013), 'Models of State-Religion Relations in Western Europe', in Allen D. Hertzke (ed.), *The Future of Religious Freedom: Global Challenges*, 202–12, Oxford: Oxford University Press.

Fox, Jonathan (2015), *Political Secularism, Religion, and the State: A Time Series Analysis of Worldwide Data*, Cambridge: Cambridge University Press.

Furseth, Inger (ed.) (2018a), *Religious Complexity in the Public Sphere: Comparing Nordic Countries*, Cham: Palgrave Macmillan.

Furseth, Inger (2018b), 'Secularization, Deprivatization, or Religious Complexity?', in Inger Furseth (ed.), *Religious Complexity in the Public Sphere*, 291–312, Cham: Palgrave Macmillan.

Giordan, Giuseppe (2012), 'Pluralism as Legitimization of Diversity', in Giuseppe Giordan and Enzo Pace (eds), *Religious Pluralism: Framing Religious Diversity in the Contemporary World*, 1–12, Cham: Springer.

Giordan, Giuseppe, and Enzo Pace (eds) (2012), *Religious Pluralism: Framing Religious Diversity in the Contemporary World*, Cham: Springer.

Goddeeris, Idesbald (2021), *Missionarissen: Geschiedenis, herinnering, dekolonisering*, Tielt: Lannoo Campus.

Hellemans, Staf, and Gerhard Rouwhorst (2020), *The Making of Christianities in History: A Processing Approach*, Turnhout: Brepols.

Hjarvard, Stig (2008), 'The Mediatization of Religion: A Theory of the Media as Agents of Religious Change', *Northern Lights*, 6 (1): 9–26.

Hjarvard, Stig (2012), 'Three Forms of Mediatized Religion: Changing the Public Face of Religion', in Stig Hjarvard and Mia Lövheim (eds), *Mediatization and Religion: Nordic Perspectives*, 1–44, Göteborg: Nordicom.

Hjarvard, Stig (2013), 'The Mediatization of Religion: Theorising Religion, Media and Social Change', *Culture and Religion*, 12 (2): 119–35.

Hjarvard, Stig, and Knut Lundby (2018), 'Understanding Media Dynamics', in Knut Lundby (ed.), *Contesting Religion: The Media Dynamics of Cultural Conflicts in Scandinavia*, 51–64, Berlin: De Gruyter.

Hjelm, Titus (2015), 'Is God Back? Reconsidering the New Visibility of Religion', in Titus Hjelm (ed.), *Is God Back? Reconsidering the New Visibility of Religion*, 1–17, London: Bloomsbury.

Holland, Tom (2019), *Dominion: The Making of the Western Mind*, London: Little, Brown.

Houtman, Dick, and Stef Aupers (2007), 'The Spiritual Turn and the Decline of Tradition: The Spread of Post-Christian Spirituality in Fourteen Western Countries (1981-2000)', *Journal for the Scientific Study of Religion*, 46 (3): 305–20.

Inglehart, Ronald (2021), *Religion's Sudden Decline: What's Causing It, and What Comes Next?*, Oxford: Oxford University Press.

Inglehart, Ronald, and Pippa Norris (2004), *Sacred and Secular: Religion and Politics Worldwide*, Cambridge: Cambridge University Press.

Kaiser, Wolfram (2017), 'Limits of Cultural Engineering: Actors and Narratives in the European Parliament's House of European History Project', *Journal of Common Market Studies*, 55 (3): 518–34.

Keysar, Ariela (2017), 'Religious/Non-religious Demography and Religion versus Science: A Global Perspective', in Phil Zuckerman and John R. Shook (eds), *The Oxford Handbook of Secularism*, 40–54, Oxford: Oxford University Press.

Kleine, Christoph, and Monika Wohlrab-Sahr (2020), *Preliminary Findings and Outlook of the CASHSS 'Multiple Secularities – Beyond the West, Beyond Modernities'*, Leipzig University, 2020.

Kluveld, Amanda (2018), 'Secular, Superior and, Desperately Searching for Its Soul: The Confusing Political-Cultural References to a Judeo-Christian Europe in the Twenty-First Century', in Emmanuel Nathan and Anya Topolski (eds), *Is There a Judeo-Christian Tradition? A European Perspective*, 241–66, Berlin: De Gruyter.

Lee, Lois (2015), *Recognizing the Non-religious: Reimagining the Secular*, Oxford: Oxford University Press.

Lewis, Martin W., and Karen Wigen (1997), *The Myth of Continents: A Critique of Metageography*, Berkeley: University of California Press.

Lövheim, Mia, and Stig Hjarvard (2019), 'The Mediatized Conditions of Contemporary Religion: Critical Status and Future Directions', *Journal of Religion Media and Digital Culture*, 8 (2): 206–25.

Lübbe, Hermann (2003), *Säkularisierung: Geschichte eines ideenpolitischen Begriffs*, Freiburg: Alber.

Lundby, Knut, Henrik Reintoft Christensen, Ann Kristin Gresaker, Mia Lövheim, Kati Niemelä, Sofia Sjö, Marcus Moberg and Árni Svanur Daníelsson (2018), 'Religion and the Media: Continuity, Complexity, and Mediatization', in Inger Furseth (ed.), *Religious Complexity in the Public Sphere*, 193–249, Cham: Palgrave Macmillan.

Mark, James, Artemy M. Kalinovsky and Steffi Marung (eds) (2020), *Alternative Globalizations: Eastern Europe and the Postcolonial World*, Bloomington: Indiana University Press.

Marzouki, Nadia, Duncan McDonnell and Olivier Roy (eds) (2016), *Saving the People: How Populists Hijack Religion*, London: Hurst.

Micklethwait, John, and Adrian Wooldridge (2009), *God Is Back: How the Global Revival of Faith Is Changing the World*, New York: Allen Lane.

Modood, Tariq (2017), 'Multiculturalizing Secularism', in Phil Zuckerman and John
    R. Shook (eds), *The Oxford Handbook of Secularism*, 354–68, Oxford: Oxford
    University Press.
Modood, Tariq, and Thomas Sealy (2019), 'Secularism and the Governance of Religious
    Diversity', *GREASE*, May. Available online: http://grease.eui.eu/wp-content/uplo
    ads/sites/8/2019/05/GREASE_D1.1_Modood-Sealy_Final1.pdf (accessed 21
    September 2021).
Nathan, Emmanuel, and Anya Topolski (2018), 'Introduction: The Myth of a Judeo-
    Christian Tradition: Introducing a European Perspective', in Emmanuel Nathan and
    Anya Topolski (eds), *Is There a Judeo-Christian Tradition? A European Perspective*,
    1–16, Berlin: De Gruyter.
Nemo, Philippe (2010), *What Is the West?*, Pittsburg: Duquesne University Press.
Neumann, Iver B. (1995), *Russia and the Idea of Europe: A Study in Identity and
    International Relations*, Abingdon: Routledge.
Neumann, Iver B. (1998a), 'Russia as Europe's Other', *Journal of Area Studies*, 6: 26–73.
Neumann, Iver B. (1998b), *Uses of the Other*, Minneapolis: University of Minnesota Press.
Nirenberg, David (2013), *Anti-Judaism: The Western Tradition*, New York: W. W. Norton.
Pasture, Patrick (2013), 'De-Christianization and the Changing Religious Landscape
    in Europe and North America since 1950: Comparative, Transatlantic and
    Global Perspectives', in Christie and Michael Gauvreau (eds), *The Sixties and
    Beyond: Dechristianization in North America and Western Europe*, 367–402,
    Toronto: University of Toronto Press. .
Pasture, Patrick (2015), *Imaging European Unity since 1000 AD*, Basingstoke: Palgrave
    Macmillan.
Pasture, Patrick (forthcoming), 'Europe's Many Easts: Why One Orient Is Not the Other',
    in Jan Vermeiren and Mark Hewitson (eds), *Europe and the East: Self and Other in the
    History of the European Idea*, London: Routledge.
Quack, Johannes (2017), 'Identifying (with) the Secular: Description and Genealogy', in
    Phil Zuckerman and John R. Shook (eds), *The Oxford Handbook of Secularism*, 138–61,
    Oxford: Oxford University Press.
RETOPEA (2020), Final Report Policy Recommendations WP-3 (Deliverable 3.7, Tartu,
    30 April).
Rosenberg, Daniel (2018), 'Exhibiting Post-national Identity: The House of European
    History', in Stefan Berger and Caner Tekin (eds), *History and Belonging: Representations
    of the Past in Contemporary European Politics*, 21–36, Oxford: Berghahn.
Roy, Olivier (2019), *Is Europe Christian?*, Oxford: Hurst.
Schnabel, Annette, Kathrin Behrens and Florian Grötsch (2017), 'Religion in European
    Constitutions – Cases of Different Secularities', *European Societies*, 19 (5): 551–79.
Schwörer, Jacob, and Belén Fernández-García (2020), 'Religion on the Rise Again?
    A Longitudinal Analysis of Religious Dimensions in Election Manifestos of Western
    European Parties', *Party Politics*, Online first. doi:10.1177/1354068820938008 (accessed
    21 September 2021).
Settele, Veronica (2015), 'Including Exclusion in European Memory? Politics of
    Remembrance at the House of European History', *Journal of Contemporary European
    Studies*, 23 (3): 405–16.
Shagan, Ethan H. (2019), *The Birth of Modern Belief: Faith and Judgment from the Middle
    Ages to the Enlightenment*, Princeton: Princeton University Press.
Stepan, Alfred (2000), 'Religion, Democracy, and the "Twin Tolerations"', *Journal of
    Democracy*, 11 (4): 37–57.

Stepan, Alfred (2011), 'The Multiple Secularisms of Modem Democratic and Non-democratic Regimes', in Craig Calhoun, Mark Juergensmeyer and Jonathan Van Antwerpen (eds), *Rethinking Secularism*, 114–39, Oxford: Oxford University Press.

Stolz, Jörg (2020), 'Secularization Theories in the Twenty-First Century: Ideas, Evidence, and Problems', *Social Compass*, 67 (2): 282–308.

Taylor, Charles (2007), *A Secular Age*, Cambridge, MA: Harvard University Press.

Taylor, Charles (2014), 'How to Define Secularism', in Alfred Stepan and Charles Taylor (eds), *Boundaries of Toleration*, 58–78, New York: Columbia University Press.

Topolski, Anya (2018), 'A Genealogy of the "Judeo-Christian" Signifier: A Tale of Europe's Identity Crisis', in Emmanuel Nathan and Anya Topolski (eds), *Is There a Judeo-Christian Tradition? A European Perspective*, 267–83, Berlin: De Gruyter.

Triandafyllidou, Anna, and Tina Magazzini (2021), 'The Governance of Religious Diversity: Challenges and Responses', in Anna Triandafyllidou and Tina Magazzini (eds), *Routledge Handbook on the Governance of Religious Diversity*, 1–10, London: Routledge.

Weir, Todd H. (2015), 'The Christian Front against Godlessness: Anti-secularism and the Demise of the Weimar Republic, 1928–1933', *Past & Present*, 229 (1): 201–38.

Wildt, Lars de, and Stef Aupers (2019), 'Playing the Other: Role-Playing Religion in Videogames', *European Journal of Cultural Studies*, 22 (5–6): 867–84.

Wintle, Michael (2016), 'Islam as Europe's "Other" in the Long Term: Some Discontinuities', *History*, 101 (344): 42–61.

Wohlrab-Sahr, Monika, and Marian Burchardt (2012), 'Multiple Secularities: Toward a Cultural Sociology of Secular Modernities', *Comparative Sociology*, 11: 875–909.

Wood, John Carter (ed.) (2016), *Christianity and National Identity in Twentieth-Century Europe: Conflict, Community, and the Social Order*, Göttingen: Vandenhoeck & Ruprecht.

Žižek, Slavoj (2001), *On Belief*, London: Routledge.

# Chapter 1

Allievi, Stefano (2005), 'How the Immigrant Has Become Muslim: Public Debates on Islam in Europe', *Revue européenne des migrations internationales*, 21 (2). Available online: doi: 10.4000/remi.2497 (accessed 21 September 2021).

Almond, Ian (2009), *Two Faiths, One Banner: When Muslims Marched with Christians across Europe's Battlegrounds*, Cambridge, MA: Harvard University Press.

Asad, Talal (2003), *Formations of the Secular: Christianity, Islam, Modernity*, Stanford: Stanford University Press.

al-Azmeh, Aziz, and Effie Fokas (eds) (2007), *Islam in Europe: Diversity, Identity and Influence*, Cambridge: Cambridge University Press.

Baddou, Ali (2021), 'Guillaume Peltier: "Je souhaite que la laïcité devienne la quatrième valeur de la devise républicaine"', *France Inter*, 21 February. Available online: https://www.franceinter.fr/emissions/questions-politiques/questions-politiques-21-fevr ier-2021 (accessed 21 September 2021).

Balibar, Étienne (2018), *Secularism and Cosmopolitanism: Critical Hypotheses on Religion and Politics*, New York: Columbia University Press.

Barkey, Karen (2008), *Empire of Difference: The Ottomans in Comparative Perspective*, Cambridge: Cambridge University Press.

Bauman, Zygmunt (1991), *Modernity and Ambivalence*, Cambridge: Cambridge University Press.

Beckford, James (2012), 'ASSSR Presidential Address: Public Religions and the Postsecular: Critical Reflections', *Journal for the Scientific Study of Religion*, 51 (1): 1–19.

Betts, Paul (2020), *Ruin and Renewal: Civilizing Europe after World War II*, New York: Basic Books.

Bialasiewicz, Luiza, and Valentina Gentile (2020), 'Spaces of Tolerance: Theories, Contested Practices, and the Question of Context', in Luiza Bialasiewicz and Valentina Gentile (eds), *Spaces of Tolerance: Changing Geographies and Philosophies of Religion in Today's Europe*, 1–20, London: Routledge.

Bistolfi, Robert, and François Zabbal (eds) (1995), *Islams d'Europe: intégration ou insertion communautaire?* Paris: L'Aube.

Bhuta, Nehal (2014), 'Two Concepts of Religious Freedom in the European Court of Human Rights', *South Atlantic Quarterly*, 113 (1): 10–36.

Brown, Callum (2001), *The Death of Christian Britain: Understanding Secularisation, 1800-2000*, London: Routledge, 2001.

Brown, Peter (2013), *The Rise of Western Christendom: Triumph and Diversity, A.D. 200-1000*, 10th Anniversary Edition, Malden, MA: Wiley-Blackwell.

Caiani, Manuela, and Tiago Carvalho (2021), 'The Use of Religion by Populist Parties: The Case of Italy and Its Broader Implications', *Religion, State & Society*, 49 (3): 211–30.

Campbell, Colin (2007), *The Easternization of the West: A Thematic Account of Cultural Change in the Modern Era*, Boulder, CO: Paradigm.

Catlos, Brian A. (2014), *Muslims of Medieval Latin Christendom, c.1050–1614*, Cambridge: Cambridge University Press.

Cesari, Jocelyne (2007), 'Muslim Identities in Europe: The Snare of Exceptionalism', in Aziz al-Azmeh and Effie Fokas (eds), *Islam in Europe: Diversity, Identity and Influence*, 49–67, Cambridge: Cambridge University Press.

Chamedes, Giuliana (2019), *A Twentieth-Century Crusade: The Vatican's Battle to Remake Christian Europe*, Cambridge, MA: Harvard University Press.

Chappel, James (2018), *Catholic Modern: The Challenge of Totalitarianism and the Remaking of the Church*, Cambridge, MA: Harvard University Press.

Chin, Rita (2017), *The Crisis of Multiculturalism in Europe: A History*, Princeton: Princeton University Press.

Classen, Albrecht (2018), *Toleration and Tolerance in Medieval and Early Modern European Literature*, New York: Routledge.

Coffey, John (2000), *Persecution and Toleration in Protestant England 1558–1689*, London: Routledge.

Conway, Martin (2006), 'The Christian Churches and Politics in Europe, 1914–1939', in Hugh McLeod (ed.), *The Cambridge History of Christianity: Vol. 9, World Christianities c.1914–c.2000*, 151–78, Cambridge: Cambridge University Press.

Dargent, Claude (2017), 'Religious Change, Public Space and Beliefs in Europe', in Pierre Bréchon and Frédéric Gonthier (eds), *European Values: Trends and Divides over Thirty Years*, 104–22, Leiden: Brill.

Davie, Grace (2000), *Religion in Modern Europe: A Memory Mutates*, Oxford: Oxford University Press.

De Cesari, Chiara (2020), '(Why) Do Eurosceptics Believe in a Common European Heritage?', in Chiara De Cesari and Ayhan Kaya (eds), *European Memory in Populism: Representations of Self and Other*, 26–46, London: Routledge.

Dessing, Nathal M., Nadia Jeldtoft and Linda Woodhead (eds) (2013), *Everyday Lived Islam in Europe*, London: Routledge.

Diamant, Jeff (2019), 'Europe Experienced a Surge in Government Restrictions on Religious Activity over the Last Decade', *Pew Fact Tank*, 29 July. Available online: https://www.pewr esearch.org/fact-tank/2019/07/29/europe-experienced-a-surge-in-government-restricti ons-on-religious-activity-over-the-last-decade/ (accessed 21 September 2021).

Ferrari, Silvio (2013), 'Models of State-Religion Relations in Western Europe', in Allen D. Hertzke (ed.), *The Future of Religious Freedom: Global Challenges*, 202–14, Oxford: Oxford University Press.

Forst, Rainer (2011), *Toleration in Conflict: Past and Present*, Cambridge: Cambridge University Press.

Forst, Robert I. (2018), *The Oxford History of Poland-Lithuania: Vol. I: The Making of the Polish-Lithuanian Union, 1385–1569*, Oxford: Oxford University Press.

Friedeburg, Robert von (2011), 'Cuius regio, eius religio: The Ambivalent Meanings of Statebuilding in Protestant Germany, 1555–1655', in Howard Louthan, Gary B. Cohen and Franz A. J. Szabo (eds), *Diversity and Dissent: Negotiating Religious Difference in Central Europe, 1500–1800*, 73–91, New York: Berghahn.

Furseth, Inger (2018), 'Secularization, Deprivatization, or Religious Complexity?', in Inger Furseth (ed.), *Religious Complexity in the Public Sphere*, 291–312, Cham: Palgrave Macmillan.

Gara, Eleni (2017), 'Conceptualising Interreligious Relations in the Ottoman Empire: The Early Modern Centuries', *Acta Poloniae Historica*, 116: 57–91.

GESIS (2019), *Special Eurobarometer 493: Discrimination in the EU*, Leibniz Institute for the Social Sciences (GESIS). Available online: https://data.europa.eu/euodp/en/data/ dataset/S2251_91_4_493_ENG (accessed 21 September 2021).

Göle, Nilüfer (2015), *Islam and Secularity – The Future of Europe's Public Sphere*, Durham, NC: Duke University Press.

Gorski, Philip S. (2000), 'Historicizing the Secularization Debate: Church, State, and Society in Late Medieval and Early Modern Europe, ca. 1300 to 1700', *American Sociological Review*, 65 (1): 138–67.

Green, Steven (2010), *The Second Disestablishment: Church and State in Nineteenth-Century America*, New York: Oxford University Press.

Haefeli, Evan (2021), *Accidental Pluralism America and the Religious Politics of English Expansion, 1497–1662*, Chicago: University of Chicago Press.

Hajdarpašić, Edin (2008), 'Out of the Ruins of the Ottoman Empire: Reflections on the Ottoman Legacy in South-Eastern Europe', *Middle Eastern Studies*, 44 (5): 715–34.

Hanebrink, Paul (2006), *In Defense of Christian Hungary: Religion, Nationalism, and Antisemitism, 1890–1944*, Ithaca, NY: Cornell University Press.

Hanebrink, Paul (2018), *A Specter Haunting Europe: The Myth of Judeo-Bolshevism*, Cambridge, MA: The Belknap Press of Harvard University Press.

Haselby, Sam (2015), *The Origins of American Religious Nationalism*, New York: Oxford University Press.

Hellemans, Staf (1990), *Strijd om de moderniteit: Sociale bewegingen en verzuiling in Europa sinds, 1800*, Leuven: Leuven University Press.

Hellemans, Staf (2020), 'Pillarization ("Verzuiling"): On Organized "Self-Contained Worlds" in the Modern World', *American Sociologist*, 51 (6): 124–47.

Hempton, David N., and Hugh McLeod (eds) (2017), *Secularization and Religious Innovation in the North Atlantic World*, Oxford: Oxford University Press.

Hjelm, Titus (2015), 'Is God Back? Reconsidering the New Visibility of Religion', in Titus Hjelm (ed.), *Is God Back? Reconsidering the New Visibility of Religion*, 1–17, London: Bloomsbury.

Inglehart, Ronald F. (2020), 'Giving Up on God: The Global Decline of Religion', *Foreign Affairs*, (September/October): 110–18. Available online: https://www.foreignaffairs.com/articles/world/2020-08-11/religion-giving-god (accessed 21 September 2021).

Johnson, Todd M., and Brian J. Grim (eds) (2020), *World Religion Database*, Leiden: Brill.

Kaiser, Wolfram, and Christopher Clark (eds) (2003), *Culture Wars: Secular-Catholic Conflict in Nineteenth-Century Europe*, Cambridge: Cambridge University Press.

Kaplan, Benjamin (2007), *Divided by Faith: Religious Conflict and the Practice of Toleration in Early Modern Europe*, Cambridge, MA: Harvard University Press.

Kastoryano, Riva (ed.) (2009), *An Identity for Europe: The Relevance of Multiculturalism in EU Construction*, New York: Palgrave Macmillan.

Krstić, Tijana (2009), 'Illuminated by the Light of Islam and the Glory of the Ottoman Sultanate: Self-Narratives of Conversion to Islam in the Age of Confessionalization', *Comparative Studies in Society and History*, 51 (1): 35–63.

Lähdesmäki, Tuuli (2012), 'Rhetoric of Unity and Cultural Diversity in the Making of European Cultural Identity', *International Journal of Cultural Policy*, 18 (1): 59–75.

Laursen, John Christian, and Cary J. Nederman (1998), 'General Introduction: Political and Historical Myths in the Toleration Literature', in John Christian Laursen and Cary J. Nederman (eds), *Beyond the Persecuting Society: Religious Toleration before the Enlightenment*, 1–12, Philadelphia: University of Pennsylvania Press.

Lee, Lois (2015), *Recognizing the Non-religious: Reimagining the Secular*, Oxford: Oxford University Press.

Leggewie, Claus (2011), *Der Kampf um die europäische Erinnerung: Ein Schlagfeld wird besichtigt*, München: Beck.

Lehner, Ulrich L. (2016), *The Catholic Enlightenment: The Forgotten History of a Global Movement*, Oxford: Oxford University Press.

Levy, Ian Christopher (2016), 'Liberty of Conscience and Freedom of Religion in the Medieval Canonists and Theologians', in Timothy Shah (ed.), *Christianity and Freedom*: *Vol. 1*, *Historical Perspectives*, 149–75, Cambridge: Cambridge University Press.

Littoz-Monnet, Annabelle (2012), 'The EU Politics of Remembrance: Can Europeans Remember Together?', *West European Politics*, 35 (5): 1182–202.

Malcolm, Noel (2019), *Useful Enemies: Islam and The Ottoman Empire in Western Political Thought, 1450–1750*, New York: Oxford University Press.

Marcos, Mar (2018), 'Religious Diversity and Discourses of Toleration in Classical Antiquity', in Lene Kühle, Jørn Borup and William Hoverd (eds), *The Critical Analysis of Religious Diversity*, 109–27, Leiden: Brill.

Mark, James, Bogdan C. Iacob, Tobias Rupprecht and Ljubica Spaskovska (2019), *1989: A Global History of Eastern Europe*, Cambridge: Cambridge University Press.

Marshall, Peter (2018), *Heretics and Believers: A History of the English Reformation*, New Haven: Yale University Press.

Martínez-Torrón, Javier (2016), 'Religious Pluralism: The Case of the European Court of Justice', in Ferran Requejo and Camil Ungureanu (eds), *Democracy, Law and Religious Pluralism in Europe: Secularism and Post-secularism*, 123–46, London: Routledge.

Marzouki, Nadia, Duncan McDonnell and Olivier Roy (eds) (2016), *Saving the People: How Populists Hijack Religion*, London: Hurst.

Mazower, Mark (2000), *The Balkans: From the End of Byzantium to the Present Day*, London: Weidenfeld & Nicolson.

McLeod, Hugh (2000), *Secularisation in Western Europe, 1848–1914*, Basingstoke: Palgrave Macmillan.

McLeod, Hugh (2010), *The Religious Crisis of the 1960s*, Oxford: Oxford University Press.

McLeod, Hugh, and Werner Ustorf (eds) (2003), *The Decline of Christendom in Western Europe, 1750–2000*, Cambridge: Cambridge University Press.

Merkel, Angela (2017), 'Rede von Bundeskanzlerin Merkel im Rahmen des 500: Jahrestages der Reformation am 31: Oktober 2017 in der Lutherstadt Wittenberg'. Available online: https://www.bundesregierung.de/breg-de/aktuelles/rede-von-bund eskanzlerin-merkel-im-rahmen-des-500-jahrestages-der-reformation-am-31-okto ber-2017-in-der-lutherstadt-wittenberg-466600 (accessed 21 September 2021).

Moore, Robert I. (2000), *The First European Revolution, c. 970–1215*, Malden, MA: Blackwell.

Moore, Robert I. [1987] (2006), *The Formation of a Persecuting Society: Authority and Deviance in Western Europe 950–1250*, Malden, MA: Blackwell.

Moyn, Samuel (2014), 'From Communist to Muslim: European Human Rights, the Cold War, and Religious Liberty', *South Atlantic Quarterly*, 113 (1): 63–86.

Müller, Jan-Werner (2011), *Contesting Democracy: Political Ideas in Twentieth Century Europe*, New Haven: Yale University Press.

Murphy, Andrew R. (1997), 'Tolerance, Toleration, and the Liberal Tradition', *Polity*, 29 (4): 593–623.

Nexon, Daniel H. (2009), *The Struggle for Power in Early Modern Europe: Religious Conflict, Dynastic Empires, and International Change*, Princeton: Princeton University Press.

Nielsen, Jorgen (2007), 'The Question of Euro-Islam: Restriction or Opportunity?', in Aziz al-Azmeh and Effie Fokas (eds), *Islam in Europe: Diversity, Identity and Influence*, 34–48, Cambridge: Cambridge University Press.

Nirenberg, David (1996), *Communities of Violence: Persecution of Minorities in the Middle Ages*, Princeton: Princeton University Press.

Nirenberg, David (2014), *Neighboring Faiths: Christianity, Islam, and Judaism in the Middle Ages and Today*, Chicago: University of Chicago Press.

Ocker, Christopher (2018), *Luther, Conflict and Christendom: Reformation Europe and Christianity in the West*, Cambridge: Cambridge University Press.

Oliphant, Elayne (2012), 'The Crucifix as a Symbol of Secular Europe: The Surprising Semiotics of the European Court of Human Rights', *Anthropology Today*, 28 (2): 10–12.

Paine, Thomas (1791), *Rights of Man: Being an Answer to Mr. Burke's Attack on the French Revolution*, 2nd Edition, London: J. S. Jordan.

Pasture, Patrick (2011), 'Religious Globalization in Post-War Europe', *Archiv für Sozialgeschichte*, 51: 63–108.

Pasture, Patrick (2013), "De-Christianization and the Changing Religious Landscape in Europe and North America since 1950: Comparative, Transatlantic and Global Perspectives', in Nancy Christie and Michael Gauvreau (eds), *The Sixties and Beyond: Dechristianization in North America and Western Europe, 1945–2000*, 367–402, Toronto: University of Toronto Press.

Pasture, Patrick (2015), *Imagining European Unity since 1000 AD*, Basingstoke: Palgrave Macmillan.

Pew Research Center (2014), 'Religious Diversity Index – Appendix 2: Religious Diversity Index Scores and Religious Adherents by Region and Country'. Available online: https://www.pewresearch.org/wp-content/uploads/sites/7/2014/04/Religious-Diversity-appendix-2.pdf (accessed 21 September 2021).

Pew Research Center (2017), *Five Centuries after Reformation, Catholic-Protestant Divide in Western Europe Has Faded*, Report, 31 August. Available online: https://www.pewfo rum.org/2017/08/31/five-centuries-after-reformation-catholic-protestant-divide-in-western-europe-has-faded/ (accessed 21 September 2021).

Pew Research Center (2018a), *Being Christian in Western Europe*, Report, 29 May. Available online: https://www.pewforum.org/wp-content/uploads/sites/7/2018/05/ Being-Christian-in-Western-Europe-FOR-WEB1.pdf (accessed 21 September 2021).

Pew Research Center (2018b), *Eastern and Western Europeans Differ on Importance of Religion, Views of Minorities, and Key Social Issues*, Report, 29 October. Available online: https:// www.pewforum.org/2018/10/29/eastern-and-western-europeans-differ-on-importance-of-religion-views-of-minorities-and-key-social-issues/ (accessed 21 September 2021).

Prügl, Elisabeth, and Markus Thiel (eds) (2009), *Diversity in the European Union*, Basingstoke: Palgrave Macmillan.

Roy, Olivier (2010), *Holy Ignorance: When Religion and Culture Part Ways*, London: Hurst.

Roy, Olivier (2017), 'Religious Freedom and Diversity in a Comparative European Perspective', *Journal of Balkan and Near Eastern Studies*, 19 (1): 86–9.

Roy, Olivier (2020), *Is Europe Christian?* Oxford: Hurst.

Safley, Thomas Max (ed.) (2011), *A Companion to Multiconfessionalism in the Early Modern World*, Leiden: Brill.

Sägesser, Caroline, Jan Nelis, Jean-Philippe Schreiber and Cécile Vanderpelen-Diagre (eds) (2018), *Religion and Secularism in the European Union*, Report, Brussels: Université Libre de Bruxelles.

al-Sayyad, Nezar, and Manuel Castells (eds) (2002), *Muslim Europe or Euro-Islam: Politics, Culture and Civilization in the Age of Globalization*, Lanham, MD: Lexington.

Schindler, David L., and Nicholas J. Healy Jr. (2015), *Freedom, Truth, and Human Dignity: The Second Vatican Council's Declaration on Religious Freedom*, Grand Rapids, MI: Wm. B. Eerdmans.

Schinkel, Willem (2017), *Imagined Societies: A Critique of Immigrant Integration in Western Europe*, Cambridge: Cambridge University Press.

Shagan, Ethan H. (2019), *The Birth of Modern Belief: Faith and Judgment from the Middle Ages to the Enlightenment*, Princeton: Princeton University Press.

Shah, Timothy Samuel (ed.) (2016), *Christianity and Freedom: Vol. 1, Historical Perspectives*, Cambridge: Cambridge University Press.

Soen, Violet (2017), 'From the Interim of Augsburg until the Treaty of Augsburg (1548–1555)', in Alberto Melloni (ed.), *Martin Luther: A Christian between Reforms and Modernity, Vol. 1*, 549–64, Berlin: De Gruyter.

Soen, Violet, Alexander Soetaert, Johan Verberckmoes and Wim François (eds) (2019), *Transregional Reformations: Crossing Borders in Early Modern Europe*, Göttingen: Vandenhoeck & Ruprecht.

Sorkin, David (2008), *The Religious Enlightenment: Protestants, Jews, and Catholics from London to Vienna*, Princeton: Princeton University Press.

Stanley, Brian (2018), *Christianity in the Twentieth Century: A World History*, Princeton: Princeton University Press.

Stepan, Alfred (2011), 'The Multiple Secularisms of Modern Democratic and Non-democratic Regimes', in Craig Calhoun, Mark Juergensmeyer and Jonathan Van Antwerpen (eds), *Rethinking Secularism*, 114–39, Oxford: Oxford University Press.

Stepan, Alfred (2014), 'Muslims and Toleration: Unexamined Contributions to the Multiple Secularisms of Modern Democracies', in Alfred Stepan and Charles Taylor (eds), *Boundaries of Toleration*, 267–96, New York: Columbia University Press.

Stevens, Ralph (2018), *Protestant Pluralism: The Reception of the Toleration Act, 1689–1720*, London: Boydell.

Taylor, Becky (2014), *Another Darkness, Another Dawn: A History of Gypsies, Roma and Travellers*, London: Reaction.

Te Brake, Wayne P. (2017), *Religious War and Religious Peace in Early Modern Europe*, Cambridge: Cambridge University Press.

Ther, Philipp (2015), *The Dark Side of Nation-States: Ethnic Cleansing in Modern Europe*, Cambridge: Cambridge University Press.

Tibi, Bassam (1998), *Europa ohne Identität, Die Krise der multikulturellen Gesellschaft*, München: Bertelsmann.

Todorova, Maria (1997), *Imagining the Balkans*, Oxford: Oxford University Press.

Trimçev, Rieke, Gregor Feindt, Félix Krawatzek and Friedemann Pestel (2020), 'Europe's Europes: Mapping the Conflicts of European Memory', *Journal of Political Ideologies*, 25 (1): 51–77.

Van den Hemel, Ernst (2019), 'Who Leads Leitkultur? How Populist Claims about "Christian Identity" Impact Christian-Democrats in Western Europe', *Interdisciplinary Journal for Religion and Transformation in Contemporary Society*, 5 (2): 312–30.

Villa, Virginia (2019), 'Religiously Unaffiliated People Face Harassment in a Growing Number of Countries', *Pew Fact Tank*, 12 August. Available online: https://www.pewresearch.org/fact-tank/2019/08/12/religiously-unaffiliated-people-face-harassment-in-a-growing-number-of-countries/ (accessed 21 September 2021).

Walsham, Alexandra (2008), *Charitable Hatred: Tolerance and Intolerance in England, 1500–1700*, Manchester: Manchester University Press.

Weiler, Joseph A. A. (2005), *L'Europe chrétienne? Une excursion*, Paris: Cerf.

Weir, Todd H. (2014), *Secularism and Religion in Nineteenth-Century Germany: The Rise of the Fourth Confession*, Cambridge: Cambridge University Press.

Weir, Todd H. (2015), 'The Christian Front against Godlessness: Anti-secularism and the Demise of the Weimar Republic, 1928–1933', *Past & Present*, 229 (1): 201–38.

Weitz, Eric D. (2008), 'From the Vienna to the Paris System: International Politics and the Entangled Histories of Human Rights, Forced Deportations, and Civilizing Missions', *American Historical Review*, 113 (5): 1313–43.

Wilken, Robert Louis (2019), *Liberty in the Things of God: The Christian Origins of Religious Freedom*, New Haven: Yale University Press.

Wood, John (ed.) (2016), *Christianity and National Identity in Twentieth-Century Europe: Conflict, Community, and the Social Order*, Göttingen: Vandenhoeck & Ruprecht.

Worden, Blair (2013), *God's Instruments: Political Conduct in the England of Oliver Cromwell*, Oxford: Oxford University Press.

Yilmaz, Ferruh (2016), *How the Workers Became Muslims: Immigration, Culture and Hegemonic Transformation in Europe*, Ann Arbor: University of Michigan Press.

Zagorin, Perez (2003), *How the Idea of Religious Toleration Came to the West*, Princeton: Princeton University Press.

# Chapter 2

Alexander, Claire, and Debbie Weekes-Bernard (2017), 'History Lessons: Inequality, Diversity and the National Curriculum', *Race Ethnicity and Education*, 20 (4): 478–94.

Angvik, Magne, and Bodo von Borries (eds) (1997), *Youth and History: A Comparative European Survey on Historical Consciousness and Political Attitudes amongst Adolescents*, Hamburg: Körber-Stiftung.

Arweck, Elisabeth (2016), 'The Matter of Context: The Case of Two Community Schools in Wales', in Elisabeth Arweck (ed.), *Young People's Attitudes to Religious Diversity*, 97–124, London: Routledge.

Arweck, Elisabeth, and Gemma Penny (2015), 'Young People's Attitudes to Religious Diversity: Socialising Agents and Factors Emerging from Qualitative and Quantitative Data of a Nation-Wide Project in the UK', *Journal of Intercultural Studies*, 36 (3): 249–73.

Arweck, Elisabeth, and Julia Ipgrave (2016), 'The Qualitative Strand: Listening in Depth', in Elisabeth Arweck (ed.), *Young People's Attitudes to Religious Diversity*, 19–30, London: Routledge.

Avest, Ina ter, Dan-Paul Jozsa, Thorsten Knauth, Javier Rosón and Geir Skeie (eds) (2009), *Dialogue and Conflict on Religion: Studies of Classroom Interaction in European Countries*, Münster: Waxmann Verlag.

Borries, Bodo von (1994), '(Re-)constructing History and Moral Judgment: On Relationships between Interpretations of the Past and Perceptions of the Present', in Mario Carretero and James F. Voss (eds), *Cognitive and Instructional Processes in History and Social Sciences*, 339–55, Hillsdale, NJ: Lawrence Erlbaum Associates.

Britt, M. Anne, and Cindy Aglinskas (2002), 'Improving Students' Ability to Identify and Use Source Information', *Cognition and Instruction*, 20 (4): 485–522.

Bruce, Steve (2002), *God Is Dead: Secularization in the West*, Oxford: Blackwell.

Council of Europe (2014), *Shared Histories for a Europe without Dividing Lines: results and conclusions*. Available online: http://shared-histories.coe.int (accessed 22 September 2021).

Davie, Grace (2000), *Religion in Modern Europe: A Memory Mutates*, Oxford: Oxford University Press.

Davie, Grace (2006), 'Vicarious Religion: A Methodological Challenge', in Nancy T. Ammerman (ed.), *Everyday Religion: Observing Modern Religious Lives*, 21–35, New York: Oxford University Press.

Eckhardt, Thomas (ed.) (2019), *The Education System in the Federal Republic of Germany 2016/2017: A Description of the Responsibilities, Structures and Developments in Education Policy for the Exchange of Information in Europe*, Bonn: German EURYDICE Unit of the Federal Government in the Federal Ministry of Education and Research. Available online: https://www.kmk.org/fileadmin/Dateien/pdf/Eurydice/Bildungswe sen-engl-pdfs/dossier_en_ebook.pdf (accessed 20 September 2021).

Eliot & Associates (2005), Guidelines for Conducting a Focus Group. Available online: https://datainnovationproject.org/wp-content/uploads/2017/04/4_How_to_Co nduct_a_Focus_Group-2-1.pdf (accessed 20 September 2021).

Ferrari, Silvio (2013), 'Religious Education in European Union', in Derek H. Davis and Elena Miroshnikova (eds), *The Routledge International Handbook of Religious Education*, 100–3, London: Routledge.

Grever, Maria, and Kees Ribbens (2007), *Nationale identiteit en meervoudig verleden*, Amsterdam: Amsterdam University Press.

Grever, Maria, Terry Haydn and Kees Ribbens (2008), 'Identity and School History: The Perspective of Young People from the Netherlands and England', *British Journal of Educational Studies*, 56 (1): 76–94

Husbands, Chris (1996), *What Is History Teaching? Language, Ideas, and Meaning in Learning about the Past*, Buckingham: Open University Press.

Hynd, Cynthia R. (1999), 'Teaching Students to Think Critically Using Multiple Texts in History', *Journal of Adolescent and Adult Literacy*, 42 (6): 428–36.

Jackson, Robert, and Ursula McKenna (2016), 'The Young People's Attitudes to Religious Diversity Project in the Context of Warwick Religions and Education Research Unit (WRERU)', in Elisabeth Arweck (ed.), *Young People's Attitudes to Religious Diversity*, 3–18, London: Routledge.

Nokes, Jeffrey D. (2010), 'Observing Literacy Practices in History Classrooms', *Theory and Research in Social Education*, 38 (4): 515–44.

Nokes, Jeffrey D., Janice A. Dole and Douglas J. Hacker (2007), 'Teaching High School Students to Use Heuristics While Reading Historical Texts', *Journal of Educational Psychology*, 99 (3): 492–504.

Onwuegbuzie, Anthony J., Wendy B. Dickinson, Nancy L. Leech and Annmarie G. Zoran (2009), 'A Qualitative Framework for Collecting and Analyzing Data in Focus Group Research', *International Journal of Qualitative Methods*, 8 (3): 1–21.

Paxton, Richard J. (1999), 'A Deafening Silence: History Textbooks and the Students Who Read Them', *Review of Educational Research*, 69 (3): 315–37.

Peck, Carla (2010), ' "It's Not Like [I'm] Chinese and Canadian: I Am in Between": Ethnicity and Students' Conceptions of Historical Significance', *Theory and Research in Social Education*, 38 (4): 574–617.

Perfetti, Charles A., M. Anne Britt and Mara C. Georgi (1995), *Text-Based Learning and Reasoning: Studies in History*, Hillsdale, NJ: Erlbaum.

Seixas, Peter (1993), 'Historical Understanding among Adolescents in a Multicultural Setting', *Curriculum Inquiry*, 23 (3): 301–27.

Seixas, Peter, and Tom Morton (2013), *The Big Six Historical Thinking Concepts*, Toronto, ON: Nelson Education.

Skeie, Geir (2009), 'Power to the People! Dialogue and Conflict in the Light of Classroom Interaction Studies', in Ina ter Avest, Dan-Paul Jozsa, Thorsten Knauth, Javier Rosón and Geir Skeie (eds), *Dialogue and Conflict on Religion: Studies of Classroom Interaction in European Countries*, 249–75, Münster: Waxmann Verlag.

Stahl, Steven A., Cynthia R. Hynd, Bruce K. Britton, Mary M. McNish and Dennis Bosquet (1996), 'What Happens When Students Read Multiple Source Documents in History?', *Reading Research Quarterly*, 31 (4): 430–56.

Štimac, Zrinka (2015), 'Religiöse Pluralität im Schulbuch: Analyse Ausgewählter Ethikbücher in Östlichen und Westlichen Bundesländern', in Christoph Bultmann and Antje Linkenbach (eds), *Religionen übersetzen: Klischees und Vorurteile im Religionsdiskurs*, 45–71, Münster: Aschendorf.

Van Havere, Timo, Kaat Wils, Fien Depaepe, Lieven Verschaffel and Karel Van Nieuwenhuyse (2017), 'Flemish Students' Historical Reference Knowledge and Narratives of the Belgian National Past at the End of Secondary Education', *London Review of Education*, 15 (2): 272–85.

Van Nieuwenhuyse, Karel (2017), 'Where Macro and Micro Histories Meet: Position, Trumps, and Pitfalls of Family History as a Form of Oral History in Flemish Education', in Kristina Llewellyn and Nicholas Ng-A-Fook (eds), *Oral History and Education: Theories, Dilemmas, and Practices*, 167–85, New York: Palgrave Macmillan.

Weston, Cynthia, Terry Gandell, Jacinthe Beauchamp, Lynn McAlpine, Carol Wiseman and Cathy Beauchamp (2001), 'Analyzing Interview Data: The Development and Evolution of a Coding System', *Qualitative Sociology*, 24 (3): 381–400.

Wineburg, Sam (1991), 'On the Reading of Historical Texts: Notes on the Breach between School and Academy', *American Educational Research Journal*, 28 (3): 495–519.

Wineburg, Sam (2001), *Historical Thinking and Other Unnatural Acts: Charting the Future of Teaching the Past*, Philadelphia: Temple University Press.

Wineburg, Sam (2004), 'Crazy for History', *Journal of American History*, 90 (4): 1401–14.

Wineburg, Sam (2018), *Why Learn History (When It's Already on Your Phone)*, Chicago: University of Chicago Press.

Yendell, Alexander (2016), 'Young People and Religious Diversity: A European Perspective, with Particular Reference to Germany', in Elisabeth Arweck (ed.), *Young People's Attitudes to Religious Diversity*, 275–88, London: Routledge.

Ziebertz, Hans-Georg, and William K. Kay (2005), *Youth in Europe 1: An International Empirical Study about Life Perspectives*, Münster: LIT.

# Chapter 3

## Primary sources

### For Austria

Lemberger, Michael (2012), *VG 2 (Durch die Vergangenheit zur Gegenwart)*, Linz: Veritas.

Lemberger, Michael (2012), *VG 3 (Durch die Vergangenheit zur Gegenwart)*, Linz: Veritas.

Lemberger, Michael (2012), *VG 4 (Durch die Vergangenheit zur Gegenwart)*, Linz: Veritas.

Scheucher, Alois, Josef Scheipl, Eduard Staudinger and Ulrike Ebenhoch (2017), *Zeitbilder 5/6*, Wien: ÖBV.

Staudinger, Eduard, Alois Scheucher, Josef Scheipl, Ulrike Ebenhoch (2012), *Zeitbilder 7/8*, Wien: ÖBV.

Wald, Anton, Alois Scheucher, Josef Scheipl and Ulrike Ebenhoch (2017), *Zeitbilder 2*, Wien: ÖBV.

### For Flanders/Belgium

Berings, Geert, Joke Brackeva, Kristoff Luyckx, Rik Van Braband and Natan Vanwildemeersch (2014), *Memoria 2*, Kalmthout: Pelckmans.

Berings, Geert, Joke Brackeva, Kelly D'Hollander and Rik Van Braband (2016), *Memoria 3*, Kalmthout: Pelckmans.

Geuens, Kevin, Saskia Boelens, Frank Hosten and Walter Smits (2015), *Memoria 4*, Kalmthout: Pelckmans.

Geuens, Kevin, Jan Bleyen, Saskia Boelens, Jan De Schutter and Frank Hosten (2015), *Memoria 5-6*, Kalmthout: Pelckmans.

### For England

Bates, Neil, Alec Fisher, Richard Kennett and John Clare (2015a), *Making Sense of History 1745-1901*, London: Hodder Education.

Bates, Neil, Alec Fisher, Richard Kennett and John Clare (2015b), *Making Sense of History 1901-Present Day*, London: Hodder Education.

Clare, John, Alec Fisher and Richard Kennett (2014), *Making Sense of History 1509-1745*, London: Hodder Education.

Cloake, Jon, Kevin Newman and Aaron Wilkes (2016), *Oxford AQA History for GCSE: Thematic Studies c790–Present Day*, Oxford: Oxford University Press.
Fisher, Alec, Ian Dawson, Richard McFahn and Neil Bates (2013), *Making Sense of History 1066–1509*, London: Hodder Education.


## For Estonia

Ezzoubi, Kattri, Pärtel Piirimäe, Regina-Maria Blauhut, Marika Mägi, Juhan Kreem and Inna Põltsam-Jürjo (2012), *Keskaeg. Õpik. II osa. 7. Klass*, Tallinn: Avita.
Kõiv, Mait, and Milvi Martina Piir (2010), *Vanaaeg: ajalooõpik 6. klassile. II osa*, Tallinn: Avita.
Kõiv, Mait, Linda Kaljundi, Mati Laur, Tõnu Tannberg and Jaan Lahe (2015), *Üldajalugu gümnaasiumile: uus õppekava*, Tallinn: Avita.
Nutt, Mart, and Lauri Vahtre (2014), *Lähiajalugu III*, Tallinn: Maurus.
Pajur, Ago, and Marten Seppel (2015), *Uusaeg, II osa. 8. Klass*, Tallinn: Avita.
Põltsam-Jürjo, Inna, Pärtel Piirimäe and Ursula Vent (2011), *Keskaeg. Õpik. I osa. 7. Klass*, Tallinn: Avita.
Värä, Einar, and Tõnu Tannberg (2016), *Lähiajalugu. 9. klassile. II osa*, Tallinn: Avita.


## For Finland

Aunesluoma, Juhana, Ulla Lehtonen, Titta Putus-Hilasvuori, Jari Ukkonen and Laura Vuorela (2016), *Historia ajassa 2: Kansainväliset suhteet*, Helsinki: Sanoma Pro.
Bruun, Jarno, Ossi Kokkonen, Milena Komulainen, Petri Lassi and Ari Sainio (2015), *Ritari 6*, Helsinki: Sanoma Pro.
Hanska, Jussi, Kimmo Jalonen and Juhapekka Rikala (2013), *Memo 8 Historia*, Helsinki: Edita.
Höyssä, Ari, Anu Lahtinen, Erika Ripatti, Jouni Similä and Jari Ukkonen (2016), *Historia ajassa 1: Ihminen ympäristön ja yhteiskuntien muutoksessa*, Helsinki: Sanoma Pro.
Päivärinta, Kimmo, Kati Solastie and Simo Turtiainen (2010), *Forum. 5, Historia*, Helsinki: Otava.


## For Germany

Baumgärtner, Ulrich, and Dagmar Feist (2010), *Horizonte: Geschichte: Gymnasium, Bayern 12*. Braunschweig: Westermann.
Baumgärtner, Ulrich, and Rainer Brieske (2016), *Horizonte 7/8, Berlin und Brandenburg*: Braunschweig: Westermann.
Brückner, Dieter, and Harald Focke (2011), *Das waren Zeiten 2, Mittelalter – Renaissance – Absolutismus, Bayern*. Bamberg: Buchner.
Dzubiel, Christine (2014), *Geschichte und Geschehen: Einführungsphase: Oberstufe: Nordrhein-Westfalen*. Stuttgart: Klett.
Gawatz, Andreas, Andreas Giessringer, Birgit Breiding and Claudia Gaull (2018), *Geschichte – Ausgabe für Gymnasien in Bayern: Schülerband 6*, Braunschweig: Westermann.
Geus, Elmar (2012), *Horizonte 10, Geschichte Realschule, Bayern.*. Braunschweig: Westermann.

Lendzian, Hans-Jürgen, Siegfried Bethlehen, Michael Bohle, and Lambert Austermann (2017), *Zeiten und Menschen 2, Nordrhein-Westfalen*. Paderborn: Schöningh.

Rauh, Robert, Nicky Born, and Robin Giffe (2017), *Forum Geschichte 7/8, Berlin/Brandenburg*. Berlin: Cornelsen.

Rauh, Robert, Dagmar Bäuml-Sotsiek, Joachim Cornelissen, and Udo Deus (2018), *Forum Geschichte 9/10, Berlin/Brandenburg*. Berlin: Cornelsen.

Sauer, Michael, and Ursula Fries (2015), *Geschichte und Geschehen 1, Nordrhein-Westfalen*. Stuttgart: Klett.

Sauer, Michael, and Tobias Dietrich (2017), *Geschichte und Geschehen 3, Nordrhein-Westfalen*. Stuttgart: Klett.

Wunderer, Hartmann, Klaus Dieter Hein-Mooren, Heinrich Hirschfelder and Ingo Kitzel (2016), *Buchners Kolleg Geschichte: Neue Ausgabe Hessen: Einführungsphase: Oberstufe*, Bamberg: Buchner.

Wunderer, Hartmann, Klaus Dieter Hein-Mooren, Heinrich Hirschfelder and Ingo Kitzel (2016), *Buchners Kolleg Geschichte: Neue Ausgabe Hessen: Qualifikationsphase: Oberstufe*, Bamberg: Buchner.

**For Switzerland**

Binnenkade, Alexandra et al. (2014), *Geschichte der Neuzeit: Recherchieren, Analysieren, Beurteilen*, Zürich: Lehrmittelverlag Zürich.

Davanzo Eva, René Aeby, Emanuel Baeriswyl, Frédéric Oberholzer, Florijan Sinik and Tobias Suter (2016), *Durchblick Geschichte: Band 1*, Braunschweig: Westermann.

Weiß, Ulrike, Birgit Stalder, Christophe Gross, Thomas Notz, K. Pflügner, Helmut Meyert and Patrick Grob (2011), *Schweizer Geschichtsbuch 1. Schülerbuch: Von der Urgeschichte bis zum Absolutismus*, Berlin: Cornelsen.

**For Spain**

Álvarez Rey, Leandro, Margarita García Sebastián, José Carlos Gibaja Velázquez, Jordi Palafox Gamir and Manel Risques Corbella (2016), *Historia del Mundo Contemporáneo, 1° BACHILLERATO*, Madrid: Vicen Vives.

Álvarez Rey, Leandro, Margarita García Sebastián, José Carlos Gibaja Velázquez, Jordi Palafox Gamir and Manel Risques Corbella (2016), *Historia del Mundo Contemporáneo, 2° BACHILLERATO*, Madrid: Vicen Vives.

Burgos Alonso, Manuel, María Concepción Muñoz-Delgado y Mérida (2017), *Geografía e Historia, Andalucía, 4° ESO*, Madrid: Grupo ANAYA.

Grence Ruiz, Teresa y Maite López.Sáez Rodríguez-Piñero (2017), *Geografía e Historia: Serie Descubre, 2° ESO*, Grazalema: Editorial Santillana.

López.Sáez, Maite et al. (2016), *Geografía e Historia: Serie Descubre, 1° ESO*, Grazalema: Editorial Santillana.

**Secondary sources**

Andreassen, Bengt-Ove (2015), 'Research on Textbooks in the Study of Religions', *Bulletin Eckert 15. Focus: Textbooks and Religion*, 9 (1): 7–9.

Barton, Keith (2012), 'Agency, Choice and Historical Action: How History Teaching Can Help Students Think about Democratic Decision Making', *Citizenship Teaching and Learning*, 7 (2): 131–42.

Berglund, Jenny. (ed.) (2018), *European Perspectives on Islamic Education and Public Schooling*, Sheffield: Equinox.

Bermudez, Angela (2019), 'The Normalization of Political Violence in History Textbooks: Ten Narrative Keys', *Historical Dialogues, Justice and Memory Network Working Paper Series*, 15: 1–22.

Bock, Annekatrin (2018), 'Theories and Methods of Textbook Studies', in Eckhardt Fuchs and Annekatrin Bock (eds), *The Palgrave Handbook of Textbook Studies*, 57–70, New York: Palgrave Macmillan. Available online: https://doi.org/10.1057/978-1-137-53142-1_4 (accessed 21 June 2021).

Borries, Bodo von (1994), '(Re-)Constructing History and Moral Judgment: On Relationships between Interpretations of the Past and Perceptions of the Present', in Mario Carretero and James F. Voss (eds), *Cognitive and Instructional Processes in History and Social Sciences*, 339–55, Hillsdale, NJ: Lawrence Erlbaum Associates.

Cajani, Luigi, Simone Lässig and Maria Grever (eds) (2019), *The Palgrave Handbook of Conflict and History Education in the Post-Cold War Era*, London: Palgrave MacMillan.

Cavanaugh, William T. (2009), *The Myth of Religious Violence: Secular Ideology and the Roots of Modern Conflict*, Oxford: Oxford University Press.

Cloake, Jon, and Aaron Wilkes (2016), *Oxford AQA History for GCSE: Thematic Studies c790–Present Day*, Oxford: Oxford University Press.

Douglass, Susan L. (2015), 'World Religions & Islam in US Textbooks', *Bulletin Eckert 15. Focus: Textbooks and Religion*, 9 (1): 18–21.

Erdmann, Elisabeth, Robert Maier and Susanne Popp (eds) (2006), *Geschichtsunterricht international/Worldwide Teaching of History/L'enseignement de l'histoire dans le monde: (Studien zur internationalen Schulbuchforschung)*, Hannover: Hahn.

Gottschalk, Peter (2019), 'Textbooks on "Hinduism": Defining an Ocean Described from Myriad Shores', *Religion*, 49 (2): 284–95. Available online: doi: 10.1080/0048721X.2018.1501872 (accessed 21 June 2021).

Härenstam, Kjell (2009), 'Images of Muslims in Swedish School Textbooks', in Staffan Selander and Bente Aamotsbakken (eds), *Nordic Identities in Transition – As Reflected in Pedagogic Texts and Cultural Contexts*, 171–90, Oslo: Novus Press.

Harris, Richard (2011), 'Citizenship and History: Uncomfortable Bedfellows', in Ian Davies (ed.), *Debates in History Teaching*, 186–96, New York: Routledge.

Hock, Klaus, Johannes Lähnemann, Wolfram Reiss and Jonathan Kriener (eds) (2012), *Die Darstellung des Christentums in Schulbüchern islamisch geprägter Länder, 3 vols. (Band 3 with W. Reiss)*, Schenefeld: EB-Verlag.

Ipsos (2017), *Global Views on Religion*, Bloomberg. Available online: https://www.ipsos.com/sites/default/files/ct/news/documents/2017-10/globaladvisor_Religion_Charts_AUSTRALIA.pdf (accessed 21 June 2021).

Jackson, Robert (2014), *Signposts: Policy and Practice for Teaching about Religions and Non-religious Worldviews in Intercultural Education*, Strasbourg: Council of Europe.

Karaca, Resul, and Sabine Schmitz (2018), 'La représentation de l'islam dans les manuels d'histoire en Espagne et en Allemagne: Une narration de plus en plus liée aux images', in Dominique Avon, Isabelle Saint-Martin and John Tolan (eds), *Faits religieux et manuels d'histoire: Contenus – Institutions – Pratiques: Approches comparées à l'échelle internationale*, 77–100, Nancy: Arbre bleu éditions.

Klerides, Eleftherios (2010), 'Imagining the Textbook: Textbooks as Discourse and Genre', *Journal of Educational Media, Memory, and Society*, 2 (1): 31–54.

Kröhnert-Othman, Susanne (2015), 'Islam in Textbooks: Negotiating Its Core, Its Diversity and Who Belongs to It', *Bulletin Eckert 15. Focus: Textbooks and Religion*, 9 (1): 22–5.

Lähnemann, Johannes (2013), 'Interreligious Textbook Research and Development: A Proposal for Standards', *European Judaism*, 46 (1): 15–25.

Liepach, Martin, and Dirk Sadowski (eds) (2014), *Jüdische Geschichte im Schulbuch: Eine Bestandsaufnahme anhand aktueller Lehrwerke (Eckert. Expertise, Band 3)*, Göttingen: V&R Unipress.

Linkenbach, Antje (2015), 'Weltreligion Hinduismus: Zur Konstruktion des Indienbildes in deutschen Schulbüchern', in Christophe Bultmann and Antje Linkenbach (eds), *Religionen übersetzen: Klischees und Vorurteile im Religionsdiskurs*, 23–44, Münster: Aschendorff Verlag.

Patrick, Margaretta L. (2015). 'A Call for More Religious Education in the Secondary Social Studies Curriculum of Western Canadian Provinces', *Curriculum Inquiry*, 45 (2): 154–75.

Patrick, Margaretta L., Vanessa Gulayets and Carla L. Peck (2017), 'A Call for Teacher Professional Learning and the Study of Religion in Social Studies', *Canadian Journal of Education/Revue canadienne de l'éducation*, 40 (4): 603–37.

Peck, Carla, Stuart Poyntz and Peter Seixas (2011), ' "Agency" in Students' Narratives of Canadian History', in Denis Shemilt and Lukas Perikleous (eds), *The Future of the Past: Why History Education Matter*, 253–80, Nicosia: Association for Historical Dialogue and Research.

Spielhaus, Riem (2018), 'Der Umgang mit innerreligiöser Vielfalt im Islamischen Religionsunterricht in Deutschland und seinen Schulbüchern', in Zrinka Štimac and Riem Spielhaus (eds), *Schulbuch und religiöse Vielfalt: Interdisziplinäre Perspektiven: Eckert. Die Schriftenreihe, band 143*, 93–116, Göttingen: V&R Unipress.

Standaert, Nicolas (2002), *Methodology in View of Contact between Cultures: The China Case in the 17th Century*. Occasional Paper, 11, Hong Kong: Centre for the Study of Religion and Chinese Society (CSCRS).

Štimac, Zrinka (2015), 'Religious Pluralism and the Textbook', *Bulletin Eckert 15. Focus: Textbooks and Religion*, 9 (1): 10–7.

Štimac Zrinka (2018), 'Religion as a Subject of Textbook Analysis: An Exemplary Overview', in Eckhardt Fuchs and Annekatrin Bock (eds), *The Palgrave Handbook of Textbook Studies*, 251–65, New York: Palgrave Macmillan. Available online: https://doi. org/10.1057/978-1-137-53142-1_18 (accessed 21 June 2021).

UNESCO (United Nations Educational, Scientific and Cultural Organization) (2006), *UNESCO Guidelines on Intercultural Education*, Paris: UNESCO Section of Education for Peace and Human Rights, Division for the Promotion of Quality Education, Education Sector. Available online: http://unesdoc.unesco.org/images/0014/001 478/147878e.pdf (accessed 21 June 2021).

Van Nieuwenhuyse, Karel (2014), 'From Triumphalism to Amnesia: Belgian-Congolese (Post)colonial History in Belgian Secondary History Education Curricula and Textbooks (1945–1989)', *Yearbook of the International Society for History Didactics*, 35: 79–100.

Van Nieuwenhuyse, Karel (2018), 'Towards a Postcolonial Mind-Set in a Post-colonial World? Evolving Representations of Modern Imperialism in Belgian History Textbooks since 1945', in Karel Van Nieuwenhuyse and Joaquim Pires Valentim (eds), *The Colonial Past in History Textbooks – Historical and Social Psychological Perspectives*, 155–76, Charlotte, NC: Information Age.

Van Nieuwenhuyse, Karel (2019a), 'Empire and Imperialism in Education since 1945: Secondary School History Textbooks', in Immanuel Ness and Zak Cope (eds), *The Palgrave Encyclopedia of Imperialism and Anti-imperialism*, 1–15,

London: Palgrave Macmillan. Available online: doi: 10.1007/978-3-319-91206-6_40-1 (accessed 21 June 2021).

Van Nieuwenhuyse, Karel (2019b), 'Between Non-human and Individual Agents: The Attribution of Agency in Flemish History Textbook Chapters on the Cold War', in Barbara Christophe, Peter Gautschi and Robert Thorp (eds), *Teaching the Cold War: International Perspectives on Memory Practices in Educational Media and in the Classroom*, 159–81, New York: Palgrave Macmillan.

Van Nieuwenhuyse, Karel, and Denise Bentrovato (2017), 'Naoorlogse leerboeken geschiedenis als toegang tot de heersende populaire historische cultuur in scholen? Casus van het Belgisch-Congolese koloniale verleden', *Tijd-Schrift. Heemkunde en lokaal-erfgoedpraktijk in Vlaanderen*, 7 (3): 84–98.

Van Nieuwenhuyse, Karel, and Joaquim Pires Valentim (eds) (2018), *The Colonial Past in History Textbooks – Historical and Social Psychological Perspectives*, Charlotte, NC: Information Age.

Wertsch, James V. (1997), 'Narrative Tools of History and Identity', *Culture and Psychology*, 3 (1): 5–20.

Wertsch, James V. (2004), 'Specific Narratives and Schematic Narrative Templates', in Peter Seixas (ed.), *Theorizing Historical Consciousness*, 49–62, Toronto: University of Toronto Press.

Wilke, Marjolein, Fien Depaepe and Karel Van Nieuwenhuyse (2019), 'Teaching about Historical Agency: An Intervention Study Examining Changes in Students' Understanding and Perception of Agency in Past and Present', *International Journal of Research on History Didactics, History Education, and Historical Culture*, 5 (1): 53–80.

Wils, Kaat, Andrea Schampaert, Geraldine Clarebout, Hans Cools, Alexander Albicher and Lieven Verschaffel (2011), 'Past and Present in Contemporary History Education: An Exploratory Empirical Research on Prospective History Teachers', *International Journal of Research on History Didactics, History Education, and Historical Culture, Yearbook 32: Analyzing Textbooks: Methodological Issues*, 217–36.

# Chapter 4

Aleksoska-Bačeva, Zaharinka, Branislava Mihajlova and Krste Bogoeski (2015), *Muzeite vo Republika Makedonija*, Skopje: MNK-IKOM Skopje.

Angelovska, Despina (2014), '(Mis)Representation of Transitional Justice: Contradictions in Displaying History, Memory and Art in the Skopje 2014 Project', in Peter D. Rush and Olivera Simić (eds), *The Arts of Transitional Justice*, 173–93, New York: Springer.

Arab, Pooyan Tamimi (2020), 'Longing for Mecca (Verlangen naar Mekka) Tropenmuseum, Amsterdam (February 2019–January 2020)', *Material Religion*, 16 (3): 394–6.

Ark (Finnish Architecture Review) (2014), 4: *Homes, Cohousing*. Available online: https://www.ark.fi/en/2014/04/ (accessed 10 September 2020).

Aronsson, Peter, and Gabriella Elgenius (eds) (2011), *Building National Museums in Europe 1750–2010: Conference Proceedings from EuNaMus, European National Museums: Identity Politics, the Uses of the Past and the European Citizen, Bologna 28–30 April*, Linköping: Linköping University Press.

Backhaus, Fritz, Rafael Gross, Sabine Kößling and Mirjam Wenzel (eds) (2016), *The Judengasse in Frankfurt: History, Politics, Culture*, Catalogue of the Permanent Exhibition of the Jewish Museum, Frankfurt: C. H. Beck.

Beeck, Clemens (2011), *Daniel Libeskind and the Jewish Museum*, Berlin: Jaron.

Blaževska, Gordana (2001), 'Likovnaizložba so primesinapolitika', *Utrinski vesnik*, December 3.

Bogoeski, Krste (2011), 'Muzeite vo Makedonija – Preživuvanje na tranzicijata', in S. Polić Radovanović (ed.), *Condition of the Cultural and Natural Heritage in the Balkan Region – South East Europe*, 31–6, Beograd: Centralni Institut za Konzervaciju u Beogradu.

Boškovska, Nada (2017), *Yugoslavia and Macedonia before Tito: Between Repression and Integration*, London: I. B. Tauris.

Bracke, Sarah, and Nadia Fadil (2008), 'Islam and Secular Modernity under Western Eyes: A Genealogy of a Constitutive Relationship', *Working Paper, EUI RSCAS, Mediterranean Programme Series*. Available online: https://cadmus.eui.eu/han dle/1814/8102 (accessed 12 June 2017).

Catlos, Brian A. (2014), *Muslims of Medieval Latin Christendom, c. 1050–1614*, Cambridge: Cambridge University Press.

Cohen, Richard I. (1998), *Jewish Icons: Arts and Society in Modern Europe*, Berkeley: University of California Press.

Cvitković, Sabina, and Mihael Kline (2017), 'Skopje: Rebranding the Capital City through Architecture and Monuments to Remake the Nation Brand', *Sociologija i prostor*, 55 (1): 33–53.

Dimitrova, Kalia (2017), 'Skopijski kameleon: Polityka rekonstrukcji i architektura oporu w mieście Skopje', *Obieg* 5.

Dimova, Rozita (2013), *Ethno-Baroque: Materiality, Aesthetics, and Conflict in Modern-Day Macedonia*, New York: Berghahn Books.

Dimova, Rozita (2018). 'Elusive Centers of a Balkan City: Skopje between Undesirable and Reluctant Heritage', *International Journal of Heritage Studies*, 25 (9): 1–16.

DW (2019), 'Director of Jewish Museum Berlin Resigns', 14 June. Available online: https://www.dw.com/en/director-of-jewish-museum-berlin-resigns/a-49214098 (accessed 20 July 2020).

European Commission (2002), 'A Community of Cultures: The European Union and the Arts: Europe on the Move', Brochure. Available online: http://aei.pitt.edu/15064/ (accessed 20 July 2020).

European Parliament (2018), 'Merkel: Nationalism and Egoism Must Never Have a Chance Again in Europe', 13 November. Available online: https://www.europarl.europa.eu/news/en/press-room/20181106IPR18316/merkel-nationalism-and-ego ism-must-never-have-a-chance-again-in-europe (accessed 1 September 2020).

Fadil, Nadia (2011), 'Not-/Unveiling as an Ethical Practice', *Feminist Review*, 98 (1): 83–109.

Flood, Finbarr Barry (2012), 'From the Prophet to Postmodernism? New World Orders and the End of Islamic Art', *Journal of Art Historiography*, 6: 31–53.

Gemeentemuseum Den Haag (2018), 'Splendour and Bliss: Arts of the Islamic World'. Available online: https://www.kunstmuseum.nl/en/exhibitions/splendour-and-bliss (accessed 5 July 2019).

Georgievski, Dzvezdan (2001), 'Nova vera nova Biblija: Novatamakedonskacrkva VMRO bešepromovirana so otkrivanjetonastariotikonostas', *Utrinski vesnik*, November 29.

Gori, Maja (2014), 'Fabricating Identity from Ancient Shards: Memory Construction and Cultural Appropriation in the New Macedonian Question', *Hungarian Historical Review*, 3 (2): 285–311.

Graan, Andrew (2010), 'On the Politics of "Imidž": European Integration and the Trials of Recognition in Postconflict Macedonia', *Slavic Review*, 69 (4): 835–58.

Graan, Andrew (2016), 'The Nation Brand Regime: Nation Branding and the Semiotic Regimentation of Public Communication in Contemporary Macedonia', *Sign and Society*, 4 (S1): S70–S105.

Hall, Stuart (1992), 'The West and the Rest: Discourse and Power', in Tania Das Gupta, Carl E. James, Roger C. A. Maaka, Grace-Edward Galabuzi and Chris Andersen. (eds), *Race and Racialization: Essential Readings: Second Edition*, 85–95, Toronto: Canadian Scholars Press.

Heath, Ian A. (2005), 'The Representation of Islam in British Museums', PhD diss., The University of Manchester.

Huntington, Samuel P. (2000), 'The Clash of Civilizations?', in Lane Crothers and Charles Lockhart (eds), *Culture and Politics*, 99–118, New York: Palgrave Macmillan.

Ivkovska, V. (2016), 'Reinventing Vernacular Traditions to Reveal National Identity: A Case Study of the "Macedonian Village"', *Traditional Dwellings and Settlements Review*, 27 (2): 71–83.

Jagdhuhn, N. (2016), 'Museum (Re)public', *Glasnik Etnografskog institute SANU*, 64 (1): 105–19.

Janev, Goran (2011), 'Narrating the Nation, Narrating the City', *Cultural Analysis*, 10: 3–21.

Janev, Goran (2016), 'Contesting Ethnocratic Spatial Order: Narrative Spaces in Skopje', *European Quarterly of Political Attitudes and Mentalities*, 5 (2): 24–35.

Janev, Goran (2017), 'Burdensome Past: Challenging the Socialist Heritage in Macedonia', *Stud. ethnol. Croat.*, 29 (1): 149–70.

Jewish Museum Berlin (2007), 'Cherchez la Femme: Wig, Burqa, Wimple'. Available online: https://www.jmberlin.de/en/exhibition-cherchez-la-femme (accessed 15 June 2020).

Jewish Museum Berlin (2009), 'Kosher & Co. On Food and Religion', ed. M. Friedlander and C. Kugelmann, Exhibition Catalogue, Berlin: Nicolai.

Jewish Museum Berlin (2013), 'Haut ab! Haltungen zur rituellen Beschneidung (Snip It! Stances on Ritual Circumcision)', Exhibition Catalogue, Göttingen: Wallstein.

Kamczycki, Artur (2015), *MuzeumLibeskinda w Berlinie: Żydowskikontekstarchitektury*, Poznań: Uniwersytetu im. Adama Mickiewicza.

Kamel, Susan (2019), 'Diversifying Islam and the Museum', *Material Religion*, 15 (3): 374–5.

Khabeer, Su'ad Abdul (2016), *Muslim Cool: Race, Religion, and Hip Hop in the United States*, New York: New York University Press.

Kirshenblatt-Gimblett, Barbara (2013), 'Why Jewish Museums? An International Perspective', *Studia Judaica*, 2 (32): 77–100.

Kirshenblatt-Gimblett, Barbara (2014), 'Theater of History', in *Polin: 1000 Year History of Polish Jews*, Exhibition Catalogue, 32, Polin Museum in Warsaw.

Korobar, Klime (1989), 'Obnova i transformacija Muzeja grada Skopja', *Informatica museologica*, 20 (3–4): 41–2.

Koszarska-Szulc, Justyna, and Natalia Romik (eds) (2017), 'Estranged: March '68 and Its Aftermath', Exhibition Catalogue, Warsaw: POLIN Museum of the History of Polish Jews.

Koziura, Karolina (2014), 'The Struggle over Memory Hidden in the Contemporary Cityscape: The Example of Skopje 2014, Macedonia', *Journal of Urban Ethnology*, 12: 103–18.

Kuculovska, Galena (1986), 'Muzejska postava narodnooslobodilačkog rata Makedonije', *Informatica museologica*, 17 (1–4): 31–3.

Kulić, Vladimir (2017), 'Building the Socialist Balkans: Architecture in the Global Networks of the Cold War', *Southeast Europe*, 41 (2): 95–111.

Majewski, Piotr (2016), 'Project "Skopje 2014" – À la recherche du temps perdu', *Ethnologia Balkanica*, 19: 167–83.

Mamdani, Mahmood (2002), 'Good Muslim, Bad Muslim: A Political Perspective on Culture and Terrorism', *American Anthropologist*, 104 (3): 766–75.

Mattioli, Fabio (2014a), 'Regimes of Aesthetics: Competing Performances Surrounding the Skopje 2014 Plan', in Tanja Petrović (ed.), *Mirroring Europe: Ideas of Europe and Europeanization in Balkan Societies*, 64–89, Leiden: Brill.

Mattioli, Fabio (2014b), 'Unchanging Boundaries: The Reconstruction of Skopje and the Politics of Heritage', *International Journal of Heritage Studies*, 20 (6): 599–615.

Mork, Andrea (2018), 'The Narrative', in Andrea Mork and Perikles Christodoolou (eds), *Creating the House of European History*, 137–41, Luxemburg: Publications Office of the European Union.

Muhić, Maja, and Aleksandar Takovski (2014), 'Redefining National Identity in Macedonia: Analyzing Competing Origin Myths and Interpretations through Hegemonic Representations', *Etnološka tribina*, 37 (44): 138–52.

Naguib, Saphinaz-Amal (2019), 'New Frames to Islam in European Museums', *Material Religion*, 15 (3): 376–7.

Nirenberg, David (2014), *Neighboring Faiths: Christianity, Islam, and Judaism in the Middle Ages and Today*, Chicago: University of Chicago Press.

Peressut, Luca Basso, and Pozzi, Clelia (eds) (2012), *Museums in an Age of Migrations*, Milano: Politecnico di Milano.

Peressut, Luca Basso, Francesca Lanz and Gennaro Postiglione (eds) (2013a), *European Museums in the 21st Century: Setting the Framework (vol. 1)*, Milano: Politecnico di Milano.

Peressut, Luca Basso, Francesca Lanz and Gennaro Postiglione (eds.) (2013b), *European Museums in the 21st Century: Setting the Framework (vol. 2)*, Milano: Politecnico di Milano.

Peressut, Luca Basso, Francesca Lanz and Gennaro Postiglione (eds.) (2013c), *European Museums in the 21st Century: Setting the Framework (vol. 3)*, Milano: Politecnico di Milano.

Peter, Frank, Sarah Dornhof and Elena Arigita (eds) (2013), *Islam and the Politics of Culture in Europe: Memory, Aesthetics, Art*, Bielefeld: Transcript Verslag.

Petkovski, Dragan (1975), 'Izgradnja muzejskih zgrada u Skopju', *Muzeologija*, 18 (1): 33–56.

Petkovski, Dragan (1976), '25 – godišnina na Muzejot na grad Skopje (1949–1974)', *Informatica Museologica*, 7 (3–4): 29–55.

Petkovski, Dragan (1987), 'Pet godina djelatnosti Muzeja na Staroj skopskoj čaršiji', *Informatica Museologica*, 18 (1–4): 62–3.

Polonsky, Antony (2013), *The Jews in Poland and in Russia: A Short History*, Liverpool: Liverpool University Press.

Popovska, Dragica (2015), *Spomenikot, memorijata i identitetot*, Skopje: Institut za Nacionalna Istorija.

Posavac, Zlatko (1987), 'Muzeji, umjetnost i povijest: Razmatranja uz raspravu Pavla Vuk-Pavlovića Umjetnost i muzejska estetika', *Prilozi*, 13 (1–2): 135–61.

Puttkamer, Joachim von (2015), 'No Future? Narrating the Past in Bosnian History Museums', *Nationalities Papers: The Journal of Nationalism and Ethnicity*, 44 (5): 789–803.

Reef, P. (2018), 'Macedonian Monument Culture Beyond "Skopje 2014"', *Südosteuropa*, 66 (4): 451–80.

Rey, Virginie (2019), 'Islam, Museums, and the Politics of Representation in the West', *Material Religion*, 15 (2): 250–2.

Rosman, Moshe (2013), 'Zdecydowanie żydowskie, wyraźnie polskie – Muzeum Historii Żydów Polskich a nowa polsko-żydowska metahistoria', *Studia Judaica*, 16 (32): 47–75.

Sazdova Kondijanova, Ljubica (2011), *Muzej na grad Skopje 1949-2011*, Skopje: Muzej na grad Skopje.

Scheid, Kirsten (2012), 'The Study of Islamic Art at a Crossroad, and Humanity as a Whole', in Benoît Junod, George Khalil and Stephan Weber (eds), *Islamic Art and the Museum: Discussions on Scientific and Museological Approaches to Art and Archaeology of the Muslim World*, 90–4, London: Saqi Books.

Shatanawi, Mirjam (2007), 'Tropical Malaise', *Bidoun Magazine*, 10: 42–4.

Shatanawi, Mirjam (2012a), 'Engaging Islam: Working with Muslim Communities in a Multicultural Society', *Curator: The Museum Journal*, 55 (1): 65–79.

Shatanawi, Mirjam (2012b), 'Curating against Dissent: Museums and the Public Debate on Islam', in C. Flood, Stephen Hutchings, Galina Miazhevich and Henri Nickels (eds), *Political and Cultural Representations of Muslims*, 177–92, Leiden: Brill.

Shaw, Wendy M. K. (2012), 'The Islam in Islamic Art History: Secularism and Public Discourse', *Journal of Art Historiography*, (6): 1–37.

Spaskovska, Ljubica (2010), 'Macedonia's Nationals, Minorities and Refugees in the Post-communist Labyrinths of Citizenship', *CITSEE Working Paper Series*, 5 (1): 1–27.

Sternfeld, Nora (2016), 'Inside the Post-representative Museum', in Carmen Mörsch, Angeli Sachs and Thomas Sieber (eds), *Contemporary Curating and Museum Education*, 175–86, Bielefeld: Transcript Verslag.

Todorovski, Zoran (2008), *Id Ego Sum*, Skopje: Makedonskareč.

Todorovski, Zoran (2009), *Memento*, Skopje: Makedonska reč.

Trajanovski, Naum (2018), ' "I Love GTC" Citizens' Initiative: A Happy Ending Story', in Gazela Pudar Draško, Irena Fiket and Srđan Prodanović (eds), *Democratic Engagement in South East Europe: Stories to Be Told*, 11–20, Skopje: Institute for Philosophy and Social Theory.

Trajanovski, Naum (2020a), 'The Three Memory Regimes of Ilinden Commemorations (2001–2018): A Prolegomenon to the Study of the Official Memory in North Macedonia', *Southeastern Europe*, 44 (1): 1–26.

Trajanovski, Naum (2020b), *Operacijata Muzej: Muzejot na makedonskata borba i makedonskata politika na sekavanje*, Skopje: Templum.

Troebst, Stefan (1997), 'Yugoslav Macedonia 1943-1953: Building the Party, the State, and the Nation', in Melissa K. Bokovoy, James A. Irvine and Carol S. Lilly (eds), *State-Society Relations in Yugoslavia, 1945-1992*, 243–66, New York: St. Martin's Press.

Vasev-Dimeska, Vesna (1983), 'Muzej na sovremenost umetnost Skopje', *Informatica Museologica*, 14 (3–4): 18–19.

Vergo, Peter (ed.) (1989), *New Museology*, London: Reaktion Books.

Vernoit, Stephen (1997), 'The Rise of Islamic Archaeology', *Muqarnas Online*, 14 (1): 1–10.

Vuk-Pavlović, Pavao (1963), 'Umjetnost i muzejska estetika', *Godišen Zbornik na Filozofskiot Fakultet Skopje*, 15 (3): 5–40.

Weber, Stefan (2018), 'Pulling the Past into the Present: Curating Islamic Art in a Changing World, a Perspective from Berlin', *International Journal of Islamic Architecture*, 7 (2): 237–61.

Whitehead, Chris, Susannah Eckersley and Rhiannon Mason (eds) (2012), *Placing Migration in European Museums: Theoretical, Contextual and Methodological Foundations*, Milano: Politecnico di Milano.

Whitehead, Chris, Rhiannon Mason, Susannah Eckersley and Katherine Lloyd (eds) (2013), *'Placing' Europe in the Museum*, Milano: Politecnico di Milano.

Winegar, Jessica (2008), 'The Humanity Game: Art, Islam, and the War on Terror', *Anthropological Quarterly*, 81 (3): 651–81.

Young, James E. (1993), *The Texture of Memory: Holocaust Memorials and Meaning*, New Haven, CT: Yale University Press.

Zdravkovski, Dragisa (1983), 'Stalnapostavka Arheološkogmuzeja Makedonije', *Informatica Museologica*, 12 (3–4): 26–8.

Žižek, Slavoj (2010), 'Liberal Multiculturalism Masks an Old Barbarism with a Human Face', *The Guardian*, 3 October. Available online: https://www.theguardian.com/commentisfree/2010/oct/03/immigration-policy-roma-rightwing-europe (accessed 15 July 2019).

# Chapter 5

A1on (2019), *'Prespav'*, still frame. Available online: https://a1on.mk/culture/serijata-pres pav-kje-se-emituva-vo-bugarija/attachment/prespav/ (accessed 22 September 2021).

Abbas, Tahir (2013), ' "Last of the Dinosaurs": *Citizen Khan* as Institutionalization of Pakistani Stereotypes in British Television Comedy', *South Asian Popular Culture*, 11 (1): 85–90.

Adewunmi, Bim (2012), *'Citizen Khan*: An Asian Sitcom Star Is Born', *The Guardian*, 22 August. Available online: https://www.theguardian.com/tv-and-radio/2012/aug/22/citi zen-khan-sitcom-star-born (accessed 22 September 2021).

Afdal, Geir (2006), *Tolerance and Curriculum: Conceptions of Tolerance in the Multicultural Unitary Norwegian Compulsory School*, Münster: Waxmann.

Ahmed, Abdul-Azim (2013), 'Faith in Comedy: Representations of Muslim Identity in British Comedy', *South Asian Popular Culture*, 11 (1): 91–6.

Akbar, Arifa (2012), 'Last Night's Viewing – *Citizen Khan*, BBC 1 Hunderby, Sky Atlantic', *The Independent*, 27 August. Available online: https://www.independent.co.uk/arts-entertainment/tv/reviews/last-nights-viewing-citizen-khan-bbc1-hunderby-sky-atlan tic-8082402.html (accessed 22 September 2021).

Aljazeera (2018), ' "I'll Be Muslim Too": Fans Embrace Liverpool's Mo Salah', 16 February. Available online: https://www.aljazeera.com/news/2018/02/liverpool-fans-embrace-mohamed-salah-muslim-chant-180216105515770.html (accessed 22 September 2021).

Alrababa'h, Ala', William Marble, Salma Mousa and Alexandra A. Siegel (2019), 'Can Exposure to Celebrities Reduce Prejudice? The Effect of Mohamed Salah on Islamophobic Behaviors and Attitudes', IPL Working Paper Series. Available online: https://osf.io/preprints/socarxiv/eq8ca/ (accessed 22 September 2021).

Anderson, Matt (2018), 'Understanding Gen Z through the Lens of YouTube', Think with Google, August. Available online: https://www.thinkwithgoogle.com/marketing-strateg ies/video/gen-z-and-youtube/ (accessed 22 September 2021).

Andy Does Stuff (2017), 'History of the Entire World, I Guess (School Edition)', YouTube, 13 May. Available online: https://www.youtube.com/watch?v=c-dmjDU7FT4&feature=emb_title (accessed 22 September 2021).

Bird, Ben (2019), 'How Mohamed Salah Inspired Me to Become a Muslim', *The Guardian*, 3 October. Available online: https://www.theguardian.com/football/2019/oct/03/mohamed-salah-inspired-me-become-muslim-liverpool-islam (accessed 22 September 2021).

Brown, Paul (2012), 'Citizen Khan – View from Abroad', *BBC Monitoring*, 7 September. Available online: https://www.bbc.com/news/entertainment-arts-19511191 (accessed 22 September 2021).

Burgess, Jean, and Joshua Green (2018), *YouTube: Online Video and Participatory Culture*, Hoboken, NJ: John Wiley & Sons.

Channel 4 (2018), 'Mo Salah: The New Egyptian King ... The Perfect Football Role Model?', YouTube, 27 May. Available online: https://www.youtube.com/watch?v=J-J9Pmyy3Kc (accessed 22 September 2021).

*Citizen Khan* (2012), [TV programme], BBC One, series 1, episode 1, 27 August.

Conlan, Tara (2013), 'Citizen Khan Creator Adil Ray: "Don't Allow Yourself to Be Offended" ', *The Guardian*, 29 September. Available online: https://www.theguardian.com/media/2013/sep/29/citizen-khan-adil-ray-sitcom (accessed 22 September 2021).

Danesi, Marcel (2012), *Semiotics in Language Education Vol. 2*, Berlin: Walter de Gruyter.

DawahCallIslam (2018), 'A Young Kid Does Mohamed Salah Celebration after Scoring', YouTube, 21 March. Available online: https://www.youtube.com/watch?v=25TkyG6EgwA (accessed 22 September 2021).

Duffy, Bobby, Ffion Thomas, Hannah Shrimpton, Hannah Whyte-Smith, Michael Clemence and Tara Abboud (2018), 'Ipsos Thinks beyond Binary: The Lives and Choices of Generation Z', report, Ipsos MORI. Available online: https://www.ipsos.com/sites/default/files/2018-08/ipsos_-_beyond_binary_-_the_lives_and_choices_of_gen_z.pdf (accessed 22 September 2021).

Flying with Haifa (2016), 'Italians React to a Muslim Girl!', YouTube, 15 June. Available online: https://www.youtube.com/watch?v=OgLTVxL7kVc (accessed 22 September 2021).

Forebears (n.d.), 'Khan Surname User-Submission'. Available online: https://forebears.io/surnames/khan (accessed 22 September 2021).

Furseth, Inger (ed.) (2018), *Religious Complexity in the Public Sphere: Comparing Nordic Countries*, New York: Palgrave Macmillan.

Gauntlett, David (2011), *Making Is Connecting: The Social Meaning of Creativity, from DIY and Knitting to YouTube and Web 2.0*, Cambridge, MA: Polity Press.

Goffman, Erving (1974), *Frame Analysis: An Essay on the Organization of Experience*, Cambridge, MA: Harvard University Press.

Gov.uk (2020), 'Population of England and Wales'. Available online: https://www.ethnicity-facts-figures.service.gov.uk/uk-population-by-ethnicity/national-and-regional-populations/population-of-england-and-wales/latest (accessed 22 September 2021).

Guardian Culture (2017), 'Muslim Women Discuss Removing Their Hijab at Work: "I Feel So Guilty" ', YouTube, 5 April. Available online: https://www.youtube.com/watch?v=uj19V0KFnkE&feature=emb_title (accessed 22 September 2021).

Gulick, Daniel (2018), 'Here's Why TV Is Still the Most Powerful Ad Medium', *Smartbrief*, 28 August. Available online: https://www.smartbrief.com/original/2018/08/heres-why-tv-still-most-powerful-ad-medium (accessed 22 September 2021).

Hale, James (2019), 'More Than 500 Hours of Content Are Now Being Uploaded to YouTube Every Minute', *Tubefilter*, 5 July. Available online: https://www.tubefilter.com/2019/05/07/number-hours-video-uploaded-to-youtube-per-minute/ (accessed 22 September 2021).

Hartley, John (2008), *Television Truths: Forms of Knowledge in Popular Culture*, Hoboken, NJ: John Wiley & Sons.

Huq, Rupa (2013), 'Situating *Citizen Khan*: Shifting Representations of Asians Onscreen and the Outrage Industry in the Social Media Age', *South Asian Popular Culture*, 11 (1): 77–83.

IMDb (n.d.), '*Citizen Khan*'. Available online: https://www.imdb.com/title/tt2334 302/?ref_=nv_sr_srsg_0 (accessed 22 September 2021).

It's Soso (2016), 'Islamophobia Social Experiment in Norway', YouTube, 9 October. Available online: https://www.youtube.com/watch?v=mDXBvrX4WGI (accessed 22 September 2021).

Jenner, Mareike (2018), *Netflix and the Re-invention of Television*, Cham: Springer.

Kabir, Nahid A. (2010), *Young British Muslims: Identity, Culture, and the Media*, Edinburgh: Edinburgh University Press.

Karim, Jovian (2014), '10 Hours of Walking in NYC as a Woman in Hijab', YouTube, 6 November. Available online: https://www.youtube.com/watch?v=mgw6y3cH 7tA&list=PLKDHaA-LN6Y6BqZaRZNQ34RZfHLsO1KAD&index=5&t=0s (accessed 22 September 2021).

Khan, Saira (2012), 'Offensive? Racist? No, Just Funny – and Oh So True!', *Mail Online*, 29 August. Available online: https://www.dailymail.co.uk/debate/article-2195 459/Citizen-Khan-Offensive-Racist-No-just-funny--oh-true.html (accessed 22 September 2021).

Kidd, Dustin (2017), *Popular Culture*, Oxford: Oxford University Press.

Kim, Jin (2012), 'The Institutionalization of YouTube: From User-Generated Content to Professionally Generated Content', *Media Culture & Society*, 34 (1): 53–67.

Kuneva, Meglena (2009). 'Keynote Speech: Roundtable on Online Data Collection, Targeting and Profiling', *European Commission*, 31 March. Available online: https://ec.europa.eu/commission/presscorner/detail/en/SPEECH_09_156 (accessed 22 September 2021).

Lais, Hasnet (2012), '*Citizen Khan*'s Alia: How the Hijab Got Sexy', *The Independent*, 2 October. Available online: https://www.independent.co.uk/voices/comm ent/citizen-khan-s-alia-how-the-hijab-got-sexy-8194410.html (accessed 22 September 2021).

Laws, Roz (2015), '*Citizen Khan* Bought by Countries across the World – and They're Remaking It in Germany', *Birmingham Mail*, 6 November. Available online: https://www.birminghammail.co.uk/whats-on/film-news/citizen-khan-tv-series-bought-10398810 (accessed 22 September 2021).

LFC Leader (2018), 'New Mohamed Salah Song – Mohamed Salah, A Gift from ALLAH – Lyrics', YouTube, 3 May. Available online: https://www.youtube.com/watch?v=XvkU x821YYg (accessed 22 September 2021).

Malik, Sarita (2002), *Representing Black Britain: A History of Black and Asian Images on British Television*, London: Sage.

Manning, Alan, and Sanchari Roy (2010), 'Culture Clash or Culture Club? National Identity in Britain', *Economic Journal*, 120 (524): F72–F100.

Marsh, Jackie (ed.) (2005), *Popular Culture, New Media and Digital Literacy in Early Childhood*, London: Routledge.

McClure, Paul K. (2016), 'Faith and Facebook in a Pluralistic Age: The Effects of Social Networking Sites on the Religious Beliefs of Emerging Adults', *Sociological Perspectives*, 59 (4): 818–34.

McGaha, Julie (2015), 'Popular Culture & Globalization: Teacher Candidates' Attitudes & Perceptions of Cultural & Ethnic Stereotypes', *Multicultural Education*, 23 (1): 32–7.

Othman, Jara (2016), 'Yara Othman Asks People's Opinions on Streets of Stockholm Sweden', YouTube, 25 March. Available online: https://www.youtube.com/watch?v=MhZ5vrh5PuQ (accessed 22 September 2021).

Peach, Ceri (2005), 'Muslims in the UK', in Tahir Abbas (ed.), *Muslim Britain: Communities under Pressure*, 18–30, London: Zed Books.

Pew Research Center (2018), 'YouTube, Instagram and Snapchat Are the Most Popular Online Platforms among Teens', 29 May. Available online: https://www.pewresearch.org/Internet/2018/05/31/teens-social-media-technology-2018/pi_2018-05-31_teenstech_0-01/ (accessed 22 September 2021).

Saha, Anamik (2013), 'Citizen Smith More than Citizen Kane? Genres-in-Progress and the Cultural Politics of Difference', *South Asian Popular Culture*, 11 (1): 97–102.

Saleh, Adam (2013), 'Praying in Public!', YouTube, 10 October. Available online: https://www.youtube.com/watch?v=ilqKn1BuS-s&t=218s (accessed 22 September 2021).

Saleh, Adam (2016), 'Pulling Hijab Off Experiment!', YouTube, 5 June. Available online: https://www.youtube.com/watch?v=HAhkyRyNV_g&t=96s (accessed 22 September 2021).

Smarthistory (2017), 'Judaism, Islam and the Survival of Ancient Greek Texts', YouTube, 13 July. Available online: https://www.youtube.com/watch?v=N1s7RtMg2Co&feature=emb_title (accessed 22 September 2021).

Snow, David A., E. Burke Rochford, Jr., Steven K. Worden and Robert D. Benford (1986), 'Frame Alignment Processes, Micromobilization, and Movement Participation', *American Sociological Review*, 51 (4): 464–81.

Spencer, Ian R. G. (1997), *British Immigration Policy since 1939: The Making of Multi-Racial Britain*, New York: Routledge.

Strangelove, Michael (2010), *Watching YouTube: Extraordinary Videos by Ordinary People*, Toronto: University of Toronto Press.

Sturgis, India (2015), 'The Only Time You See Muslims on TV Is as Terrorists', *Daily Telegraph*, 27 October. Available online: https://www.telegraph.co.uk/culture/tvandradio/11958400/The-only-time-you-see-Muslims-on-TV-is-as-terrorists.html (accessed 22 September 2021).

TED (2010), 'Chris Anderson: How YouTube Is Driving Innovation', YouTube, 14 September. Available online: https://www.youtube.com/watch?v=X6Zo53M0lcY (accessed 22 September 2021).

TED-Ed (2014), 'It's a Church. It's a Mosque. It's Hagia Sophia. – Kelly Wall', YouTube, 14 July. Available online: https://www.youtube.com/watch?v=KRPp3jzv1Tw (accessed 22 September 2021).

The Economist (2017), 'The World's Most Valuable Resource Is No Longer Oil, but Data', 6 May. Available online: https://www.economist.com/leaders/2017/05/06/the-worlds-most-valuable-resource-is-no-longer-oil-but-data (accessed 22 September 2021).

The Redmen TV (2018), ' "I'll Be Muslim Too!" WITH LYRICS Porto v Liverpool | New Mo Salah Song | Learn LFC Chants', YouTube, 14 February. Available online: https://www.youtube.com/watch?v=b-icmPutQDk (accessed 22 September 2021).

We Are Social and Hootsuite Digital (2019), 'Digital 2019', report. Available online: https://p.widencdn.net/kqy7ii/Digital2019-Report-en (accessed 22 September 2021).

Wurtz, Bill (2017), 'History of the Entire World, I Guess', YouTube, 10 May. Available online: https://www.youtube.com/watch?v=xuCn8ux2gbs&t=660s (accessed 22 September 2021).

Yusuf, Hanna Onyi (2013), 'Promoting Peaceful Coexistence and Religious Tolerance through Supplementary Readers and Reading Comprehension Passages in Basic Education Curriculum', *International Journal of Humanities and Social Science*, 3 (8): 224–32.

# Chapter 6

Ajuntament de Barcelona (2015), 'Refugees Welcome', Ajuntament de Barcelona. Available online: http://www.bcn.cat/barcelonainclusiva/es/fitxa_refugees_welcome_715.html (accessed 29 March 2021).

Alcalde, Javier, and Martín Portos (2018), 'Refugee Solidarity in a Multilevel Political Opportunity Structure: The Case of Spain', in Donatella della Porta (ed.), *Solidarity Mobilizations in the 'Refugee Crisis': Contentious Moves*, Florence: Palgrave MacMillan.

Alternative für Deutschland (2017a), *Der Islam gehört nicht zu Deutschland!* Available online: 2017-07-20_afd-btw_faltblatt_islam-nicht-zu-deutschland.pdf (accessed 29 March 2021).

Alternative für Deutschland (2017b), *Der Islam als politische Herausforderung. Pressekonferenz der AfD am 18: September 2017 in Berlin: Kozeptpapier Islam.* Available online: A (afdkompakt.de) (accessed 29 March 2021).

Arigita, Elena (2011), 'Spain and the al-Andalus Legacy', in Stig Jarle Hansen, Atle Mesoy and Tuncay Kardas (eds), *Borders of Islam: Exploring Samuel Huntington's Faultlines from al-Andalus to Virtual Ummah*, 223–34, New York: Columbia University Press.

Arigita, Elena (2019), 'En el punto de mira: Los imames como líderes y mediadores del islam en España', In Luz Gómez (ed.), *Islam y Desposesión: Resignificar la pertenencia*, 23–41, Madrid: Ediciones de Oriente y del Mediterráneo.

Armbruster, Heidi (2019), ' "It Was the Photograph of the Little Boy": Reflections on the Syrian Vulnerable Persons Resettlement Programme in the UK', *Ethnic and Racial Studies*, 42 (15): 2680–99.

Assmann, Aleida (2016), *Shadows of Trauma: Memory and the Politics of Postwar Identity*, trans. Sarah Clift, New York: Fordham.

Assmann, Aleida (2020), *Das neue Unbehagen der Erinnerungskultur*, 3rd Edition, Munich: C. H. Beck.

Barreira, David (2019), 'Los 10 episodios favoritos de Vox en la historia de España: Así sucedieron de verdad', *El Español*, 23 January. Available online: https://www.elespanol.com/cultura/historia/20190123/episodios-favoritos-vox-historia-espana-sucedieron-verdad/370464067_0.html (accessed 29 March 2021).

BBC News (2015a), 'Big Rise in German Attacks on Migrant Homes in 2015', 9 October. Available online: https://www.bbc.com/news/world-europe-34487562 (accessed 29 March 2021).

BBC News (2015b), 'Migrant Crisis: Hungary Crossings Echo 1989 and 1956', 9 September. Available online: https://www.bbc.com/news/world-europe-34168084 (accessed 29 March 2021).

Bélanger, Danièle, and Cenk Saracoglu (2019), 'Syrian Refugees and Turkey: Whose "Crisis?"' in Cecilia Manjivar, Marie Ruiz and Immanuel Ness (eds), *The Oxford Handbook of Migration Crises*, 280–94, Oxford: Oxford University Press. Available online: doi: 10.1093/oxfordhb/9780190856908.013.67 (accessed 29 March 2021).

Brownlie, Siobhan (2020), *Discourses of Memory and Refugees: Exploring Facets*, Cham: Palgrave Macmillan.

Bocskor, Ákos (2018), 'Anti-immigration Discourses in Hungary during the "Crisis Year": The Orbán Government's "National Consultation" Campaign of 2015', *Sociology*, 52 (3): 551–68. Available online: https://doi.org/10.1177/0038038518762081 (accessed 29 March 2021).

Büscher, Wolfgang, Martin Lutz and Till-Reimer Stoldt (2016), 'Die meisten waren frisch eingereiste Asylbewerber', *Welt*, 7 January. Available online: https://www.welt.de/poli tik/deutschland/article150735341/Die-meisten-waren-frisch-eingereiste-Asylbewer ber.html (accessed 29 March 2021).

CEAR (2016), *Informe 2016: Las Personas Refugiadas En España y Europa*. Available online: https://www.cear.es/wp-content/uploads/2016/12/informe_cear_2016_ok.pdf (accessed 29 March 2021).

Dainotto, Roberto Maria (2007), *Europe (in Theory)*. Durham: Duke University Press.

Dearden, Lizzie (2016), 'Cologne Sexual Assaults: Vigilante Gangs Attack Asylum Seekers after Vowing to "Clean Up" German City', *The Independent*, 12 January. Available online: https://www.independent.co.uk/news/world/europe/cologne-sexual-assaults-vigilante-gangs-attack-asylum-seekers-after-vowing-clean-german-city-a6807021.html (accessed 29 March 2021).

De Cesari, Chiara, and Ann Rigney (2014), 'Introduction', in Chiara De Cesari and Ann Rigney (eds), *Transnational Memory: Circulation, Articulation, Scales*, 1–28, Berlin: De Gruyter.

De Cesari, Chiara, Ivo Bosilkov and Arianna Piacentini (2020), '(Why) Do Eurosceptics Believe in a Common Heritage?', in Chiara De Cesari and Ayhan Kaya (eds), *European Memory in Populism: Representations of Self and Other*, 26–46, London: Routledge.

Deutsche Welle (2019), 'Deutschland und die Flüchtlinge: Wie 2015 das Land veränderte', 11 February. Available online: https://www.dw.com/de/deutschl and-und-die-fl%C3%BCchtlinge-wie-2015-das-land-ver%C3%A4nderte/a-47459712 (accessed 29 March 2021).

EFE (2016), 'Sánchez, a Un Refugiado Sirio: España Comprende El Drama de Una Guerra Civil', *El Diario*, 18 May. Available online: https://www.eldiario.es/politica/sanchez-refugiado-espana-comprende-guerra_1_3990484.html (accessed 29 March 2021).

Erll, Astrid (2011), 'Travelling Memory', *Parallax* 17 (4): 4–18.

Europa Press (2015), 'Exparlamentarios recuerdan el exilio español y exigen atender a los refugiados sirios', *El Diario*, 23 September. Available online: https://www.eldiario.es/politica/exparlamentarios-recuerdan-espanol-atender-refugiados_1_2471650.html (accessed 29 March 2021).

Feldman, David (2011), 'Why the English Like Turbans: Multicultural Politics in British History', in D. Feldman and J. Lawrence (eds), *Structures and Transformations in Modern British History*, 281–302, Cambridge: Cambridge University Press.

Fernández Parrilla, Gonzalo, and Carlos Cañete (2018), 'Spanish-Maghribi (Moroccan) Relations beyond Exceptionalism: A Postcolonial Perspective', *Journal of North African Studies*, 24 (1): 1–23. Available online: https://doi.org/10.1080/13629387.2018.1459262 (accessed 29 March 2021).

Ferreño, Paula Villaverde, and Itzel E. Cruz Pérez (2019), 'El Papel de Las Regiones En La Acogida de Refugiados: Comparativa entre España y Alemania', *Revista Internacional de Estudios Migratorios*, 9 (2): 197–230.

Ferris, Elizabeth and Kemal Kirişci (2016), *The Consequences of Chaos: Syria's Humanitarian Crisis and the Failure to Protect*. Washington: Brookings Institution Press.

Freedman, Jane (2019), 'A Gendered Analysis of the European Refugee "Crisis"', in Cecilia Manjivar, Marie Ruiz and Immanuel Ness (eds), *The Oxford Handbook of Migration Crises*, Oxford: Oxford University Press.

García-Sanjuán, Alejandro (2020), 'Weaponizing Historical Knowledge: The Notion of Reconquista in Spanish Nationalism', *Imago Temporis. Medium Aevum*, XIV: 133–62.

Goździak, Elżbieta M. (2019), 'Using Fear of the "Other", Orbán Reshapes Migration Policy in a Hungary Built on Cultural Diversity', *MPI*, Migration Policy Institute, 10 October. Available online: Using Fear of the "Other," Orbán Reshapes Migration Policy in a Hungary Built on Cultural Diversity | migrationpolicy.org (accessed 29 March 2021).

Goździak, Elżbieta M., and Brigitte Suter (2020), 'Concluding Thoughts', in Elżbieta M Goździak, Izabella Main and Brigitte Suter (eds), *Europe and the Refugee Response: A Crisis of Values?*, 286–92, London: Routledge. Available online: https://doi.org/10.4324/9780429279317 (accessed 29 March 2021).

Halbwachs, Maurice (1992), *On Collective Memory*, Chicago: University of Chicago Press. Translated from *Les cadres sociaux de la mémoire*, Paris: Presses Universitaires de France, 1952; originally published in *Les Travaux de L'Année Sociologique*, Paris: F. Alcan, 1925.

*Hansard* (2015a), HC Deb, vol. 599, cols. 33–4, 7 September. Available online: https://publications.parliament.uk/pa/cm201516/cmhansrd/cm150907/debtext/150907-0001.htm#1509074000002 (accessed 29 March 2021).

*Hansard* (2015b), HC Deb, vol. 603, cols. 1552–3, 16 December. Available online: https://www.parliament.uk/globalassets/documents/publications-records/house-of-commons-publications/hcbv603.pdf (accessed 29 March 2021).

*Hansard* (2016), HC Deb, vol. 617, cols. 549, 29 November. Available online: https://hansard.parliament.uk/Commons/2016-11-%2029/debates/16112935000003/RefugeeFamilyReunion(ImmigrationRules)#contribution-AA89C6E4-1D83-4FF4-9CAB-B62D45334E49 (accessed 22 September 2021).

Herrmann, Therese (2020), 'Crisis and Willkommenskultur: Civil Society Volunteering for Refugees in Germany', in Elżbieta M. Goździak, Izabella Main and Brigitte Suter (eds), *Europe and the Refugee Response: A Crisis of Values?*, 201–19, London: Routledge. Available online: https://doi.org/10.4324/9780429279317 (accessed 29 March 2021).

Höcke, Bernd (2017), 'Gemütszustand eines total besiegten Volkes', *Der Tagesspiegel*, 19 January. Available online: https://www.tagesspiegel.de/politik/hoecke-rede-im-wortlaut-weizsaeckers-rede-zum-8-mai-1945-war-gegen-das-eigene-volk/19273518-3.html (accessed 29 March 2021).

Holmes, Seth M., and Heide Castañeda (2016), 'Representing the "European Refugee Crisis" in Germany and Beyond: Deservingness and Difference, Life and Death', *American Ethnologist*, 43 (1): 12–24. Available online: https://escholarship.org/content/qt0xr0m9rr/qt0xr0m9rr.pdf (accessed 29 March 2021).

Huntington, Samuel P. (1997), *The Clash of Civilisations and the Remaking of World Order*, London: Simon & Schuster.

*Index* (2015), 'Orbán: Gazdasági bevándorlóknak nem adunk menedéket', 1 November. Available online: https://index.hu/belfold/2015/01/11/orban_gazdasagi_bevandorlok nak_nem_adunk_menedeket/ (accessed 20 September 2021).

Kallius, Annastiina (2017), 'The East-South Axis: Legitimizing the "Hungarian Solution to Migration"', *Revue Européenne des Migrations Internationales*, 33 (2 and 3): 133–55.

Karlsson, Klas-Göran (2010), 'The Uses of History and the Third Wave of Europeanisation', in Malgorzata En Pakier and Bo Stråth (eds), *A European Memory?*, 38–55, New York: Berghahn Books.

Kingsley, Patrick (2016), 'Hungary's Refugee Referendum Not Valid after Voters Stay Away', *The Guardian*, 2 October. Available online: https://www.theguardian.com/ world/2016/oct/02/hungarian-vote-on-refugees-will-not-take-place-suggest-first-poll-results (accessed 29 March 2021).

Körber, Carsten (2015), German National Parliament, 18th legislature, 122nd session, 11 September, 12727 C, Berlin. Available online: https://www.bundestag.de/mediat hek?videoid=5767597&url=L21lZGlhdGhla292ZXJsYXk=&mod=mediathek#url=L21l ZGlhdGhla292ZXJsYXk/dmlkZW9pZD01NzY3NTk3JnVybD1MMMjFsWkdsaGGRHa GxhMjkyWlhKc1lYaz0mbW9kPW1lZGlhdGhlaw==&mod=mediathek (accessed 22 September 2021).

Körösényi, András, Gábor Illés and Attila Gyulai (2020), *The Orbán Regime: Plebiscitary Leader Democracy in the Making*, London: Routledge.

Kovács, János Mátyás, and Balázs Trencsényi (2020), 'Introduction: Historicizing an Anti-Liberal Turn', in János Mátyás Kovács and Balázs Trencsényi (eds), *Brave New Hungary*, Lanham: Lexington Books.

László, Surán (2017), 'Felelet Timmersmans biztos úrnak', *Magyaridok*. Available online: https://www.magyaridok.hu/velemeny/felelet-timmermans-biztos-urnak-1921 621/ (accessed 29 March 2021).

Leipziger Städtische Bibliotheken (2015), 'Banner am Neuen Rathaus thematisiert Flucht 1945 und heute', Leipziger Städtische Bibliotheken. Available online: Banner am Neuen Rathaus thematisiert Flucht 1945 und heute - Stadt Leipzig (accessed 29 March 2021).

Leruth, Benjamin, and Peter Taylor-Gooby (2019), 'Does Political Discourse Matter? Comparing Party Positions and Public Attitudes on Immigration in England', *Politics*, 39 (2): 154–69. Available online: https://journals.sagepub.com/doi/10.1177/026339571 8755566?icid=int.sj-full-text.similar-articles.3 (accessed 22 September 2021).

Llopis, Sandra (2015), '¿Exiliados pero Libres?', Asociación Para la Recuperación de la Memoria Histórica. Available online: https://memoriahistorica.org.es/exiliados-pero-libres/ (accessed 29 March 2021).

MacDonald, Sharon (2013), *Memorylands: Heritage and Identity Today*, London: Routledge.

Mark, James, Artemy M. Kalinosvky and Steffi Marung (2020), 'Introduction', in James Mark, Artemy M. Kalinovsky and Steffi Marung (eds), *Alternative Globalizations: Eastern Europe and the Postcolonial World*, Bloomington: Indiana University Press.

McGuiness, Terry (2017), 'The UK Response to the Syrian Refugee Crisis', Research briefing, UK Parliament, House of Commons Library, 14 June. Available online: https://commonslibrary.parliament.uk/research-briefings/sn06805/ (accessed 29 March 2021).

Melegh, Attila (2020), 'The Fear of Population Replacement', in János Mátyás Kovács and Balázs Trencsényi (eds), *Brave New Hungary*, Lanham: Lexington Books.

Merkel, Angela (2011), 'Bericht der Vorsitzenden der CDU Deutschlands', 9 September. Available online: http://www.karlsruhe2010.cdu.de/images/stories/docs/101115-Rede-Merkel.pdf (accessed 22 September 2021).

Merkel, Angela (2015), 'Sommerpressekonferenz von Bundeskanzlerin Merkel: Thema – Aktuelle Themen der Innen- und Außenpolitik', 31 August, *Bundesregierung de*. Available online: https://www.bundesregierung.de/breg-de/aktuelles/pressekonferen zen/sommerpressekonferenz-von-bundeskanzlerin-merkel-848300 (accessed 29 March 2021).

Middaugh, Ellen, Browyer Benjamien and Joseph Kahne (2016), 'U Suk! Participatory Media and Youth Experiences with Political Discourse', *Youth & Society*, 49 (7): 1–21.

Montagut, Marta, and Carlota M. Moragas-Fernández (2020), 'The European Refugee Crisis Discourse in the Spanish Press: Mapping Humanization and Dehumanization Frames through Metaphors', *International Journal of Communication*, 14: 69–91.

Monzón, Ismael, Enric Bonet, Víctor David López, Aldo Mas, Gabirela Sánchez and Icíar Gutíerrez (2019), 'Los discursos contra la inmigración que hemos escuchado en campaña están copiados de la extrema derecha de otros países', *El Diario*, 26 April. Available online: https://www.eldiario.es/desalambre/discurso-antiinmigratorio-calc ado-espana_1_1580619.html (accessed 29 March 2021).

Mueller, Jan-Werner (2016), 'Angela Merkel's Misunderstood Christian Mission', *Foreign Policy*, 18 March. Available online: https://foreignpolicy.com/2016/03/18/angela-merk els-misunderstood-christian-mission-eu/ (accessed 29 March 2021).

MTI (2015), 'Varga Mihály: A magyarok válasza ma is az, mint 1956-ban', *Infostart*, 23 October. Available online: https://infostart.hu/belfold/2015/10/23/varga-mihaly-a-magyarok-valasza-ma-is-az-mint-1956-ban-768393 (accessed 29 March 2021).

Neiman, Susan (2019), *Learning from the Germans: Confronting Race and the Memory of Evil*, Allan Lane: Penguin.

*Nemzeti konzultáció a bevándorlásról és a terrorizmusról* (2015). Available online: https://2015-2019.kormany.hu/download/4/d3/c0000/Bev%20konz ult%C3%A1ci%C3%B3%20eredm%C3%A9nyei.pdf#!DocumentBrowse(accessed 29 March 2021).

News Wires (2016), 'Cologne Braces for Far-Right Rally after New Year's Violence', *France 24*, 9 January. Available online: https://www.france24.com/en/20160109-germany-colo gne-pegida-far-right-rally-new-year-violence-sexual-assaults-women-migrants-ref (accessed 29 March 2021).

Olmos Alcaraz, Antonia (2012), 'Discurso Político e Inmigración: Análisis crítico de discurso a propósito de la reforma gubernamental realizada al sistema de salud pública en España', *Discurso & Sociedad*, 6 (4): 739–58.

Orbán, Viktor (2015), 'Orbán Viktor beszéde a Mgyar Diaszpóra Tanács V. ülésén', 2 December. Budapest: miniszterelnok.hu. Available online: https://miniszterelnok.hu/ orban-viktor-beszede-a-magyar-diaszpora-tanacs-v-ulesen/ (accessed 29 March 2021).

Orbán, Viktor (2016), 'Prime Minister Viktor Orbán's Speech at the Official Ceremony Marking the 60th Anniversary of the 1956 Revolution', *miniszterelnök.hu*, Budapest, 23 October. Available online: http://www.miniszterelnok.hu/prime-minister-viktor-orb ans-speech-at-the-official-ceremony-marking-the-60th-anniversary-of-the-1956-rev olution/ (accessed 29 March 2021).

Orbán, Viktor (2017), 'Prime Minister Viktor Orbán's Speech on the 61st Anniversary of the 1956 Revolution and Freedom Fight', *miniszterelnök.hu*, Budapest, 23 October. Available online: http://www.miniszterelnok.hu/prime-minister-viktor-orbans-spe

ech-on-the-61st-anniversary-of-the-1956-revolution-and-freedom-fight/ (accessed 29 March 2021).

*Országgyűlési Napló* (2015), Session on 20 February 2015 of the Hungarian Parliament. Available online: https://www.parlament.hu/documents/10181/308218/ny150220. pdf/7817140d-c961-441d-b21c-29c26963684c (accessed 29 March 2021).

Ostrand, Nicole (2015), 'The Syrian Refugee Crisis: A Comparison of Responses by Germany, Sweden, the United Kingdom and the United States', *Journal of Migration and Human Security*, 3 (3): 255–79.

Ottermann, Philip (2020), 'How Angela Merkel's Great Migrant Gamble Paid Off', *The Guardian*, 30 August. Available online: https://www.theguardian.com/world/2020/ aug/30/angela-merkel-great-migrant-gamble-paid-off?CMP=Share_iOSApp_Other (accessed 29 March 2021).

Pérez Baquero, Rafael (2020), 'Narrar La Historia, Recordar el Trauma: Memoria y Olvido de la Guerra Civil española, Ochenta años después', PhD diss., Universidad de Murcia.

Pérez Baquero, Rafael (2021), 'Europa Como "Comunidad Mnémica": El Recuerdo Del Holocausto Entre Memorias Cosmopolitas y Multidireccionales', *Pasado y memoria: Revista de historia contemporánea*, 23: 384–406.

*Propeller* (2015), 'Kósa Lajos: A mai demokráciánk 1956-ban gyökeredzik', 23 October. Available online: https://propeller.hu/itthon/3166089-kosa-lajos-mai-demokraci ank-1956-ban (accessed 29 March 2021).

Propuesta de No Ley (2015), Grupo Parlamentario Partido Socialista, 29 September, Diario de Sesiones del Congreso de los Diputados Pleno y Diputatción Permanente, n. 307. Available online: http://www.congreso.es/public_oficiales/L10/CONG/DS/PL/ DSCD-10-PL-307.PDF#page=31 (accessed 29 March 2021).

Roose, Joshua M. (2021), *The New Demagogues: Religion, Masculinity and the Populist Epoch*, London: Routledge.

Rothberg, Michael (2009), *Multidirectional Memory: Remembering the Holocaust in the Age of Decolonization*, Stanford, CA: Stanford University Press.

Sarrazin, Manuel (2015), German National Parliament, 18th legislature, 130th session, 15 October, Berlin, 12574 (B). Available online: http://dipbt.bundestag.de/dip21/ btp/18/18130.pdf (accessed 29 March 2021).

Scholten, P. (2012), 'Agenda Dynamics and the Multi-Level Governance of Intractable Policy Controversies: The Case of Migrant Integration Policies in the Netherlands', *Policy Sciences*, 46 (3): 217–36.

Sharples, Caroline (2012), 'The Kindertransport in British Historical Memory', in Andrea Hammel and Bea Lewkowicz, *The Kindertransport in Britain 1938/39: New Perspectives*, The Yearbook of the Research Centre for German and Austrian Exiles Studies, Vol. 13, Institute of Germanic and Romance Studies, University of London, 15–28, Amsterdam: Brill.

Spencer, Nick (2016), 'Angela Merkel: How Germany's Iron Chancellor Is Shaped by Her Christianity', *Christian Today*, 6 January. Available online: https://www.christiantoday. com/article/angela.merkel.how.germanys.iron.chancellor.is.shaped.by.her.christian ity/75803.htm (accessed 29 March 2021).

Strømmen, H., and Schmiedel, U. (2020), *The Claim to Christianity: Responding to the Far Right*, London: SCM Press.

Szirtes, George (2016), 'Hungarians Fought for Freedom in 1956, not Viktor Orban's Rabble-Rousers', *The Guardian*, 1 October. Available online: https://www.theguard ian.com/commentisfree/2016/oct/01/hungary-freedom-viktor-orban-rabble-rousers-migrants-refugees-racism (accessed 29 March 2021).

Tarrés, Sol, and Javier Rosón (2014), 'Los origines de la institutionalizción des Islam en España: Bases y fundamentos (1900–1992)', *Awraq: Estudios sobre el mundo árabe e islámico contemporáneo*, (9): 147–69.

Timmermans, Frans (2015), 'Situation of Fundamental Rights in the EU', European Parliament, PV 07/09/2015 – 21, Strasbourg, 7 September. Available online: https://www.europarl.europa.eu/doceo/document/CRE-8-2015-09-07-ITM-021_EN.html (accessed 29 March 2021).

Toth, Gergely (2015), 'Menekültek voltak az első magyarok is, akikkel találkoztam', *index*, 31 May. Available online: Index - Belföld - Menekültek voltak az első magyarok is, akikkel találkoztam (accessed 29 March 2021).

Trimçev, Rieke, Gregor Feindt, Félix Krawatzek and Pestel Friedemann (2020), 'Europe's Europes: Mapping Conflicts of European Memory', *Journal of Political Ideologies*, 25 (1): 51–77. Available online: https://doi.org/10.1080/13569317.2019.1696925 (accessed 29 March 2021).

UKIP (2015), *Valuing Our Christian Heritage*. Available online: http://www.support4th efamily.org/UKIPChristian_Manifesto-1.pdf (accessed 29 March 2021).

UNHCR (2014) *2014 Syria Response Plan*. Available online: 2014 SYRIA REGIONAL RESPONSE PLAN (unhcr.org) (accessed 29 March 2021).

UNHCR (2020), *Global Trends: Forced Displacement in 2019*, The UN Refugee Agency. Available online: https://www.unhcr.org/5ee200e37.pdf (accessed 29 March 2021).

Vertovec, Steven, and Susanne Wessendorf (2009), 'Introduction: Assessing the Backlash against Multiculturalism in Europe', in Steven Vertovec and Susanne Wessendorf (eds), *The Multiculturalism Backlash: European Discourses, Policies and Practices*, 1–31, London: Routledge.

Weiss, Julia (2020), 'What Is Youth Political Participation? Literature Review on Youth Political Participation and Political Attitudes', *Frontiers in Political Science*, 2 (1). Available online: doi.org/10.3389/fpos.2020.00001(accessed 11 November 2021).

*Welt* (2015), 'Gauck spricht von Dunkeldeutschland', 26 August. Available online: https://www.welt.de/politik/deutschland/article145651584/Gauck-spricht-von-Dunkeldeut schland.html (accessed 29 March 2021).

Wilms, Valerie (2015), German National Parliament, 18th legislature, 130th session, 15 October, Berlin, 12727 C. Available online: http://dipbt.bundestag.de/dip21/btp/18/18130.pdf (accessed 29 March 2021).

Winkel, Carmen (2019), 'The German Refugee Crisis: Narratives of Empathy and the Politics of Memory', *Journal of Arts & Humanities*, 8 (7): 16–27.

Wodak, Ruth (2015), 'Critical Discourse Analysis, Discourse-Historical Approach', in Karen Tracey (ed.), *The International Encyclopedia of Language and Social Interaction*, Hoboken, NJ: Wiley & Blackwell. Available online: https://doi.org/10.1002/9781118611 463.wbielsi116 (accessed 29 March 2021).

Zapata-Barrero, Ricard (2003), 'The "Discovery" of Immigration in Spain: The Politicization of Immigration in the Case of El Ejido', *Journal of International Migration and Integration*, 4 (4): 523–39.

Zapata-Barrero, Ricard, Elisabet González and Elena Sánchez Montiijano (2008), *El discurso político en torno a la inmigración en España y en la Unión Europea*, Madrid: Ministerio de Trabajo e Inmigración. Available online: El_discurso_polxtico_en_torno_a_la_inmigracixn_en_Espaxa_y_en_la_UE.pdf.pdf (inclusion.gob.es) (accessed 29 March 2021).

# Chapter 7

A1 (2002a), 'Ramkovniot dogovor klucen stolb na uspesnoto resenie na krizata', *A1*, 13 August.

A1 (2002b), 'Priznanie za liderite za sproveduvanjeto na Ramkovniot dogovor', *A1*, 13 August.

A1 (2002c), 'SP: Ramkovniot dogovor e sramno predavstvo', *A1*, 13 August.

A1 (2002d), 'Edna godina od potpišuvanjeto na Ramkovniot dogovor', *A1*, 13 August.

A1 (2006), 'Pet godini od Ramkovniot dogovor', *A1*, 13 August.

Ackermann, A. (2001), 'On the Razor's Edge: Macedonia Ten Years after Independence', *OSCE Yearbook 2001*: 117–35.

Ahern, Bertie (2008), 'Speech by the Taoiseach … to the Institute for British-Irish Studies Conference "From Conflict to Consensus: The Legacy of the Good Friday Agreement", … 3 April 2008', Copy in Linen Hall Library, Belfast.

Aleksovska, Marija (2015), 'Trust in Changing Institutions: The Ohrid Framework Agreement and Institutional Trust in Macedonia', *East European Quarterly*, 43 (1): 55–84.

Anderson, Benedict (1983), *Imagined Communities: Reflections on the Origin and Spread of Nationalism*, London: Verso.

Andonovski, Stefan (2018), 'The Effects of Post-conflict Constitutional Designs: The "Ohrid Framework Agreement" and the Macedonian Constitution', *Croatian International Relations Review*, 24 (81): 23–50.

Andonov, Z. (2019), 'Zaginatite braniteli kaj Karpalak ḱe dobijat spomenik po vlezot vo NATO i relaksiranje na meguetničkite odnosi, veli Stojanče Angelov', *Sakam da kažam*, 8 August. Available online: https://sdk.mk/index.php/dopisna-mrezha/zaginatite-braniteli-kaj-karpalak-ke-dobijat-spomenik-po-vlezot-vo-nato-i-relaksirane-na-meg uetnichkite-odnosi-veli-stojanche-angelov/ (accessed 24 September 2021).

Assmann, Aleida (2010), 'The Holocaust – a Global Memory? Extensions and Limits of a New Memory Community', in A. Assmann and S. Conrad (eds), *Memory in a Global Age: Discourses, Practices and Trajectories*, 97–117, Basingstoke: Palgrave Macmillan.

Bell, Christine (2008), 'Peace Agreements: Their Nature and Legal Status', *American Journal of International Law*, 100 (2): 373–412.

Bellamy, Alex J. (2002), 'The New Wolves at the Door: Conflict in Macedonia', *Civil Wars*, 5 (1): 117–44.

Bieber, Florian (2008), 'Power-Sharing and the Implementation of the Ohrid Framework Agreement', in *Power-Sharing and the Implementation of the Ohrid Framework Agreement*, 7–40, Skopje: Friedrich Ebert Stiftung – Office Macedonia.

Bliznakovski, Jovan (2013), 'Symbolic Aspects of Nation-Building: The Story of Three Versions of the Preamble of the Macedonian Constitution', *Politička misla*, 11 (44): 115–22.

Bogumił, Zuzanna and Malgorzat Glowacka-Grajper (2019), *Milieux de mémoire in Late Modernity: Local Communities, Religion and Historical Politics*, Berlin: Peter Lang.

Brewer, John D., Gareth I. Giggins and Francis Teeney (2011), *Religion, Civil Society and Peace in Northern Ireland*, Oxford: Oxford University Press.

Brunnbauer, Ulf (2002), 'The Implementation of the Ohrid Agreement: Ethnic Macedonian Resentments', *Journal on Ethnopolitics and Minority Issues in Europe*, 1: 1–25.

Church of Ireland (2018), 'Joint Statement to Mark the 20th Anniversary of the Good Friday/Belfast Agreement by Archbishop Richard Clarke and Archbishop Eamon Martin', 9 April. Available online: https://www.ireland.anglican.org/news/7881/joint-statement-to-mark-the (accessed 20 September 2021).

Clayer, Nathalie (2007), *Aux origines du nationalisme albanais: La naissance d'une nation majoritairement musulmane en Europe*, Paris: Karthala.

Conway, Brian (2010), *Commemoration and Bloody Sunday: Pathways of Memory*, Basingstoke: Palgrave Macmillan.

Čupeska, Ana (2013), *Kulturnite identiteti vo politikata: Aspekti na multikulturalizmot*, Skopje: Fondacija Konrad Adenauer, Kancelarija Skopje/Makedonija.

Dimova, Rozita (2013), *Ethno-Baroque: Materiality, Aesthetics, and Conflict in Modern-Day Macedonia*, New York: Berghahn.

*Dnevnik* (2002), 'Krevok mir i raznišana meguetnička doverba', 14 August. Available online: http://star.dnevnik.com.mk/default.aspx?pbroj=1924&stID=6249 (accessed 24 September 2021).

*Dnevnik* (2003), 'Noḱni pukotnici ečat vo Skopsko, policijata ne znae što se slučuva', 11 August. Available online: http://shorturl.at/tFGY0 (accessed 24 September 2021).

*Dnevnik* (2005), 'Venci od taga i gorčina', 9 August. Available online: http://shorturl.at/blpET (accessed 24 September 2021).

Elliott, Marianne (2009), *When God Took Sides: Religion and Identity in Ireland – Unfinished History*, Oxford: Oxford University Press.

Eyerman, Ron (2019), *Memory, Trauma, and Identity*, Basingstoke: Palgrave Macmillan.

Falconer, Alan (ed.) (1988), Second Edition, A. Falconer and J. Liechty (eds) (1998), *Reconciling Memories*, Blackrock: Columba Press.

Fenton, Siobhán (2018), *The Good Friday Agreement*, London: Biteback.

Frawley, Ooona (ed.) (2014), *Memory Ireland: Volume 3: The Famine and the Troubles*, Syracuse, NY: Syracuse University Press.

Frčkoski, Ljubomir D. (2011), 'Reconciliation and Transitional Justice in Macedonia, Ten Years Later', *Mediterranean Journal of Social Science*, 2 (3): 43–51.

Gensburger, Sarah (2016), *National Policy, Global Memory: The Commemoration of the 'Righteous' from Jerusalem to Paris, 1942–2007*, New York: Berghahn.

Georgieva, Lidija, Ardit Memeti and Ali Musliu (2011), 'Patterns of Conflict Resolution in the Republic of Macedonia', *Institute for British-Irish Studies Discussion Paper*, 8: 1–25.

Gray, Peter, and Oliver Kendrick (2004), *The Memory of Catastrophe*, Manchester: Manchester University Press.

Grayson, Richard S., and Fearghal McGarry (eds) (2016), *Remembering 1916: The Easter Rising, the Somme and the Politics of Memory in Ireland*, Cambridge: Cambridge University Press.

Harris, Erika, and Hannes Baumann (2019), 'Identity and War: Comparisons and Connections between the Balkans and the Middle East', *East European Politics*, 35 (4): 401–14.

Horowitz, Donald L. (2014), 'Ethnic Power-Sharing: Three Big Problems', *Journal of Democracy*, 25 (2): 5–20.

Ilievski, Zoran, and Stefan Wolff (2011), 'Consociationalism, Centripetalism and Macedonia', *Crossroads: The Macedonian Foreign Policy Journal*, 2 (4): 31–44.

Irish Democrat (2003), 'Good Friday Agreement – 5th Anniversary Meeting'. Available online: https://archive.irishdemocrat.co.uk/news/2003/gfa-5th-anniversary (accessed 20 September 2021).

Irish Foreign Ministry (2013), '15th Anniversary of the Good Friday Agreement', YouTube, 10 September. Available online: https://www.youtube.com/watch?time_continue=9&v=15X1YOJ0_Xc&feature=emb_logo (accessed 20 September 2021).

Irish Times (2008), 'An Anniversary of Deep Significance', 10 April 2008: 17.

Janev, Goran (2011), 'What Happened to the Macedonian Salad: Ethnocracy in Macedonia', *Ethnologia Balkanica*, 15 (1): 33–44.

Jarman, Neil (2019), 'A Bitter Peace: Flag Protests, the Politics of No and Culture Wars', in C. I. Armstrong, D. Herbert and J. E. Mustad (eds), *The Legacy of the Good Friday Agreement*, 109–32, Cham: Palgrave Macmillan.

Kaiser, Wolfram (2012), 'The European Parliament as an Institutional Memory Entrepreneur', in L. Bekemans (ed.), *A Value-Driven European Future*, 113–24, Brussels: European Interuniversity Press.

Kubik, Jan, and Michael Bernhard (2014a), 'A Theory of the Politics of Memory', in Jan Kubik and Michael Bernhard (eds), *Twenty Years after Communism: The Politics of Memory and Commemoration*, 7–37, Oxford: Oxford University Press.

Kubik, Jan, and Michael Bernhard (2014b), 'The Politics and Culture of Memory Regimes: A Comparative Analysis', in Jan Kubik and Michael Bernhard (eds), *Twenty Years after Communism: The Politics of Memory and Commemoration*, 261–96, Oxford: Oxford University Press.

Latifi, Veton (2001), 'Religious Strife Fuels Macedonian Conflict', *IWPR's Balkan Crisis Report*, 262 (1). Available online: https://reliefweb.int/report/former-yugos lav-republic-macedonia/religious-strife-fuels-macedonian-conflict (accessed 24 September 2021).

Makfaks (2012), 'Otvoren muzej na ONA vo Slupčane', *Makfaks*, 21 November. Available online: https://makfax.com.mk/makedonija/296917/ (accessed 24 September 2021).

Markovikj, Nenad, and Ivan Damjanovski (2018), 'The EU's Democracy Promotion Meets Informal Politics', *Region*, 7 (2): 71–96.

Marschall, Sabine (2013), 'Collective Memory and Cultural Difference: Official vs. Vernacular Forms of Commemorating the Past', *Safundi: The Journal of South African and American Studies*, 14 (1): 77–92.

Mayer, Wendy (2013), 'Religious Conflict: Definitions, Problems and Theoretical Approaches', in W. Mayer and B. Neil (eds), *Religious Conflict from Early Christianity to the Rise of Islam*, 1–20, Berlin: De Gruyter.

McBride, Ian (ed.) (2001), *History and Memory in Modern Ireland*, Cambridge: Cambridge University Press.

McConnell, Taylor (2019), 'Memory Abuse, Violence and the Dissolution of Yugoslavia: A Theoretical Framework for Understanding Memory in Conflict', *European Journal of Social Science Research*, 32 (3): 331–43.

McGrattan, Cillian, and Stephen Hopkins (2017), 'Memory in Post-conflict Societies: From Contention to Integration?', *Ethnopolitics*, 16 (5): 488–99.

MCIC (2010), 'Macedonia and Northern Ireland Exchange Experience', *MCIC*, 22 March. Available online: https://mcms.mk/en/news-and-publicity/news/825-most-makedon ija-severna-irska-razmena-na-iskustva.html (accessed 24 September 2021).

Milenkovska, Marija, and Frosina Taševska Remenski (2016), 'Macedonia after the 2001 Conflict: Towards Social Cohesion and Reconciliation', *Southeast European and Black Sea Studies*, 16 (3): 447–59.

Morrow, Duncan et al. (2019), *Sectarianism in Northern Ireland: A Review*, Belfast: Ulster University.

Muhić, Maja, and Aleksandar Takovski (2014) 'Redefining National Identity in Macedonia: Analyzing Competing Origin Myths and Interpretations through Hegemonic Representations', *Etnološka tribina*, 37 (44): 138–52.

Newman, Edward, Paris Roland and Oliver P. Richmond (2009), *New Perspectives on Liberal Peacebuilding*, Tokyo: UNU Press.

Northern Ireland Statistics and Research Agency (2012), *Census 2011: Key Statistics for Northern Ireland*, Belfast: NISRA.

O'Kane, Eamonn, and Paul Dixon (2019), 'The Northern Ireland Peace Process: Political Issues and Controversies', in Charles I. Armstrong, David Herbert and Jan Erik Mustad (eds), *The Legacy of the Good Friday Agreement*, 15–33, Cham: Palgrave Macmillan.

Opetčeska, I. (2006), 'Branko Crvenkovski: So čista sovest go potpišav ramkovniot', *Vreme*, 19 August. Available online: http://shorturl.at/fhkB7 (accessed 24 September 2021).

Pandevska, Maria (2012), 'The Term "Macedonian(s)" in Ottoman Macedonia: On the Map and in the Mind', *Nationalities Papers*, 40 (5): 747–66.

Pandevska, Maria, and Makedonka Mitrova (2019), 'The Concept of the Millet in Turkish Dictionaries: Its Alteration and the Impact on Ottoman Macedonia', *Balcanica Posnaniensia*, 26 (1): 171–92.

Phillips, John (2002), *Macedonia: Warlords and Rebels in the Balkans*, London: I. B. Tauris.

Pickering, John Al. (2009), *Drumcree*, Belfast: Ambassador.

Pohoryles, Ronald J. (2019), 'The Persistence of Divided Memories – Is it Unavoidable?', *Innovation: The European Journal of Social Science Research*, 32 (3): 291–2.

Prime Minister's Office (2013), 'Statement on Anniversary of Good Friday Agreement', 10 April. Available online: www.gov.uk/government/news/statement-on-anniversary-of-good-friday-agreement (accessed 20 September 2021).

Queen's University Belfast (2018), 'Building Peace: The Belfast/Good Friday Agreement 20 Years On'. Available online: http://www.qub.ac.uk/Research/GRI/mitchell-institute/good-friday-agreement-20-years-on/ (accessed 20 September 2021).

Ragaru, Nadège (2008), 'Macedonia: Between Ohrid and Brussels', *Cahiers de Chaillot*, 2008: 41–60.

Ramet, Sabrina P., Ola Listhaug and Albert Simkus (eds) (2013), *Civic and Uncivic Values in Macedonia: Value Transformation, Education and Media*, London: Palgrave Macmillan.

Reef, Paul (2018), 'Macedonian Monument Culture beyond "Skopje 2014"', *Südosteuropa*, 66 (4): 451–80.

Reka, B. (2011), 'Ohridski ramkoven dogovor – nova politička filozofija za funkcioniranje na multietnička država', in B. Reka (ed.), *Deset godini od Ohridskiot ramkoven dogovor: Dali Makedonija funkcionira kako multietnička država?*, 11–20, Tetovo: Univerzitet na Jugoistočna Evropa.

Richmond, Oliver P. (2014), 'The Dilemmas of a Hybrid Peace: Negative or Positive?', *Cooperation and Conflict*, 50 (1): 50–68.

Ristevska, S. (2006), 'Nikogaš nema da mu prostam na Bučkovski', *Vreme*, 7 August. Available online: http://shorturl.at/fhkB7 (accessed 24 September 2021).

Sinn Féin (2003), 'Ó Caoláin – Fifth Anniversary of Agreement Marks Crucial Stage in Peace Process', 15 April. Available online: www.sinnfein.ie/ga/contents/394 (accessed 20 September 2021).

Smyth, Jim (ed.) (2017), *Remembering the Troubles: Contesting the Recent Past in Northern Ireland*, Notre Dame, IN: University of Notre Dame Press.

Spaskovska, Ljubica (2011), 'Macedonia's Nationals, Minorities and Refugees in the Post-communist Labyrinths of Citizenship', *CITSEE Working Paper Series*, 5: 1–27.

Spaskovska, Ljubica (2012), 'The Fractured "We" and the Ethno-National "I": The Macedonian Citizenship Framework', *Citizenship Studies*, 16 (3–4): 383–96.

Stojanov, Darko, Jana Kocevska, Vlora Reçica and Bozho Bubalo (2019), *Revisiting 2001*, Skopje: Forum Civil Peace Service.

Sturgeon, Brendan, Neil Jarman and Olivia Lucas (2018), *Next Generation: Ireland-Northern Ireland*, Belfast: British Council.

Trajanovski, Naum (2020a), '"Skopje 2014" Reappraised: Debating a Memory Project in North Macedonia', in A. Milošević and T. Trošt (eds), *Europeanisation and Memory Politics in the Western Balkans*, 151–76, London: Palgrave Macmillan.

Trajanovski, Naum (2020b), 'The Three Memory Regimes of Ilinden Commemorations (2001–2018): A Prolegomenon to the Study of the Official Memory in North Macedonia', *Southeastern Europe*, 44 (1): 28–52.

Vest (2003), 'DUI kani na gala priem na Šapka', *Vest*, 13 August. Available online: http://star.vest.com.mk/default.asp?id=65194&idg=4&idb=930&rubrika=Makedonija (accessed 24 September 2021).

Viggiani, Elisabetta (2014), *Talking Stones: The Politics of Memorialization in Post-conflict Northern Ireland*, New York: Berghahn.

Visoka, Gëzim, and Elvin Gjevori (2013), 'Census Politics and Ethnicity in the Western Balkans', *East European Politics*, 29 (4): 479–98.

Vreme (2008), 'Otvoren Muzej na ONA', *Vreme*, 29 November. Available online: http://shorturl.at/gmvC4 (accessed 24 September 2021).

Zelizer, Barbie (2014), 'Memory as Foreground, Journalism as Background', in Barbie Zelizer and K. Tenenboim-Weinblatt (eds), *Journalism and Memory*, 32–50, Basingstoke: Palgrave Macmillan.

Aleksander, A., and Kenneth Morrison (2014), 'The Orthodox Churches of Macedonia and Montenegro: The Quest for Autocephaly', in Sabrina P. Ramet (ed.), *Religion and Politics in Post-socialist Central and Southeastern Europe*, 240–62, Basingstoke: Palgrave Macmillan.

# Chapter 8

## Main documentary sources

The Amman Interfaith Message (2005). Amman: The Royal Hashemite Court.

Bin Bayyah, Abd Allah (2016a), 'Framework Paper for the Conference: Abridgment of the Rights of Religious Minorities in Muslim Majority Communities: Its Legal Framework and a Call to Action', *Special Edition of the Marrakesh Declaration Conference*, 25 January. Available online: http://www.marrakeshdeclaration.org/Files/Booklet-eng.pdf (accessed 20 October 2019).

Bin Bayyah, Abd Allah (2016b), 'Framework Paper for the Conference: Abridgment of the Rights of Religious Minorities in Muslim Majority Communities: Its Legal Framework and a Call to Action' (original text in Arabic), *Special Edition of the Marrakesh Declaration Conference*, 25 January. Available online: http://www.marrakeshdeclaration.org/Files/Booklet-ara.pdf (accessed 20 October 2019).

Bin Talal, Gazi bin Muahmmad (ed.) (2006), *True Islam and the Islamic Consensus on the Amman Message*, Amman: The Royal Aal al-Bayt Institute for Islamic Thought.

García Luján, José Antonio (1998), *Treguas, guerra y capitulaciones de Granada (1457–1491)*, Granada: Diputación Provincial.

Garrido Atienza, Miguel (ed.) (1910), *Las capitulaciones para la entrega de Granada*, Granada: Paulino Ventura Traveset.

The Mardin Declaration (2010). Available online: http://www.alhabibali.com/en/news/the-mardin-declaration/ (accessed 4 September 2019).

Maqqarī, al- (1968), *Nafḥ al-ṭīb min guṣn al-Andalus al-raṭīb*, ed. Iḥsān ʿAbbās, 8 vols, Beirut: Dār Ṣādir.

Melo Carrasco, Diego (2015), *Las alianzas y negociaciones del sultán*, Murcia: Editum.

Wansharīsī, al- (1996), *Asnà al-matāŷir*, ed. Ḥ. Muʾnis, Al-Qāhira: Maktabat al-Ṯaqāfa al-Dīniyya.


### Other references

Arcas Campoy, María (2003), 'Justicia y tolerancia en el marco legal de las relaciones humanas: el caso de la frontera oriental nazarí', in Abdeluahed Akmir (coord.), *Actas del I Coloquio Internacional sobre 'La civilización musulmana en al-Andalus y los aspectos de la tolerancia'*, 11–26, Rabat.

Argente del Castillo Ocaña, Carmen (1988), 'Los cautivos en la frontera entre Jaén y Granada', in Cristina Segura Graíño (coord.), *Relaciones exteriores del Reino de Granada: IV del Coloquio de Historia Medieval Andaluza*, 211–25, Almería: Instituto de Estudios Almerienses.

Baylocq, Cédric (2018), 'From Conservative Islam to the "Theology of acculturation": The Social and Religious Trajectory of a French Imam', in M. Hashas, J. J. de Ruiter and N. V. Vinding (eds), *Imams in Western Europe: Developments, Transformations, and Institutional Challenges*, Amsterdam: Amsterdam University Press.

Browers, Michaelle (2011), 'Official Islam and the Limits of Communicative Action: The Paradox of the Amman Message', *Third World Quarterly*, 2 (5): 943–58.

Caeiro, Alexandre (2011), 'Transnational Ulama, European Fatwas, and Islamic Authority: A Case Study of the European Council for Fatwa and Research', in M. van Bruinessen and S. Allievi (eds), *Production and Dissemination of Islamic Knowledge in Western Europe*, 121–41, London: Routledge.

Carriazo y Arroquia, Juan de Mata. (2002), *En la frontera de Granada*, Granada: Universidad de Granada.

Chalmeta Gendrón, Pedro (2004), *Invasión e islamización: La sumisión de Hispania y la formación de al-Andalus*, Jaén: Universidad de Jaén.

'A Common Word between Us and You' (2009), Amman: The Royal Ahl al-Bayt Institute for Islamic Thought. Available online: https://www.acommonword.com/downloads/CW-Booklet-Final-v6_8-1-09.pdf (accessed 6 September 2019).

Fahy, John (2018), 'The International Politics of Tolerance in the Persian Gulf', *Religion, State & Society*, 46 (4): 311–27.

Fierro, María Isabel (1991), 'La emigración en el Islam: Conceptos antiguos, nuevos problemas', *Awraq*, 12: 11–41.

Galán Sánchez, Ángel (2008), 'Fuqahāʾ y musulmanes vencidos en el Reino de Granada (1485–1520)', in Ana Echevarría Arsuaga (ed.), *Biografías mudéjares o la experiencia de ser minoría: Biografías islámicas en la España cristiana*, EOBA, 15: 329–84, Madrid: CSIC.

García Sanjuán, Alejandro (2015), 'Del dār al-islām al dār al-ḥarb: la cuestión mudéjar y la legalidad islámica', in *Coexistencia y conflictos: Minorías religiosas en la península ibérica durante la Edad Media*, 13–24, Granada: Universidad de Granada.

Gómez, Luz (2018), *Entre la sharía y la yihad: una historia intelectual del islamismo*, Madrid: Los Libros de la Catarata.

Gómez, Luz (2019), *Diccionario de islam e islamismo*, Madrid: Editorial Trotta.

Hoover, Jon (2016), 'Ibn Taymiyya between Moderation and Radicalism', in Elisabeth Kendall and Ahmad Khan (eds), *Reclaiming Islamic Tradition: Modern Interpretations of the Classical Heritage*, 177–203, Edinburgh: Edinburgh University Press.

Kayaoglu, Turan (2015), 'Explaining Interfaith Dialogue in the Muslim World', *Politics and Religion*, 8 (2): 236–62.

Kern, Karen M. (2011), *Imperial Citizen: Marriage and Citizenship in the Ottoman Frontier Provinces of Iraq*, New York: Syracuse University Press.

Kutelia, Murman (2011), 'Egyptian Enlightener Rifa'a at-Tahtawi', *IBSU Scientific Journal*, 5 (1): 83–92.

Makdisi, Ussama (2000), *The Culture of Sectarianism: Community, History, and Violence in Nineteenth-Century Ottoman Lebanon*, Los Angeles: University of California Press.

Managhan, Tina (2020), *Unknowing the 'War on Terror': The Pleasures of Risk*, New York: Routledge.

Melo Carrasco, Diego (2012), 'Las treguas entre Granada y Castilla durante los siglos XIII a XV', *Revista de Estudios Histórico-Jurídicos [Sección Historia del Derecho Español]*, 34: 237–75.

Michot, Yahya (2006), *Muslims under Non-Muslim Rule: Ibn Taymiyya*, London: Interface.

Michot, Yahya (2011), 'Ibn Taymiyya's "New Mardin Fatwa": Is Genetically Modified Islam (GMI) Carcinogenic?', *The Muslim World*, April: 130–81.

Monferrer Sala, Juan Pedro, and Rafael Pinilla Melguizo (1998), 'Tres documentos árabes granadinos sobre las treguas de 1469 y 1472', *Revista del Centro de Estudios Históricos de Granada y su Reino*, 12: 231–62.

Mu'nis, Ḥusayn (1996), *Asà al-mutājir*, Al-Qāhira: Maktabat al-Ṯaqāfa al-Dīniyya.

Paradela Alonso, Nieves (2001), 'Belicismo y espiritualidad: una caracterización del yihad islámico', *Militarium Ordinum Analecta*, 5: 653–67.

Peyret, Sophie De (2019), *Nation et religion: l'expérience marocaine*, Paris: Institut Thomas More.

Quran (1980), *The Message of the Qur'ān*, trans. Muhammad Asad, Gibraltar: Dar al-Andalus.

Ramadan, Tariq (2002), *El islam minoritario: cómo ser musulmán en la Europa laica*, Barcelona: Bellaterra.

Ramadan, Tariq (2012), *The Quest for Meaning: Developing a Philosophy of Pluralism*, London: Penguin Books.

Rodríguez Molina, José (1997), 'Relaciones pacíficas en la frontera con el Reino de Granada', in Pedro Segura Artero (coord.), *Actas del Congreso 'La frontera nazarí como sujeto histórico (s. XIII–XVI)'*, 253–88, Almería: Instituto de Estudios Almerienses.

Seeberg, Christine (2017), 'The Amman Message as an Invitation to Interfaith Dialogue: A Christian Response', in Mike Hardy, Fiyaz Mughal and Sarah Markewicz (eds), *Muslim Identity in a Turbulent Age: Islamic Extremism and Western Islamophobia*, 160–92, London: Jessica Kingsley.

Shalabi, Jamal al- and Mahmoud al-Khalayleh (eds) (2007), *Political Islam: Amman Message as a Model*, Zarka: Hashemite University.

Velázquez Basanta, Fernando Nicolás (2002), 'La relación histórica sobre las postrimerías del Reino de Granada, según Aḥmad al-Maqqarī (s. XVII)', in Celia del Moral Molina (ed.), *La frontera nazarí como sujeto histórico (siglos XIII–XVI)*, 481–554, Granada: Grupo de Investigación CABEI.

Verskin, Alan (2015), *Islamic Law and the Crisis of the Reconquista: The Debate on the Status of Muslim Communities in Christendom*, Leiden: Brill.

Vidal Castro, Francisco (2000), 'Historia política', in M. J. Viguera Molíns (coord.), *El reino nazarí de Granada (1232–1492)*, 8–3 of *Historia de España de Menéndez Pidal*, J. M. Jover Zamora (dir.), 48–248, Madrid: Espasa Calpe.
Viguera Molíns, María Jesús (1997), 'Guerra y paz en la frontera nazarí desde las fuentes árabes', in P. Segura Artero (coord.), *La frontera nazarí como sujeto histórico (siglos XIII–XVI)*, 79–92, Almería: Instituto de Estudios Almerienses.
The White House (2009), 'Remarks by the President at Cairo University, 6-04-09', 4 June. Available online: https://obamawhitehouse.archives.gov/the-press-office/remarks-president-cairo-university-6-04-09 (accessed 10 September 2020).
Zomeño, Amalia (2015), 'Los notarios musulmanes de Granada después de 1492', *Cuadernos del CEMYR*, 22: 195–209.

# Chapter 9

Alouti, Feriel (2018), 'Dans les écoles, l'association Coexister rappelle, entre autres, qu'on peut être "musulman et laïque" ', *Le Monde*, 23 February. Available online: https://www.lemonde.fr/societe/article/2018/02/23/dans-les-ecoles-l-association-coexister-rappe lle-entre-autres-qu-on-peut-etre-musulman-et-laic_5261717_3224.html (accessed 21 September 2021).
Ash, Timothy Garton (2016), *Free Speech: Ten Principles for a Connected World*, Kindle version, London: Atlantic Books.
Axcent (n.d.a), 'About Axcent'. Available online: https://www.axcent.org/en/axcent/about-axcent (accessed 21 September 2021).
Axcent (n.d.b), 'Ik levensbeschouw jou', DVD. Available online: https://www.axcent.org/index.php/nl/jeugd/dvd (accessed 21 September 2021).
Bakkouch, Radia (2016), 'Association Coexister: face à la diffamation, nous répondons laïcité', *Marianne*, 14 January. Available online: https://www.marianne.net/agora/tribu nes-libres/association-coexister-face-la-diffamation-nous-repondons-laicite (accessed 21 September 2021).
Balibar, Étienne (2018), *Secularism and Cosmopolitanism: Critical Hypotheses on Religion and Politics*, trans. G. M. Goshgarian, New York: Columbia University Press.
Bauman, Zygmunt (2000), *Liquid Modernity*, Cambridge: Polity.
Becker, Françis (ed.) (2016), *Becoming Citizens of a Plural Europe: Interconvictional Spaces and Practices*, Paris: Publibook.
Beckford, James (2012), 'ASSSR Presidential Address Public Religions and the Postsecular: Critical Reflections', *Journal for the Scientific Study of Religion*, 51 (1): 1–19.
Bock, Jan-Jonathan, John Fahy and Samuel Everett (eds) (2019), *Emergent Religious Pluralisms*, Cham: Palgrave Macmillan.
Bonding Beyond Borders (2018), 'Campaign Summary: Facebook Digital Global Challenge'.
Boubekeur, Amel, and Olivier Roy (eds) (2012), *Whatever Happened to the Islamist? Salafis, Heavy Metal Muslims and the Lure of Consumerist Islam*, London: Hurst.
Brandsma, Bart (2016), *Polarisatie: Inzicht in de dynamiek van wij-zij denken*, Culemborg: BB in Media.
Browers, Michaelle (2011), 'Official Islam and the Limits of Communicative Action: The Paradox of the Amman Message', *Third World Quarterly*, 2 (5): 943–58.

Cavanaugh, William T. (2009), *The Myth of Religious Violence*, Oxford: Oxford University Press.

Coexister (2016), 'La Laïcité en 3 minutes', YouTube, 3 September. Available online: https://www.youtube.com/watch?v=fx50d_aqaUo (accessed 21 September 2021).

Coexister (2020), 'Rapport Moral 2019–2020'. Available online: https://www.coexister.fr/wp-content/uploads/2020/11/1920-Rapport-moral-Coexister.pdf (accessed 21 September 2021).

Coexister (n.d.), 'Que faisons-nous?'. Available online: http://www.coexister.fr/que-fais ons-nous/ (accessed 21 September 2021).

Expertisepunt IDB (n.d.), 'Wie zijn wie - Presentatie'. Available online: http://www.idkb.be/nl/wie_zijn_wij/presentatie-3.html (accessed 21 September 2021).

Fahy, John (2018a), 'The International Politics of Tolerance in the Persian Gulf', *Religion, State & Society*, 46 (4): 311–27.

Fahy, John (2018b), 'International Relations and Faith-Based Diplomacy: The Case of Qatar', *Review of Faith & International Affairs*, 16 (3): 76–88.

Fahy, John, and Jeffrey Haynes (eds) (2018), 'Interfaith on the World Stage', Special Issue, *Review of Faith & International Affairs*, 16 (3): 1–188.

Fahy, John, and Jan-Jonathan Bock (eds) (2020a), *The Interfaith Movement: Mobilising Religious Diversity in the 21st Century*, Abingdon: Routledge.

Fahy, John, and Jan-Jonathan Bock (2020b), 'Introduction: Interfaith and Social Movement Theory', in John Fahy and Jan-Jonathan Bock (eds), *The Interfaith Movement: Mobilising Religious Diversity in the 21st Century*, 1–27, Abingdon: Routledge.

Furseth, Inger, Lars Ahlin, Kimmo Ketola, Annette Leis-Peters, Pål Repstad, Bjarni Randver Sigurvinsson and SivertSkålvoll Urstad (2018), 'Faith and Worldview Communities and Their Leaders – Inward or Outward Looking?', in Inger Furseth (ed.), *Religious Complexity in the Public Sphere: Comparing Nordic Countries*, 251–90, New York: Palgrave Macmillan.

Galal, Lise Paulsen, Louise Lund Liebmann and Magdalena Nordin (2018), 'Routes and Relations in Scandinavian Interfaith Forums: Governance of Religious Diversity by States and Majority Churches', *Social Compass*, 65 (3): 329–45.

Griera, Mar, and Maria Forteza (2011), 'New Actors in the Governance of Religious Diversity in European Cities: The Role of Interfaith Platforms', in Jeffrey Haynes and Anja Hennig (eds), *Religious Actors in the Public Sphere: Means, Objectives, and Effects*, 113–31, London: Routledge.

Griera, Mar, and Alexander-Kenneth Nagel (2018), 'Interreligious Relations and Governance of Religion in Europe: Introduction', *Social Compass*, 65 (3): 301–11.

Halafoff, Anna (2013), *The Multifaith Movement: Global Risks and Cosmopolitan Solutions*, Dordrecht: Springer.

Harris, Sam, and Maajid Nawaz (2015), *Islam and the Future of Tolerance: A Dialogue*, Cambridge, MA: Harvard University Press.

Haynes, Jeffrey (2018), 'The United Nations Alliance of Civilizations and Interfaith Dialogue: What Is It Good For?', *Review of Faith & International Affairs*, 16 (3): 48–60

Hellyer, H. A., and Michele Grossman (2019), 'A Framework for Understanding the Relationship between Radicalisation, Religion and Violence', *GREASE*, May. Available online: http://grease.eui.eu/wp-content/uploads/sites/8/2019/05/GREASE_D1.2_Hell yer-Grossman_Final1-1.pdf (accessed 21 September 2021).

Hjelm, Titus (2015), 'Is God Back? Reconsidering the New Visibility of Religion', in
Titus Hjelm (ed.), *Is God Back? Reconsidering the New Visibility of Religion*, 1–17,
London: Bloomsbury.

Karam, Azza (2021), 'A Counter-Narrative? Ruminations around Holocaust Memorial
Day', *Inter Press Service*, 2 February. Available online: http://www.ipsnews.net/2021/02/
counter-narrative-ruminations-around-holocaust-memorial-day/ (accessed 21
September 2021).

Kayaoglu, Turan (2015), 'Explaining Interfaith Dialogue in the Muslim World', *Politics and
Religion*, 8 (2): 236–62.

Kazanjian, Victor (2016), 'Promoting Peace and Reconciliation to Counter Violent
Extremism. Focus on Faith', *Briefing of the United Nations Department of Public
Information*. Available online: https://uri.org/uri-story/20160205-promoting- peace-
and-reconciliation-counter-violent-extremism (accessed 21 September 2021).

Klinkhammer, Gritt (2020), 'Interreligious Dialogue Groups and the Mass Media', *Religion*,
50 (3): 336–52.

Klinkhammer, Gritt, Hans-Ludwig Frese, Ayla Satilmis and Tina Seibert (2011),
*Interreligiöse und interkulturelle Dialoge mit MuslimInnen in Deutschland. Eine
quantitative und qualitative Studie*, Bremen: Universität Bremen. Available
online: https://nbn-resolving.de/urn:nbn:de:gbv:46-00102006-15 (accessed 21
September 2021).

Kniss, Fred, and Paul Numrich (2007), *Sacred Assemblies and Civic Engagement: How
Religion Matters for America's Newest Immigrants*, New Jersey: Rutgers University Press.

Kollar, Nathan R. (2016), 'The Interfaith Movement in a Liminal Age: The
Institutionalization of a Movement', *Journal of Ecumenical Studies*, 51 (1): 7–30.

Lamine, Anne-Sophie (2013), 'Singular Pluralities: A Critical Review of Religious
Pluralism', *Religion and Society: Advances in Research*, 4 (1): 150–66.

Lee, Lois (2015), *Recognizing the Non-religious: Reimagining the Secular*, Oxford: Oxford
University Press.

Lehmann, Karsten (2020a), 'Interreligious Dialogue in Context: Towards a Systematic
Comparison of IRD-Activities in Europe', *Interdisciplinary Journal for Religion and
Transformation in Contemporary Society*, 6 (2): 237–54.

Lehmann, Karsten (2020b), 'Interreligious Dialogue as a Response to Processes of
Secularization: A New Perspective on the World's Parliament of Religions', *Interdisciplinary
Journal for Religion and Transformation in Contemporary Society*, 6 (2): 513–32.

Lehmann, Karsten (ed.) (2020), 'Interreligious Dialogue in Context: A European
Comparison', Special Issue, *Interdisciplinary Journal for Religion and Transformation in
Contemporary Society*, 6 (2): 237–561.

Mandaville, Peter, and Melissa Noze (2017), 'Engaging: Religion and Religious Actors
in Countering Violent Extremism', United States Institute of Peace – Special Report
(413). Available online: http://www.jstor.com/stable/resrep12243 (accessed 21
September 2021).

Melnik, Sergey (2020), 'Types of Interreligious Dialogue', *Journal of Interreligious Studies*,
31: 48–72.

Merrigan, Terrence (2017), 'Introduction: Rethinking Theologies of Interreligious
Dialogue', in Terrence Merrigan and John Friday (eds), *The Past, Present, and Future of
Theologies of Interreligious Dialogue*, 1–16, Oxford: Oxford University Press.

Moyaert, Marianne (2013), 'Interreligious Dialogue', in David Cheetham, Douglas Pratt and David Thomas (eds), *Understanding Interreligious Relations*, 201–12, Oxford: Oxford University Press.

Nagel, Alexander-Kenneth, and Mehmet Kalender (2014), 'The Many Faces of Dialogue: Driving Forces for Participating in Interreligious Activities', in Wolfram Weiße, Katajun Amirpur, Anna Körs and Dörthe Vieregge (eds), *Religions and Dialogue: International Approaches*, 85–98, Münster: Waxmann.

Neumaier, Anna, and Gritt Klinkhammer (2020) 'Interreligious Contact and Media: Introduction', *Religion*, 50 (3): 321–35.

Orbit (2017a), 'Interlevensbeschouwelijke ontmoeting'. Available online: http://www.orbit vzw.be (accessed 21 May 2018).

Orbit (2017b), 'Kwaliteitsnota: De Bondgenotenstrategie: Een strategie om racisme aan te pakken en maatschappelijke verandering na te streven'. Available online: https://www. orbitvzw.be/wp-content/uploads/2017/11/Kwaliteitsnota-bondgenotenstrategie-ORBI T031017defkleur.pdf /(accessed 21 September 2021).

Pasture, Patrick (2009), 'Religion in Contemporary Europe: Contrasting Perceptions and Dynamics', *Archiv für Sozialgeschichte*, 49: 319–50.

Patel, Eboo, and Patrice Brodeur (eds) (2006), *Building the Interfaith Youth Movement: Beyond Dialogue to Action*, Lanham: Rowman & Littlefield.

Pérou, Olivier, and Clément Pétreault (2020), 'Coexister, une association dans le collimateur du gouvernement', *Le Point*, 25 November. Available online: https://www. lepoint.fr/politique/coexister-une-association-dans-le-collimateur-du-gouvernem ent-25-11-2020-2402716_20.php (accessed 21 September 2021).

Phan, Peter (2012), 'Interreligious and Ecumenical Dialogue at Vatican II', *Conversations on Jesuit Higher Education*, 42 (article 5): 12–17. Available online: https://epublications. marquette.edu/cgi/viewcontent.cgi?article=1769&context=conversations (accessed 21 September 2021).

Quilliam Foundation (n.d.), 'About Us'. Available online: http://www.quilliaminternatio nal.com/about/ (accessed 31 May 2018).

Religions for Peace (2014), 'The Abu Dhabi Statement: Rejecting Violent Religious Extremism and Advancing Shared Well-Being', 13 December. Available online: https:// www.unaoc.org/wp-content/uploads/Statement-of-Multi-Religious-Action-Engl ish-13-December.pdf (accessed 21 September 2021).

Religions for Peace (2018), 'Violent Religious Extremism'. Available online: https://rfp.org/ act/stop-war/violent-religious-extremism/ (accessed 31 May 2018).

Sclafani, Robin (2019), 'Interconvictional Dialogue as a Way to Combat Extremism', *Our World*, 18 December. Available online: https://www.ourworld.co/interconvictional-dialogue-as-a-way-to-combat-extremism/ (accessed 21 September 2021).

Shagan, Ethan H. (2019), *The Birth of Modern Belief: Faith and Judgment from the Middle Ages to the Enlightenment*, Princeton: Princeton University Press.

Tracy, David (1987), *Plurality and Ambiguity Hermeneutics, Religion, Hope*, Chicago: University of Chicago.

UNESCO (n.d.), 'Intercultural Dialogue'. Available online: http://www.unesco.org/new/en/ culture/themes/dialogue/intercultural-dialogue/ (accessed 21 September 2021).

United Religions Initiative (n.d.), 'Who We Are'. Available online: https://www.uri.org/ who-we-are (accessed 21 September 2021).

Youth for Peace (n.d.), 'Projects'. Available online: https://youth-for-peace.ba/en/projects (accessed 21 September 2021).

Yukich, Grace, and Ruth Braunstein (2014), 'Encounters at the Religious Edge: Variation in Religious Expression across Interfaith Advocacy and Social Movement Settings', *Journal for the Scientific Study of Religion*, 53 (4): 791–807.

# Chapter 10

Abiline, Toomas (2013), 'Uue vaimsuse eelkäijad: antroposoofia, teosoofia, vabamüürlus ja parapsühholoogia Eestis 1918–1940', in Marko Uibu (ed.), *Mitut usku Eesti III: Valik usundiloolisi uurimusi: uue vaimsuse eri*, 37–78, Tartu: Tartu Ülikooli Kirjastus.

Altnurme, Lea (2006), *Kristlusest oma usuni*, Tartu: Tartu Ülikooli Kirjastus.

Altnurme, Lea (2009), 'Interdenominational Friendship Circles in Estonia in the 1970s and 1980s', in Riho Altnurme (ed.), *History of Estonian Ecumenism*, 194–225, Tartu: University of Tartu/Estonian Council of Churches.

Altnurme, Lea (2010), 'Mida võiks kirik teada eestimaalaste individuaalsest religioossusest', in Eerik Jõks (ed.), *Astu alla rahva hulka: Artikleid ja arutlusi Eesti elanikkonna vaimulaadist*, 193–212, Tallinn: Eesti Kirikute Nõukogu.

Altnurme, Lea (2013), 'Uus vaimsus – mis see on?', in Marko Uibu (ed.), *Mitut usku Eesti III: Valik usundiloolisi uurimusi: uue vaimsuse eri*, 18–36, Tartu: Tartu Ülikooli Kirjastus.

Altnurme, Lea (2018), 'Mittekristlikud usundid ja usugrupid', in Riho Altnurme (ed.), *Eesti kiriku-ja religioonilugu*, koostaja, 300–8, Tartu: Ülikooli Kirjastus.

Au, Ilmo, and Ringo Ringvee (2007), *Usulised ühendused Eestis*, Tallinn: Allika.

Bouma, Gary D., and Rod Ling (2009), 'Religious Diversity', in Peter B. Clarke (ed.), *The Oxford Handbook of the Sociology of Religion*, 507–24, Oxford: Oxford University Press.

Clarke, Peter B. (2005), *New Religions in Global Perspective: A Study of Religious Change in the Modern World*, London: Routledge.

Ellermäe-Reimets, Eve (2004), 'Hare Krišna liikumine Eestis', in Lea Altnurme (ed.), *Mitut usku Eesti: Valik usundiloolisi uurimusi'*, 96–116, Tartu: Tartu Ülikooli Kirjastus.

Forst, Rainer (2017), 'Toleration', in Edward N. Zalta (ed.), *The Stanford Encyclopedia of Philosophy*, Center for the Study of Language and Information, Stanford University. Available online: https://plato.stanford.edu/archives/fall2017/entries/toleration (accessed 21 September 2021).

Hall, Stuart (2007), 'The Hippies: An American Moment', in Ann Gray, Jan Campbell, Mark Erickson, Stuart Hanson and Helen Wood (eds), *CCCS Selected Working Papers*, Vol. 2, 146–67, New York: Routledge.

Hanegraaff, Wouter (1996), *New Age Religion and Western Culture: Esotericism in the Mirror of Secular Thought*, Leiden: Brill.

Hanegraaff, Wouter (2006), 'Introduction', in Wouter Hanegraaff, Antoine Faivre, Roelof van den Broek and Jean-Pierre Brach (eds), *Dictionary of Gnosis & Western Esotericism*, vii–xiii, Leiden: Brill.

Heelas, Paul (1996), *The New Age Movement: The Celebration of the Self and the Sacralization of Modernity*, Oxford: Blackwell.

Kent, Stephen A. (2001), *From Slogans to Mantras: Social Protest and Religious Conversion in the Late Vietnam War Era*, Syracuse, NY: Syracuse University Press.

Mäll, Linnart, Märt Läänemets and Teet Toome (2006), 'Vägivaldsusetus', in *Ida mõtteloo leksikon*, Vol. II, 246, Tartu: Tartu Ülikooli Orientalistikakeskus.

Mayring, Philipp (2014), *Qualitative Content Analysis: Theoretical Foundation,*

*Basic Procedures and Software Solution*, Social Science Open Access Repository. Available online: http://nbn-resolving.de/urn:nbn:de:0168-ssoar-395173 (accessed 21 September 2021).

Murphy, Andrew R. (2020), 'Toleration', Britannica. Available online: https://www.britann ica.com/topic/toleration (accessed 21 September 2021).

Pasture, Patrick (2011), 'Religious Globalisation in Post-war Europe', *Archiv für Sozialgeschichte*, 51: 63–107.

Pekko, Indrek, and Katre Koppel (2013), 'Püha kolmainsus kui ema-isa-laps: uus vaimsus ja luteri kirik', in Marko Uibu (ed.), *Mitut usku Eesti III: Valik usundiloolisi uurimusi: uue vaimsuse eri*, 139–66, Tartu: Tartu Ülikooli Kirjastus.

Põlenik, Ave (2004), 'Budismist Eestis', in Lea Altnurme (ed.), *Mitut usku Eesti. Valik usundiloolisi uurimusi*, 67–95, Tartu: Tartu Ülikooli Kirjastus.

Stolz, Jörg, and Thomas Engelberger (2016), 'Values and Change of Values', in Jörg Stolz, Judith Könemann, Mallory Schneuwly Purdie, Thomas Englberger and Michael Krüggeler (eds.) , *(Un)Believing in Modern Society: Religion, Spirituality and Religious-Secular Competition*, 97–108, London: Routledge.

Sutcliffe, J. Steven, and Ingvild Saelid Gilhus (2014), 'Introduction: "All Mixed Up" – Thinking about Religion in Relation to New Age Spiritualities', in Steven J. Sutcliffe and Ingvild Saelid Gilhus (eds), *New Age Spirituality: Rethinking Religion*, 1–16, London: Routledge.

Tamm, Kaidi (2012), 'Lilleoru keskus', in Lea Altnurme (ed.), *Uued usulised ja vaimsed ühendused Eestis*, 85–9, Tartu: Tartu Ülikooli Kirjastus.

Taylor, Charles (2002), *Varieties of Religion Today: William James Revisited*, Cambridge: Harvard University Press.

Tipton, Steven M. (1982), *Getting Saved from the Sixties: Moral Meaning in Conversion and Cultural Change*, Berkeley: University of California Press.

Uibu, Marko (2012), 'Võitlus teaduse nimel', *Ajalooline Ajakiri*, 3/4 (141/142): 337–57.

Uibu, Marko (2015), 'Elu tõelise olemuse tunnetamine, moodsa aja religioon või umbluu – uue vaimsuse erinevad nimetamis – ja käsitlusviisid Eestis', *Usuteaduslik Ajakiri*, 2 (69): 99–121.

Uibu, Marko (2016), 'Reemerging Religiosity: The Mainstreaming of New Spirituality in Estonia', *Journal of Baltic Studies*, 47 (2): 257–74.

# Index

Abascal, Santiago 132–3
Abdallah II, King of Jordan 170
Abdülhamid II, Sultan 21
Afghanistan 57, 114
Africa 4, 16
  North Africa 18, 116, 120, 122, 129, 164
  North African backgrounds 118
  South-Africa 101, 151
agnosticism 3, 28, 186
Ahern, Bertie 150–2
Ahmeti, Ali 146–7
al-Andalus 2, 13–15, 18, 56, 63, 74, 120–1,
    131, 159–62, 164–5, 170–2, 177
  Andalusian Parliament 132
  Andalusis 166
Amman Message 160, 170
anti-Semitism 1, 9, 21–3, 76, 87, 124, 181,
    183, 187
Arab Spring 57
Asia 16
  Asian culture 195
  Asian Muslims 103
  atheism 3, 5, 12, 23–4, 186
  Central Asia 28
  South Asian immigrants 100
  Southeast Asia 4, 15
Atatürk, Mustafa Kemal 88
Austria 20–1, 24, 52, 54, 63, 117, 124–5,
    176 (*see also* Habsburg Empire)
Axcent 176, 183, 186

Balkans 12, 22, 28, 69, 75, 83, 94–7, 99,
    112, 187
  Balkan corridor 116–17
  Balkan route 117
  post-imperial 140
Battle of the Somme 137, 153
Belgium 21, 24, 28, 37–8, 52, 54, 58, 63,
    101, 182
  Flanders 38, 46, 54, 58–9, 187

Bible 202–3
Bin Bayyah, Abd Allah 166
Blair, Tony 150–2
Bonding Beyond Borders 187
Buddhism 53, 108, 191, 194, 195, 196
  new spirituality subculture 199 (*see also*
    New Spirituality)
Bulgaria 22, 24, 28, 101, 138, 186
Bush, George W. 9, 151
  Cameron, David 123, 127, 152
capitalism 68, 164, 192, 193
Catholicism 16, 44, 57, 105, 150
  Catholic Church 8, 20, 22–3, 27, 29, 56,
    60, 178
  Catholic monarchs 17–18, 159, 163, 169
  Catholic school 41, 43–4
  Catholic states 19, 21
  national-catholic imagination 132
*Charlie Hebdo* 117, 134
Christian Democracy 23–4, 122, 128
Christianity 3–4, 6, 10, 13, 24, 31, 33, 37,
    53, 56, 58–9, 61–2, 65, 82, 88, 102,
    108–9, 120, 122, 132–5, 170, 173, 186,
    195, 197–8, 201
  Christendom 2, 4–5, 15–17, 30,
    75–6, 121
  Christian values 27, 122
  (re-)Christianization 2, 28
  de-Christianization (*see* secularization)
  conversion (converted) to 161, 166, 170
  Judeo-Christianity 3, 27, 122, 132, 135
  Orthodox Christians (Christianity) 2,
    84, 86, 96, 99, 137, 140, 156, 195
Church *see* Christianity; denomination
citizenship 141, 164–5, 168, 171
commemoration 125, 138–9, 142–4, 146,
    148, 150–1, 153, 157
Constitution of Medina 161, 168, 171
Creasy, Stella 122
Coexister 176–7, 180, 182–3, 186, 188–9

Cold War 2, 23, 64, 68
  Iron Curtain 68, 76, 125
  post-Cold War era 55, 57, 62
colonialism 22, 55, 68
  decolonization 4, 22, 193
  European colonization 163
communism 3, 26, 78
  anti-communism 124
  in Eastern Europe 24, 76
counterculture 191–3, 196
Crusades 41, 56, 58–9, 62–3
  Crusaders 161
Church *see* Christianity; denomination

democracy 13, 21, 23, 27, 29, 31, 69, 76,
    81, 89, 117, 131, 141
  democratization 6, 76, 78
denomination 57, 109, 198
  denominational boundaries 198, 210
  denominational (and non-
    denominational) teaching of
    religion 37
dictatorship 81, 132
discourse 4, 12–13, 28, 52, 67, 69, 71, 73–4,
    81, 84, 85, 104, 113–15, 117, 119–20,
    122–4, 132–5, 146–8, 171, 194
  identity 8, 77
  media 43, 118
  memory 142–5, 148
  political 72, 82, 113–15, 118, 121–5,
    129, 131, 133–5
docutube 33, 38, 49, 113

Easter Rising 137
Egypt 81, 116, 164
Enlightenment 16, 27, 68, 71, 74
  humanistic-secular values 27, 122, 135
Erdogan, Recep Tayyip 108
Esteve, Esperanza 130
Estonia 34, 37–8, 42, 52, 54, 58, 61,
    194–9, 203–4
ethnicity 15, 20, 74, 122, 135, 140
  multi-ethnicity 67
European Broadcasting Union
    (EBU) 106, 111
European Union (EU) 15, 68, 74, 110, 114,
    126, 130, 133–4, 141, 175
  European Commission 34, 68, 111,
    116, 126

European Court of Justice 106
European Parliament 68, 126
House of European History 11, 68
unity in diversity 4, 15, 68
Expertisepunt IDB (*Interreligieuze Dialoog
    van de Kerk in Brussel*) 176, 178,
    183, 185

Facebook 92, 185–6
Farage, Nigel 123, 132
First World War 21, 83–4, 87, 154, 164
France 17, 19, 21, 24, 28–9, 34, 37, 54, 119,
    129–30, 132, 161, 168, 182–3, 186–7
  Huguenots 123
  French 'republican values' 186
  French Revolution 10–11, 20, 68
  Louvre 70, 72, 74
  *Laïcité see* secularism
Frayling, Nicholas 151
freedom 13, 18, 42, 76, 80, 95, 104, 123,
    160, 168–9, 193, 202
  of conscience 5, 19, 20
  of expression (speech) 28, 133
  Museum of Freedom 146
  religious (of religion) 7, 16–17, 19–23,
    28–9, 141, 161, 164–5, 170–1, 176,
    186, 195
  spiritual 201
fundamentalism 12, 28, 57

Gandhi, Mahatma 192
Gauck, Joachim 128–9
Generation Z 93, 97
Germany 3, 12, 21, 24, 34, 37–8, 41–2, 46,
    52, 54–5, 58, 97, 101, 114, 117–19,
    121, 122, 125, 127–35, 177, 180,
    182, 187
  *Alternative für Deutschland*
    (*AfD*) 122, 132–3
  Christian Democratic Union
    (CDU) 122, 128
  German Lutherans 59
  German-Jewish history 80
  historical duty 121–2
  National Socialism 22
  *Willkommenskultur* 118, 122, 129
Ginsberg, Allen 191
Good Friday Agreement 13, 86, 138, 149
  (*see also* Northern Ireland)

Gorriarán, Carlos Martínez 131
Granada 42
  capitulation of 120, 162–3, 165,
    169–70, 172
  Nasrid kingdom 18, 159, 162–3,
    168–70, 172
  Toma de Granada, 133
Greece 2, 10, 28–9, 116, 118–19, 138, 146
  Ancient 108
  Greek antiquity 68
  Greek Orthodox Church 18

Habermas, Jürgen 179
Habsburg Empire 18, 21
Halbwachs, Maurice 114, 138–9
ha-Levi, Samuel 80
heritage 13, 42, 69, 72, 74, 78, 87, 123,
  135, 145
  cultural 47, 67, 68, 72, 88
  discourses 71
  European 11, 68, 133
  institutions 70
  Islamic 69–70, 73–4
  Jewish 69, 76–7, 80
  Judeo-Christian 3, 27, 122, 132, 135
  Pakistani 102
  socialist 85
hippie 191–3, 196 (*see also* counterculture)
Hinduism 53, 82, 194, 196, 198
Holocaust 11, 22, 27, 41–2, 69, 76–8, 81,
  86, 115, 121 (*see also* anti-Semitism)
  Auschwitz 186–7
  Shoah 76–7, 80–1
homogeneity 2, 4, 14, 19, 22–3, 30–1,
  114, 187
Howarth, Gerald 123
Hungary 12, 17, 21, 28–9, 37, 82,
  114, 116–17, 124–6, 128,
  131–2, 134–5 (*see also* Orbán, Viktor)
  Fidesz 117, 124–5, 131, 133–5
  Christian center of Europe 135

Iberian Peninsula 2, 18, 75, 133, 159,
  161–2, 164–5
Ibn Taymiyya 167–8
identity 2, 7, 21, 30, 45, 70, 72, 86, 114,
  118, 132, 146, 171, 175, 178, 184,
  186–8, 201
  Christian 117, 121

construction (building) 3, 12, 139
  European 68, 114, 116, 120, 131, 135
  identity-marker 4, 11, 84, 140–1
  Jewish 76
  Macedonian 87, 146
  national 3, 23, 34, 100, 137, 146
  religious 121, 140, 167
  Spanish 118, 120–1, 131, 135
Ilinden Uprising 137, 143
image 9, 70, 74, 103, 119, 130, 180
immigration 4, 23, 29, 99–100, 117–18,
  120, 128, 133, 175
  anti-immigration 117, 119, 125–6, 131,
    133, 135
  as 'invasion' 29, 117, 120, 132, 134
  immigration countries 124
  welfare immigration 134
imperialism 22, 30, 55, 133
India 5, 17, 85, 99, 101
  British India 100
institutional religion 5, 193, 197,
  200–2, 204
Ireland 8, 137, 140, 149, 151, 155
  Republic of 138, 149–50, 152
  Unionist 149–51
  united 150
Iraq 62, 114, 116, 119, 124, 161, 171, 180
Islam 2–3, 9, 11, 13, 17–18, 25, 27, 30–1,
  34, 43–5, 53–4, 56, 59, 62, 65, 69–74,
  82, 88, 99, 102–3, 106–9, 111, 120–3,
  159–62, 164, 167–8, 170–3, 176, 185
  Arab-Islamic culture 17, 120
  Euro-Islam 25
  Federation of Islamic Organizations in
    Europe 168
  hajj 73
  Islamic civilization 70, 88, 133
  Islamic empires 16, 30
  Islamic law 167, 172
  Islamic Tatars 17
  Islamist religious extremists 59, 60, 63, 65
  Islamist terrorism 31, 43, 57, 189 (*see
    also* terrorism)
  (re-)Islamization 118, 132–3, 135
  Islamo-Christian zone 2
  Islamophobia 1, 28–9, 107, 121, 160,
    164–5, 176, 183, 188
  'middle-ground' 167, 170
  representation of 71–2, 106, 176

western Islamdom 164
Israel 9, 57, 76, 81–2, 182
Italy 21, 24, 29, 37, 54, 110, 118–19, 132

Jerusalem 56, 161
jihad 161, 167, 171
Joseph II, Emperor 20
Judaism 9, 11, 53–4, 69, 76–7, 82, 88, 108,
   120, 186
   Ashkenazi culture 78
   Sephardic Jews 80, 164
Judeo-Christian 128–9
Jung, Burkhard 3, 27, 122, 132, 135

Kazanjian, Victor 179
*Kindertransport* 127, 131
King Abdullah bin Abdulaziz International
   Centre for Interreligious
   and Intercultural Dialogue
   (KAICIID) 176, 180, 182, 184
Koolmees, Wouter 71, 74
Körber, Carsten 128–9
Kósa, Lajos 125
Kosovo Liberation Army (KLA) 146

Latin America 118, 129–30
*Leitkultur* 27–8, 122
Libeskind, Daniel 80
liberty 18, 21, 125
   individual 6, 24
   political 25
   religious 8, 20
Louis XIV, King 19

Mardin Conference 160, 166–7
   Mardin Declaration 168, 170
Marrakesh Declaration 160, 170–1
Mecca 161, 163
memory (memories) 2, 22, 68–9, 76, 80–1,
   130–1, 141–5, 120, 148, 186
   collective 52, 114–15, 120, 134, 137, 157
   historical 95, 138–9
   memorialization 147, 156
   national 124–5, 129
   politics of 84, 114, 121–2, 139
   transnational 12, 113–15, 119, 133–5
Merkel, Angela 15, 69, 117, 122
Middle Ages 2, 16, 55–6, 58, 60, 62–3, 65,
   69, 78, 162, 164

Middle East 119, 122, 164, 176–7, 187
Milan I, King 96
Milošević, Slobodan 28
minorities 18, 21–2, 70, 72, 81, 88, 137, 187
   Christian 21, 124
   ethnic 69, 100
   religious 9, 11, 30, 67, 170–1, 185
Moors 120, 131, 163
Moriscos 18, 120, 131, 133, 163–4, 166–7
Morocco 160, 171, 185
multiculturalism 11, 26, 45, 67, 81, 86, 95,
   134, 145
   toleration 123, 134, 183

National Liberation Army
   (NLA) 140, 146–8
nationalism 4, 8, 22, 27, 69, 81–2, 140, 150,
   155, 164, 175
   Christian 8
   ethnonationalism 142
   Irish 150, 155
   methodological 3, 114
   religious 22
Nazism 21
   Nazi dictatorship 81
   Nazi Germany 80, 122, 135 (*see also*
      Germany)
   Nazi regime 41, 121
Netherlands 7, 21, 24, 34, 37, 57,
   72, 106
   Dutch Calvinists 57
   Dutch Muslim 72–3, 106
   Dutch Republic 19
New Spirituality 3, 6–7, 12, 14, 25, 191,
   193–204
   New Age 192–3
North Atlantic Treaty Organisation
   (NATO) 142, 144, 146, 148
Northern Ireland 13, 23, 137–9,
   149–53, 155–6
   Anglo-Irish Treaty 138
   Irish Republican Army (IRA) 149–51
   Troubles 138–9, 149–51, 153, 155
North Macedonia 13, 84, 86, 137–9, 141,
   143, 153, 156
   Democratic Union for Integration (DUI)
      142–4, 146–7, 157
   Macedonian Orthodox Church
      (MOC) 141

Social Democratic Union of Macedonia
(SDSM) 144
VMRO-DPMNE 85, 143–6

Obama, Barack 159
Ohrid Framework Agreement 13, 84,
86, 138, 141, 143 (*see also* North
Macedonia)
Orbán, Viktor 28, 117, 124–5, 133–4
Orbit 176–7, 180, 183, 186, 188
Organization for Security and
Co-operation in Europe (OSCE) 142
Ottoman Empire 2, 14–15, 18–19, 21–2,
74, 137, 140, 164
confessionalization 18
invasions 18
Ottoman Turks 2, 19

Pakistan 100–1
Palestine 57, 76, 82, 164, 182
*Patriotische Europäer gegen die
Islamisierung des Abendlandes*
(PEGIDA) 118
Paty, Samuel 7, 28
pluralism 4, 6–7, 20, 77–9, 81, 171, 177,
186, 194
Poland 8, 25, 29, 100, 128
Jews in 78–9 (*see also* Judaism)
Poland-Lithuania 18
polarization 4, 8, 21, 52, 112, 148–9, 180,
184, 187–8
polytheism 41
Roman polytheistic believers 55–6,
58–9, 61–2
popular culture 12, 25, 43, 91–4, 97
populism 4, 8, 13, 26, 28–9, 82, 118
far-right populist movements 122,
132–3, 135, 156
populist Islamophobia 28–9
post-secular(ism) *see* secular
presentism 1, 47, 65, 173
propaganda 110, 117, 133
anti-religious 195
jihadist 162
political 82, 124
Protestantism 57, 61
Protestant Church 19
Protestant countries 19, 22–3
Orangemen 153

public opinion 67, 113
public sphere 8, 92, 115, 123, 141

Quran 102–3, 111, 160, 168, 185

race 29, 76, 81, 122, 134–5
racism 22, 81, 183, 188
radicalization 12, 28, 112, 183, 185, 187–8
Reconquista 17, 132
referendum 117, 119, 132, 150, 152
Reformation 14–15, 20, 41, 57–8, 109
refugee 4, 18, 25, 39, 81, 130–5
asylum seeker 117–18, 126, 134
Calais 119
crisis 12, 114–27, 132–5
*Willkommenskultur* 118, 122, 129
Religions for Peace (RfP) 176–7,
180–2, 185
religiosity 6, 33, 107, 156
representation 1, 13, 30, 35, 40, 48, 59,
62–3, 66, 74, 88, 100, 104, 112–13,
121, 127, 129, 135, 139, 142, 159, 178
of Islam 71–2, 106, 176
media 42
misrepresentation 94
of the past 14, 51, 84
of religion (religious diversity) 8–10, 15,
43–4, 46–7, 49, 83, 91–2
Roman Empire 16, 55, 58–62
Russia 2–3, 24, 34, 101, 128
(see also *Soviet Union*)
Russian Empire 18, 21, 195

Salah, Mohamed 106–7
Salvini, Matteo 28
Sánchez, Pedro 130
Saudi Arabia 161, 176
Second World War 8, 22–3, 31, 42, 64, 76,
89, 95, 99, 118, 128–9, 140, 143, 164,
176, 187, 198
secular 6, 10, 19, 20, 22, 23, 27, 29, 31, 54,
102, 132, 164, 175, 177, 179, 183, 187,
188, 189
liberal/ secular values 122, 133, 135? 186
post-secular 12, 31, 179, 187
secularity 7, 135
secular Christendom 21
secularism 5, 7, 11, 24, 27, 30–1, 55, 57,
60–2, 65, 133, 186, 207

*laïcité* 5, 21, 183, 186
secularization 2, 4–6, 9, 14, 21–5, 28, 30,
    33, 187, 188, 195
de-Christianization 5, 20, 23–4
de-secularization 28
Serbia 83, 94–5, 116, 140
    Serbian Kingdom 96
    Serbian Orthodox Church 96
Sharia 17, 166, 168
Soviet Union 22, 25, 195–6, 198
Spain 2, 12, 17, 21, 23, 34, 37–8, 52, 54, 56,
    63, 80, 106, 114, 118, 120–1, 129–35,
    167, 178
    Castile 80, 162, 168–70
    fortress of Christian Europe 121
    Franco regime 129, 132–3
    Granada 13, 18, 42, 120, 133, 159–60,
        162–3, 165, 168–70, 172
    Islamic 133
    *Partido Popular* 118
    Spanish Civil War 129–31
    VOX 132–3
stereotype 43, 48, 53, 70–1, 76, 100, 102, 173
    anti-Muslim 133
    deconstruction of
        (deconstructing) 45, 59
    generalization 34
    historical 81, 121
    negative 29, 132, 180, 198
    religious 8, 103
Surján, László 126
Syria 62, 114, 116, 124, 128–9, 164,
    171, 180
    civil war 116, 130 (*see also* refugee)
    Syrian Regional Response Plan 116
    Syrian Vulnerable Persons Relocation
        Program 119

terrorism 43, 57, 62, 127, 133, 160,
    164–5, 189
    terrorist attack 7, 8, 28, 60–1, 117, 184, 187
Thatcher, Margaret 149
Timmermans, Frans 126
Todorovski, Zoran 85
tolerance *see* toleration
toleration 13, 15–16, 19–20, 30–1, 33, 37,
    55–6, 68–9, 71–3, 89, 95–6, 110, 122,
    131, 145, 157, 160, 165, 170, 173, 191,
    194, 196–8, 204

intolerance 7, 16, 18, 30–1, 33, 42, 45,
    55, 61, 81, 87, 192
    myths of 135
    religious 67, 92, 94, 105, 107, 111–12,
        124, 159, 197
*tasāmuḥ* 171, 173
Turkey 2, 27, 31, 41, 116–17, 119, 166
    Hagia Sophia 108
    (*See also* Ottomans)

United Kingdom (UK) 10, 12, 23, 34,
    37–8, 42, 44, 52, 54, 63, 100–1,
    106, 114, 119, 122, 124, 127, 131–5,
    137, 149–50, 152, 155, 166, 176, 182
    Brexit 28, 119, 132 (*see also* referendum)
    Britain 82, 94, 99–103, 111–12, 119,
        123, 127
    British Isles 2, 19
    British Museum 70, 72
    British Pakistani Muslim 94, 101–2,
        104, 111
    Britishness 42, 102
    United Kingdom Independence Party
        (UKIP) 132–3
United Nations High Commissioner for
    Refugees (UNHCR) 116, 119
United Religions Initiative (URI) 176–7,
    180–2, 184
United States (US) 8, 16, 20, 60, 63, 132,
    141, 176–7, 191
    9/11 63, 160, 165
    America 3, 20, 143, 150, 163
    American imperialism 30
    American Revolution 20
    evangelicalism 8–9
    Institute of Peace 175
    native American 199

Wars of Religion 15–16, 18
West 3, 30, 33, 63, 65, 117, 126, 132, 176, 196
    Christian West 129
    Western, Christian man 134 (*see also*
        Orbán, Viktor)
    Western Christian Medieval society 60
    Western civilization 6
    Western Europe 16, 21–6, 28–9, 77, 94,
        112, 116, 124, 133, 172
    Western secular ethics 29
    Western values 27

Westphalia, Peace of 16, 57, 61
William of Orange, King 153
Williams, Roger 14, 20
Wilms, Valerie 121
World Congress of Religions 187
Wurtz, Bill 108

YouTube 12, 36, 43–4, 91–4, 105–8, 111
    YouTuber 110

Yugoslavia 22, 26, 28, 89, 139, 147, 187 (*see*
    *also* Balkans)
    communist regime 28, 84, 140
    Kingdom of 83, 137
    Tito 84
    Yugoslav Macedonia 69, 83–4
    Yugoslav wars 11, 28, 57

www.ingramcontent.com/pod-product-compliance
Lightning Source LLC
Chambersburg PA
CBHW050409280326
41932CB00013BA/1793